BLACK THEOLOGY IN BRITAIN

I hope that this book will be an inspiration and encouragement. Thank you for all of your support and encouragement over the years. It May not show but it does pay off!!

Bless You.

Robert Beckford

27/6/08

With best wishes on your journey Michael

Keep on keeping on! peace & Love!

Cross Cultural Theologies

Series Editors: Jione Havea and Clive Pearson, both at the United Theological College, Australia, and Anthony G. Reddie, Queens Foundation for Ecumenical Theological Education, Birmingham

This series focuses on how the "cultural turn" in interdisciplinary studies has informed theology and biblical studies. It takes its leave from the experience of the flow of people from one part of the world to another.

It moves beyond the crossing of cultures in a narrow diasporic sense. It will entertain perspectives that arise out of generational criticism, gender, sexual orientation, and the relationship of art and film to theology. It will explore the sometimes competing rhetoric of multiculturalism and cross-culturalism and will demonstrate a concern for the intersection of globalization and how those global flows of peoples and ideas are received and interpreted in localized settings. The series will seek to make use of a range of disciplines including the study of cross-cultural liturgy, travel, the practice of ministry and worship in multi-ethnic locations and how theologies that have arisen in one part of the world have migrated to a new location. It will look at the public nature of faith in complex, multicultural, multireligious societies and compares how diverse faiths and their theologies have responded to the same issues.

The series welcomes contributions by scholars from around the world. It will include both single-authored and multi-authored volumes.

Published

Global Civilization:
Challenges to Society and to Christianity
Leonardo Boff

Dramatizing Theologies:
A Participative Approach to Black God-Talk
Anthony G. Reddie

Bibles and Baedekers:
Tourism, Travel, Exile and God
Michael Grimshaw

Art as Theology:
The Religious Transformation of Art from the Postmodern to the Medieval
Andreas Andreopoulos

BLACK THEOLOGY IN BRITAIN
A READER

edited by
Michael N. Jagessar
and
Anthony G. Reddie

LONDON   OAKVILLE

Published by

UK: Equinox Publishing Ltd
Unit 6, The Village
101 Amies St.
London, SW11 2JW

US: DBBC
28 Main Street
Oakville, CT 06779

www.equinoxpub.com

British Library Cataloguing-in-Publication Data
A catalogue record for this book is available from the British Library.

Library of Congress Cataloging-in-Publication Data
Black theology in Britain : a reader / edited by Michael N. Jagessar and
Anthony G. Reddie.
      p. cm. -- (Cross cultural theologies)
   Includes bibliographical references and index.
   ISBN 978-1-84553-059-4 (pb)
   1. Black theology. 2. Blacks--Great Britain--Religion. 3. Theology,
Doctrinal--Great Britain. I. Jagessar, Michael N., 1955- II. Reddie,
Anthony.
   BT82.7.B575 2007
   230.089'96041--dc22
                                    2006101426

ISBN-13   978 1 84553 059 4   (paperback)

Typeset by CA Typesetting Ltd, www.publisherservices.co.uk
Printed and bound in Great Britain by Lightning Source UK Ltd., Milton Keynes and
Lightning Source Inc., La Vergne, TN

Contents

Foreword

This undertaking has been an emotional rollercoaster of excitement and despair, coupled with a marked sense of duty and awesome responsibility. One of the editors can assert the belief that without Black theology he would not be in the church at the time of writing.[1] Both the editors would describe themselves as being on the 'Liberationist' or 'Deconstructionist' wing of Black Christianity in Britain. Whilst we are shaped by and have been socialized within Caribbean social mores with their concomitant Christian emphases, we, nonetheless, have both sought to challenge and reinterpret the normative boundaries and restrictive thought forms of these traditions. In short, we are not your average Black Christians.

We do not claim any privileged identity when making this form of statement, nor would we wish to assert any sense of estrangement from the broader hinterland of normative Black Christianity in Britain. In short, by identifying ourselves in this way, we wish to delineate our own perspectives and ideological presuppositions behind the task of compiling and constructing this reader in Black theology in Britain.

Talk of creating a reader in Black theology in Britain was first mooted during conversations at the then 'Centre for Black and White Christian Partnership' during one of the monthly Black theology forums[2] in Birmingham in 1999. Many of the 'major players' at the time were involved in discussions around commencing such an undertaking. Conversations came and went and the project did not get past 'first base', namely, the broad agreement as to what shape and form this proposal might take.

After this abortive attempt, the trail of the Black theology in Britain reader went cold for a number of years. Renewed talk of reviving the proposal came to life around the time of the 10th anniversary International Conference in Black theology held in Sheffield, but once again, the warm mist of animated discussions evaporated in the cool air of reality.

The reality of which we speak was the realization that the majority of the adherents in the Black theology in Britain movement do not occupy academic positions nor are able to luxuriate in the space to concentrate solely on this area of commitment. Essentially, many of our peers in the movement are in full-time pastoral ministry, or in employment outside of the church. The failure to initiate the developments for undertaking a Black theology in Britain reader was not due to any lack of ability or passion from many of our colleagues. Rather, it was one mainly of constraints of time.

It was in the spring of 2005 that Reddie approached Jagessar (the two work together closely as editor and reviews editor, respectively, of the only

Black theology journal in the world, *Black Theology: An International Journal*) with the idea of bringing to life this often talked-about undertaking.

The editors of this work are, at the time of writing, two of a relatively small group of Black theologians in Britain, engaged in teaching and scholarship within the academy. As such, we have been afforded the space and the time in which to undertake the necessary archival, editorial work and writing in order to complete this text, the first ever reader in Black theology in Britain.

In some respects, we are deeply honoured and extremely fortunate to have found ourselves in the position of being able to undertake this work, for we are quite clear in our minds that other Black colleagues could have done this task and accomplished it with great skill and alacrity. The honour of accomplishing this much needed task of producing this resource fell to us and we remain deeply moved and grateful for that opportunity.

Acknowledgements

There are many people to thank for enabling us to complete this task and it would be invidious to attempt to name them all, but it would be equally remiss of us if we did not identify some key people and organizations in this process.

In the first instance, we are both grateful to the Queen's Foundation for Ecumenical Theological Education for supporting us in this work. The library at Queen's remains one of the best stocked provisions of Black theological texts in Britain and we have raided its archives on numerous occasions, finding material that has sought to give life to the reader. We would like to thank Michael Gale, the librarian at Queen's, for his assistance in finding material within the deeper recesses of the library.

We would also like to thank our colleagues at Queen's, particularly Dr Mukti Barton, the tutor in Black and Asian theology at Queen's, who forms, with ourselves, perhaps the most concentrated triumvirate of Black theological specialism in any institution in Britain. We need also to acknowledge our 'other' Black colleague at the time of writing, Carol Troupe, whose work on the Living Out Faith project[1] often goes overlooked. Carol has been instrumental in being our 'objective third eye' in reading through the material as a whole, in addition to assisting Jagessar in the compilation and editing of the chapter on Reddie's work (which, for reasons that should be readily apparent, he did not wish to be directly involved).

In thanking our colleagues at Queen's, we also need to recognize the sterling work of Diane Johnson. Diane's connection with Queen's is by way of marriage to one of our colleagues, but in her own right she is a talented and accurate copy typist, whose unerring ability to decipher badly written scrawl and to type up old documents, essays and articles from long-deleted publications saved us incalculable amounts of time.

Reddie would like to thank the Methodist Church in particular for their special support that has enabled him to not only work on this reader, but to undertake ongoing work in the development of Black theology in Britain as a whole.

In thanking British Methodism for Reddie's Research Fellowship in Black Theological Studies (the only one of its kind in Britain, if not the world), Jagessar and Reddie would also like to thank the Methodist Churches' Multi Racial Projects Fund (MRPF), overseen by Naboth Muchopa, the Connexional (National) Secretary of Racial Justice, for their invaluable financial assistance that facilitated archival research and the extensive typing up of numerous old documents, reports and essays.

Similarly, the Churches Commission for Racial Justice (CCRJ) within Churches Together in Britain and Ireland (CTBI) should be thanked for their most generous grant that provided the necessary funds that have supplemented the gift from MRPF. We wish to thank the likes of Naboth Muchopa, the late James Ozigi and Arlington Trotman for their moral, in addition to the financial, support we have received.

We wish to thank many of our colleagues, peers and students further afield for the intangible but no less important support. Their vibrant conversation and sharp incisive input has invigorated and enabled us to complete this task. The monthly Black Theology Forum in Birmingham remains a space that continues to feed our minds and inspire us to write and edit work for both the promotion of Black theology in Britain and for the wider needs of social transformation and Black empowerment of ordinary Black people in Britain.

Particular thanks are reserved for all the participants in this project who kindly agreed to have their work published in this reader. We thank the publishers of previously published work for allowing us to reproduce extracts in the text.

Last but not least, special thanks are offered to Janet Joyce, the Managing Director of Equinox and to the other editors of the 'Cross Cultural Theologies' series (Jione Havea and Clive Pearson) for agreeing and supporting this venture. From our previous connections with Janet, by way of the *Black Theology* journal, we know that Equinox is deeply supportive and appreciative of Black theology in Britain and across the world. From the moment Reddie met with Janet Joyce in a restaurant in Harborne, Birmingham and she communicated the initial bad news that Continuum (the previous publishers of the journal) were intending to 'drop us' from their operations, but that she was going to resign, create her own company and continue to publish the journal, Equinox have remained a stellar operation in the support of Black theology in Britain.

This work is the second Black theology text they have published under the 'Cross Cultural Theologies' series,[2] and Reddie has now joined Havea and Pearson as a co-editor, in order to assist in developing more Black theology work for Equinox. All this is in addition to the sterling support Equinox have given towards the international journal.

To all the people who have inspired, encouraged and supported us in this mammoth undertaking, you have our heartfelt thanks and gratitude.

Michael Jagessar and Anthony Reddie

Permissions

Permission to reproduce the writings in this reader has been kindly granted by the various copyright holders (authors and publishers). Every effort has been made to track all copyright holders.

Chapter 2: Roots of Black British Religiosity

Roswith Gerloff, 'The African Diaspora in the Caribbean and Europe: From Pre-emancipation to the Present Day', in Hugh McLeod (ed.), *The Cambridge History of Christianity*. Vol. IX. *World Christianities c. 1914– c. 2000* (Cambridge: Cambridge University Press, 2006), 219–35. Copyright © 2006. Reproduced with permission from the Roswith Gerloff and Cambridge University Press.

Lorraine Dixon, 'The Nature of Black Presence in England before the Abolition of Slavery'. Unpublished research material. Copyright © 2006 Lorraine Dixon. Reproduced with permission from the Lorraine Dixon.

Edson Burton, 'Post Emancipation Religious Stratification in Jamaica 1865– 1948'. Unpublished PhD thesis, University of West England, 2004. Copyright © 2004 Burton. Reproduced with permission from Edson Burton.

Claire Taylor, 'British Churches and Jamaican Migration: A Study of Religion and Identities 1948 to 1965'. Unpublished PhD thesis, Anglia Polytechnic University, 2002. Copyright © 2002 Taylor. Reproduced with permission from Claire Taylor.

Chapter 3: Remembering the Forgotten Voices

Valentina Alexander, 'Passive and Active Radicalism in Black Led Churches', in 'Breaking Every Fetter? To What Extent has the Black Led Church in Britain Developed a Theology of Liberation?' Unpublished PhD thesis, University of Warwick, 1996. Copyright © 1996 Alexander. Reproduced with permission from Valentina Alexander.

John Wilkinson, 'Black Theology at Queen's: The First Steps'. Personal reflections from his time at Queen's College (includes unpublished materials as appendix). Copyright © 2006 Wilkinson. Reproduced with permission from John Wilkinson.

Chapter 4: Dread and Rahtid: Robert Beckford's Canon

Robert Beckford, 'Jah would never give the Power to a Baldhead': Bob Marley as a Black Liberation Theologian', in Robert Beckford, *Jesus is Dread:*

Black Theology and Black Culture in Britain (London: Darton, Longman and Todd, 1998), 115–27. Copyright © 1998. Reproduced with permission from the publisher Darton, Longman and Todd Ltd.

Robert Beckford, 'Liberation Theological Praxis (LTP)', in Robert Beckford, *Dread and Pentecostal: A Political Theology for the Black Church in Britain* (London: SPCK, 2000), 150–55. Copyright © 2000. Reproduced with permission from the publisher SPCK.

Robert Beckford, 'Kingdom of God and God of the Rahtid', in Robert Beckford, *God of the Rahtid* (London: Darton, Longman and Todd, 2001), 41–47. Copyright © 2001. Reproduced with permission from the publisher Darton, Longman and Todd Ltd.

Robert Beckford, 'Whiteness', in Robert Beckford, *God and the Gangs* (London: Darton, Longman and Todd, 2004), 74–78. Copyright © 2004. Reproduced with permission from the publisher Darton, Longman and Todd Ltd.

Robert Beckford, 'Dub, Signification and the Trickster Motif', in Robert Beckford, *Jesus Dub: Theology, Music and Social Change* (London: Routledge, 2006), 74–80. Copyright © 2006. Published by Routledge and reproduced by permission of Taylor and Francis Books UK.

Chapter 5: What are the Sistas Saying?

Kate Coleman, 'Black Theology and Black Liberation: A Womanist Perspective', *Black Theology in Britain: A Journal of Contextual Praxis* 1 (October 1998), 59–69. Copyright © 1998. Reproduced with permission from Equinox and the editor (Anthony Reddie).

Kate Coleman, 'Black Women and Theology', *Black Theology in Britain: A Journal of Contextual Praxis* 3 (November 1999), 51–65. Copyright © 1999. Reproduced with permission from Equinox and the editor (Anthony Reddie).

Lorraine Dixon, 'bell hooks: Teller of Truth and Dreamer of Dreams', in Anthony Reddie (ed.), *Legacy: Anthology in Memory of Jillian Brown* (Peterborough: Methodist Publishing House, 2000), 97–108. Copyright © 2000. Reproduced with permission from Lorraine Dixon and Anthony Reddie.

Lorraine Dixon, 'Are Vashti and Esther our Sistas?: The Stories of Two Biblical Women as Paradigmatic of Black Women's Resistance in Slavery', in Anthony Reddie (ed.), *Legacy: Anthology in Memory of Jillian Brown*

(Peterborough: Methodist Publishing House, 2000), 129–35. Copyright © 2000. Reproduced with permission from Lorraine Dixon and Anthony Reddie.

Valentina Alexander, 'Afrocentric and Black Christian Consciousness: Towards an Honest Intersection', *Black Theology in Britain: A Journal of Contextual Praxis* 1 (October 1998), 11–18. Copyright © 1998. Reproduced with permission from Equinox and the editor (Anthony Reddie).

Valentina Alexander, 'A Black Woman in Britain Moves Towards an Understanding of her Spiritual Rites', in Anthony Reddie (ed.), *Legacy: Anthology in Memory of Jillian Brown* (Peterborough: Methodist Publishing House, 2000), 119–25. Copyright © 2000. Reproduced with permission from Valentina Alexander and Anthony Reddie.

Maxine Howell Baker, 'Towards a Womanist Pneumatological Pedagogy', *Black Theology: An International Journal* 3.1 (2005), 32–54. Copyright © 2005. Reproduced with permission from Equinox and the editor (Anthony Reddie).

Chapter 6: Interpreting Texts

Hyacinth Sweeney, 'The Bible as a Tool for Growth for Black Women', in Joe Aldred (ed.), *Sisters with Power* (London and New York: Continuum, 2000), 114–22. Copyright © 2000. Reproduced with permission from the publisher, Continuum, and Hyacinth Sweeney.

Kate Coleman, 'Being Human: A Black British Christian Woman's Perspective', in her unpublished PhD thesis, 'Exploring Metissage: A Theological Anthropology of Black Christian Women's Subjectivities in Postcolonial Britain' (University of Birmingham, 2006), 327–46. Copyright © 2006 Coleman. Reproduced with permission from Kate Coleman.

Mukti Barton, 'Hermeneutical Insubordination Toppling Worldly Kingdom', in Joe Aldred (ed.), *Sisters with Power* (London and New York: Continuum, 2000), 24–35. Copyright © 2000. Reproduced with permission from the publisher, Continuum, and Mukti Barton.

Joe Aldred, 'Paradigms for a Black Theology in Britain', *Black Theology in Britain: A Journal of Contextual Praxis* 2 (1999), 9–32. Copyright © 1999. Reproduced with permission from Equinox and the editor (Anthony Reddie).

Michael Jagessar, 'Spinning Texts—Anancy Hermeneutics', *The Journal of the College of Preachers* 117 (July 2004), 41–48. Copyright © 2004. Reproduced with permission from Michael Jagessar and the editor (Mark Wakelin).

Valentina Alexander, 'Onesimus's Letter to Philemon', *Black Theology in Britain: A Journal of Contextual Praxis* 4 (May 2000), 61–65. Copyright © 2000. Reproduced with permission from Equinox and the editor (Anthony Reddie).

Chapter 7: Communicating Black Theology: Anthony Reddie's Writing

Anthony Reddie, 'Faith Stories and the Experience of Black Elders', in Anthony G. Reddie, *Faith, Stories and the Experience of Black Elders* (London and Philadelphia: Jessica Kingsley Publishers, 2001), 14–26. Copyright © 2001. Reproduced with permission from Anthony Reddie.

Anthony Reddie, *Nobodies to Somebodies: A Practical Theology for Liberation and Education* (Peterborough: Epworth Press, 2003) 2–36, 74–106. Copyright © 2003. Reproduced with permission from Anthony Reddie.

Anthony Reddie, 'Acting in Solidarity: *Black Voices*', in Anthony G. Reddie, *Acting in Solidarity: Reflections on Critical Christianity* (London: Darton, Longman and Todd, 2005), 109–19. Copyright © 2005. Reproduced with permission from Anthony Reddie.

Anthony Reddie, 'Accessing the Dramatic: Using Drama as a Medium for Doing Black Theology', in Anthony G. Reddie, *Dramatizing Theologies: A Participative Approach to Black God-Talk* (London and Oakville: Equinox, 2006). Copyright © 2006. Reproduced with permission from Anthony Reddie.

Chapter 8: Black Theology in Pulpit and Pew

Kate Coleman, 'Arise and Build', in Joe Aldred (ed.), *Preaching with Power: Sermons by Black Preachers* (London: Cassell, 2000), 111–21. Copyright © 1998. Reproduced with permission from the publisher Continuum.

Wilfred Wood, 'The Good Neighbour', in Wilfred Wood, *Keep the Faith Baby!* (Oxford: Bible Reading Fellowship, 1994), 28–33. Copyright © 1994. Reproduced with permission from Wilfred Wood.

Inderjit Bhogal, 'A Table in the Wilderness', in Inderjit Bhogal, *A Table for All* (Sheffield: Penistone Publications, 2000), 27–35. Copyright © 2000 by Inderjit Bhogal. Reproduced with permission from Inderjit Bhogal.

Michael Jagessar, 'The (Un)forgiving King', *Journal of the College of Preachers* 119 (July 2005), 64–66. Copyright © 2005. Reproduced with permission from Michael Jagessar and the editor Mark Wakelin.

Anthony Reddie, 'Freedom', in Anthony Reddie, *Growing into Hope*. Vol. II: *Liberation and Change* (Peterborough: Methodist Publishing House, 1998), 106–108. Copyright © 1998. Reproduced with permission from Anthony Reddie.

Chapter 9: Roots and Routes

Ronald Nathan, 'Caribbean Youth Identity in the United Kingdom: A Call for a Pan-African Theology', *Black Theology in Britain: A Journal of Contextual Praxis* 1 (October 1998), 19–34. Copyright © 2000. Reproduced with permission from Equinox and the editor (Anthony Reddie).

George Mulrain, 'The Music of African Caribbean Theology', *Black Theology in Britain: A Journal of Contextual Praxis* 1 (October 1998), 35–45. Copyright © 1998. Reproduced with permission from Equinox and the editor (Anthony Reddie).

Emmanuel Lartey, 'An Intercultural Approach to Pastoral Care and Counselling', in Emmanuel Y. Lartey, *In Living Colour: An Intercultural Approach to Pastoral Care and Counselling* (London: Jessica Kingsley, 2003 [1997]), 21–35. Copyright © 1997 by Emmanuel Lartey. Reproduced with the permission of Emmanuel Lartey and the publisher Jessica Kingsley.

Michael Jagessar, 'Navigating the World of "White" Ecumenism: Insights from Philip Potter', in *Wereld en Zending* 31.4 (2002), 32–41. Copyright © 2002 by Michael Jagessar. Reproduced by permission of Michael Jagessar and the editor (Gerard van 't Spijker).

Chapter 10: Future Trajectories

Emmanuel Lartey, 'After Stephen Lawrence: Characteristics and Agenda for Black Theology in Britain', *Black Theology in Britain: A Journal of Contextual Praxis* 3 (November 1999), 79–91. Copyright © 1999. Reproduced with permission from Equinox and the editor (Anthony Reddie).

1 Black Theology in Britain? Discerning a Rationale for this Work

Historic Roots

'What is this about colours in theology? Surely there is only one true theology—that revealed by God in the Bible! And why on earth would you want a Black theology anyway?'[1] These words are the opening paragraph to the editorial for the first issue of *Black Theology in Britain: A Journal of Contextual Praxis*. The words were written by the founding editor, Emmanuel Lartey, who at the time was a senior lecturer in Pastoral Theology in the Department of Theology at the University of Birmingham.

Black theology as a self-named discipline and a radical form of Christian practice emerged in its present form in the 1960s, in the USA. It has grown out of the experiences of Black people of the African Diaspora as they have sought to re-interpret the central ideas of Christianity in light of their experiences. But Black theology is not simply a North American affair.

If Black theology can be defined as the radical re-interpretation of the revelation of God in Christ, in light of the struggles and suffering of Black existence in order that de-humanized and oppressed Black people might see in God the basis for their liberation, then there has been a form of Black theology in operation in Britain since the epoch of slavery.

It is, therefore, most timely that this seminal volume should come to fruition in 2007. 2007 marks the 200th anniversary of the abolition of the slave trade in Britain. Although there has been a Black presence in Britain since Roman times, the often troubled existence of Black people in Britain can be traced to the Elizabethan era and the influx of Black slaves from Africa and the Americas.

This text seeks to outline the development of Black theology in Britain from the eighteenth century through to our contemporary era. By means of re-investigating popular texts and previously unpublished groundbreaking material, the editors offer a comprehensive and challenging interpretation of the development of the eclectic and distinctive voice that is Black theology in Britain.

In this opening chapter we hope to analyse the development of Black Christianity in the African Diaspora. This development has grown out of the ongoing struggle of Black peoples to affirm their identity and very humanity in the face of seemingly insuperable odds.[2] The 'invention' of Blackness, as opposed being 'African', is a construction of the enlightenment.[3] Although there already existed deep-seated, racialized depictions of people of darker skin within the cultural imagination of Europeans, influenced in no small measure by Greek philosophical thought, nevertheless the construction of an overarching doctrine of racial inferiority ascribed to people of African descent reached its apotheosis during the epoch of slavery, aided and abetted by specious notions of pseudo-science.[4] In short, somewhere across the 'Middle Passage' and the 'Black Atlantic', Africans became 'negroes'.[5]

The use of the term 'Black' as a qualifying nomenclature for any particular theological or ecclesiological entity remains a contested and even controversial notion. In using the term 'Black' with reference to a particular understanding, development and intent of Church, embodying the Body of Christ, we are drawing upon a particular theological, philosophical and ideological tradition that finds its roots in the epoch of slavery. This particular understanding of the term 'Black', having its roots in the slave epoch, adopted an academic conceptualization in the development of Black theology in the 1960s, during the Civil Rights and Black Power era in the United States of America.

In seeking to define a notion of Black Christianity, we are drawing upon a body of literature that has identified African Diasporan Christian religious experience as a struggle for a more affirmed, realized and nuanced humanity that is more than the crude construction of racialized inferiority imposed upon Black people by White Christian hegemony. Anthony Pinn has called this ongoing struggle the 'quest for complex subjectivity'.[6] Complex subjectivity is the attempt by Black people of the African Diaspora to construct notions of their own humanity on terms that are more amplified and nuanced than the reified strictures of fixed objectification that was a feature of the construction of the 'negro'.[7]

The roots of Black Christianity lay in the counter-hegemonic struggles of Black peoples in the Americas, the Caribbean and Britain to challenge the worst excesses of oppressive Christian inspired supremacist practices, through a radical re-interpretation of the central tenets of the Christian faith. This dialectical tension between White normalcy and the Black subversive hermeneutical response can be found in the apposite words of John Wilkinson who writes:

> But the heart of Black Christianity lay not with the teaching of the white missionaries but with the form of Christianity which the slaves fashioned for themselves arising out of their *own* experience and needs.[8]

The roots of Black Christianity can be found in the radical and subversive re-interpretation of Christianity by Black slaves in the so-called New World, during the eighteenth and nineteenth centuries. Black people, having being exposed to the tendentious Christian education of the exploitative planter class in the Americas and the Caribbean, began to 'steal away' from beneath the close confines of their slave masters to worship God in their own existential spaces.[9]

The desire of Black people to form their own ecclesial spaces was the process of a long period of history, arising from the 'Great Awakening' in the middle of the eighteenth century.[10] It is beyond the scope of this introductory chapter to mount a detailed analysis of the historical development of Black Christianity in the African Diaspora, but it is worth noting the importance of Black existential experience and context to the historical manifestation of such developments. Black Christianity begins with Black existential experience and not historic mandates born of the often abstract philosophical musings as to the nature of Jesus as the Christ. Black Christianity was born of the existential need to create a means by which the Black self could create the basic rubrics of what it meant to be a human being.[11]

Black Christianity subsequently gave birth to independent Black churches. The birth of independent Black churches in the Caribbean can be traced to the arrival in Jamaica in 1783 of approximately four hundred White families, who migrated from the United States, preferring to live under British rule than in the newly independent Thirteen colonies. Amongst the White migrants were two Black Christians, George Liele and Moses Baker.[12]

In the United States, activists such as Richard Allen used Christian teachings and a nascent Black existential theology as their means of responding to the need for Black subjectivity. Richard Allen, a former slave, became the founder of the African Methodist Episcopal Church (AME), which seceded from the American Episcopal Church due to the endemic racism of the latter.[13] Henry McNeal Turner, a descendant of Allen in the AME church, began to construct an explicit African-centred conception of the Christian faith, arguing that an alignment with Africa should became a primary goal for Black Americans. This focus upon African ancestry would enable subjugated objects of Euro-American racism to find a suitable terrain for the subversive activism that would ultimately lead to liberation.[14] Pinn acknowledges the link between the African-centred strictures of the AME church and the later Black nationalism of Marcus Garvey and the *Black Star Line* 'Back-to-Africa' movement of the early twentieth century.[15]

Responding to the ongoing threat of non-being has been one of the central aims of the Black church that has emerged from the existential experiences of oppressed Black peoples of the African Diaspora. Harold Dean Trulear, writing on the importance of Black Christian religious education within the Black Church in the US, states:

> Rather it [religious education] has carried upon its broad shoulders the heavy responsibility of helping African Americans find answers for the

following question: What does it mean to be Black and Christian in a
society where many people are hostile to the former while claiming allegiance to the latter?[16]

So the historic roots of Black Christianity emerge from the Black experience of struggle and marginalization during the era of slavery and it was
a determined and self-conscious attempt to create liminal spaces where
the subjected and assaulted Black self could begin to construct a notion of
selfhood that extended beyond the dictates of White illegitimate power.

Defining Black Theology in Britain

When speaking of Black theology, we are referring to the specific self-
named discipline of re-interpreting (predominantly) Christian traditions
and practices in light of liberationist themes and concepts, which arise out
of Black experiences. This approach is one that makes Blackness and Black
experience the initial point of departure. This point of departure sits in
dialogue with 'Holy Scripture' and is not one that sees the Bible alone as
sole authority as a source and the primary hermeneutical lens by which
the message of God's liberating agency is discerned. In effect, Blackness
becomes the prime interpretative framework of re-interpreting and reimaging God and the Christian faith.

There has been a tendency in recent times to assert the belief that all
theology done by Black people is Black theology. To suggest this is then to
rob Black theology of any specificity. In that case, then *all* theology done by
Black people is Black theology. If Black theology is so generic, it, in effect,
ceases to exist. The best analogy the editors can make in order to shed light
on this contention is to point to the parallel discipline of Feminist theology.
Not all women who do theology are feminists, therefore not all women
who are engaged in doing theology are feminist theologians! Similarly, not
all Black people doing theology are necessarily engaged in doing Black
theology.

Black theology cannot be reduced to the notion that conservative
Black Christian approaches to the Bible can be deduced as Black theology. Black theology stands and falls on its commitment to situational
analysis, liberation and social transformation. Those wanting to invoke
the term 'Black theology' without wishing to engage in the dangerous and
often controversial work of this approach, simply want to have the luxury
of using the terminology whilst still holding to the creedal building blocks
of normative (White) Christianity.

The editors would assert that Black theology is not reducible to what
all Black Christians say or write. Rather, we would argue that there are

important and essential sources and norms for the doing of Black theology. To our mind, describing oneself as an evangelical stands in direct tension with the notion of Black theology. We feel it is fairer and more accurate to define many Black evangelicals as coming within the tradition of 'Black Christian religious experience'[17] as opposed to Black theology. Reddie defines Black Christian religious experience as

> the 'folk' orientated approach to Christian traditions which arise out of Black experiences, but which do *not necessarily* have a political or explicitly transformative agenda. Neither does this approach necessarily see Blackness as being a primary hermeneutical lens for re-interpreting the Christian faith, nor is it the case that one necessarily begins with Black experience as the normative source for doing theology.[18]

Black theology begins with the material reality of the Black experience as its point of departure. Scripture sits in dialectical tension with the Black experience and does not precede it. To suggest that Scripture is the primary or even the only site of revelation is to fail to take the Black experience and the material reality of the Black self seriously.

Black theology, like all liberation theologies, is governed by the necessity of ortho-praxis rather than orthodoxy. It is important to note that those who would still adhere to normative evangelicalism will tend to emphasize traditional Christian teaching as opposed to the exigencies of the Black experience.

Whether in the work of James Cone,[19] Delores Williams[20] or Robert Beckford,[21] Black and Womanist theologians have not been afraid to jettison traditional Christian teachings in order to affirm the new revelation that arises from Black experience. In the case of Cone, sin becomes a systemic material evil emanating from the inhuman practices of oppressors and not a cosmic metaphysical phenomenon that emerges from early Christian mythology.[22] Similarly, Williams completely re-orientates atonement theories in light of the suffering and oppression of Black women.[23] Black Christian religious experience is simply unwilling to engage in this form of deconstructionist work in order to remake Christian teaching commensurate with the realities of Black negation and struggle.

So, this edited text is concerned with Black theology in Britain—an academic discipline and a form of praxis that is committed to re-interpreting the Christian faith in light of the exigencies of the Black experience, in order that Black people can challenge the societal and structural forces that marginalize and oppress them. This text is not concerned with the more generic enterprise of detailing the Black Christian experience in Britain that tends to emanate from Black evangelical Christians, who whilst acknowledging Blackness, will not prioritize it in their theological construction.

Who is the 'Black' in Black Theology in Britain?

Black theology in Britain, much like the development of Black identities, can be viewed as plural, hybrid and dynamic entities that eschew any simplistic attempt to essentialize or to reify cultures.[24]

Indeed, one could quite legitimately theorize in an inordinate fashion and still never exhaust the seemingly endless ways in which one could seek to identify and construct a working paradigm for the nature and intent of Black theology in Britain.

The opening chapter of this work is an attempt to create a working paradigm for the development of Black theology in Britain. Given the immensity of the task, in collating, documenting and re-interpreting previously published texts and hitherto, unpublished works, we have had to undertake the difficult and discriminating task of deciding what becomes part of this text and what does not.

This text is concerned with the development of Black theology in Britain. In invoking the term Black we are aware of the multiple ways in which this term has been used within academic discourse in Britain. The term Black has to be understood within the context of Britain with all its peculiarities and inconsistencies. The use of the term Black does not simply denote one's skin pigmentation but is rather a political statement relating to one's sense of marginalization within the contested space that is Britain. Using the term Black is to identify oneself as a socially constructed 'other' when juxtaposed with the dominant Eurocentric discourses that dominate the normative gaze and trajectory of what it means to be *authentically British*. This tradition of political mobilization around the once maligned and socially constructed term of Black has roots in the political left and the rise of coalition politics in the 1970s. The work of political activists and commentators such as Sivanandan[25] and Ramdin[26] has been supplemented by the inter-textual work of cultural studies and postcolonial exponents such as Kobener Mercer,[27] R.S. Sugirtharajah,[28] and the doyen of critical studies in Britain, Stuart Hall.[29]

These inter-cultural perspectives that incorporate African, Caribbean and Asian dimensions has been the basic default position of both *Black Theology in Britain* and *Black Theology: An International Journal* since their inception in 1998 and 2002, respectively. Talk of the Black experience has never been an exclusively African affair. The work of scholars such as Inderjit Bhogal[30] and Mukti Barton[31] has been instrumental in defining the trajectory and character of Black theology in Britain. The Asian presence has often been a hidden and overlooked component of the Christian scene in Britain.

Despite this honourable and important coalition of voices in the development of the Black Christian presence in Britain, the authors have chosen to concentrate their efforts on documenting the largely Black Caribbean perspective on Black theology in this text. The reasons for doing so are largely practical and should not be taken as exclusionary.

In the first instance it worth noting that there remain important semantic and definitional questions regarding the juxtaposition of Black and Asian theologies as analogous terms. Black, as we have seen, is a socially constructed term that has no natural habitus beyond the popular imaginations that have sought to give it life. In short, there are no naturally Black people. People are no more literally Black than they are literally White. Scholars such as James Perkinson have investigated the theological and socio-political and cultural meanings of such contested terms.[32] The term Asian refers to the identities of a set of peoples who are bound together by geography, languages, religions, cultures, shared histories, mythologies, colonialism and migration.

Like all forms of ethnicity (unlike 'race') it has an embodied reality beyond mere social construction. Comparing Black and Asian theologies, although *de rigueur* within socio-political and cultural discourse, is, nonetheless, something of a misnomer. The more acceptable analogous juxtaposition is that of 'African' and 'Asian'. But this then gets us into another contested discourse around the relationship between 'African' theologies and Black theology.

The previous point has been an important semantic detour from our main task of detailing the development of Black theology in Britain, but it is necessary in order to highlight the contested and elusive nature of language in intellectual discourse. The editors should assert, however, that our decision to concentrate on Black Caribbean perspectives in the development of Black theology has largely been a pragmatic decision and was not influenced unduly by the previous discussion on the relationship between Black and Asian theologies.

Rather, in talking about pragmatism we are being cognizant of the abundance of literature available from predominantly Black Caribbean writers in the development of Black Christianity in Britain as a whole and Black theology in particular. Given the limitations of space and the need to construct a coherent and 'linear' text, it soon became apparent to the editors that critical and painful decisions would have to be made concerning what was included (and not) in this Reader. Consequently, we have chosen to highlight the dominant and visible literature, but want to pay homage and give respect to those tireless and prophetic voices whose presence has illuminated the whole and hope to include them in a future publication.

This Reader is an attempt to tell our own story. This is the story of being Black people in an allegedly Christian nation that has rarely lived up to such an exalted billing. This Reader is told through the prism of important extracts from seminal texts that seek to articulate perspectives on what it means to be Black and Christian in Britain, from early modernity through to the present day.

This academic gaze is not a pseudo objective, disinterested arid tome created by two neutral observers. Rather, the editors identify themselves as a part of the Black theology in Britain movement and see this work as a passionate polemic for the self-determined spirit of liberation that resides within the Black British self. This work incorporates a narrative and pastoral dimension.

This Reader seeks to offer an indicative trajectory for the development of Black theology in Britain by way of re-examining significant texts that have played an important role in assisting to define the nature of this discipline and practice. In many respects, the development of Black theology in Britain has become synonymous with one individual—Robert S. Beckford, to whom a whole chapter is dedicated. It is important to remember that prior to Beckford there were the important landmark texts of *A Time to Speak*[33] and its sequel, *A Time to Act*.[34]

Both texts were edited by Raj Patel, a Christian of Asian descent and Paul Grant, a Black Christian sociologist. Both were connected with a grassroots Christian campaigning group named 'Evangelical Christians for Racial Justice', which was based in Birmingham, in the West Midlands. The development of Black theology in Britain took a more distinctive and formidable turn with the publications of these two books.

Whilst Beckford has been the dominant voice in the articulation of Black theology in Britain, this text seeks to highlight the work of such scholars as Kate Coleman, Lorraine Dixon and Inderjit Bhogal.[35] It is interesting to note that the latter three figures are ordained Black Christians in historic churches in Britain. We state this fact simply to remind ourselves that Black theology in Britain has always been a pan-denominational or plural Christian movement and is not simply reducible to Black British Pentecostalism, as many would seem to imply.[36]

The *Black Theology in Britain* Journal(s)— Outlining a Way Forward

If one were to outline a critically important year in the development of Black theology in Britain one might be tempted to say 1998 was that appointed 'Kairos time'. That year saw not only the publication of the first self-authored book on Black theology in Britain, Robert Beckford's *Jesus Is Dread* (on which in-depth work has already been done by other Black theologians in Britain[37]), but it also marked the birth of *Black Theology in Britain*.[38] The first issue of the journal was launched in Birmingham on the

October 10, 1998 at the George Cadbury Hall. The founding editor was The Revd Dr Emmanuel Lartey, then a senior Lecturer in Pastoral Theology in the department of Theology at the University of Birmingham. The meeting was chaired by Bishop Dr Joe Aldred, then the Executive Director of the 'Centre for Black and White Christian Partnership' based in Selly Oak Birmingham, who was also the Founding Chairman of the Editorial Board. Other speakers included Kate Coleman who was one of the contributors to that first issue, along with Anthony Reddie. The journal represents the first ongoing, collective enterprise for the development of Black theology in Britain. Whereas Patel and Grant's twin edited volumes were stand-alone pieces and Beckford's *Jesus Is Dread* a single authored work, *Black Theology in Britain* was the first self-conscious attempt to create a sustainable framework for the articulation of Black theology in Britain in written form. Further analysis of the development of the journal can be found in Anthony Reddie's *Black Theology in Transatlantic Dialogue*.[39]

Black Theology in Britain: A Journal of Contextual Praxis (hereafter detailed as BTIB) emerged as a direct response to the desire to locate a repository that would harness the burgeoning developments of this discipline and ongoing practice in Britain. BTIB was an important means of making Black theology in Britain a more visible and respected academic discipline within the theological academy in Britain. Prior to the emergence of the journal there was little, if any, explicit mention of Black theology within academic publishing in Britain.

The birth of BTIB was the result of lengthy negotiations between Emmanuel Lartey, Joe Aldred and Inderjit Bhogal in addition to a number of others on the fledgling editorial group. The journal was essentially a four-way partnership between the Centre for Black and White Christian Partnership, headed by Joe Aldred, Department of Theology at the University of Birmingham, represented by Emmanuel Lartey, Queen's College, represented by Robert Beckford and the Urban Theology Unit (an ecumenical, but largely Methodist run theological institution) in Sheffield, headed by Inderjit Bhogal. Other significant players included Ron Nathan and Patricia Gowrie.[40]

The Black theology journal has, since 2002, become an internationally renowned publication under the editorship of Anthony Reddie. Its move from being identified as a parochial organ towards becoming the main international publication for the dissemination of Black theology across world was testament to the hard work of a number of people and the vision of Janet Joyce, the Managing Director of Equinox (publishers of the journal and this Reader).

At the time of writing, *Black Theology* is not only the sole *international journal* dedicated to Black theology in the world, it is, incidentally, the *only Black theology journal* in the world (now listed in ATLA), following the demise of the *Journal of Black Theology in South Africa*, which was produced by the staff of the theology department at the University of South Africa (UNISA). The Black theology journal (in both guises) provides a good deal of the material that will be featured in this Reader. Over the years, all the major figures in the development of Black theology in Britain have written pieces for this publication. Clearly, it has been possible to include no more than a brief microcosm of the wealth of scholarly work that has contributed to the growth and importance of *Black Theology*, but we have highlighted particular texts for the insights they offer towards the ongoing narrative that is Black theology in Britain.

Black Theology in Britain and the Challenge to the Ongoing Threat of Racism

This Reader has been constructed in order to give testimony to the fortitude and theological insight of Black people in Britain. Whilst Black Christian faith can be defined in a number of ways, as this opening section of the Reader has shown, there is, nevertheless, a sense in which Black theology in Britain has remained the most vociferous of opponents in the ongoing threat of the non-being of Black people.

As Beckford has demonstrated, one can chart a genealogy of racism in European intellectual thought that has exerted a disproportionately negative hold on the life experiences of Black people.[41] Scholars such as Eze have shown the extent to which the allegedly enlightened thinking of such 'luminaries' as Hume and Kant was infected with the stain of White supremacist thought.[42]

The construction of the binary of Blackness and Whiteness is a product of the modernity.[43] The chief legacy of transatlantic slavery was the unleashing of the rampageous and ravenous animal that is racism. The construction of racialized notions of fixed identity and restricted perspectives on Black human selfhood were the dangerous offspring of the chattel slavery of the Black Atlantic.[44] The outworking of an immutable hierarchical manipulation of humanity did not disappear when the Act to abolish the British slave trade was passed in Britain in 1807. The act brought the making of slaves to an end but racism, the notion of White supremacist norms, most certainly did not end.

Whilst the bulk of the literature pertaining to the abolition of slavery has tended to emphasize the important role played by White abolitionists, this text is a testament to the legacy of not only those first Black protagonists, but also their descendents. The teaching and learning about the epoch of slavery in Britain has largely cast Black people as invisible players, in which their Black bodies were the integral subtext that underpinned the whole drama.

The likes of Clarkson and Wilberforce have set the scene for an ongoing drama that has exorcized Black presence from British history. The dependency culture of White liberal paternalism acting on behalf of the bedraggled mass of Black humanity has been set in motion since the late seventeenth and early eighteenth centuries. The partnership between White and Black has been likened to that between the rider and the horse.[45] Black people have been used to having to carry the responsibility for effecting reconciliation between Black and White even though we have been the 'sinned against' in the ongoing drama of slavery and racism.

This text is an attempt to chronicle the development of Black theology in Britain from the eighteenth century onwards. The inhuman institution of slavery found a willing accomplice in the allegedly egalitarian doctrines and practice of Christianity and the Christian church. The injunction that all human beings are created in the image of God (Genesis 1:27) or that all people are engaged in a holy covenant with the one God (Malachai 2:10) were largely ignored as White capitalism and expansionist greed rode roughshod over supposedly universal Christian values.

In an attempt to bolster its own morally bankrupt religio-cultural framework, White Euro-American hegemony sought refuge within specious ideological tenets of pseudo enlightenment science whilst plundering the scriptures in an effort to secure the services of God in their racist practices. Scholars such as Johnson[46] have demonstrated how White Euro-American hegemony constructed notions of the otherness of Black bodies juxtaposed with White normality in their use of the mythical 'Curse of Ham' as depicted in Genesis 9. The idea of Ham, the divinely sanctioned slave of Shem (Genesis 9:26) as the progenitor of all Black people, was a key biblical and theological resource for the moral apologetic of chattel slavery.[47]

The Pauline injunctions for slaves to obey their masters (Colossians 3:22; Ephesians 6:5) or Paul's pastoral advice to Philemon to treat his slave Onesimus better (but not to set him free) were taken as proof texts for the God-given institution of slavery.

And yet, the antecedent for the development of Black theology in Britain lay in the ability of the Black slaves across the Black Atlantic to 'read against' the text in order to break the closed hermeneutical circle of allegedly Scriptural authority. Clearly, the early Christian communities in first-century Palestine and across the Greco-Roman world could accommodate slavery within their seemingly egalitarian practices. Paul may have instituted a more expansive religious faith based upon the invocation of the Holy Spirit as opposed to the Jewish law, but he was not inclined to end the ownership of one person of another within the body of Christ. Paul was struggling to effect a seismic change in the socio-political and cultural milieu of the first-century 'Near East'.[48]

Unlike those within the Black Christian religious experience whose adherence to the immutable authority of Scripture is such that they seek to justify Paul's work or lack of it (he was against slavery but was being tactical in his dealings with the Romans),[49] Black theological work has always been adept at reading against the text.[50]

Those first Black slaves were also able to re-read biblical texts in light of their own experiences in order to fashion a theological response to their existential plight. Paul may have said that slaves should obey their masters or that all government is ordained and sanctioned by God (Romans 12), but slaves like Sam Sharpe in Jamaica[51] or Equiano in Britain[52] were able re-read biblical texts in order to move beyond the literal meaning of scripture.

The ability to read against the text was the liberationist theological norm that enabled abolitionists (Black and White) to break the closed hermeneutical cycle that had given power to the oppressive forces that subjugated Black humanity.

Black theologians in a more modern vein, whether in terms of cultural analysis[53] or educational method,[54] have continued to struggle with Scripture and Christian tradition in order to construct Christian inspired approaches to prayerful action for systemic change. Black theology in Britain has sought to reconfigure Christianity, offering alternative forms of hermeneutics for understanding the Christian faith in light of Black experience.

When Black theologians challenge White authority over the deaths of Black people in police custody[55] or analyse the systemic violence against Black people within the body politic of the nation,[56] they are drawing upon a Black political conception of liberation theology that utilizes multiple sources for talking about God, drawing upon Black history, cultures, experience, revelation and scripture.[57]

This text reader has been produced in honour of all those who have preceded the editors of this work and the largely living scholars who have contributed towards its production. *Black Theology in Britain: A Reader*— published in 2007, the 200th Anniversary of the act to abolish the slave trade in Britain—is a testament to the subversive and protesting resilience of Black Christian faith in Britain and across the broader contours of the African Diaspora.

The Nature of Black Theology in Britain

Within the British context, the term 'Black theology' has taken on a more generic conception to mean the doing and articulation of theology arising out of the Black experience from within a variety of disciplines. Unlike the US[58] or South Africa,[59] where the articulation and definition of Black theology is largely determined in terms of systematic or constructive theology or ethics (the main exception in either context being Randall Bailey[60] in the US and Itumeleng Mosala[61] in South Africa, who are both biblical scholars), Black theology in Britain is interdisciplinary.

In Britain, for example, there exist a number of Black theology forums, with Birmingham (the biggest and most established of the different group-ings) existing alongside those in Sheffield and London. These forums are dedicated spaces for the articulation of Black scholarly work in this country. The working definition of Black theology in each of these meet-ings is an eclectic and plural one, with people coming from a variety of backgrounds.

Some are theology students, others are educationists, psychologists, pastors, plus those who defy any form of categorization, but who simply want to be part of a radical and creative Black space. The meetings are not self selective, and are open to all Black and Asian people who simply want to relate Black religious thinking to life. Black theology is the discipline that unites us.

Whilst Beckford's work in cultural analysis and criticism (see Chapter 4) remains the most visible in terms of popular readership, the work of Reddie, for example, in the area of education and formation has been significant in highlighting the importance of conscientizing and mobilizing the thinking of grassroots believers outside of the academy (see Chapter 7). In terms of the latter, whilst there have been occasions when others have not perceived this work as being a part of the Black theology in Britain movement,[62] Reddie's work in education has, nonetheless, offered schol-arly and practical resources for reimaging the nature of Christian formation and learning for Black people from within a Black liberationist framework.

At the time of writing, postgraduate students, mainly within the Uni-versity of Birmingham and the Queen's Foundation, are pursuing research in a diverse range of areas, including political theology, education, faith development, hip-hop music, biblical studies, spirituality and self-determi-nation and psychology. We hope that this text illustrates both the eclectic and creative character of Black theology in Britain, particularly since the epoch of the Black theology journals in the late 1990s.

The Methodological Framework of the Book

This text has been conceived in order to provide an indicative snap-shot of the historical and thematic development of Black theology in Britain. The structure of the work has been developed in order to amplify many of the salient features of Black liberative theological construction in this context. Before we proceed to outline the major themes and overarching structure of the book, it is perhaps prudent that we say something of the genesis of this particular approach.

Black theology in Britain is neither a new discipline nor a disconnected solo exercise by allegedly neutral and unbiased thinkers and activists. We make these twin claims in order to justify our particular approach to structuring this work. To say that Black theology is not a new discipline is to recognize and take seriously the historic antecedents for the development of this discipline and practice in the UK.

Whilst Robert Beckford can be rightly credited with being the first important solo author of a major Black theology text, it would be remiss of us if we did not recognize the many individuals dating from the 1970s onwards. Often lacking an academic platform for the sustenance of their work, these pioneering individuals, while still pastors, began to write articles and essays outlining a nascent Black theology in Britain.

And yet, even these writers would be forced to concede that, prior to their emergence, there existed fledgling Black communities that produced inspiring individuals who argued for the egalitarian tenets of Christianity as a basis for proclaiming the dignity of the Black human subject. But, preceding all these individuals and the emergent communities from which they came was the Black presence during the epoch of slavery in Britain. The roots of Black theology in Britain traverse the chasm of history, and find their beginnings in the indefatigable work of the likes of Equiano, Sancho and Mary Prince.[63]

Whilst this text argues that there are a number of elemental factors that constitute the nature and identity of Black theology (to which the movement in Britain clearly adheres), the editors would argue that these constituent themes are no less in evidence in the work of those seventeenth- and eighteenth-century slaves as is the case in the lives of their descendents.

The development of Black theology in Britain in its modern scholarly articulation has been influenced greatly by the defining tenets of Black self-determination. Prior to the emergence of scholarly work on the Black Christian religious experience in Britain, it was not uncommon to find the bulk of theological reflections on Black people undertaken by White scholars. The scholarly development of Black theology in Britain has emerged from within a rubric of Black people wanting to document their own experiences and articulate their own perspectives in their own words. The emergence of the Black theology journal, for example, was accomplished with this sense of the necessity of visible Black writing uppermost in the collective thinking of those who helped to birth this pioneering initiative.[64] This importance of the defining doctrine of self-determination and articulation can be found in the following words of Aldred, who, writing a few years later in one of his edited texts, states:

> A tragedy of our time is that some cultures, in particular black cultures, are
> pigeonholed, stigmatized even, as 'oral', while others, in particular white
> European culture, are regarded as 'literary'. Clearly, all cultures enjoy both
> elements in their traditions to some extent. However, an unfortunate, if
> inevitable, result of this stereotyping is that black cultures in Britain are
> not encouraged to write: the literary cultures have traditionally written for
> them and about them. This collection challenges this paradigm.[65]

Aldred's desire that Black folk in Britain should begin to document their
experiences and knowledge of God is a crucial maxim for this edited project.
In keeping with Aldred's charge for Black people not to be stereotyped as
purely 'oral' communities, but also to do justice to the collectivist ethic of
Black British scholarship (it should be noted that the majority of Black British
religious writing is found in edited works rather than sole authored books—
Aldred, Barton, Beckford and Reddie excepted), this text draws on the *actual*
words of Black British theologians and not paraphrased commentaries. It
would be too easy, and an erroneous move to our mind, if this edited reader
were to proceed on the basis of 'speaking for' rather than 'dialoguing with'
this exceptional cast of Black theological players in this ongoing drama.

The selection of the material in this Reader corresponds to the criteria
as we have defined it at an earlier juncture in this chapter. We have been
quite intentional in acknowledging those pieces of work that can be readily
identified as being 'Black theology' as opposed to 'Black Christian religious
experience'.

Clearly, in a single-volume text, we have had to make some hard choices
in terms of what is included. Whilst there are, inevitably, some value judgements being made in terms of what has been included and omitted, we
want to assure the reader, and those authors of the pieces that have been
left out, that we value *all* Black British Christian writing in its totality. It is
simply the case that one has to construct some form of criteria in order to
accomplish this type of undertaking.

The editors have chosen to highlight excerpts from significant texts that
encapsulate an important feature or theme within Black theology in Britain.
Each section and the segments within that section are extracts from larger
pieces of work, the majority of which have been published previously
in whole or in part, in an alternative setting. On a number of significant
occasions we have chosen to highlight important work that has previously
remained unpublished. The majority of this work has been written by Black
women in Britain. Perhaps the non-published status of these works may
be an indictment of the patriarchal nature of Christian/scholarly publishing
in Britain. The editors are pleased to be in a position to enable extracts of
these important pieces of work to receive a deserved, wider audience for
such scholarly excellence.

The Shape of Each Chapter

Black Theology in Britain: A Reader is made up of a number of chapters, each one detailing a significant theme or methodological concern in the development and articulation of the discipline and practice in this country.

Each chapter begins with a brief overview of the rationale for this section of the text and reasons why the work within it is of significance and scholarly import. These opening reflections have been written in order to place the following extracts in that chapter into a broader situational and analytical context. In what ways are the various pieces in each chapter of significance to the overarching development of Black theology in Britain? How do the various pieces relate to one another (in that particular chapter) and to the overall shape and flow of the book?

The opening reflections to each chapter are essential in order to provide the necessary continuity to the book and to prevent it from becoming a series of un-related and de-contextualized, a-historical extracts in an unsatisfactory whole. The editors have sought, in these pieces, to detail the context, emergence and importance of each extract. Clearly, undertaking this type of editorial work leads inevitably to some subjective judgements on our part. This cannot be helped, but the authors acknowledge their bias and subjective concerns and interpretation of the work of others.

Following the opening reflections each chapter then proceeds with the individual extracts. The extracts themselves are preceded by some opening comments by the editors to detail the larger work from which the piece was taken and offer some brief comments on the identity of the author. Full citation details are provided for each extract and we encourage all readers of this text to refer to the larger body of work from which each piece is taken.

Part of our aim in compiling this text is to alert all readers to the wealth of Black British theology material that exists in a number of disparate and sometimes obscure places in this country. All the work in this text deserves to be read in its entirety and we would warmly encourage you to do so. In the first instance, however, this text provides an opportunity to read a snapshot of important work that has contributed to the ongoing development of Black theology in Britain.

Outline of the Chapters

Chapter 1 (which you are presently reading) offers a contextual narrative to the development of Black theology in Britain and the rationale and construction of this text reader. Little more needs to be said in this opening section save for the fact that, like the greater whole, it does not pretend that this rendering of Black theology in Britain is a definitive articulation. Rather, the editors have provided a rationale and a substantive thematic structure and method for the interpretation, definition and theological intent of Black theology in Britain. Others may disagree with our assessment and, of course, it is their right to do so. But it should be noted that this project has been undertaken by the present editor and reviews editor of the only Black theology journal in the world, so the initiators of this work are not without authority in this discipline.

Chapter 2 looks at the roots of Black British religiosity. In this chapter we offer extracts that seek to chart the development of Black Caribbean Christianity, in the many islands where a significant number of Black British Christians trace their immediate antecedents.[66] How did the introduction of Black slaves to a religion that was meant to pacify, de-politicize and subjugate oppressed and dehumanized peoples become one of the primary tools for them to re-conceive their ontological and existential humanity, even in the midst of unimaginable horror?[67]

This chapter uses both previously published material and work that has not been published before in order to offer a brief vignette for the nascent seeds of the subversive and prophetic version of Christianity that emerged from within the life experiences of incarcerated and oppressed Black Atlantic Caribbean bodies.[68]

Chapter 3 offers two significant texts, each of which offers us an interesting and illuminating look at particular examples of the manifestation of Black theology in Britain. The first is by John Wilkinson, a White Anglican Priest and former tutor in Pastoral theology at the then Queen's College (now called the Queen's Foundation). Wilkinson can be credited with helping to create one of the very first programmes in Black Christian Studies at Queen's in the early 1990s, which, in turn, became a forerunner to the more explicit development of Black theology overseen by Wilkinson and Robert Beckford.

The second piece in this chapter is by one of the unheralded 'Sheroes' of the Black theology in Britain movement, namely, Valentina Alexander. The work of Alexander features extensively in this text, as she has been one of the most important Black woman theologians in the UK. Whilst many of her later published articles and essays have been rightly included in this text, her groundbreaking PhD thesis (reputed to be the first thesis in religious studies and theology by a Black woman in Britain) has remained unpublished. We are glad to report that a significant section of her thesis has been published for the first time in this text. The development of Black theology owes much to these two often neglected and sometimes forgotten voices.

Chapter 4 details the canon of Robert Beckford, the most visible of all the Black theologians in Britain. His work is significant in that it offers a radical, Caribbean rooted apologetic for a Pentecostal orientated conception of Black theology in Britain. Beckford's method, which utilizes a post-Tillichian framework, established more recently by David Tracey as 'Revised Critical Correlation' as noted by Elaine Graham,[69] has sought to combine the sources and norms of Pentecostalism with the concepts and epistemologies of Black expressive cultures, particularly those which emerge from within reggae music and Rastarfari.

Beckford's canon is an impressively large one, and we have chosen to concentrate on his first five sole authored books, namely *Jesus Is Dread*,[70] *Dread and Pentecostal*,[71] *God of the Rahtid*,[72] *God and the Gangs*[73] and *Jesus Dub*.[74] We feel these are the seminal texts that have assisted in shaping the development and identity of Black theology in Britain.

Chapter 5 is concerned with the contribution of Black British Christian women's writing to the development of Black theology in Britain. Of particular import in this chapter is an extract from the aforementioned Valentina Alexander's thesis.[75]

In addition to Alexander's work we are pleased to present extracts by many of the leading Black women theologians in Britain, including Kate Coleman and Lorraine Dixon, two of the stalwarts of the movement dating back to the early days of the journal.[76] This chapter is the largest in the whole text, but being mindful of the patriarchal and androcentric nature of the theological academy in Britain, and the fact that two men are editing this venture, we felt it prudent that extra space be given over to the pioneering, but often overlooked, contribution of Black women to the development of Black theology in Britain.

Chapter 6 deals with the ways in which Black theologians in Britain have attempted to engage with and interpret the Bible, seeking to develop a Black hermeneutic in order that the Bible might be a tool for empowerment and liberation.[77] This chapter highlights how Black theology in Britain has to engage with the biblical text, whether in terms of searching for the spaces within the text in order to gain a sense of 'what has not been said' by those who have been marginalized,[78] or in terms of offering new strategies for reading scripture.[79] As Reddie has stated on a previous occasion:

> Given that Black folk are not going to let go of the Bible any time soon, how can we become more attuned to the subtle and not so oblique ways in which the Bible has been used as a weapon against us?[80]

This chapter seeks not only to answer this specific question, but more positively it demonstrates how the enduring power of the 'Word' remains a vital resource for inspiring and energizing Black theologians in their ongoing task of challenging the dehumanizing structures that limit the human potential of the Black self.

Chapter 7 is concerned with the work of Anthony Reddie, who, along with Beckford, is one of the most prolific writers on Black theology in Britain and is also editor of *Black Theology: An International Journal*. Reddie's canon has been mostly undertaken within the purview of practical theology (although his later work has seen a shift in perspective).[81] His work has attempted, consistently, to use educational method and pedagogy as a means of 'translating' the central tenets of Black theology into an accessible form, so that ordinary Christians can engage with its ideas and be inspired and transformed for new, liberating forms of Christian praxis.

Whilst his canon has lacked the verve and iconoclastic status of Beckford's work (his work is far less known within the British context), it has, nonetheless, offered a more practical and accessible approach to Black theology for clergy and laity alike in the ongoing work of Christian ministry in the local church.

Chapter 8 is concerned with the way in which Black theology in Britain has used the medium of preaching as a means of articulating their commitment to the liberating dimensions of the Gospel. Black preaching is always drawn from the Bible. The Bible has always been a fundamental source and norm in Black theology.[82] One of the distinctive strengths of Black theology in Britain when compared with her older and more established sibling in the US, for example, is that the movement in this context has not become overly 'professionalized' and therefore removed from the challenges and needs of Christian ministry and the Black church (in all its guises). Preaching, therefore, rooted in the ongoing lives of church communities across the country, is the practical theological discipline that attempts to connect academic Black theology with the needs of ordinary Black Christians.

At the time of writing, the editors cannot think of one major Black theologian in Britain who is completely divorced from or undertakes their work without some cognizance of the importance of the church in and to scholarly output. It is this commitment to the tangible praxis of the church and the realization that the Bible remains the most potent of tools in the theological task of effecting liberation[83] that has led many Black theologians to interpreting texts in order to preach their Black theology.

Chapter 9 examines the roots and routes of Black theology and Black peoples in Britain. African Caribbean peoples and their identities have been forged in the process of colonial and postcolonial history, from the continent of Africa to the Caribbean and now Britain.[84] This chapter offers a number of brief vignettes of the way in which Black theology in Britain has been suffused with and has responded to the insights and analysis of the 'outsider's' voice. Whether that voice has emanated from the Caribbean, African or the South Asian context, Black theology in Britain, particularly through the Black theology journal, has provided a unique repository for a 'pan-recipe'[85] of ingredients that have given rise to a distinctive Black British theological flavouring.

Chapter 10 finds the editors reflecting upon the journey of Black theology in Britain to date, and using this analysis as a means of discerning a future trajectory for the movement. How will Black theology in Britain respond to the ever deepening epoch of postmodernism? How and in what ways can and will Black theology respond to the mounting challenges of globalization, nationalism and fundamentalisms? Will Black theology become weighed down by theological minutiae and seemingly clever semantic arguments around often arcane scholarly developments in post-structural discourse? Or will the continued travails of mainly poor Black people (despite what some of the Marxists and neo-Marxists have professed, poverty has *always had a colour*), working class and underclass peoples in Britain and across the world continue to inspire Black theologians to speak, write and act? Raj Patel and Paul Grant, the editors of the first British texts to carry the words 'Black theology' in the title, once professed that it was 'A Time to Speak'[86] and 'A Time to Act'[87]—to what end is Black theology in Britain seeking to speak and act in this and future epochs?

This final chapter seeks to ask what we can learn from the development of Black theology in Britain. How will *Black Theology* react to the future challenges that face Black people in this country? How and in what ways will Black theology remain a radical and challenging framework for systemic and structural change?

In conclusion, then, we can say that Black theology in Britain arises out the experiences of Black people of the African Diaspora as they have sought to re-interpret the central ideas of Christianity in light of their experiences. This text demonstrates most ably that Black theology is not simply a North American affair.

If Black theology can be defined as the radical re-interpretation of the revelation of God in Christ, in light of the struggles and suffering of Black existence in order that de-humanized and oppressed Black people might see in God the basis for their liberation, then there has been a form of Black theology in operation in Britain since the epoch of slavery.

This reader text, therefore, will be the first text of its kind and a key resource for courses in Black British history, cultural studies, critical theory and popular culture, Black theology, religious studies and citizenship studies (the Black contribution to civic life in Britain).

2　Roots of Black British Religiosity

It is an undoubted truism that all people come from somewhere. All of us are in some sense the products of history. One does not have to subscribe entirely to this notion in order to see the importance of assessing the development of one's antecedents as a means of understanding contemporary reality and experience.

This chapter contains extracts from four pieces, which detail the antecedents of Black theology in Britain. Each extract is taken from a larger, more substantive piece of work. Not all of these pieces can be construed as Black theology per se, but they do represent aspects of the historical development of Black Christian faith in the eighteenth and nineteenth centuries that were to give rise to the development of Black theology in Britain in its more academic and articulated form in the latter part of the twentieth century.

As we have detailed in the first chapter, Black theology is not necessarily a new form of Christian inspired practice. The roots of Black theology in Britain date back to the substantive formative period in Black life in this country. In order to appreciate the distinctive character and intent of Black theology in Britain one must go back in time to assess the development of Black Christian expression—in effect to investigate the roots of Black religiosity.

The first piece in this chapter is by Roswith Gerloff and is entitled 'The African Diaspora in the Caribbean and Europe: From Pre-emancipation to the Present Day'. Gerloff was formerly the first Executive Director of the 'Centre for Black and White Christian Partnership' that was based in Selly Oak, in Birmingham. At the time of writing, Gerloff is a Visiting Lecturer in African Christian Studies at the University of Leeds. Gerloff's extract is taken from her contribution to an edited text by Hugh Mcleod of the University of Birmingham. Gerloff's piece is significant for this study since she provides a Diasporan African gaze, particularly around the Caribbean, in order to locate the historic roots for the development of Black Christian faith in Britain. In order to understand the work of the Black abolitionists in the eighteenth and nineteenth centuries in England one has to understand the nature of colonial history and the role of the British Empire in exporting imperial Christianity into the minds (if not the hearts) of predominantly Caribbean people.

The second piece in this chapter is from the Revd Lorraine Dixon who is an Anglican priest in the Church of England. Her piece is entitled 'The Nature of the Black Presence in England before the Abolition of Slavery' and is taken from her research work undertaken at the University of Birmingham. Dixon outlines the nature of the Black presence in Britain prior to the abolition of the slave trade in 1807. Dixon's piece analyses the historic backdrop against which the pioneering work of the likes of Equiano and Sancho were undertaken. In what ways has the discipline of English history sought to encapsulate the Black presence in the historic frame, long before the advent of the SS Empire Windrush on June 22, 1948?

The third contribution to this chapter comes from Edson Burton. Burton's piece is entitled 'Post Emancipation Religious Stratification in Jamaica 1865–1948' and is an extract from his unpublished PhD thesis with the University of the West of England. Burton's research considers the development of Black religiosity in Jamaica, the largest of the English speaking islands in the Caribbean, from the viewpoint of the Morant Bay Rebellion in 1865 through the arrival of the first post-war Caribbean migrants in Britain in 1948. His work offers an inter-religious discourse on the nature of Black faith formation in the epoch immediately following the abolition of slavery. This work provides an important link between the earlier historical work of Gerloff and Dixon and the more modern assessment of Black religious faith in the piece that follows.

The final piece in this chapter is from Claire Taylor. Claire Taylor is a Methodist minister and her work details the arrival of Caribbean people in and their relationship to the church in this country in that early post-war period. This piece is also extracted from a comparatively recent unpublished PhD thesis in Church History from the University of East Anglia. Her doctoral thesis is entitled 'British Churches and Jamaican Migration: A Study of Religion and Identities 1948 to 1965'.

The African Diaspora in the Caribbean and Europe: From Pre-emancipation to the Present Day

Roswith Gerloff

[This essay is abridged from Gerloff's essay in Hugh McLeod (ed.), *The Cambridge History of Christianity.* Vol. IX. *World Christianities c. 1914– c. 2000* (Cambridge: Cambridge University Press, 2006), 219–35. Whilst there are multiple tributaries that form the antecedents for Black communities in Britain, the bulk of the early post-war migrants to this country, often termed in popularist discourse the 'Windrush generation', can trace their immediate origins to the Caribbean. Roswith Gerloff traces this historical and religious development in her essay 'The African Diaspora in the Caribbean and Europe from Pre-emancipation to the Present Day'. This work offers an invaluable account of the social, political, cultural and theological background to the later developments of Black theology in Britain. The following is an extract of the account of African resistance in the Caribbean, especially by the Native Baptists in Jamaica. When the Baptists declined, Gerloff goes on to argue in the remainder of the essay, Pentecostalism became the new organizing power based on grassroots expressions.]

The concept 'African Diaspora' has become, at least for those once forcibly removed from their homelands, and their descendants, a viable instrument of *empowerment*, based on the biblical imagery of Exodus and the history of endurance, survival and perseverance of human values. Some European academics question the term because of the historical difference between a past enforced exile and present voluntary migration from Africa, and also because the concept can exegetically and linguistically provoke negative connotations of persecution in Jewish history. Yet, we give priority to the *self-expression* of blacks who, inspired by liberational biblical stories, for centuries identified with Israel seeking the 'Promised Land' and developed physical, cultural and spiritual means to resist bondage. For the slaves, in particular with the development of strong Ethiopian ideas in the Caribbean and North America in the eighteenth and nineteenth centuries, the concept *African Diaspora* confirmed *continuity in variations*; it granted them access to alternative interpretations of power and destiny, and can therefore be used as the description of past and present processes. Significantly, African and Caribbean youths on both side of the Atlantic today are increasingly guided by similar concepts and values spelt out in Pan-Africanism and Afrocentricity.

Spanish Catholicism, while enslaving indigenous populations and, after their extinction, enslaving the imported Africans, at least did not deny their humanity; they taught them a memorized form of 'main truth' called the *Doctrina Christiana*, and made steps to secure their baptism. In contrast, Protestant powers, in a capitalist economy compelled by new technologies in the sugar complex, cheap supply of labour, and rivalries with trading competitors, treated African slaves as mere chattel and property. Although the imported Black population constituted a large majority in all the islands, they were not to be instructed in literacy or the Christian faith or to be baptized. The Church of England as the church of the plantocracy was the dominating Christian body in Barbados from 1625, in Nevis, Antigua and Montserrat from 1634, and in Jamaica from 1655. Clergy and parishioners, intrinsically tied to vested interests, had no desire to address the appalling conditions of the slaves or include them in civil society.

More, as an episcopal church without bishops in the region until 1824,[1] and as part and parcel of English society and restorative politics, they perceived themselves as the 'nation at prayer', or mere voyagers across the

Atlantic to virtually uninhabited lands. Humanitarian efforts such as the work of the Society for the Propagation of the Gospel in Foreign Parts (SPC, 1701), appeals by individuals such as Bishop Edmund Gibson (London, 1727) or Sir Christopher Codrington, governor of Barbados (1704; Codrington estates bequeathed to SPC in 1703) which were Anglican attempts of moderate reform or 'progressive amelioration', and the foundation of Codrington College, a quasi-monastic community based on Black labour, proved powerless to change the overall system of subordination and cruelty.[2] A few, among them James Ramsey, a Scot in St. Kitts, in a 'courageous duel' with the planters against slave trade and slavery, strongly influenced the abolitionist movement in the pre-emancipation period.[3] Precursors were the Quakers, especially in Barbados (George Fox visiting there in 1671), who acted on a liberational biblical interpretation of human life and thus helped to prepare the ground for the non-conformist missionaries.[4] The striking feature of the period, however, was 'not the failure of the established church to launch a mission for the slaves, but its failure to make any impact on the lives of the free and white members of colonial society'.[5]

Against this background of an ecclesiastical life based on the dominance of European thought, rituals and values and the de-culturization and de-spiritualization of human beings, there arrived another mission motivated by a personal approach and care for the slaves: the Moravians, ushered in by a meeting between the German Pietist Count Zinzendorf from Herrnhut, and the slave Anthony Ulrich in Copenhagen, in St. Thomas in 1732, and Jamaica in 1754; the African American Baptists, George Liele from Georgia and Moses Baker from the Bahamas in Jamaica in 1783; the Methodists, led by John Baxter and Thomas Coke from London in Barbados and Jamaica in 1787 and 1789, respectively; the Congregationalists from London in Guyana in 1807; and the Presbyterians in Jamaica in 1827. *Coastlands and Islands*[6] mentions five strongholds for this Evangelical mission: (1) Places entered by planter invitation, made use of by the Moravians. (2) The significance of free converts, particularly urban freed slaves, starting points for the Methodists. (3) The significance of slave migration, enforced and voluntary, within the Caribbean. (4) The role played by the army, such as in Liele's escape from America to Jamaica. (5) Mission stations opened—besides the *Unitas Fratrum* from 1732—by various London-based missionary societies inaugurated to shape Christian expansion from 1790: the Wesleyan-Methodist Missionary Society (1789), Baptist Missionary Society (BMS, 1792), London Missionary Society (LMS, mainly Congregationalists, 1795), Scottish Missionary Society (1796), and later the Society of Jesus (Jesuits).[7]

From a Eurocentric perspective, the Caribbean pre-emancipation movement is interpreted as part of those fundamental changes in human politics, economics and philosophy that emerged in the outgoing eighteenth century:

It was only in the 1780s, at the earliest, that colonial slaves began to find a place within the rights-of-man philosophy—at least a half-century lag behind similar demands for Europeans.[8]

The slow fall of the plantation complex, a drawn-out process throughout the nineteenth into the twentieth century, economic studies which emphasized the long-term non-profitability of slavery, the democratic revolutions in America (War of Independence, 1776–83) and France (1789) sweeping away old regimes, the Haitian revolution (Toussaint L'Ouverture, 1791) impacting on the West Indies, the Napoleonic wars triggering revolts in the Spanish Caribbean colonies, the Enlightenment emphasizing individual human rights—all these developments strengthened the abolitionists, active in the British and Foreign Antislavery Society or Société des Amis des Noirs. Eventually, inhuman coercion came to be morally condemned and legally abandoned. However, as Curtin points out, there was a convenient chronological distinction between two separate Acts, abolishing the slave trade (1807), and abolishing slavery (Britain, 1833; France, 1848; Cuba and Brazil, 1880).[9] When emancipation came, it brought 'freedom' without equality, 'tolerance' without cultural recognition, religious pluralism without basic human respect. The predominance of European sociopolitical interests remained guaranteed through the industrial revolution, and new developments in technology, food production and international trade. They ensured that the former racist patterns lingered on into the nineteenth and twentieth centuries. 'The antislavery campaign…went hand in hand with *laissez-faire* capitalism'.[10]

From the perspective of the African Diaspora, slaves and emancipated slaves, the story must be told differently. From the onset, there was passive and active resistance often fuelled by religion. Harsh suppression did not produce lasting submission nor quench the spirit of freedom and the hope for liberation. Of the more than fifty major slave revolts in three hundred years, besides the Maroon wars, mention should be made here of later major uprisings: Rebellions in Jamaica (Tacky, 1760), Berbice and Suriname (1763 and 1772), Belize (1773), and—with emancipation approaching—in Barbados (1804 and 1816), Trinidad (1819 and 1825), Demerara (1823), and the 'Jamaica Baptist War' (Sam Sharpe, 1831). Without exception they ended in arrests, reprisals and executions. In the midst of inhuman treatment, the Africans held on to their religious world views: 'Uprooted from their homeland, they maintained some of their identity and so filled the vacuum to which the church only paid attention in an inadequate way.'[11]

Imagine the white non-conformist missionaries in opposition to older ecclesiastical traditions would have, if not allied, at least sympathized with non-violent black resistance! Some few indeed did, led by an emphasis on experience, evangelistic zeal, equalitarian beliefs, and practical morality.[12]

But primarily, the Evangelical mission was motivated by insider-oriented themes such as religious voluntarism, personal evangelism, and individual freedom. In an attempt to prevent cruelty and eradicate the evils of 'sin', corruption, 'heathenism' and immorality, they concentrated on the personal conversion of the slaves. In an utterly senseless and destructive world, they preached a gospel of salvation sympathetic and meaningful to the conditions and demands of plantation life; they therefore helped the oppressed to arrive at personal integrity and moral conduct. As they did not need 'organized' religion, they turned the converted into effective evangelists for others and spread the faith rapidly. Unwittingly, though cloaked in European cultural values, they introduced an intercultural interface, if not yet synthesis, between biblical and African-creole elements.

In this way, they posed a serious threat to the establishment and the planters' interests which would later force them to take an unambiguous stand in the antislavery campaign. For the time being, their understanding of Christianity referred to one's personal relationship to God, and not at all to civil and political affairs. It called people to repentance from 'sin' to be liberated spiritually, not politically: absolute neutrality, therefore, in the slavery issue was a matter of necessity in mission policy. So the white missionaries tried to turn Africans into even more useful servants, and did not challenge the socio-political system nor called the slaves to rebellion. When in the ensuing years they themselves became engulfed in conflicts and persecution, they still regarded it as irresponsible to encourage violence and advocated only 'amelioration' of the system brought on by constitutional reforms. However, this 'missionary gradualism' on the slavery and injustice issues, the missionaries' ambiguity and ineptitude to engage in earnest cross-cultural encounters, could not satisfy black Christians. The missionaries 'accepted the blacks abstractly as equal, while rejecting the cultural expressions which defined black life'.[13]

As an outstanding example, we concentrate on the mission, strategies and theology of the Black Baptists who entered Jamaica in 1783 (Trinidad, 1812).[14] They recruited the rural and urban masses, became the most critical opponents of the authorities' and planters' attitude and practice towards the slaves, influenced the pre-emancipation as well as post-emancipation periods throughout the nineteenth century, and introduced a Black theology of liberation and interculturation. A key figure is George Liele (or Lile), often called the 'Negro prophet of deliverance'. He was born a slave in Virginia, but in 1773 set free by his master to exercise his spiritual gifts, ordained and licensed in 1775 to preach and sing salvation to the oppressed. He was, besides the Baptists William Byrd, Andrew Bryan, David George (later in Sierra Leone) and the Methodists Absalom Jones and Richard Allen (founder of the 'Free African Society' in Philadelphia in 1894, organized as the African Methodist Episcopal Church in 1816), one of the first African preachers and pioneers of independent Baptist churches in North America. His church in Silver Bluff in South Carolina and the Yamacraw Baptist Church in Georgia were the first in a string of well-organized congregations under black leadership along the Savannah River which, distinct from mission stations, schools, or mere permission to attend camp-meetings, became the social and cultural home of thousands of freed slaves after the Civil War.

When his master's children tried to re-enslave him, he escaped with 400 white families and 5,000 freed blacks and slaves after Independence on an army ship to Jamaica, where he was moved by the plight of his sisters and brothers. While in service to the governor, he obtained the license to preach and founded the first 'Ethiopian Baptist Church' at Kingston Race Course in 1784. In a sermon on Romans 10:1, he compared the fate of the slaves with Israel's bondage in Egypt who needed to be set free, and referred to the God of the Bible as the God of the *African cosmos* who would turn oppression and suffering into victory—a first synthesis of African traditions and historical experience with the biblical message. Thirty years before the arrival of the British Baptists, he laid together with other American ex-slaves, George Gibbs, Moses Baker and Thomas Nicholas Swigle, the foundation for overt African expressions of the Christian faith and the 'freedom of the African soul'. In the *'Covenant of the Anabaptist Church, Begun in America, Dec 1777, and in Jamaica, Dec 1783'* he placed the Baptist work formally under the protection of 'King, Country and Law' and allowed only those into membership of the church who obtained permission from their masters. Swigle soon started a second congregation less dependent on the plantocracy which is understood as initiating the process of further Africanization. Both Liele and Baker called for support from the BMS in London, motivated by lack of finance, the need to counteract mounting persecution and tightened legal restrictions (from 1807; Jamaica slave code against licensing non-conformist preachers, 1816), and to channel the mission into more orderly Baptist patterns.

The Methodists, in pursuit of 'Christian perfection' and Wesley's stance against slavery as a human 'villainy', recruited initially most converts from among the 'free people of colour' in towns, but also reached white settlers, and turned into a church for the mixed-race middle class. By 1824, they were based in St. Vincent, St. Kitts, Barbados, Dominica, Nevis, Tortola, Jamaica, the Bahamas, Anguilla, Haiti, Guyana and Trinidad.[15] Concerned about the violent hostility of the white upper classes, they chose political passivity and pious moderation. Coke wrote: 'However just my sentiments may be concerning slavery, it was ill-judged of me to deliver them from the pulpit.'[16] However, this policy did not shield the Wesleyans from being reputed as an extremely disruptive force by the Jamaican legislature. [...]

The resistance of Christian black and free coloured converts before emancipation warranted its continuance into the nineteenth and twentieth centuries. August 1, 1834 was without exception celebrated as the 'Day of Jubilee' (Lev. 25).[17] By then half of the Jamaican ex-slave population pronounced themselves Methodists, Baptists, Moravians or Presbyterians. They understood Christianity as protecting basic liberty and equality. The missionary churches seemed to offer them self-respect, 'respectability based on British non-conformist models',[18] much-needed education, assistance in accessing land, and social upward-mobility. Since previous conflicts between the denominations had given way to some kind of mutual acquiescence and cooperation, even Anglicans were now accepted as the church able to bestow propriety and political influence on the black and mixed-race middle class. They all expanded. However, when the euphoria had passed, the majority discovered that socio-politically and economically they were not set free, and the assumed intercultural partnership between black and white missions was not to take place. Hope began to fade and gave way to disillusionment. After the period of 'apprenticeship' (1834–1838), perceived by Africans as half-slavery, the plantation owners carried on with their usual techniques in order to keep control of the labour force. The industrial revolution[19] had brought immense wealth to Europe which in turn meant new demand for tropical products. So the European influence in the Caribbean increased throughout the nineteenth century. The import of indentured labour from the Indian subcontinent because of labour shortage, voluntary migration within and between regions including Panama, Cuba and North America, and schemes developed by the British and French for continued (partly coerced) migration from West Africa, all facilitated further exploitation, but also aided more adaptability among shifting populations, granting them access to added, even revolutionary, ideas.

Between 1840 and 1870, the European missions embarked on widespread humanitarian and educational programmes, established schools (helped by Parliamentary and other educational grants) and founded theological training colleges (Anglicans: Codrington 1830, Baptists: Calabar 1843). They also began work in Africa. However, with the exception of the Baptists, they dismally failed to develop an indigenous leadership. When, in 1853, the black priest Robert Gordon applied to enter the Anglican ministry in his homeland Jamaica, the bishop urged him to work in Africa.[20] By and large western churches were convinced that authority and governance had to be white; they had to introduce colonial citizens to British culture, and only vigilant supervision, strict moral discipline, and preaching an 'undefiled' Christian gospel would free blacks from 'pagan' rituals and 'superstitions' and thus avert church life and theology from becoming syncretistic. They certainly were eager to 'ameliorate' the conditions of the underclass faced with impoverishment, natural disasters and diseases, but they ignored other forces and remedies at work. Racism, based on colour of skin, cultural superiority and social status, was even to intensify in the second half of the century.

Only the Baptists, particularly native Baptists, followed a different direction. 'Native Baptist', according to Turner, is the generic term for a proliferation of groups in which blacks 'developed religious forms, more or less Christian in content, that reflected their needs more closely than the orthodox churches, black or white'.[21] Led by congregational, non-hierarchical principles, and gathered in hundreds of 'free villages', they developed a local leadership of African 'mammies' and 'daddies', applied a 'class-ticket and leader' system which augmented independent membership, and expressed themselves in often unorthodox styles. Recent studies from 1990 such as by Stewart, Gordon, Segal, Lawson, Austin-Broos and others have thrown light on this lasting legacy surviving to the present. Stewart speaks of Caribbean Baptist activists and 'Baptist politics' with three objectives: to develop a theology of mission steeped in human affairs, help achieve electoral franchise, and strengthen economic independence.[22] Lawson explores it further: The story, he affirms, 'is one historic example of the unpredictable nature of the struggle between the dynamic social forces of race, religion and politics in any society',[23] be it in the colonies, South Africa, the States or modern Europe. This concurs with the debate, from the mid-twentieth century, about African retentions in the diaspora anywhere, or what Aleyne has called an 'African continuum in variations'.[24] It confirms two conflicting cosmologies, two cultures, two theologies, one European and one African, in mutual encounter or intercultural interplay which, ever refreshed by ongoing contacts with Africa, introduced a process of cross-fertilization, allowed for a creative synthesis of different traditions, and made syncretization in various degrees inevitable.[25] Curtin, for the years 1830–1865, coined the term 'two Jamaicas': Native Baptists had become 'another religion competing with the Christianity of the European missionaries.'[26]

The Nature of Black Presence in England before the Abolition of Slavery

Lorraine Dixon

[The following essay is an extract from some unpublished research undertaken by Lorraine Dixon in the late 1990s and subsequently published in extract form in *Black Theology: An International Journal* 5.2 (July 2007). The author, a Black Anglican priest, undertakes important work in the area of

Black Church history and outlines the historical context in which the abolitionist movement against slavery was conducted. One of the important
aims of this Reader is to uncover important work that has not been given a
public or a more prominent airing, hitherto. This work is such an example.
Given that this year marks the 200th anniversary of the abolition of the
slave trade in Britain, this piece is an apposite piece of work detailing the
cultural and theological context that gave rise to the outlawing of the slave
trade in this country.]

Black British History: A Black Atlantic Perspective

Historians in recent decades have begun to chronicle Black history in Britain.[27]
This has been a hidden chronicle in the scheme of British history and thus a
much needed corrective. However, this narrative has been somewhat insular,
fragmenting the story of Black peoples into geographic areas. It should be
stated that Paul Edwards and James Walvin do concede that 'Africans came
to Britain individually or in batches, directly from Africa or indirectly by way
of the American and West Indian plantations'.[28] In contrast, Paul Gilroy's
book *The Black Atlantic: Modernity and Double Consciousness*[29] has been
an important contribution to the notion of a 'Black Atlantic'. Slavery thrust
different African ethnic groups together in the slave forts of West Africa, on
the slave ships of the 'middle passage' and most significantly on the slave
plantations and the huge houses of the rich in the Caribbean, America and
Britain. As the letters and autobiographies of Africans such as Ignatius Sancho,
Ottobah Cugoano and Olaudah Equiano testify, there was also movement
between these three locations for those who were enslaved.

As Africans came into contact with White people in Europe as well as in
the Americas, this resulted in a 'Black Atlantic' culture that was a complex
hybrid of Black and White influences from Africa, the Caribbean, America
and Britain. Gilroy refers to this particular culture as a 'transcultural [and]
international formation…'[30] Modern popular music has illustrated this very
point. Talking about the music of Black British soul band 'Soul II Soul' who
rose to prominence in the 1980s, Gilroy describes their record 'Keep on
Moving' as a creative cultural mix of Black British, African Caribbean and
African American ingredients. He states that

> [t]his formal unity of diverse cultural elements was more than just a power-
> ful symbol. It encapsulated the playful Diasporic intimacy that has been a
> marked feature of transnational black Atlantic creativity…[31]

Gilroy goes on to make the point that the Black Atlantic is not a new
concept but one that has marked out the migration of African peoples ever
since slavery. He says that the

> history of the black Atlantic…continually crisscrossed by the movements
> of black people—not only as commodities but engaged in various strug-

gles towards emancipation, autonomy, and citizenship—provides a means to re-examine the problems of nationality, location, identity, and historical memory.[32]

For Gilroy the Black Atlantic is about the fluid nature of Black identities, cultures and geographies which are not specifically African, Caribbean, American or British but are an amalgam of all of these at once. The concept of the 'Black Atlantic' has begun to feed into historical discourse providing 'a means to re-examine the problems of nationality, location, identity, and historical memory'.[33]

Here to Stay: A Brief History of Black People in England

Despite the cautionary note of the previous section, that Black British history is a Black Atlantic history, the rest of this chapter will focus on the nature of Black presence in England up to abolition. This coincides with the time frame and emphasis of my research.

According to Peter Fryer, Black people have been a part of the British Isles and its historical narrative for 2,000 years.[34] This narrative navigates itself between silence and speech in terms of this presence. Nevertheless, Fryer is still able to explore Black involvement in Roman Britain as part of the military and slave presence as well as in Ancient Ireland and Scotland.

In the early modern era, the evidence that Black people have contributed to British life especially in England is slightly easier to gather. A Black trumpeter called John Blanke was employed as one of King Henry VIII's court musicians. Fryer posits that he was 'pretty certainly the man who is twice portrayed in the painted roll of the 1511 Westminster Tournament, held to celebrate the birth of a son to Catherine of Arragon'.[35] He is depicted on horseback, playing a trumpet, liveried in yellow and grey plus a turban. A few decades later, in 1555 John Locke introduced five Black 'slaves' as a result of his trading between Africa and England. They were taught English and returned to the Guinea Coast as translators to further English commercial interests. These interests increased as other English travellers and merchants visited Africa. John Hawkyns was the first English trader to seek a profit from the sale of African slaves. Fryer reveals that on Hawkyns's

> triangular voyage, in 1562-3, he acquired at least 300 inhabitants of the Guinea coast... He took these people to the Caribbean island of Hispaniola (now Haiti and the Dominican Republic), where he sold them to the Spaniards for £10,000 worth of pearls, hides, sugar, and ginger.[36]

Hawkyns's example opened the way for increasing trade in African flesh. It is not possible to accurately date when trading in slaves began on British soil. Both Folarin Shyllon and Peter Fryer cite William Bragge receiving monies from the East India Company in 1621 for thirteen 'negroes or

Indian people' possibly revealing their Asian identity as opposed to an African one. Other historians such as Kenneth Little suggest that 'English participation in the slave trade did not become significant until about the time of the Restoration in 1660'.[37]

This coincided with a period of stability, influenced by the restoration of the monarchy and an attendant oligarchy, following the power struggles after Oliver Cromwell's death. With colonies in America and the Caribbean, the importance of sugar and tobacco to the British economy was being discovered. 'The Company of Royal Adventurers Trading in Africa' was formed in 1663. This was superseded by the Royal African Company in 1672 which held the monopoly on British slave interests until 1698, by which time the pressure to engage in free trade proved irresistible. Shyllon states that with

> free trade and the increasing demands of the sugar plantations, the volume of the British slave trade rose enormously. The Royal African Company, between 1680 and 1686, transported an annual average of 5,000 slaves. In the first nine years of free trade, Bristol alone shipped 160,950 black slaves to the sugar plantations. In 1760, 146 ships sailed from British ports for Africa, with a capacity for 36,000 slaves. By 1771 the number of ships had increased to 190 and the total number of slaves to 47,000.[38]

As Britain took over former Spanish colonies, this resulted in a near monopoly regarding the slave trade. Although the British slave trade did not become significant until possibly the second half of the seventeenth century, there is evidence to suggest that Black people were living in Britain on a constant basis from the sixteenth century. Fryer draws attention to a number of people mentioned in parish and other records. These are sometimes named, sometimes unnamed and often described as negroes belonging to somebody.

> In 1570 one Nicholas Wichehalse of Barnstaple in Devon mentioned 'Anthony my negarre' in his will. The illegitimate daughter of Mary, described as a 'negro of John Whites', was baptized in Plymouth in 1594, the supposed father was a Dutchman.[39]

Fryer also records the presence of Clare, Maria, Jesse or Lewse and Marea who were Black servants based at various residences. To further underline their precarious position, he proposes that the options for Black people in this period were in the main limited to that of domestic servant/slave,[40] prostitute, sailor or entertainer. However, it was as a slave/servant that most Black people found their employment. The reasons for this being that it was fashionable for royalty, the aristocracy and the newly rich, including merchants and slave ship captains, to have Black servants on their staff.

This fashion was probably started by West Indian planters who, returning to Britain continued to use their slaves, and set a pattern that others wanted to emulate. Domesticated Blackness was appropriated in this case as a marker for White affluence and vanity. The portraits of slaves in a number of aristocratic homes, including that of Dido Elizabeth Lindsay in the residence of Lord Mansfield, bear witness to this. It is difficult to put an accurate figure on the numbers of Black people in Britain at this time, but their presence especially in London must have been significant in order for Queen Elizabeth I to twice attempt to have them deported, first in 1596 and then again in 1601. The Queen in her letter to the Lord Mayor of London on July 11, 1596, is concerned with the numbers of 'blackmoores' being brought into the country and wishes to have them confiscated from their masters (who should 'be served by their owne countrymen then with those kinde of people...'[41]). The deportations probably did not have the desired effect as the Queen issued another proclamation in 1601 demanding the removal of 'blackmoores' from her realm. However, the outcome of increasing British presence in the slave trade was that Black people were to form a continuous and an increasingly visible presence.

By the eighteenth century, the Black community had grown considerably. The size of this community can only be estimated, as the population census came into being in 1801. People of colour were peripheral to this as ethnicity was not recorded. Norma Myers in her book *Reconstructing the Black Past*, first presents the usual view of historians who 'assume that the Black population increased following the influx of black American Loyalists in 1784, and subsequently experienced a decrease in the nineteenth century'.[42] She then seeks to interrogate this view and obtain a more accurate figure. Myers contends that numbers of the Black population were inflated because of racist concerns. She gains this view from eighteenth-century newspapers such as the *Daily Journal* that report in a hysterical manner about the growing Black population in London and irrational fears on the part of reporters, perhaps speaking for other White people particularly in London, of being swamped by such people.

Myers proposes that estimates of the period such as twenty, thirty or even forty thousand were inflated, estimates that have been perpetuated by historians ever since. In a pamphlet published in 1773 by the West Indian agent for Barbados, Samuel Estwick stated that 'there are already fifteen thousand Negroes in England and scarce is there a street in London that does not give many examples of that'.[43] Other contemporary observers cite similar figures and gradually exaggerate the numbers. 'By 1788', Myers states, 'Gilbert Francklyn estimated the size of the black population to be over forty thousand.'[44] In none of these estimated figures are distinctions made regarding the numbers of each gender or whether the Black people referred to are free or slave, in London or in the country as a whole. Myers settles for a figure of around 10,000 Blacks by utilizing analysis of various records such as those connected with baptisms, the criminal justice system and poor law relief. In this estimation, Myers' view is shared by fellow historians Folarin Shyllon and Seymour Drescher.

As stated above, most Africans who were slaves in the households of the aristocracy and the rich could be found not only in the prosperous slave ports of London, Liverpool or Bristol but isolated in the homes of the landed gentry in rural areas up and down the British Isles. Their *raison d'être* was to service the needs of rich families; they were in bondage not in service. Little suggests, rather provocatively, that aristocratic ladies wanted Black boys as personal attendants to 'better show off the whiteness of their own skins'.[45] Black people were perceived as commodities and as such were advertised for sale in papers and bought and sold in taverns.

Once bought they were given a new name, often a Latin one,[46] a metal collar with the owner's name or coat of arms, and became the opulently dressed chattels and pets[47] of their master and mistress. Black people existed on the margins of social life, becoming somewhat invisible to mainstream British life. However, at times

> they emerged...to establish their own families and homes. In doing so, they entered the records, the baptismal, marriage and death registers, enabling us to catch a glimpse of otherwise obscure individuals.[48]

There was a gender imbalance among the slaves, in that the majority of them were overwhelmingly male. This may have occurred because initially males were wanted by the planters to work their plantations. According to Edwards and Walvin, the gender situation was worse in Britain than in the colonies. This inevitably led to relationships between these Black men and White women, leading to marriage or long-term and casual partnerships.[49]

Black people who were unable to obtain a position in a household or who chose to escape slavery as a 'runaway' became part of the army of multi-ethnic poor who attempted to survive life on the streets of London and other slave ports as street entertainers, peddlers, beggars or petty criminals.[50] Black soldiers, who fought on the British side in the American war of independence, also expanded this horde as well as stowaways from the so-called West Indies. The Black poor became so numerous in parts of the east end of London that they were known as the 'St Giles' Blackbirds'.

Not all Black people in Britain at this time were slaves or part of the poor classes. Folarin Shyllon speaks of a small number of royal African youths sent to England to be educated including Peter Panah, John Naimbanna and Philip Quaque, as well as others who visited the British Isles such as Paul Cuffee, a successful African American merchant and shipbuilder.[51] Nonetheless, life for the vast majority of Black people in England was limited by bondage or poverty.

The Dynamic of 'Race' and Slavery

Slavery has had a long history in the narrative of human experience and so the Atlantic slave trade was not unique by any means. For over a millennia, conquering nations have enslaved the vanquished, especially male warriors, and sold them on for political favours, goods or money. The Atlantic slave trade grew out of the needs of the early planters in the Caribbean and Americas to produce cash crops such as tobacco, sugar and cotton. Initially, indigenous populations were used, but disease, overwork and abuse decimated them. European 'Indentured' workers were then brought in to take on this work.

Although the

> white labourers were able to stand up to the hard work and harsh treatment…the disadvantage [for the planters was] that they had to be freed after the term of their contract was over, usually five or ten years. Then they expected to receive a plot of land of their own.[52]

The only alternative seemingly for the plantation owners, so that they could gain higher returns from their plant yields, was to obtain 'slave labour from Africa. The slave was cheaper money which might buy a white man's services for ten years, would buy a slave for life.'[53]

The genesis of this particular slave trade came out of 'explorations' of Africa by various European countries, in particular Spain, Portugal and subsequently Britain from the fifteenth century in search of gold. They found gold in two forms, one was the precious metal and the other was Black gold—African slaves. The trade in Black flesh to provide virtually free labour on the plantations in the Americas and Caribbean proved to be very profitable. Moreover, the kings of West Africa colluded with the trade, by selling their prisoners of war for arms and manufactured goods. The goods and capital gained by these rulers ensured that they engaged in more frequent wars against neighbouring communities.

European slave traders sought to encourage these wars in order to maintain their wealth. The Atlantic slave trade was a horrific and brutal system. On the slave ships, women and men were chained together and kept in very dirty, restrictive spaces that frustrated any attempts to move freely. Malnutrition and disease were part of the life of the slaves on these ships. As well as the cruelty of beatings, African women also faced the outrage of rape and sexual abuse. Most of the slaves were taken to the Caribbean. They were either kept on the islands or dispatched to other parts of the Americas. The plantations were just as brutal as the slave ships, with abuse and cruelty part of the everyday existence of these Africans. The institution of slavery attempted to deny Black people their humanity or place in the world except a subordinate one. The social construct of racism and flawed theological reflection were used as an apologetic to maintain the economic interests of slavery. Legislation and political will further institutionalized and legitimated the system.

Myths about Africa and her people abounded in the sixteenth and seventeenth centuries that helped to justify the enslavement of African peoples. Peter Fryer states:

> Such fantasies [included]...the notion that Africans were inherently care-free, lazy, and lustful... Such myths eased English consciences about enslaving Africans and thereby encouraged the slave trade... They were sub-human savages, not civilized human beings like us. So there could be no disgrace in buying or kidnapping them, branding them, shipping them to the New World, selling them, forcing them to work under the whip.[54]

However, the slave traders and explorers that visited Africa possessed views of the country and its people that were already part of the European imagination from more ancient times. Unlike the modern world of these adventurers, the ancient world was a mixed one where different ethnic groups and peoples existed side by side. The dynamic of 'race' and a value system that denigrated people on the basis of their skin colour did not exist. Yet, there is evidence that

> there was a definitive colour symbolism within Greco-Roman culture, by which whiteness was positively evaluated and blackness negatively evaluated. Blackness was associated with death and a conception of an under-world.[55]

However, the situation was further complicated by Blackness being seen as a desirable quality by other ancient sources. So, the attitude to Blackness and Black people was fluid and unclear. The Middle Ages are what proved to be most significant in the genesis of racialized thought in European consciousness. The ideas and traditions of the ancient world were refracted through the lens of Christianity. An idea that survived on into the Middle Ages was the concept of 'monstra'. According to Robert Miles:

> monstra defined unusual individual or anomalous births, but its meaning was extended through the Middle Ages to include whole populations of people supposedly characterised by anomalous phenotypical characteristics... [V]arious human physical features (some imaginary) were signified as monstrous, one of which was skin colour.[56]

The Church viewed particular people as being under the wrath of God and as the embodiment of sin and the Devil. Christianity had inherited the colour symbolism of the ancient world and this was reinterpreted into a racialized dichotomy. This led to a 'discourse of the Other'[57] where physical, religious and societal differences from a perceived norm were becoming fixed in the minds of European thinkers as 'monstrous'.

At first this 'othering' was directed at Muslim North Africans who were viewed as the direct opposite of Christian Europeans. They were depicted as uncivilized, depraved and tyrannical and such representation fuelled the desire for the holy Christian war or Crusades against those perceived as 'heathens'.

However, this concept of the 'Other' was directed at other non-European peoples, especially in Sub-Saharan Africa and Asia, as they were encountered in the travels of European traders and explorers. The written accounts of these travellers became an important source of how Africans were represented. Fantastical tales were written about African peoples and their communities which

> served to identify the abnormal characteristics of the people with whom contact was established… [T]he reporting often stressed precisely those aspects of African life that were most repellent to the West and tended to submerge the indications of a common humanity.[58]

With the rise of the British role in slavery and the need for cheap labour, these negative representations of African peoples were increasingly important in the production of an apologetic for the Atlantic slave trade and the brutalization of an alleged sub-human 'race'.

The Road to Abolition

Despite the racialized discourse that surrounded the institution of slavery, the existence of the buying and selling of human flesh raised questions about the validity of ownership of a fellow human being in English common law. The Yorke-Talbot decision in 1729 sought to clear up a confused situation. It was determined by the Solicitor-General and Attorney General that baptism did not effect the freedom of slaves on British soil and that they remained the property of their masters who could send them to the colonial plantations if they so chose.

Although this ruling seems unjust and horrific, Gretchen Gerzina reminds us readers that the eighteenth century was a harsh and brutal era where crime and punishment, child labour and high infant mortality and oppressive work situations for poor White people were part of the very fabric of English life. In this sort of context, slavery was perceived as playing its part in the economic life of the country. Cotton, sugar and other benefits that were gained from this industry made it seemingly indispensable.

In this economic climate, those who argued for the retention of the slave trade had powerful allies. Racist ideas about Black people as less than human, as lascivious, as lazy, as base brutes, were also appropriated in the fight to maintain this system. Those who were struggling for the abolition of slavery had an uphill battle. They employed stories of Black people who were literate or who had converted to Christianity to argue that such people were harmless, domesticated and naive.[59]

The Yorke-Talbot ruling remained active until it was challenged on behalf of a slave called James Somerset. Somerset ran away from his master after arriving in England. Upon his recapture he was put on a boat bound for Jamaica. Granville Sharp managed to rescue him before he was removed from the country. After a long legal battle, Lord Chief Justice Mansfield finally ruled in June 1772 that a slave could not be removed forcibly from Britain. This ruling did not effect the abolition of slavery, because sales and kidnaps of Black people continued, but it gave ammunition to the abolitionists' struggle.

Black people themselves were acting on their own behalf to gain their freedom. Some slaves escaped the brutality of the Caribbean plantations by stowing away or working their passage on ships in order to gain freedom on English soil. Many undertook such actions because the laws relating to the institution of slavery were not as clearly defined in England as in the colonies. Those who chose to liberate themselves by running away from their masters were often the subject of advertisements in the newspapers of the era. Folarin Shyllon cites an early example of such a notice.

> Went away 22nd July last, from the house of William Webb, in Limehouse Hole, a negro man, about 20 years old, called Dick, yellow complexion, wool hair, about five foot six inches high, having on his right breast the word 'Hare' burnt. Whosoever brings him to the said Mr. Webb's, shall have half-a-guinea reward and reasonable charges.[60]

Others sought baptism as they believed that once they were baptized they should be as free as their 'Christian' brothers and sisters who were their masters and mistresses. Dinah Black of Bristol in 1667

> told her mistress, following her baptism, that she wished from henceforth 'to live under the teaching of the Gospel', whereupon the Christian mistress had Dinah Black bound and gagged and put on board a ship going to America.[61]

She was saved by some truly Christian souls who gained her freedom. Furthermore, some Black people bought their own freedom and spoke out against the heinous crime of slavery through political autobiography. Their impetus was their understanding of Christianity and their theology could be said to be an early form of Black theology—a seeking of freedom from the dehumanizing effects of slavery and racism. Such Black people included Ukawsaw Gronniosaw, Olaudah Equiano, Mary Prince, Mary Seacole and Ottabah Cugoano. Black people connected to Christianity in their own oppositional way. It is a story of both survival strategies and radical action in the face of hostility and racism in the church and society. It was such struggles of many within the Black British community, as well as the well-known advocates of the Anti-slavery movement such as Granville Sharp and William Wilberforce, that saw the abolition of British slavery in 1834.

Concluding Thoughts

The story of Black people in England did not stop with their emancipation. They disappeared into the margins of their communities marrying, working, struggling for survival up and down the country, but their descendants are still part of the urban life of the nation, peoples who have reshaped the nature of England as a multicultural and multiethnic diverse tapestry.

> From London to Liverpool they walk the same streets as their ancestors, with lineage that goes back, for some, even to the sixteenth and seventeenth centuries. They have intermarried and become inextricably entwined in England's past and present. While individuals have doubtless been long forgotten, theirs is nonetheless an unbroken living legacy, a continual and very English presence.[62]

Post Emancipation Religious Stratification in Jamaica 1865–1948

Edson Burton

[This extract is taken from Burton's unpublished doctoral thesis 'From Assimilationism to Anti-Racism: The Church of England's Response to Afro-Caribbean Migration 1948–1981' (University of West England, 2004). Burton's thesis is concerned with the Church of England and her relationship to Black people in Britain between the years 1948 and 1981. This extract seeks to place the development of the later Anglican approaches to Black theology in Britain.]

Despite the downturn in enthusiasm in Britain, missionary Christianity and education achieved the partial assimilation of the Afro-Jamaican populace. During the nineteenth century adherence to Christianity became a social cement that bound the many differing strata on the island to a shared set of values.[63] But this cannot be separated from a wider identification with British culture that was occurring on these islands. [...]

The social stratification that had begun during slavery deepened in the post-emancipation period. By inculcating the notion that assimilating English mores was a sign of social worth, the West Indies came to a position of a class colour stratification that was common to nearly all post-emancipation societies. Whites were at the apex of the social ladder, the Browns, those who could claim a white ancestor, at the centre and the Black population at the bottom.[64]

As was implicit in our earlier allusions to church affiliation, church attendance became a barometer of social stratification. Adherence to Christianity was a mark of respectability.[65] Clergy and congregations reinforced perceptions of respectability. Peter Wilson hints at the importance of female agency in this regard.

> Not only is the Church the ultimate authority for the definition of respectability it is outside the home, the principal public domain of sociability for women, who more or less control the activities of the church even through such key positions as pastor and deacon are controlled by men.[66]

The denomination to which one belonged conferred further respectability. Membership of the Anglican Church, for example, became an outward sign of social mobility as despite disestablishment the Church of England continued to represent the metropolitan religion and the religion of the White social elite. Ranked hierarchically below the Anglican Church were the various denominations. The Methodists were on many islands the church of the aspirant Brown and Black classes while the Baptists and Afro-Christian sects were the churches of the poor. This hierarchy was sometimes reversed on other islands depending on the respective strengths and weaknesses that existed between the denominations.

As church affiliation was a sign of social prestige, it was not uncommon for individuals or for generations within the same family to 'progress' from Baptist to Methodist and thence to Anglican status as their position in society improved.[67]

But the extent of conformity to Christianity that existed among the population fell far short of what was expected by the missionaries and clergy. Christian commentators bemoaned the continuance of African syncretic forms.[68] The Christian writer E.W. Thompson perceived these to be the vestiges of African beliefs:

> West African superstition survives in the West Indian Negroes. The Voodooism of the thickets of Haiti and other West Indian islands is only African paganism in its most degraded form without the dignity that national or tribal use lend to it.[69]

Elements of African belief flourished by way of either compartmentalization or fusion with Christianity. Belief in obeah evidences the former since unlike the Myal tradition it has not fused with Christianity. As in slavery, practising obeah was generally despised but was nonetheless believed in by much of the black population well into the twentieth century. By contrast the trend witnessed in Myalism towards the assimilation of Christian elements continued throughout the nineteenth century. This assimilation was implicit in the fact that from the early onset of Christian mission in Jamaica, Myal men invoked the Holy Spirit as the force of possession rather than an African deity and, marking a later change on this continuum, during the 1860 revival Myal men referred to themselves as 'Angel-men'. As suggested earlier Myalists assimilated Christian elements as a veneer for the practice of African traditions which were otherwise illegal. Post-slavery assimilation continued to serve such a legitimizing function.

The encounter between Myalism and Christianity led to the creation of new religious forms that were offshoots of both traditions. 'Convince' was the earliest form of Myalism and is not well documented in the litera-ture. According to Gardner, Convince began, in the years before slavery's abolition, as an attempt by Myalist leaders to gain official recognition by introducing Christian elements.[70] Gardner reports that its name is derived from the conversion experience of its adherents:

> [E]vidence for conversion and qualification for baptism was sought not so much in repentance and faith as in dreams, but if the applicant had expe-rienced a convince, that is, had swooned away, and while in that state had a vision, or passed through a stage of great excitement, attended by physi-cal contortions, then all was well.[71]

The 'followers' of Convince, known as Bongo men, added God and Christ to the Myalist pantheon but do not invoke them directly.[72] Despite the assimilation of Christian elements there are obvious continuities with the African stream of religious practice. As with Gardner's description of the worship of Accompong, supreme beings—God, Jesus—were seen as above human affairs unlike the lesser deities and it was these spirits that Convince members invoked. Furthermore, Convince devotees would be mounted or possessed by the spirits they invoked thus demonstrating the continual importance of the possession experience in the development of Afro-Jamaican syncretism. The role of preaching in Convince demon-strates continuity with Myalism. The emphasis in Convince was on a style of preaching that would invoke the possession.

Kongolese Africans who came to Jamaica as indentured servants in the 1840s revitalized the Myal stream.[73] However, the Kongolese indentured labourers are more strongly associated with *Kumina*.[74] Owing to the relative recentness of its importation, Kumina has retained many African features.[75] Kumina has a largely African pantheon with, typically, the deities being of more importance than the Creator God. Kumina demonstrates the additive nature of African religions in that it has assimilated Christian saints and the Yoruba God Shango into its pantheon. The main concern of Kumina is with the worship and invocation of ancestral spirits.

In contrast to the rural base of earlier and coexisting Afro-Christian sects, the Revivalists are concentrated in the more urban centres such as West Kingston, and the deprived areas outside Kingston and Morant Bay. Unlike Convince, Revival sects display the tradition in Myalism that attempted to solidify the Myal religious community into a structured leadership and following that was differentiated by roles. Revivalists assimilated aspects of Christianity within a Myal framework. As in Convince, Revivalists do not call on God or Christ to effect change in the world. They assemble figures drawn from the Bible and African religions into what is functionally a pantheon of higher and lower deities. These figures, which include Elijah, Moses, Daniel, Isaiah, Mark, Luke, Michael, Gabriel, Peter, Paul, James, and a deity called 'Madhouse', are believed to have particular powers and functions. Possession or, as it is called by the Revivalists, 'trumping', is central to Revivalist worship. Possession is seen as vital to the revelation of spiritual truth.[76] As in Myalism, Revivalists believe that spiritual forces cause physical illness. The Revival leader role is to diagnose, root out and protect their followers from malign spiritual forces.

A further example of African syncretism with Christianity is demonstrated in the early twentieth-century movement in Jamaica, 'Pocomania'. In many respects, Revivalism and Pocomania share similar traits and indeed coexist chronologically except that Pocomanians place more emphasis on 'singing' and 'spiritual' dancing and less stress on biblical preaching. In fact Simpson comments that many of his respondents conflated the two.[77]

Most commentators agree that is difficult to ascertain the strength of the Afro-Christian sects on the island. They did not, for example, keep membership records. But while they enjoyed some measure of support among the Black masses, in the society at large, where Englishness promised success, they lost religious authority to the white denominations. The Afro-Christian sects were viewed by Whites, Browns and more socially successful Blacks as the churches of the poor, the churches of the powerless, the moral outcasts.[78] In fact the negative view of the Afro-Christian sects partly explains their adoption of Christian elements.

The unity, which made them a vehicle of protest, also seemed to have dissipated by the twentieth century. Discussing the Afro-Christian sects in Jamaica, Trinidad, and Grenada, Simpson makes the following observation:

> All these groups are intensely competitive and the survival of a given 'church' depends upon the personality and ingenuity of the leader. Shifting memberships and secessions are common, and a leader who loses all or most of his following simply tries to recruit another.[79]

In the twentieth century however, the emergence of two very distinct religious phenomena, Rastafarianism and Pentecostalism, have represented quite distinct examples of the assimilation of Christian elements by the Afro-Jamaican population.

The importation of Pentecostalism in the twentieth century demonstrates in striking form both continuities and departures from earlier Myal traditions. The last decades of the nineteenth century and the turn of the twentieth century witnessed a new revival that swept through Europe and the Americas. A number of evangelical, charismatic and millenarian sects were born out of this revival. Two broad streams can be discerned: the

Sabbatarian and the Pentecostal. These streams are comprised of a number of different churches expressing particular nuances of Pentecostal or Sabbatarian belief. This thesis will focus upon the Pentecostal churches. The Pentecostal churches can be divided into three main traditions, the Trinitarian, Oneness Apostolic and Latter Rain Movement.

The Trinitarian churches are so called as they baptize in the name of the Trinity. They include the largest group of Pentecostal churches, the Church of God and the Church of God of Prophecy. Both churches have their headquarters in Cleveland Tennessee. In the United States, they are White majority churches. The Apostolic or Oneness churches baptize solely in the name of Jesus. This has been a source of much antagonism between the Apostolic and Trinitarian movement. Included in the Oneness churches are the First United Church of Jesus Christ and a number of smaller churches. In the United States, membership of these churches is particularly strong among the urban Black poor. In the Caribbean, their influence spread rapidly among the rural peasantry. The Latter Rain movement is a far more recent manifestation of Pentecostalism. The Latter Rain churches lay particular emphasis upon the laying on of hands and harnessing spiritual power. It is not, however, relevant to our present discussion.[80]

The Pentecostal movement began in 1906 in what is commonly known as the Azusa street revival. The revival refers to the first Pentecostal church in Azusa Street USA founded by the African-American W. J. Seymour. Seymour preached on divine healing for the imminent Second Advent. But the most significant theme was that speaking in tongues (diaglossia) was a sign of the Baptism of the Holy Spirit.[81] This experience harked back to the biblical day of Pentecost in which the Holy Spirit possessed Christ's disciples.[82] Seymour envisaged the revival as a solution to the political divisions in contemporary American society, particularly the racial segregation. At its inception, the church was racially mixed but this was short-lived. Beset by the internal and external politics of race in the USA, the revival split along racial lines.[83]

White North American, West Indians and British missionaries disseminated Pentecostalism through the Caribbean.[84] The new faith grew unremarkably until the period between 1940 and 1960, which saw a massive growth in Pentecostal adherence. For example, in 1943 the largest Pentecostal denomination, the Church of God, was seventh in denominational membership with 43,560 members (3.5 per cent of the population); by 1960 this figure had risen to 200,000 members (12 per cent of the population).[85] […]

This movement towards social conformity is reflected in the belief and worship practices often found in Pentecostal churches. In the context of the Jamaican African past, Pentecostalism witnesses the most extensive assimilation of European Protestant notions of Christianity. There is, for example, little deviation from the central importance of the Trinity. Saints are not accorded powers of possession and ancestors are not commemorated. Unlike Kumina or Pocomania there is no African ritual dance or music in Pentecostalism that we can speak of in terms of survival, or retention. Yet it is the Myal past that helps to explain the attractiveness of Pentecostalism in Jamaica and the Caribbean generally.[86] Pentecostalists, like their Myal forebears, continue to be concerned with the immanence of evil; its emphasis upon malign and benign spiritual forces demonstrate that there is no division between the spiritual and the material realm. Possession—a rite of passage towards individual renewal—has a central place in Pentecostal belief. Possession is brought on through music and through the unique oratorical power of Black preaching.[87]

Rastafarianism by contrast involved a comprehensive rejection of the European Jamaica. The roots of Rastafarianism can be traced to the Ethiopian movement of the late nineteenth century. However, the idealization of Ethiopia found widespread appeal in the Caribbean through the activities of Marcus Mosiah Garvey. Garvey was the founder of the largest, to date, Pan-African movement, the Universal Negro Improvement Association (UNIA). At its peak the UNIA had branches in the USA and in West and Southern Africa throughout the Caribbean.[88]

Garveyism was ostensibly a secular creed with a romantic attachment to Africa. However, Garvey's vocabulary was suffused with religious imagery. He called upon Blacks to worship Christ in their image:

> [J]ust as the White and the yellow man worship God in their own image that we as Negroes believe in the God of Ethiopia, the everlasting God… we shall worship him through the spectacles of Ethiopia.[89]

Garvey's key contribution to Rastafarianism lay in his emphasis upon identification with Africa. Garvey's identification with Africa expanded into a conviction that Blacks in the Diaspora should return to the African continent. Garvey highlighted Ethiopia in particular as the nation with which Africans in the Diaspora should identify. Furthermore, Garvey seemed to point towards the emergence of an African monarch that would redeem Africa's heritage, a heritage that he considered to be tarnished by European imperialism. His 'prophecy' was enshrined in the catechism of the UNIA: 'Princes come out of Egypt, Ethiopia shall stretch forth her hands to God.'[90] Garvey was also reported to have said before his departure to the USA in 1916, 'Look to Africa for the Crowning of a Black King, he shall be the Redeemer.'[91]

Garvey's pronouncements seemed to be borne out by the coronation of Ethiopia's monarch Haile Selassie. The symbolism of the event was heightened by Haile Selassie's additional titles 'King of Kings', 'Lords of Lords', 'Conquering Lion of the Tribe of Judah'. Perhaps most importantly he was regarded as a direct descendant of King Solomon.

In the context of Jamaica in which political events were furnished with religious significance Haile Selassie's Coronation was interpreted as a sign of a revelation from God.[92] The former Garveyites Leonard Howell, Joseph Hibert, Archibald Dunkley, Robert Hinds and Altamont Reid propagated the belief in the divinity of Haile Selassie. The first Rastafarians, as they became known, were drawn from the poor landless peasantry that had settled in the shantytowns of Kingston. Having taken root in Kingston its key thinkers began to spread the doctrine across Jamaica.

The main tenets of Rastafarianism evolved during the 1930s. Rastafarianism inherited the Black nationalism of Garveyism and added new resistance symbols such as the flag, the drum, the chalice, the locking of the hair and a new religious vocabulary. Some of these were in sharp counterpoise to the ideals of Jamaican society. But according to Chevannes in its worship—drumming, the choice of Sankey hymns, its religious nomenclature—Rastafarianism combined the worship practices common to Revivalism.[93] However, unlike Revivalism, Rastafarianism was less ambiguous in its celebration of Blackness.[94] Rastas also borrowed from the resistance struggles that were taking place in the Diaspora. For example, one explanation for the locking of the hair among Rastas is that the circulation of images of Kenya's Mau Mau fighters with their hair long and matted in the Jamaican press in 1953 inspired Rastas to do likewise.[95] Not only were the Mau Mau a symbol of proud resistance but also within the context of Jamaican aesthetics matting the hair was anathema to the prevailing fashion for straightening the hair in order for it to appear more European.[96] Rastas also found theological justification for locking the hair in the Bible.[97] As suggested by this, the Bible remained central to Rasta belief. Rastas interpreted the Bible as a chronicle of the struggles of Africans, the true Israelites.

Rastafarians were opposed to what they saw as the white misinterpretation of scripture. However, as recorded by Robert Owen, Rastas were also suspicious of the association between the churches and the colonial state. He records how the 'amalgamation of powers of the Church and state fits the Rasta theory of widespread conspiracy to deprive Blacks of their rights.'[98] It is of course important to contextualize Rastafarianism in the Jamaican religious milieu. But of vital interest to this study is the society's perception of Rastas before and during the migration to Britain. The establishment in Jamaica regarded Rastas as a threat to public order. Furthermore, the colonial Government was alarmed by its Pan-Africanism, particularly its identification with Ethiopia during the *Italo*-Abbyssian War. The conservative Jamaica newspaper *The Gleaner* regularly portrayed the movement as a threat to Whites. This seemed to be confirmed by violent clashes between Rastas and the police in 1959 and 1961. Yet, among the working classes there were those who celebrated the craftsmanship and entrepreneurial skill of Rastas.[99]

But whether viewed as misguided or revolutionaries it was clear to non-Rastafarians that Rasta was diametrically opposed to the Europeanized Jamaica. The particular relevance of Rastafarianism to the religious milieu of West Indians in Britain will become clear in later chapters. Suffice to say here that many Jamaicans who migrated to Britain in the key years of Caribbean migration between 1948 and 1962 would have had a perception of the movement. This would come to inform their attitudes to the movement once it re-emerged among second-generation Afro-Britons. On a broader scale, the complex trends towards syncreticism and assimilation represented by Rastafarianism, Pentecostalism and the European churches were to re-emerge in Britain.

British Churches and Jamaican Migration: A Study of Religion and Identities 1948 to 1965

Claire Taylor

[This extract is taken from Taylor's unpublished PhD thesis 'British Churches and Jamaican Migration: A Study of Religions and Identities 1948–1965' (Anglia Polytechnic University, 2002). Taylor, a Methodist minister, has undertaken invaluable research into the relationship between British churches and Jamaican migration from 1948 to 1965. This extract covers the first six years of the 'Windrush' epoch and offers an insight into the experiences of those first post-war Caribbean migrants and their experiences with various churches in Britain.]

The First Period—1948–1954
The first generation of migrants arriving in Britain from Jamaica after the Second World War had grown up in colonial Jamaica. Their image of Britain was as the 'mother country', the source of most authority. Their teachers, doctors, government officials and church ministers were all White and British. Their education was the same as that of many other British children and most could name the streets in London and reel off the list of British kings and queens throughout history, though they were taught very little about African or Caribbean history. Many had had a taste of life in Britain during the war when they had been proud to be serving the 'mother country'.

Jamaica has a culture of migration. From the slave trade onwards, people have been very used to travelling in and out of the island for economic and later, political, reasons. With a largely seasonal agricultural economy, the island has, for much of its history, been unable to sustain all of its population. So people have migrated either internally, from the rural areas to the city of Kingston, or externally to work for periods in Panama, Cuba, America and elsewhere. Finance sent by migrants back to their families in Jamaica has been important to the Jamaican economy for generations. Travelling to Britain was therefore not regarded as a potentially life-changing move; it was simply the latest move in search of work. The novelist, Andrea Levy, reflected on her father's migration on the *Windrush*:

> Far from the idea that he was travelling to a foreign place, he was travelling to the centre of his country... Jamaica, he thought, was just Britain in the sun.[100]

That meant that many migrants had made little preparation before they left Jamaica, considering this migration to be temporary like all the others. Most were young men, many of whom had left behind wives and children, since they were planning to make enough money to be able to return and to create a comfortable life back home in Jamaica.

In this way, churches in Jamaica lost a whole generation of potential leaders, though few regarded it as a problem at least initially. Migration is so much part of life that it was no surprise at all that people should simply take off, leaving choirs without members and Sunday Schools without teachers.

One migrant, for example, described how he had made no preparations for his move to Britain other than scratching together enough money for his fare on the boat. When they arrived in Britain, he simply followed another passenger from the boat, who had been met by relatives in London. He stayed with this family for a week or two, and then simply wandered the streets. He ended up persuading officers at a police station to let him sleep in a cell for three nights, until he met another Jamaican who allowed him to share his rented room. That meant him sleeping in the bed at night while the other man was on a night shift and then swapping over during the daytime.[101] These were proud British citizens who regarded their migration as 'coming home to mother', and they fully expected 'mother' to take care of them.

The shock they experienced has been well documented. It was far colder than they had ever expected, and the majority had come without sufficient warm clothing. There were White people sweeping railway platforms and working in factories, when the only White people they had ever met before had been in professional positions of authority. It was difficult to adjust to a dirty urban environment since most had come from a rural life of space and fresh air. Doors were always closed, chimneys belched out fumes, and people walked past them without saying 'Good morning'. Many migrants also expressed their shock at the hygiene habits of British people. Several spoke in horror of seeing unwrapped bread being carried along streets, and fish and chips being served out of newspaper. This was at a time when one of the criticisms levelled at migrants by prejudiced people in Britain was that *they* had dirty habits.

The 1948 British Nationality Act was just completing its passage through Parliament when the *Windrush* docked at Tilbury. It declared that citizens of any United Kingdom colony were British subjects. There was absolutely no doubt that the migrants from the Caribbean had every right to settle in Britain, and yet no Government department wanted to take responsibility for the newly arriving migrants. The Colonial Office, the Home Office and the Ministry of Labour engaged in a *'furious spate of buck-passing'*.[102] This prevarication continued as other ships arrived in Britain in subsequent years, and it was often left to voluntary organizations, the churches among them, to respond in practical ways to the needs of migrants arriving in this bewildering 'mother country'. For example, in June 1950, the British Cabinet decided that a National Advisory Committee should be set up to bring together Government and voluntary organizations in order to address the needs of migrants and to pool resources, yet a month later they changed their minds and declared that such a Committee would best be established by the voluntary organizations.

The churches could have taken a similar view to that of Government departments, concerned about the potential formation of 'ghettos', or simply unable to deal with the unexpected arrival of people from the other side of the world on their doorsteps. No doubt that was the response of some, but by and large, the churches in British cities, confronted with the needs of migrants, lost no time in responding. It was a very practical, appropriate and 'joined up' approach, which appeared to come totally naturally to many church bodies and communities at the time.

Accommodation and employment were very soon established as the main problems confronting migrants in many British cities. They were the victims both of the post-war housing shortage in British cities and of a bubbling racism that overflowed once British people were suddenly confronted with Jamaican neighbours and work colleagues. Many migrants initially joined family members or friends they had known from home, renting a room in the same house. This was good news for unscrupulous landlords who even converted kitchens into bedrooms in order to get another family's rent, relegating the cooker to a landing to be shared by anything up to fifteen families. Most migrants were very keen to save as much money as possible to support families back home, to set themselves up for their return home, or to pay for the next member of their family to travel to Britain. Therefore they crammed in together rather than paying out for more space elsewhere, even if there had been much else to choose from. It was not at all unusual in the 1950s to see signs in windows which proclaimed: *'Rooms to let—no children, no dogs, no Blacks'*.

Churches were responding far earlier than other agencies and also in a far more organized way. The British Council of Churches became crucial in this early period, enabling churches and church leaders to share information and ideas, and advising churches that were seeking to respond appropriately to the issues concerning migrants and migration. The British Council of Churches held an important conference in 1951, not even three years after the arrival of the *Windrush*, and long before any other agency had developed such a coordinated response. Initially the aim of conference was to promote Christianity to migrants, but as it was being planned, it became clear that the focus would need to change. The resulting conference therefore debated the possibilities of integrated social action and welfare issues, in response to migrants arriving in Britain.

The conference was held over three days and brought together a diversity of people including: bishops, other church leaders, representatives of voluntary organizations, academics, and representatives from statutory bodies such as the Colonial Office and the Ministry of Labour. It was remarkable for many reasons. This was not just one denomination or one church responding, but it involved commitment from right across the ecumenical spectrum. The change in the intended focus for the conference also showed how the British Council of Churches was prepared to *develop* their understanding in reaction to changing needs. This conference even debated the idea of bringing Black clergy to Britain at that early stage. In addition, the churches were not just operating in isolation, but they brought people together from many different organizations, with many different priorities.

The example of this early conference indicates that churches were leading other agencies in their response to migrants. In time, it became clear that even the statutory bodies were often looking to the churches to provide answers and assistance.

The church press, however, still fell into the habit, common in society in general, of describing migration as a 'problem'. Much discussion was held in the correspondence columns of the church newspapers about the theological implications of this 'new' phenomenon, notably about the concept of 'race' in relation to the biblical idea of a 'chosen race', and also concerning issues around intermarriage.

Churches may have been responding in a very positive and coordinated way at the level of their denominational and ecumenical national leadership, but in individual churches, responses were much more varied. From the start some churches were keen to show a different response to that encountered by many migrants in the rest of society. So they tackled prejudice, but were not always so aware of the prejudice, at varying levels of subtlety, that existed within their own church communities. Some migrants faced outright rejection in churches, often with the excuse by clergy that the rest of the congregation would not like to worship with Black people. Such attitudes were often criticized in the church press of the period. Others found a 'cold shoulder' and little social contact when they went to worship in British churches. This was a total mystery to them. It was often explained away by British congregations as the 'British reserve' with the implication that it was something migrants would simply have to get used to.

The following was the response of one migrant in Brixton recalling a situation that many found themselves in:

> I have heard from experiences of people going to church. And every pew they sit in 'Oh you can't sit there because it's Mrs. So-and-so's seat' or 'no it's Mr so-and-so's seat, you can't sit there', and they might eventually go to the back. One lady had such an experience. The vicar—when she was going out—the vicar told her, he said, 'its nice to see you coming to church and things like that, but I would ask you not to come back because the parishioners don't like it, and we wouldn't like to lose them'. An Anglican church—Church of England![103]

There was much discussion concerning the most appropriate way forward. Some churches elected to incorporate elements of more formal worship into special 'Anglo-Caribbean Services'. Others were concerned that different sorts of services would cause more prejudice and division. This was an ongoing debate throughout the period for some churches, though others remained unaware of any of these issues.

In most British cities there were churches and individuals making a huge difference. Some church workers were going to British ports and railway stations and simply standing there as crowds of migrants arrived. They held placards saying things like 'Can I help?' or 'Methodist?—we can help you'. They provided warm clothing for migrants who were unprepared for the temperature of a British winter, and also helped people to find their relatives, made suggestions about accommodation, and gave them information about churches. This gave migrants what they most needed, a welcome in a very new, and at times, a very shocking environment.

Many of the churches in Brixton were seeking to respond appropriately. One Methodist minister, the Rev. Leonard Webb (minister of Railton Road Methodist Church), went so far as to put a banner outside his church which read 'West Indians welcome to worship with us'. He did not make himself popular in the process, but that did not stop him. He collected names and addresses of newly arrived migrants from the housing offices in order to welcome them, rather than waiting for migrants to turn up for worship. He also began to invite people to lead worship who had been to Jamaica, and he introduced elements of worship that were familiar to the migrants.

3 Remembering the Forgotten Voices

This chapter offers fruits of two important pieces of work by two individuals, whose profiles at the time of writing remain remarkably 'low key'. John Wilkinson and Valentina Alexander are, in many respects, the 'forgotten voices' in the developmental narrative of Black theology in Britain. Whilst in more recent times, the likes of Robert Beckford, Inderjit Bhogal, Anthony Reddie, Joe Aldred and Mukti Barton have tended to predominate in the public consciousness of those who are interested followers in the development of Black theology in Britain, there can be no doubting the importance of Alexander and Wilkinson. We have shared some of their importance in our opening reflections in the first chapter.

Reddie first met Valentina at the inaugural Black theology forum he attended in the autumn of 1994. Valentina was still living in Birmingham in those days, and for a group of largely nervous postgraduate students at the University of Birmingham, she was something of a luminous trailblazer in our midst. On Reddie's first attendance at the forum in the 1990s, Valentina was the only Black British-born student connected with the Black Theology in Britain forum who was within touching distance of completing her doctorate. Valentina's PhD thesis was completed not without its trauma and difficulties. Despite such difficulties and struggles, she nevertheless completed her work. Like all trailblazers, she paved the way for many to follow.

Whilst there were Black women prior to Valentina Alexander who had undertaken invaluable theological work,[1] Valentina's thesis remains unique, not only for being arguably the first doctorate, but also for the fact that it is unequivocally an example of Black British Liberation theology.

In terms of John Wilkinson, Reddie has noted his importance to the development of Black theology in his more recent account of the ongoing progress of Black theology in Britain.[2]

For many years, prior to the emergence of Mukti Barton,[3] David Isiorho[4] and Glynne Gordon-Carter,[5] John Wilkinson's *Church in Black and White*[6] remained one of the standard bearing texts for detailing the experience and the role of Black people within the Church of England. Time has not diminished the importance of Wilkinson's work, but most tellingly, as a White middle-class male, he has recognized the need to remove himself from the forefront of the discourse in this country. It is not often the case that one meets eminent White scholars, who through the inevitable dictates of patronage and White hegemony finding themselves as the 'experts on

Black folks', have the foresight and the grace to remove themselves from that vantage-point of privilege and importance. Having known John for many years, he will not mind us saying that he is much too savvy to relax in the assumed ignorance of believing himself to be beyond the contaminating stains of racism and privilege that is the unearned lot of so many White middle-class males in Britain.

We salute John Wilkinson not because his actions are exemplary, but simply because we recognize the important role he has played in helping to establish the position and intent of Black theology as an academic discipline in Britain, particularly within theological education.

Following the contemporaneous reflections from Wilkinson, we have also included some additional, supporting material on the development of the Black Christian Studies course that ran at Queen's, under the stewardship of John Wilkinson (with the support of his wife Renate) and later, Robert Beckford. The editors are aware of the significant developments in Black theological curricula since that time. These are represented in the later curricula work overseen by Robert Beckford during his time at Queen's (1992–1998), by Mukti Barton, his successor as Tutor in Black (and Asian) Theology at Queen's (1998–) and through the MA in Black Theology, at the Graduate Institute for Theology and Religion, Elmfield House, University of Birmingham, initiated by Emmanuel Lartey and later overseen by Robert Beckford. We have highlighted the background materials to Black Christian Studies and not subsequent documents, primarily as a mark of the historical precedence of the former, and not as any form of rebuff for the importance of these later developments.

So this chapter celebrates the work of these two unheralded, but hopefully, not forgotten heroes and sheroes in the development of Black theology in Britain.

Passive and Active Radicalism
in Black Led Churches

Valentina Alexander

[This extract is from Alexander's unpublished PhD thesis 'Breaking Every Fetter? To What Extent Has the Black Led Church in Britain Developed a Theology of Liberation?' (University of Warwick, 1996). Alexander is reputed to be the first Black British woman to complete a PhD in religious studies and theology. Her thesis remains a groundbreaking piece of work; in it she poses the question as to whether the Black-led church[7] in Britain has developed a Black theology of Liberation. Like all good scholars, Alexander synthesizes the prevailing literature at the time (her work predates that of

Aldred, Beckford and Reddie, for example), critiquing it for its veracity and accuracy, and then, most crucially, she proceeds to outline a radical and yet sympathetic vision for a pragmatic radicalism for Black-led churches in Britain. We are proud to offer an extract from this groundbreaking thesis for publication.]

> I love Black Churches, I'm proud of Black Churches because it's about self determination and Black-led Churches are the only organization from slavery downwards, that is about Black organization, Black people in power, Black people leading, Black people participating... To me it's about self determination, it's about Black people on our own, serving God and through the castles of our own skin.[8]

> What I'm saying is that if people are going to use the term Black-led Church, then it's got to have some meaning behind it... on a social level as well as on a spiritual level.[9]

This study has presented a picture of two spheres of liberational response made by Black British Churches in response to their local context. The first, an internal response, is characterized by the nurturing of a pragmatic and holistic spiritual identity. The second, an external response, refers to the way in which the Church has, through this spiritual identity, attempted to identify and respond to the social needs of its congregations and their communities through a range of self-help services. Both the internal and external activities of the Church can be described as contextual, firstly in that they have emerged as a syncretized expression of African and European theologies and secondly in that they represent a unique response to the wider social and political conditions the Church has been made to relate to, both in its contemporary life and throughout its historical development.

This chapter will continue to explore the reality and nature of liberation within the Churches by assessing the manifested identity against the criteria summarized in previous chapters. In brief these are that for a theology to be defined as liberational it must (a) be contextual; (b) be holistic; (c) engage in social analysis; (d) engage in critical reflection on liberational praxis; (e) be dialogical and ecumenical in approach and (f) be expressed at popular, pastoral and professional levels of the Church. This chapter concerns itself with the third and fourth of these criteria.

Social Analysis as Facilitator of Liberation Theology

It has been suggested that Liberation Theology needs to engage with tools of social analysis where they serve to give meaning to causes and mechanisms of oppressive practice and ideology. The paradigm of Latin American theology in particular has illustrated how the application of methods of social science can aid in an effective analysis of the nature of oppressive society—its present realities as well as its historical development. From this basis, theologians such as Boff and Gutierrez have been able to nurture a liberative theological praxis through which their contextual concerns of oppression are confronted.

The issue of theology's engagement with social analysis requires an understanding of the way in which theology works at popular, pastoral and professional levels. Thus far the study has concentrated on the first two of these theological levels; the present discussion will continue in this vein. What is essentially under discussion here is the way in which, at popular and pastoral levels, the BLC has engaged in an analysis of the social conditions with which its members have been confronted. Popular and pastoral levels of the BLC have already been identified as engaging in holistic and contextual theology. It is from this foundation that the extent of its interaction with social analysis must also come to be understood.

Liberational Spirituality as Passive Radicalism

The Church's engagement with social analysis is inextricably intertwined with its manifestation of liberative spirituality. This spirituality, which has been understood as holistic and fundamentally connected to the social experiences and realities of believers, is the overriding medium through which, at pastoral and popular levels, the BLC interprets and analyses the social context of those believers. Liberative spirituality is, therefore, the key epistemological tool at these levels. The contextual development of the Church means that it has most often been, however, essentially an implicit tool enabling believers to identify, challenge and overcome the various levels of their ideological and material oppression without necessarily seeking out its socio-historical source and without making an explicit theological alignment with that liberative process. To the extent that this manifestation of social analysis within the BLC would seem to represent yet another paradox, it has been identified in this study as *passive radicalism*. Social analysis through passive radicalism describes how the BLC has sought to undermine the ideologies and practices of race, class and gender oppression within the everyday, holistic expression of its spirituality. It is useful to begin an exploration of the radical component within the principle before going on to examine its limitations.

The *radical* component of the BLC's engagement with social analysis relates to the way that it has created a contextual understanding of the experiences of racism and disadvantage. Its own unique existence as an institution during the past fifty plus years of Black British history is evidence of its commitment to interpret and respond to the social realities with which its members are surrounded. Indeed its attraction as a subject of study for social scientists and religionists over the years has been precisely because it exists not purely as a series of religious organizations but, more significantly, of Black organizations. In so doing, it represents a form of Black community mobilization. The BLC's engagement with social analysis at popular and pastoral levels, therefore, cannot be understood as a distanced theoretical exercise but must be viewed contextually, as an integrated process within the holistic Church experience.

Interpreting Social Analysis in the BLC

This fundamental reality has been variously interpreted by researchers of the BLC over the years. For example, Clifford Hill, writing in the early 1960s, regarded the Churches as harmful sects which stood ultimately 'against the long term interests of the immigrants'.[10] Malcolm Calley, writing in 1965, saw the Church in terms of a pernicious fringe establishment and its adherents as having been 'hardened' into a pattern of 'religious apartheid' activity that made it impossible for integration to take place.[11] Ironically, whilst Calley's description of the Church implicitly indicates his awareness of its existence as a religious, social and even political reality, he is nonetheless unable to credit this reality with legitimacy since for him it is a dysfunctional response to a society where such political acts are not needed:

> Perhaps in Jamaica the saints, seeking religious consolations for hopeless poverty and social disorganization is inevitable, their position is indeed hopeless. But in England the position of the West Indian minority is far from hopeless... *Britain does not have an acute race relations problem... The migrant is not caught in a closed system.* He can overcome the undoubted disadvantages of having a dark skin, and often does...[12]

Hence in spite of the political and ideological overtones of the term 'religious apartheid' and of his implied accusation of the Church as a separatist movement, Calley sees the existence of the BLC in Britain essentially as an act of escapism and withdrawal, devoid of any legitimate social analysis or response:

> The thoroughgoing obsessive, ritual withdrawal of the saint from the world *appears to be out of all proportion to the actual difficulty of the situation he is withdrawing from.* I think this can only be understood historically... There is in the West Indies a long tradition of seeking magico-religious rather than practical solutions to problems. This is particularly true of Jamaica, whence nearly all of the sect members have come.[13]

In addition to a superficial understanding of Jamaica's historical religious traditions, what Calley illustrates here are the problems which can be encountered when a researcher attempts to understand the position of the Church *vis-à-vis* its place in society from the outside. That is to say Calley approaches his study as a middle-class, White, male researcher and interprets social reality on behalf of his research subjects, thus relegating the entirety of their religious behaviour to the level of withdrawal. He is unable or unwilling to take seriously the experiences of the migrants in a racist and unwelcoming British society. Nor is he able, therefore, to consider the development of their faith from an historical perspective alongside the impositions of a dominant missionary-led Christianity which also went hand in hand with the forces of slavery, colonialism and racial oppression. Essentially, therefore, despite being able to recognize that the identity of the BLC holds political implications, researchers such as Calley and Hill have been unable to understand the *radicalism* inherent within this identity. This is necessarily the case since their research emerges not from the position of those needing to engage in liberation but from those representing those structures which are being resisted.

Subsequent White researchers have been able to avoid some of the more obvious errors of Calley and Hill and have consequently come closer to exploring the implicit radicalism in the existence of the BLC in Britain. Both Roswith Gerloff[14] and Iain MacRobert,[15] for example, have approached their studies by taking seriously the socio-religious and historical contexts of the BLC. Gerloff, for example, when describing the collective identity of the BLC, writes:

> They are part and parcel of Black culture with its wholesome approach to human life. They are the guardian of a radical or prophetic strand of Christianity, and the precise political response to the situation of Blacks in a White racist society.[16]

Her study, which takes a very detailed look at the African sources and Caribbean development of Sabbatarianism and Oneness Pentecostalism, is at pains to illustrate the political potential inherent in holistic Black spirituality. She identifies the communal qualities of the Church as being a major source of empowerment for oppressed Black adherents and is also able to recognize the liberative functions in the central principles of Black theological expression.[17] In this respect, Gerloff's study can be aligned with the work of liberation theologians in America, South Africa and the Caribbean who, as the second chapter has explored, have understood the essential culture of Black faith in the Churches to be one of resistance and liberation.

Iain MacRobert picks up on the theme of holistic liberation in his study and focuses particularly on the centrality of *experience* within the Black liberational tradition. From the very beginning of his study he is keen to point out the difficulties of himself as a White researcher—and of Western theology in general—gaining academic access to something which he has identified as being 'primarily experiential in cognitive terms'.[18] This foundational assumption of the emotional, as opposed to rational, nature of Black Pentecostal spirituality will necessitate further exploration.

Like Gerloff and unlike Calley and Hill, MacRobert traces the contextual development of the Pentecostal Church. He understands it as essentially a syncretized faith which has needed, throughout its history, to respond to both the physical as well as ideological realities of racism with which it has continually been confronted. To the extent that the BLCs have created for themselves internal spiritual defences against the effects of both physical and ideological racism, MacRobert argues that they have attempted to undermine the prevailing hegemony of oppression. In so doing, he suggests, BLCs have thereby engaged in a 'psychological liberation' which has its heart in a Black leitmotif grounded in experiential reality and manifested through an implicit theology.[19]

Ironically, although these later studies of the BLC in Britain adopt a more sympathetic and sensitive approach towards the contextual development of the Church, they (in particular MacRobert) appear to share in common an understanding which lays strong emphasis on the experiential and anti-intellectual nature of Black radicalism within the manifested theology. This theme is echoed in the work of John Wilkinson[20] and in the more anthropological accounts of Roy Kerridge.[21] It is an emphasis that serves to limit the way these studies are able to identify the level of social analysis carried out by the Church itself since it does not tell, as the theologian Cecil Cone has argued, 'the whole story'.[22]

Whilst this study has sought to argue, like these latter studies, that liberation within the BLC is inextricably tied to a resistant spirituality which takes its implicit impetus from an African world view, it distinguishes itself from them in its attempt to define this spirituality as not only liberational but, most significantly, holistically so. That is to say that whilst the experience of liberation certainly is mediated through the 'emotions, body and mind…all committed to worship and celebration of life',[23] the holistic experience of liberation within the Churches cannot be understood without reference to the continual cycle of social analysis carried out at pastoral and popular levels.

The apparent dichotomy that exists, therefore, in MacRobert's account between cognitive and experienced liberation in the BLC is a false one. Moreover, to insist on the essentially emotional and anti-intellectual nature of the BLC is to veer dangerously towards ideologies of cultural racism such as that expressed by missionary Christianity in the nineteenth-century Caribbean.

It may in fact be the case that, as Elaine Foster suggests, the most useful representation of social analysis in the BLC can be found in 'whe dem seh (that is what is said by the people themselves)'.[24] Certainly a most welcome addition to the writing on the BLC, both in its historical development and contemporary status, has been those African Caribbean writers who have emerged, in particular, from within the ranks of popular and pastoral theological tradition in Britain. These contributions will form part of the focus of the second set of criteria for consideration in this chapter. Their principal value in the present discussion is to highlight the degree to which the social analysis emerging from the BLC is represented not only through the experiential-based leitmotif of liberational spirituality but also through theoretical analysis and reflection. This is particularly well represented in the works of Selwyn Arnold, Elaine Foster and Ira Brooks, as will be examined later.[25]

The radical element in *passive radicalism* seeks to acknowledge the ways in which the core identity of the BLC engages in an implicit form of social analysis through both experiential and cognitive means. Yet when seeking evidence for such a claim it is essential to approach the Church from its own contextual placing: it is particularly important to allow the Church, as it were, to speak for itself. A useful model for such an approach is provided by Patricia Hill Collins in her projection of an Afrocentric feminist epistemology.[26] Collins, as stated in the introduction to this study, begins by critiquing what she identifies as the 'masculinist knowledge validation process', the ultimate aim of which is to present a 'white male standpoint' regardless of the various manifestations such a process one may take.[27] She goes on to assert the inappropriateness of such hegemonic epistemologies when applied to the experiences of Black women. At the heart of the concept of radicalism as it is used in the term *passive radicalism*, then, is an embracing of an alternative epistemology for the BLC—one that is able to take seriously the reality of the social analysis implicit in an holistic liberational spirituality.

Collins's counter-hegemonic epistemology involves four key components. These are (1) concrete experience as a criterion of meaning; (2) the use of dialogue in assessing knowledge claims; (3) the ethic of caring, and (4) the ethic of personal accountability.[28] Each of these will prove useful in identifying the nature of social analysis in the Churches.

Firstly, according to Collins's analysis, it is vital for the epistemology of BLC members to be clearly identified with the experience of day-to-day realities. This is not the same thing as saying that members of the Churches are only able to respond to their social realities through the medium of their emotions; to the contrary, it highlights the fact that their means of cognitively analysing their social conditions must be inextricably aligned with their material experience of those realities. The purpose of social analysis, therefore, should not be to create abstract social-scientific formulas about the meaning of oppression and the means of liberation; it should rather be to clarify—to shed light upon—an experienced reality so as better to respond to that reality in pragmatic terms. This, in Collins's analysis, is symbolic of the separation between decontextualized *knowledge* systems and those Africentric epistemologies which rely upon contextual and holistic *wisdom*. For purposes of clarity her original term 'Black women' has been substituted by BLC members:

> This distinction between knowledge and wisdom, and the use of experience as the cutting edge dividing them, has been key to *BLC members'*

survival. In the context of race, gender, and class oppression, the distinction is essential. Knowledge without wisdom is adequate for the powerful, but wisdom is essential to the survival of the subordinate.[29]

It is, therefore, 'concrete experience' which serves as a catalyst to social analysis and not remote theories of social analysis which are made to somehow fit in to the mould of the BLC.

Secondly, Collins's analysis suggests that the existence and the centrality of community relations within the BLC experience contributes towards another key element of its alternative epistemology. The significance of dialogue, facilitated by the supporting communal environment, allows for the promotion of holism rather than diametricism. Hence the Church is able to exist with what appear to be, through the medium of dominant epistemologies, stark contradictions and dichotomies. Moreover, since communal action and response lies at the heart of the BLC experience, its engagement with social analysis is necessarily dependent on that community for its sense of legitimization.

Thirdly, the epistemological approach of the BLC is one which, as has already been acknowledged in most studies, takes seriously the imperative of emotion. The ethic of caring means that the obligation which the Church places on itself to embrace the essential humanity of its members and the communities they represent is part and parcel of its holistic analysis. Moreover, the expressing of emotion is a rational and experiential part of its epistemology since it indicates a commitment to what Collins refers to as 'the validity of an argument'.[30]

Finally, the ethic of personal accountability means that the social analysis of the BLC will not take place in a spiritual vacuum. Those who engage in social analysis on behalf of the Church must first give account of their own spiritual standing. In the language of the Church, this involves clarifying 'where they stand in the Lord'. However, since a declaration of 'true' Christian faith is also, for the believers, an announcement of allegiance with the spiritual and material forces of right, then the ethic of accountability also becomes an affirmation of allegiance with the oppressed. In this way the social analysis of the BLC stands as an independent and counter-hegemonic epistemology. As Collins highlights:

> Emotion, ethics, and reason are used as interconnected, essential components in assessing knowledge claims... Values lie at the heart of the knowledge validation process such that the inquiry always has an ethical aim.[31]

It is possible to argue, therefore, that the BLC engages with social analysis, not as a disinterested or objective science but as an essential and concrete part of its experienced reality. Moreover, it is in this way, through its engagement with an alternative epistemological framework, that members of the BLC are able to become what the theologians Boff and Boff have described as 'social subjects of the historical process'.[32] This means that they are able to make sense of their position in the social world in the light of their own efforts at self liberation rather than by the strategies of those who oppress them.

Social Analysis as Passive Radicalism

It is clear then that the nature of social analysis within the BLC needs to be considered from the vantage point of an alternative epistemology to that usually engaged in by positivistic social science. This study has therefore employed the model provided by Collins as an appropriate contextual and phenomenological alternative. Through this model it is possible to see how the BLC, in its existence as a Black institution which nurtures the characteristics which have been identified in previous chapters,[33] stands itself as a testament to its own engagement with social analysis. This analysis, moreover, is both experiential and cognitive.

In its contextual reality and as an ongoing commitment to its active analysis of the social world, the Church provides an essential vehicle for the empowerment of its adherents. It does not simply create an imitation power base in which individuals can, as it were, play at liberation. Rather, it creates an *alternative* power house in which believers are able to put into practice a counter-hegemonic epistemology which constantly enables them to challenge and reaffirm their own existence in the social world. This is essentially what makes passive radicalism liberational.

Before moving on to the process of identifying the passive counterpart to the radicalism manifested through the social analysis of the Church, it is useful to provide some concrete examples of the working out of this radicalism. The overwhelming evidence from the research carried out for this study illustrated the many ways in which believers were motivated to resist the obstacles placed against them by their race, class or gender because of their spiritual convictions nurtured within the context of the BLC. As one respondent shared: 'I try to break down barriers that exist, I never leave them. I always try to go through them and break them down.'[34] At the foundation of each church, therefore, is firstly an acknowledgement of the oppression that faces believers and secondly an implicit commitment to equip believers with the holistic spiritual power to overcome it:

> In work I realize that in this society there's only so far that you can get... Whatever you're doing in life, if it's what God wants then nobody can stop it. They can hinder it but they can't stop it. My pastor always says, what's for you can't not be for you. If it's for you then it's for you. It may take some time to get there but if it's for you then nobody can stop you.[35]

Since the impetus for social analysis within the Churches is a liberational spirituality grounded in concrete social experience, its manifestation operates on two distinct levels. The first involves asserting believers' claim to full access into the material benefits of life in British society:

> I believe in a Christian having the best house, the best car… I don't believe that a Christian should walk around being destitute because God's people should have the best because all things belong to God and God would not have his children suffering.[36]

The above illustrates a theological imperative for the material struggle for equality which emerges from the implicit analysis in which the Church engages. Secondly, however, the counter-hegemonic nature of the Church's epistemology means that it promotes an alternative sense of values and priorities which allow its members to define their own legitimacy not in material but in spiritual terms:

> I'm happy with who I am and I'm not out earning mega bucks and I can't buy the designer clothes that I like but I'm happy. So I'm not gonna place my happiness and who I am on what I can get materially… I'm a young Black woman who's got a strong faith in Jesus and believes that the situation that I'm in at the moment is materially not so hot but it will change and I've got work to do for the kingdom and it might mean that my material wealth increases, it might mean that it stays the same but you know that doesn't really matter. I can't base who I am on what I have.[37]

> What is power? I believe if you're happy, well balanced and you believe in yourself you can gain power. You can get a good job and if you have a good stable family that is power for you. Not every individual wants to run the country, but if you can still make yourself happy then that is a certain amount of power in itself.[38]

The influence of an African epistemology becomes apparent in the above quotation through the maintenance of the theme of continuity. Believers retain an understanding of themselves as whole beings, having implicit value and power as children of God which cannot be eradicated by external conditions. Simultaneously the theme of conflict is also extended as believers determine to resist the conditions that would deny them this humanity in social and material terms. The *radical* element of passive radicalism which stands as an inherent part of the social analysis of the Church was also reinforced by an interview question which asked respondents whether their faith helped them to deal with racism and injustice. Seven primary responses were collected and these were:

1. Faith offered comfort and encouragement, it encouraged the belief that God would open up a way, and inspired confidence.
2. Faith confirmed that the negative attitudes of society can be moderated through faith inspired behaviour.
3. Faith enabled an easing of the load and provided grace to bear oppression.

4. Faith confirmed the power of prayer as a lifeline.
5. Faith facilitated the mutual sharing and support at church which helped.
6. Faith enabled self empowerment.
7. Faith reminded believers that ultimately oppression would be met by vengeance from God.

Collectively, then, liberational faith manifested as passive radicalism provided believers with the necessary grace to bear discrimination and empowered them also to tackle and oppose it. Moreover, underlying both approaches was the confident understanding that nothing could stand in the way of what God wanted them to achieve.

The eschatology of the Churches which is most often cited as the most significant limitation to liberation did not, from the evidence of research findings, necessarily work in that way. Even where respondents felt strongly that oppression would never be eliminated in its earthly form, they nonetheless utilized passive radicalism to enable them to deal with its social consequences in the present time while awaiting a more permanent solution:

> I wouldn't say faith is a solution because you're going to always have injustice. It's just like an easing of a load… It's like you're adding oil to a wound, that's the way I see it… My faith helps in coping with difficult situations.[39]

> It's not going to get any better, it's not supposed to. Faith eases it for me but I don't want to be in a comfortable position and say, oh, because God's looking out for me, stuff everybody else… As far as possible, if I can help somebody then I will.[40]

In keeping with its epistemological imperative, these kinds of views were often accompanied by accounts of personal experiences of overcoming oppression. In such instances the story was given in order to illustrate how the believer's personal life and Christ-like example could overcome and alter the oppressive behaviour of another individual or even an organization. The key to this particular type of response is summed up succinctly by the following:

> I'm not really interested in fighting. I'm interested in winning and you don't necessarily have to fight to win. You can still get what you want, if you're really smart, without even fighting. You can end up in the position that you want to end up.[41]

Just how this winning without fighting takes place is essentially a matter of personal empowerment. A foundational element of the implicit social analysis of the BLC is an unshakeable confidence in the power of right to overcome wrong in concrete everyday experiences:

I feel no way threatened by being Black... If it's a white environment I feel as though they feel threatened by me... I know that, on a personal level, I'll always come through and that is really, for me, my faith in God. He always brings me through any problems that I have whether it's racism or something else... As long as I'm in the right, I get God on the case and God deals with it and either He'll change their mind, move them out of the way or whatever it takes, but I'm coming through.[42]

...I know who I am in God. I'm special. If I wasn't a Christian I wouldn't believe so... So because I believe that God did so much for me then I've got that confidence. I'm a confident person because I know that I'm not by myself, I've got God on my side.[43]

If you understand the true value of prayer then prayer does literally move mountains and it opens the doors so that you then need very little physical effort... You could be doing a lot of physical effort and just ending up with mountain after mountain to climb, just coming against brick walls. So for me, the first thing anybody ought to do is to pray about the situation and deal with it in a spiritual realm so that the physical wall will more or less come tumbling down.[44]

Social analysis through passive radicalism, then, indicates a clear engagement of the Church with the social realities of the believers. As has been evidenced from the responses of members and leaders of the Churches in the study thus far, the implicit social analysis not only identifies the hardships that exist for Black people in British society but also commits itself to a particular strategy for overcoming these difficulties through a process of self actualization. This means that members are encouraged to pursue maximum educational achievement and to extend to the highest levels of their chosen careers. In practice this has resulted in a growing level of professional status of members within the Churches:

As a Christian your faith helps you to believe in yourself that you can do anything according to your ability and according to the Lord's will. If you have a positive view of yourself and if you are encouraged by other people and if you are willing to be patient and work at it, then I think you can achieve anything. For instance, in my church there are lots of very well-educated people.[45]

The social analysis of the Church engages in something of a symbiotic relationship. Within the context of the life of the Church it enables believers to bring to bear, through spiritual expression, what they know cognitively and experientially, about the social world. At the same time, outside of the Church, believers carry with them what Joel Edwards has described as their 'mobile sanctuaries' which enable them to apply their spiritual imperatives to their social realities. It is in this way that passively radical social analysis is able to engender social, economic and political purpose. It undermines the ideologies of racism by reaffirming the holistically spiritual capabilities of each member, on their own and as supported by a like-minded group.

Through passively radical analysis the Church is able to react against the alienating effects of divide-and-rule influences inflicted on Black people throughout the history of their oppression. It not only asserts the basic humanity of all people and the special potential of men and women of God, but in so doing it also contradicts the processes of internalized racism so often manifested as self hate. It also combats the processes of disempowerment created by race, class and gender oppression by providing a source of divine and thereby superior power. This divine empowerment removes the believer from his and her marginalized position within British society and increases self-worth which in turn inspires a greater vision for success in this world and the next.

The radical and liberational qualities of a social analysis based on passive radicalism, therefore, are pervasive and clear. However, since the nature of this liberation has nonetheless been described as passively radical then there are obviously some limitations to its manifestation. These will be explored now.

Limitations of Passively Radical Social Analysis
Regardless of the given benefits of the social analysis of the Church at pastoral and popular levels, its full liberational potential is hindered by the very nature and manifestation of its radicalism. This becomes distinct in three principal and related areas. Firstly, social analysis as passive radicalism has a uni-dimensional understanding of social transformation. Secondly, it does not manifest itself in an explicit way, and thirdly, it contains no real 'historico-analytical' element.[46]

1. *A uni-dimensional understanding of social transformation*
The social analysis of the BLC is primarily geared towards creating and nurturing strategies of survival which serve to challenge the effectiveness of oppression in the lives of the believers. It does not, therefore, seek to dismantle systems of oppression but merely to develop appropriately resistant *responses* to them. James Cone has more closely defined this 'art of survival' within the BLC experience:

> It is called *survival* because it is a way of remaining physically alive in a situation of oppression without losing one's dignity. We call it *grace* because we know it to be an unearned gift from him who is the giver of 'every good and perfect gift'. This is what Black people mean when they sing: 'We've come this far by faith, leaning on the Lord, trusting in his holy Word'.[47]

Whilst the radical implications of the strategy of survival for the individual believer have already been made apparent, it is nonetheless appropriate to describe 'the art of survival' as a means of individuals *coping with* rather than *altering* oppressive structures within society. As such it is essentially a passively radical approach which carries with it further implications for the nature of liberation in society.

According to Boff and Boff, in order for liberation to be fully effective, it needs to capture for itself a 'transforming energy...that will lead to individual change (conversion) and change in history (revolution)'.[48] What passively radical social analysis does is to attempt to effect the second element by exclusive dependence on the first. In other words, individuals who are transformed through repentance and conversion will eventually contribute towards a final, eschatological revolution. Such an approach results in what could be described as a uni-dimensional vision of societal transformation.

As has already been demonstrated from interview responses, sin is considered to be interchangeable with oppression in that the latter is very much a product of the former within the epistemology of the BLC. It follows, therefore, that the most consistent social analytical finding should be that change in the social world be experienced through a process of direct conversion of those who offend society by their oppression. Although, epistemologically, this conversion is both holistic and contextual in that it symbolizes the repentance of the oppressor and a shift to their alignment with the oppressed,[49] it needs, nonetheless, to be placed alongside wider strategies for societal transformation. A multi-dimensional vision of transformation would more easily accommodate change in the structures and systems of society as well as in offending individuals. Strategies with which a wider transformation could be achieved will be considered in latter discussions.

2. The consequences of non-explicit social analysis

Passive radicalism means that social analysis, as has been described, takes place as an implicit, even subconscious, part of the Church's identity. Both congregation and pastor benefit from, as well as contribute to, its processes—but only occasionally is it formerly vocalized and explicitly identified as a key feature of BLC theological reality. There would appear to be two principal explanations for this and both of them relate to the contextual nature of development within the Churches as outlined previously in the themes of continuity and conflict and innovation and conservatism. To recap briefly, the idea of continuity reflects the commitment of African Caribbean peoples to maintain a sense of self-worth and identity by retaining the influence of an African heritage throughout their struggles in the 'New World'. This has also been defined broadly as an Afrocentric epistemology. Conflict, however, manifests itself in three distinct forms. Firstly, by the way in which this effort at maintaining humanity is forced to do battle with material and ideological forces of oppression which have the effect of denying such humanity. Secondly, in the ideological pressure exerted by dominant theologies to ensure an 'authentic', largely fundamentalist, reading of theology. And thirdly, through the legacy of a syncretized theological development which, having been created under the backdrop of ideological racism, has developed a kind of inherent ambiguity in its working out of liberational practice.

A perhaps inevitable outcome of conflict has been a dual force of innovation and conservatism which has come to symbolize the manifestation of liberation within the BLC. This is what essentially is being expressed in the term passive radicalism.

The first explanation for the implicit rather than explicit nature of social analysis within the Churches is that it facilitates the process of dual identity which has elsewhere been identified as double-speak.[50] On the slave plantations of the Caribbean, dual identity originated as a pragmatic means of giving the appearance of loyalty to the enforcement of doctrines and theologies which went blatantly against the enslaved African's commitment to continuity. After the abolition of slavery the pressures to conform to dominant theology altered from a physical to ideological plane as Eurocentric Christianity established itself as the benchmark for social status in the new society in the nineteenth and early twentieth century. Nonetheless the continued experience of dual church membership was able to perpetuate believers' identification with two distinct theological traditions. In a contemporary British society which is increasingly pluralist and secular, however, this dual identity has not been motivated by physical threat or the search for social status. It has therefore been able to contain itself within the religious experience of a single church body.

Consequently, what started out as a conscious and strategic manifestation of resistance has since become an implicit characteristic of BLC identity. In this way African Caribbean Christian believers take seriously their commitment to the dominant imperatives of fundamentalist faith as expressed, for example, through codes of morality, the language of 'authentic' Christian identity and, most significantly, the separation of secular and spiritual realities. For example, since Eurocentric fundamentalism regards its own theology as being universally valid, then the identification and articulation of a theology as being 'Black' or even 'liberational' involves transgressing against the completeness and legitimacy of the 'true gospel'. Since fundamentalism divides the world into spiritual and secular realms, then even to consciously identify with the cause of the socially oppressed—and certainly to seek a structural solution to their condition—is somehow to compromise one's commitment to spirituality. What this means, essentially, is that the explicit and vocalized identity of the BLC maintains a formal allegiance to the principles of dominant theology. This injects a critical level of conservatism into its theological expression thereby rendering the implications of liberational spirituality, implicit and passive. The spirit of continuity is advanced through the practical social analysis of the Church, and as such it continues to offer a serious critique of, and challenge to, dominant theology and the wider systems of social oppression. However, since the message of radicalism is encoded by the requirements of dominant theology, these have to be deciphered by those external to the immediate BLC experience in order to be understood. This means that the fundamental identity of social analysis as a mechanism of holistic liberation for the BLC and the wider oppressed community is compromised.

The second possible explanation for radicalism as implicit within the Church returns the discussion to the ambiguous nature of syncretism as a liberational process. The central paradox which lies at the heart of ACC belief has already been identified. It is, in essence, that the syncretized faith of believers necessitates that they draw upon, as a tool for holistic liberation, a phenomenon which in its extracted form has been used as an ideological justification and instrument of their oppression.

It has already been suggested that the social analysis of the Church represents an epistemological approach which runs counter to that of positivist social science. However, the very ambiguous nature of its syncretistic origins and development disable it from articulating a *consistently* holistic liberational challenge to wider hegemonies of domination. Hence the Church manifests behaviour which is sometimes innovative and liberational whilst at other times conservative. Occasionally it finds both manifestations in the same act.

One illustration of this is found in the Christology of the Church. Christ stands as a powerful symbol of divine deliverance and holistic salvation as has already been explored. The Pentecostal Churches sing the chorus 'Jesus breaks every fetter and he will set you free'. The young woman exhorter of the NEW TESTAMENT CHURCH OF GOD youth night service encouraged her fellow believers 'to remember that with Jesus we've got a 100% guarantee of deliverance'.[51] It is clear from the research data and observation notes collected that the BLC's understanding of divine deliverance is an holistic one and yet the starting point for these liberating experiences is, for these believers, the blood of Jesus which washes them 'whiter than snow'.[52] Liberational transformation, then, often comes through the symbols of not just literal but ideological Whiteness. Whilst the portraits of a white, blue-eyed Jesus may no longer 'bless the houses' of the younger generation of believers it is harder to determine the extent to which the realness of such an image has been removed from their consciousness.

The connections that many of the BLCs continue to make with their White headquarter branches provide further illustration of the limiting influence of dominant theological values on the localized social analysis of the Churches in Britain. The Wesleyan Holiness Church, Seventh Day Adventists and New

Testament Church of God, for example, regard themselves as members of an international religious network with standardized theologies and doctrines which are determined by these original or headquarter branches.

In many instances international communication of ideas is maintained through official denominational journals such as the New Testament Church of God's *Evangel* which overviews the work of the Church around the world. In spite of the multi-cultural representation of the journal,[53] the epistemological approach of its theology is one which clearly rests comfortably within a wider hegemony of cultural imperialism. An edition in October 1991, for example, carries an article entitled 'Pursuit for God—Then and Now' which relates a brief history of men who have been motivated for world mission. The article's account begins with Christopher Columbus who had a 'desire to serve Christ and carry His light to heathen lands'.[54] It continues with the Pilgrims and Puritans in their journeying to America 'for the glory of God and the advancement of the Christian faith'.[55] Another article in the same edition relates how 'Africa, once considered the dark continent, is now receiving the light of the glorious gospel of Christ'.[56] Such uncritical theological approaches are carried through in the articles of both Black and White contributors. Moreover, the essentially conservative fundamentalism represented in these dominant theologies are often brought even closer to home, and even to those denominations who don't have formal or historical links with such denominations, through the mission and healing campaigns of evangelists such as Morris Cerullo and Benny Hinn who are supported, in the main, by BLC members.

The unwillingness or inability of BLC theology to distance itself from dominant theology means therefore, as Shaw and Stewart have argued, that implicit social analysis runs the danger of having no 'authentic niche' which is able to extend 'beyond the reach of colonial power'.[57] Hence whilst this study has thus far argued that syncretism in the Caribbean constituted the *first act* of Liberation Theology, it is also the case that this same act of syncretism has defined the nature of that theology. It has given it an internal ambiguity which highlights once again the sense of paradox within the liberational tradition of the BLC.

3. *The absence of an 'historico-analytical' approach*
A third and final dimension of the *passive* component in passive radicalism is the absence of what Boff and Boff have referred to as a 'historico-analytical' approach.[58] Within their introduction to Liberation Theology they use the terms historical and social analysis interchangeably; however, for the purposes of this study, it is most useful to consider the historical elements of social analysis as a separate entity. This more easily demonstrates the limitations of a passively radical approach to understanding the social world.

For Boff and Boff the purpose of engaging in historical analysis is to try to understand the reasons for oppression as it exists in the social world. A theologically liberative approach, therefore, should either assess current theories which seek to understand the historical causes of oppression or should apply their own knowledge systems to the same task.

Although the Church does manifest a certain degree of historical aware-ness in terms of its own spiritual calling to Britain in the midst of a racist and morally and spiritually bankrupt society,[59] it does not appear to extend to a broader collective analysis of the historical processes of race, class and gender oppression. This is particularly the case at the popular level of lib-erational expression. The absence of historical analysis is partly supported by the afore-mentioned uni-dimensional approach to societal transforma-tion. For example, since emphasis is placed on overcoming sin/oppression in the here and now, it becomes less important for believers to explore its historical causes or dimensions since those cannot be redeemed. Moreover, since conversion must ultimately come from an individual act of repent-ance both in the past and present, discussion on causes of oppression are limited to an understanding of individual rather than structural sinfulness. This further affects the degree of historical analysis in which the Church is able to engage.

As will be explored in the following section, although this lack is partially redressed through the process of critical reflection, it still means there is no consistent attempt at popular level to understand and acknowledge the roots of race, class and gender oppression as it has affected Black communities over the years. This means that although contextual social analysis is able to tackle the contemporary conditions of oppression—and through that process to apply practical responses to those conditions—it fails to explore adequately the historical causes. In so doing it detracts from the holistic nature of that analysis and thereby contributes to its essentially passive nature.

Passive radicalism, then, suggests that although the BLC does engage in social analysis, it is limited in so doing by certain features which have themselves been part of its contextual development. The extent to which these shortcomings can be identified and addressed depend on the level of critical reflection which the Church can lay claim to.

Black Theology at Queen's: The First Steps

John Wilkinson[60]

[John Wilkinson was for many years a tutor at the Queen's College, in Edgbaston, Birmingham. In the following piece he outlines the pioneering developments in Black theology in Britain from an era that predates the visible, epoch-defining work of Robert Beckford in the 1990s. Whilst some of this work has been recounted in a previous publication,[61] the author of that text will readily assert that he was working from archive documents and published texts, as he was not around at the time these events were unfolding. Wilkinson, who was privy to the seismic developments in the emergence of Black theology in the 1980s and early 90s first hand, so to speak, recounts the formative period in the emergence of a nascent Black theology in Britain, a good deal of which was located within the Queen's College in Birmingham—which at the time of writing remains the one institution in the British theological education system where Black theology is a core component of the curriculum.]

Encounter

Robert Beckford, perhaps Britain's leading Black theologian, was my successor as Tutor in Black Theology at the Queen's College Birmingham and later Lecturer in Black Theology at the University of Birmingham. He tells how he would begin his classes each year with his mainly White student body at the University, namely by asking them to write down what it means to be White. Invariably, White students would sit puzzled and write little or nothing; Black students on the other hand had no difficulty in responding to the task of defining Whiteness. It is a telling illustration of why Black theology, or come to that any reflection on Black experience, cannot take place in isolation—by definition it has implications for White people as well!

And yet, as Robert noted in an interview on Radio 4, 'White Studies' is a discipline that is still in its infancy. Indeed, on the shelves of the library of Birmingham University, only one book examines White Christian existence in relation to Black from a White perspective, namely *Church in Black and White: The Black Christian Tradition in 'Mainstream' Churches in England—a White Response and Testimony.*[62]

This book claims that a White response to the Black presence within the church has to start with White Christians hearing the 'cry' of Black people.[63] It notes how leading African American Black theologian James Cone recalls the Black Christian tradition's identification of the suffering of Black people with the death of Christ:

> Through the experience of being slaves, [Black people] encountered the theological significance of Jesus' death: through the crucifixion Jesus makes an unqualified identification with the poor and the helpless and takes their pain upon himself. If Jesus was not alone in his suffering, they were not alone in their slavery. Jesus was with them! He was God's Black Slave who had come to put an end to human bondage. Herein lies the meaning of the resurrection… Through Jesus' death, God has conquered death's power over his people.[64]

Hearing the cry of Black people thus means hearing the cry of 'God's Black Slave' from the Cross. This cry has two aspects. Firstly, it is the cry of *judgement*; it is the cry which accuses the White crucifiers and makes plain to them what they have done. Secondly, it makes an *appeal for repentance* to White Christians. It declares that Whites not only should repent but may and can repent; it is not beyond them to make the 'quantum leap' in imagination to grasp what their victims have suffered and to be moved from within.

It is in this perspective that the process which led to the teaching of Black theology at Queen's College should be understood. It is also the perspective in which, as author of *Church in Black and White*, I should briefly note a number of events and experiences which proved formative for me. These include:

- Being moved by the story of early nineteenth-century Anglican Evangelical social reformers in a children's Lent course in my home church. These included Wilberforce and the 'Clapham Sect', with whom I identified in my imagination.
- Identifying with the struggle against apartheid whilst at school and university, and the role of some Christians within that struggle.
- Identifying with the Civil Rights struggle in the United States whilst at university and especially its Christian leadership.
- Two years' (1965–67) teaching at Stann Creek High School in Belize, with Voluntary Service Overseas. One of my tasks there was to introduce a Caribbean History syllabus, replacing one which taught the history of the British Empire from an imperial standpoint. Thus I found myself teaching the history of slavery to descendents of its victims.
- Ten years (1974–84) as Vicar of St James, Aston, a largely Black (African-Caribbean) congregation.
- My 'discovery' of Liberation Theology whilst Research Fellow at Queen's College 1984–85, notably Gutierrez's elucidation of the nature and process of conversion to the poor.[65]

1. Antecedents

The concern that Church of England theological education presupposes a middle-class identity and ethos is not new. In 1985, the Archbishop of Canterbury's Commission on Urban Priority Areas reported that the Church is supplied with clergy 'positively unfitted' for urban ministry whilst at the same time clergy who come from working-class urban contexts lose their roots and identity in training.[66] In so far as this concern is well grounded, the 'underside' of the Church is doubly disadvantaged. This is a danger which takes on a new sharpness when the issues of 'race' and ethnicity are added to those of class. From 1981, however, three specific needs gradually emerged in the consciousness of the Church. These needs are: (i) the need to train all students for ministry in a multi-cultural, multi-racial and multi-faith society, (ii) the need to prepare White students to minister to Black and multi-racial congregations, and (iii) the need to enable Black students to develop their skills, vision and practice of ministry on the basis of a Black identity.

In 1980, the Black Methodist minister, Robinson Milwood, published the booklet *Let's Journey Together*. In it, he bases his strategy on the self-affirmation of Black people. His vision for Black ministry, and thus for theological education, comes from a self-aware Black base in local Methodist churches, circuits and districts. Unfortunately, he does not spell out the implications of this for theological education, except to say that 'contact with theological colleges' is 'assumed'.[67]

The report *Blind Leaders for the Blind?*, an enquiry into the way theological students are prepared for ministry in a multi-cultural society, was published in 1981 by AFFOR, a community-based anti-racist organization in Birmingham. It contains useful findings about awareness among colleges and students and outlines a theology of anti-racism and of ministry in a multi-faith society, but it makes no mention whatever of Black theology or Black Christians, and seems not to have envisaged them as partners in the theological task. This report belongs to the era of Black invisibility.[68]

In 1983, another Methodist document, *Race and Theological Education*, was published. It affirms the multi-racial nature of the Methodist Church, notes the need to tackle 'questions of race and racism' in theological education, and accurately summarizes the experience of Black Methodists.[69] A brief theological basis for multi-racialism is provided out of which six guidelines for theological education are given. These involve a shift away from White ethnocentric traditions and values, affirmation of multi-racialism in church and society, and the necessity of experiencing other cultures, including 'experience in churches with a number of black members'. The guiding principle was *permeation* of the course by these insights. The authors were concerned to avoid 'add-on' marginalized courses about 'race' and racism which would leave the main syllabus untouched. This paper is a marked advance on *Blind Leaders for the Blind?* in that it addresses the inner life and table fellowship of the church and aims to avoid marginalization.

The report, however, has three weaknesses: firstly, it does not list what the 'issues of race and racism' actually are, thus leaving much work to be done on the practical implementation of its principles. Secondly, it fails to recognize that both the 'permeation' and the 'add-on' approaches have advantages as well as disadvantages—an 'add-on' course may be marginal, but by its very focusing and creation of concentrated 'space' it can have an element of power that is rarely found through the permeation approach. To be effective, 'permeation' depends on the commitment and awareness of a complete college or course staff, which is simply not a realistic expectation.[70] Thirdly, the faith, culture and resources of Black people are not 'named' or affirmed. The concern to 'fight racism' seems to have obscured a potent weapon for that fight, namely God's revelation to a Black Christian community of faith.

It is only when we come to David Moore's unpublished paper, 'Pre-Theological College Training', also written in 1983, that we find a programme of theological education which is both true to the inheritance of Black Christianity that is also developed in detail. Moore advocates a one-year full-time pre-college course for Black candidates for ministry. The educational programme, an integrated pattern of academic study, spiritual life and practical experience, seeks to foster in students the development of self-confidence and self-worth on the basis of their own culture and its values. It recognizes the importance of Liberation Theology and other contextual theologies for this task and articulates a vision of ministry as 'participation in the struggle of the poor'.

2. *Wesley Daniel*
In 1987, Wesley Daniel, a young Black Methodist training for ministry at Queen's College, presented to his home church, Harlesden Methodist, a paper entitled 'The Question of Race and Theological Education',[71] which was a reflection on his time in college. In it, he describes how, as a Black student, he has found himself facing two theological agendas, one set by his College and the other arising from his own identity. He was, he says, accepted by his colleagues, but only as long as 'thorny issues' of race and racism were not raised. When, in the aftermath of the Brixton and Tottenham disturbances, these issues *were* raised, he had become isolated as the realization dawned that his White fellow-students were living in a 'different world' from himself.

He had also come to realize that, although Black Methodists were proud of their Methodist heritage and although the Methodist Church took pride in its Black members, theological students were not being shown the implications of this for ministry. Queen's was taking only marginal and incidental note of Black theology whilst other colleges, it seemed, had nothing at all. In both College and Church, the real theological issues raised by the presence of Black people were at best relegated to the 'pastoral' area, or placed among the many items to be addressed under the 'social responsibility' heading.

Daniel's attempts at raising issues of racism had met with resistance both in college and in the wider church. Daniel believed that many White students left college without resolving even such basic questions as why Black people name themselves as 'Black' or why they at times need to meet separately (this being often described as 'apartheid in reverse'!). To Daniel, this in effect meant, 'become white, allow us to dictate your course of action', a sentiment reinforced by his experience that theology was taught as substantially a White subject, with 'Third World' or 'Black theology' at best a peripheral appendage.

The remedy lay in a 'systematic approach to the issue'. Firstly, tutors were needed who are 'able to represent the experience of Black people, their spirituality, tutors with prophetic insight able to put their finger on the nerve of the situation Black people face and interpret it to the church'. Secondly, Black students must study *together*: it was difficult to be the only Black student in college, doubly so when one knew there were other students isolated elsewhere. Whilst numbers remained small, a proper programme should be developed in one place before being duplicated elsewhere. Thirdly, a curriculum should be devised in which the Black tradition—preaching, pastoral care, music, prayer, socio-economic existence and its relationship to religion—was taught as a unit. The idea that existing courses could be 'permeated' with Black insights was unrealistic. Finally, Daniel was clear that study of the Black tradition was equally important for Black and White students. White students would understand their own identity better, and be better equipped to minister to White and Black people. Black students, he concluded, 'must be equipped...to realize that they can make a significant contribution to the future of church and theology, and that they can provide inspiration to future Black Methodist ministers in this country, through preparation that has taken into account who they are, where they have come from and where they are going'.

Daniel's paper should be recognized as a landmark in the development of theological education. Its starting point is a description of the cost of remaining authentically Black, of remaining true to Black roots, inheritance of faith and upbringing. It develops from that the inheritance of a liberative praxis, namely a detailed programme by which a neglected 'invisible' community can take its rightful place at the table of theological comprehensiveness. This process will involve pain and cost as White theology is purified and transformed by its encounter with Black theology, but Daniel ends with a universal vision: *both* groups of students would know themselves better, and be better equipped to minister to both communities.

The presentation of this paper to a College staff meeting in July 1987 was perhaps the first occasion in which a specifically Black critique, with demands for action, was made directly to a White theological institution in Britain. The primary challenge was spiritual: could the College 'hear' and 'name' the Black Christian tradition? Was it willing to acknowledge its own identity in relation to that challenge, take repentant action and so develop the 'new common life' of a truly Black and White church? Three developments were agreed: about raising of awareness, about the general curriculum of the college, and about a course specifically for

Black students. Firstly, *Racism Awareness Training* was made mandatory in the curriculum; it was later included in staff in-service training. This training was later judged generally successful in its aims, and had a significant impact on the general consciousness of the College.

Secondly, staff members agreed to a review of courses in the light of the criticism that theology was being taught as a 'White' subject. This was the most sensitive area of response since it involved the revision of the syllabuses of individual tutors. Thoroughly pursued, it would involve, for example, acknowledging Black hermeneutics as a distinctive contextual approach to the Bible, or including Black Church history and Black traditions of pastoral care in their respective subject areas. It would involve examining the issue of solidarity with the oppressed, which Black Christianity makes the touchstone of discipleship for White people, in both spirituality and systematic theology classes.

Staff agreed to invite Bishop Patrick Kalilombe, the eminent Malawian theologian and at the time Director of the Centre for Black and White Christian Partnership, to assist in the review. However, many of his suggestions were not acted upon, though some modifications to the curriculum took place. Willingness to engage in the practice of 'permeation' varied greatly from tutor to tutor and was not monitored.

Thirdly, it was agreed to offer to Black students a *Black Christian Studies course* with the aim of providing opportunity to study theology and prepare for ministry on the explicit basis of Black identities, work collaboratively towards a British Black theology and find mutual support.

3. *Black Christian Studies*[72]

The course began in October 1987. Early meetings were taken up with determining basic principles, aims and methods, which were then worked on by the Revd John Wilkinson, Tutor in Pastoral Studies at Queen's and two associate tutors: the Rt Rev Dr Patrick Kalilombe, Director of the Centre for Black and White Christian Partnership in the Selly Oak Colleges and the Revd Rajinder Daniel, Bishop's Adviser for Black Ministries in the Diocese of Birmingham.

The following statement of aims was agreed:[73]

The Black Christian Studies course aims to provide Black students with the opportunity to:

    a. study the inheritance of Black Christianity and explore their own experience,

    b. study theology and prepare for ministry on the basis of a Black identity,

    c. work collaboratively towards a British Black theology,

    d. find mutual support.

Four issues proved especially important, namely: eligibility for the course, its relationship to other studies, assessment, and teaching staff. The following excerpts from the November 1989 version of the course prospectus describe how these were resolved:

> a. *Eligibility.* For the first two-year cycle of the course, only Black students were admitted. This was necessary particularly for the fulfilment of the fourth aim (mutual support for Black students). From September 1989 a small number of white students with appropriate experience have been admitted.[74] However, the course will continue to be made up of a majority of Black students. The course is normally restricted to students of Queen's College and the WMMTC,[75] though applications from others are considered.

> b. *Relationship to other studies.* Students are able to take the course without adding to their total workload. Normal commitments may therefore be modified, by arrangement with the student's personal tutor. Enrolment for the course is not obligatory.

> c. *Assessment.* Each student is to submit one seminar presentation or one essay per term, to be marked in the usual way. Tutors in other subjects may be asked to agree essay titles to which a student could respond from a Black perspective, whilst covering College essay requirements for that subject. Second-year students, additionally, choose a study topic in the first term in consultation with the course tutors and students. A paper of up to 5,000 words is submitted on this topic at the beginning of the third term.

> d. *Teaching staff* The participation of Black clergy with appropriate theological skills is sought, whilst the role of the tutor from College (who is not Black) is primarily to coordinate and administer. The collaborative style of the course should make it the 'property' of all participants.

The curriculum explored Black theological method and then pursued it in four basic areas of theology: History, Systematics, Ministry and Mission, and Social Context. The full text of the statement of methodology and of the curriculum is appended. The course fulfilled Daniel's criteria by using as far as possible Black and Asian tutors (notably Bishop Patrick Kalilombe), by bringing Black students together, and by devising a Black curriculum undiluted by 'permeation'. It marked distinct progress in that it enabled Black students, for the first time in British theological education, to drink unambiguously from their own wells.

Wesley Daniel had asked that whilst numbers of Black students remained small, a proper programme should be developed in one place before being duplicated elsewhere. In responding to this need, Queen's College was doing more than simply creating a critical mass which would make the course viable; it was also creating a 'safe space' for Black self-expression and exploration. In fulfilling both aims, the course was eminently successful. As we have noted, a number of White students were admitted, but this was subject to certain restrictions. One was that White students had to remain in a small minority. Another was that Black students should in fact be discreetly consulted about the suitability of a White applicant to the course. As course co-ordinator, John Wilkinson strongly supported the view of course members that this potentially explosive right of veto was vital to the course's success. Nothing would have been more damaging than the erosion of the protected forum in which, as one Black student put it, 'we can tell the truth without having to deal with a whole load of nonsense in return'.

At the same time, it should be noted that course tutors could not assume in Black students a consciousness that would immediately understand or agree with the aims of the course. Some students welcomed it and immediately realized its potential for responding to questions thrown up by their Blackness in a White-majority society and church. Others articulated anxiety and even reluctance. However, as far as course tutors are aware, no students finished the course feeling it had failed them, nor did anyone ever say they regretted joining.

Here are three student evaluations:

> In September of 1987 I was invited with three other students to join a course at Queen's College, Birmingham. The subject was Black theology. I went with a lot of anxieties because I was not sure what this would involve. After the first session I became less nervous and wanted to go back. We explored many areas in our history, looking on our African heritage, the move to the West Indies, the Americas and later to the United Kingdom. By this time my adrenalin was really active because I could connect a lot of history to today's living. We studied the life and work of many of our freedom fighters such as Malcolm X, Marcus Garvey and Martin Luther King.
>
> Not only did we study in these areas, we also looked at the biblical implications and its relevance to us and our 'blackness'. What is Jesus Christ saying to me as a black person and how black would he have to be to liberate me?
>
> We were able to use all these materials in our context and match them beside our life. This course has transformed me not only in my thinking but in my general lifestyle and attitudes. It has been a year of pain and joy, a time of tremendous growth and healing.
>
> I now look forward to another year, this time with eagerness. From the syllabus for this year I know more will be revealed about the God of the oppressed—the God who promises to set his people free.
>
> ****
>
> As preparation for a ministry which neither devalues nor diminishes my experiences as a black person, I find Black Christian Studies relevant and stimulating.
>
> ****

> When I arrived at Queen's eighteen months ago it was clear that any seri-
> ous attempts to study theology had to include my perspective of God and
> what he means to me as a black woman training for ministry. My experi-
> ence of life had to be taken seriously by the College and consequently the
> quality of training I received.
>
> It must be said then that without the Black Christian Studies group on
> Tuesdays I would not have survived with my integrity intact.
>
> This group gave me the opportunity not only to find the right books, but
> it also gave me the chance to explore my faith in the light of my black
> experience. The group helped me to organize my thoughts—it gave me
> a chance to deal systematically with the issues, for example, 'What does
> God mean to me when society would have me believe that others are
> more in the image of God?'
>
> But above all the group is a place of refuge. Refuge because in an all-white
> environment it would be easy to go under or play the 'We are all one in
> Christ' game. Of course we are, but the fact remains that as black people
> we need to plug into our own spiritual and cultural tradition if we are to
> remain sober, or if our theology is to remain authentic. We must learn to
> be, and to love the company of our own people. This group gives me that
> chance—without it I would not have survived College.

At the same time, discreet vigilance was required to try to discover Black
ordinands in the church at large and encourage then to come to Queen's,
or at least make sure they were aware of what Queen's had to offer a
Black student. Eventually, the Methodist Church's Division of Ministries did
support the College's efforts to attract Black students. In at least one case,
a Black student allotted by the Methodist Church to Wesley College Bristol
was permitted to travel to Birmingham every Tuesday with travel costs
paid by her College. Things were more difficult in the Church of England
because of its more diffuse diocesan structures and the alleged bias against
an ecumenical institution of some Diocesan Directors of Ordinands.

At first, all students were of African-Caribbean descent and ethnicity,
though several had been born in the Caribbean. However, interesting issues
had to be faced when a Black student of African or Asian descent joined
the course. For them, the definition of Blackness had to be explored using
tools additional to those from North America which included the narrative
of slavery. For example, appropriate resources of history and theology had to
be gathered quickly when a student of Nigerian descent joined the course,
and when an outside student of Gujarati Moslem background also joined. By
1992, the Course was open not only to ordinands and their spouses but also
to Black students from beyond the College and the associated West Midlands
Ministerial Training Course and to appropriate Black lay people as well, for
example local preachers or others of equivalent theological training.

4. Simon of Cyrene Theological Institute

In September 1989, the Simon of Cyrene Theological Institute opened in Wandsworth. Whereas the developments at Queen's had been built on the slenderest of local resources and much good will, the Institute came from the 'centre' of the Church of England. After the publication of *Faith in the City*, a small steering group had been formed which in only two years secured ACCM funding,[76] obtained accommodation in Wandsworth, turned a purely Anglican committee into an ecumenical body, appointed Sehon Goodridge from Codrington College, Barbados, as the first Principal, and developed a statement of aims and some preliminary course outlines.

The Institute's aim was 'research and action towards a just and reconciled society' which it was to promote by developing the articulation of a British Black theology, as well as through 'dialogue' and addressing White church structures. It sought to train Black lay people and to prepare Black candidates for ministry for subsequent training at a theological college or course. It also offered Pastoral Studies Units (PSUs) for students already in training. These were advertised as for 'white and black' students, but inevitably were in practice White events, since the overwhelming majority of students in training were White.

The Institute claimed to be a facility 'devised and developed by Black Christians, and one which they can own with the help of the whole Church'.[77] But in comparison with what happened at Queen's, it seems to have suffered from a number of practical and conceptual flaws. First, by being separate from colleges and courses, it ran the risk of seeming patronising and having a 'remedial' role. Black students might well ask why they should be singled out to do an extra, preliminary year and then be sent to other institutions which were unaffected by its Black perspective. Secondly, its Black identity was in practice compromised by its financial dependence on White students being signed up for Pastoral Studies Units. Thirdly, as Wesley Daniel had pointed out in 1986, Black theology is not a 'pastoral' need but the life-blood of Black Christian discipleship and of all who seek to be in relationship with Black Christians in the Church.

In practice, it could not help being in competition with Queen's, which was able to offer serious Black theological education in the midst of the wider formation offered by the Church and not as a preliminary to it. The marked reluctance of the Simon of Cyrene Theological Institute, and of the Association of Black Clergy which supported it, to respond to overtures from Queen's that the two bodies should co-operate and work out their respective roles together is regrettable.

5. Queen's College and the West Midlands Course

By 1989, Black Christian Studies and Racism Awareness had become established parts of the curriculum and of College and West Midlands course life.

But there remained considerable limitations in the teaching programme of the White majority of students. This had been acknowledged in the response of the College Principal to a 1988 ACCM enquiry into racism in theological education:

> We would have to acknowledge that some students still go out of College without seriously grappling with the issues or reading the basic literature. Many will have little or no contact with Black Methodist or Anglican congregations or with Black-led Churches. Moreover, our programme…is not really a sustained programme, but is made up of bits and pieces put together over two or three years.[78]

A new curriculum introduced in 1990 sought to address this last issue. In it, the various elements of (i) an experiential Pastoral Studies Course *Christian Ministry in a Multi-cultural Society*, (ii) *Racism Awareness Training* and (iii) a course *Introduction to Black Christianity* were brought into a coherent relationship to each other and are part of the core-course taken by all students. But the crucial task of monitoring the general curriculum remained. Progress was clearer in some subjects than others—evidence of continued dependence on the priorities and consciousness of individual tutors. The College finally took the step to this problem, and at the same time to provide Black tutorial leadership for the Black Christian Studies course, by employing a Tutor for Black theology.

In September 1992, Robert Beckford, a young theologian from a Black-led church in Birmingham, was appointed as the first such tutor in British theological history. His appointment carried the additional promise of building bridges between 'mainstream' and 'Black-led' churches. In November 1992, Robert took over responsibility for the Black Christian Studies course.

4   Dread and Rahtid:
Robert Beckford's Canon

This chapter is something of a departure from the two sections that have preceded it. The difference lies in the fact that this section does not contain the eclectic thematic structuring of varied Black theological extracts from different writers. Instead, in this chapter we have given over space to one scholar: that scholar is Robert Beckford.

Robert Beckford has been a colleague of ours for many years. Anthony Reddie first met Robert soon after he had been appointed Tutor in Black Theology at Queen's College in Birmingham, way back in 1992. Beckford was the first person to be appointed to teach Black theology within the British theological education system in Britain.

Robert Beckford is the most charismatic and luminous member of the 'Black theology in Britain' movement. We are convinced that more Black scholars have been persuaded to undertake undergraduate and postgraduate work, having been provoked by Beckford's insistent, restless and playful energy than having read non-descript and largely inaccurate promotional literature. Such has been Reddie's testimony.

Beckford's appointment to the Queen's College[1] was a landmark moment. Being the first Black person to be appointed to the staff of a theological training institution with the express intention of teaching Black theology was a major paradigm shift for the production of theological work in this country. Working alongside John Wilkinson, Beckford pioneered the development of Black Christian Studies (later Black Theology), as a core part of the curriculum for initial ministerial training and formation. This was the first of its kind in the early 1990s, and, at the time of writing, remains so within the British theological education system.

This chapter of the reader is dedicated to the canon of Robert S. Beckford. Giving Beckford a chapter to himself is a clear ideological statement of intent. As we have indicated in the opening chapter, the editors have made a clear demarcation between Black Christianity in Britain and Black theology. We have not suggested that the two areas are so distinct as to have no relationship with each other, but we are also clear that they are not necessarily one and the same thing.

The editors would assert that theology undertaken by Black people does not necessarily render it Black theology any more than any theology undertaken by women is necessarily Feminist theology.

In terms of an explicit re-interpretation of the Christian faith in light of Black experience, in solidarity with a particular identified group, for the purposes of social transformation and systemic political change, Beckford remains the most visible and widely read member of this, somewhat limited, club. For whilst Black Christianity as reflected in the works of Black Christian scholars, and in the work of such bodies as the Council for Black-Led Churches, the African Caribbean Evangelical Alliance and its parent body, the Evangelical Alliance, are well attended and numerically thriving entities, Black theology, due to its radical and non-traditional approach to re-interpreting Christianity, remains more of a minority pursuit.

In terms of 'Black theology in Britain', Robert Beckford remains the key 'organic intellectual', whose canon has and continues to exert a profound influence upon the development of the movement in this country.

In order to emphasize the iconoclastic nature of Beckford's work, we propose to highlight some of the salient features and emphases in his work by way of a number of key extracts from Beckford's published texts. As the editors were preparing this text they were keenly aware of the limited nature of this chapter as it relates to Beckford's canon. For alongside a number of highly influential books, Beckford has carved out a parallel career as an award-winning mainstream television presenter. In the last few years, a steady stream of documentaries have emerged, all fronted by Robert Beckford. At the time of writing, his major documentaries are *Britain's Slave Trade* (Channel 4, 1999), *Black Messiah* (BBC 4, 2001), the BAFTA award-winning *Test of Time* (BBC Education, 2001), *Blood and Fire* (BBC 2, 2002), *Ebony Towers* (BBC 4, 2003), *God Is Black* (Channel 4, 2004), *Who Wrote the Bible?* (Channel 4, 2004), *The Gospel Truth* (Channel 4, 2005), *The Empire Pays Back* (Channel 4, 2005), *The Real Patron Saints* (Channel 4, 2005), *The Passion: Films, Faith and Fury* (Channel 4, 2006).[2]

The editors are aware of Beckford's media work, particularly his documentaries, but have chosen instead to concentrate on his literary output. Our reasons for doing so are relatively simple and linked with the particular nature of this Reader and the ideological claims that are inherent within the nomenclature of Black theology that defines its existence.

There is no doubting that Beckford's documentaries represent the most visible medium for the articulation of predominantly religiously related themes, especially as they affect Black people in Britain. Clearly, given the dominant role television plays in our collective social, cultural and political consciousness, more people will have seen Beckford when compared to those who have read his work. One viewing of his influential *Who Wrote the Bible?* (broadcast on Christmas Day on Channel 4, 2004) will have attracted more people than the cumulated numbers undertaking preparatory Adult Christian education courses or classes in 'How to read the Bible'. Our assessment of Beckford's written work, as opposed to his media output, is not some form of hierarchical snobbery against the claims of so-called 'popularism' and pop-culture. We recognize the visibility and accessibility of his media work and in no way wish to suggest that such output is not worthy of scholarly analysis or to be prized and celebrated in its own right. No doubt there are others, particularly, within the realms of cultural studies, who are undertaking this form of analysis of his documentary work as we speak.

Our reasons for confining our scholarly gaze to Beckford's literary work can be found in the nature and intent of this Reader. This book is concerned with detailing and discerning the nature, intent and development of Black theology in Britain. Beckford's written work (particularly the first three books) has been a consistent apologetic for the development of a Pentecostal inspired approach to Black liberation theology that is informed by Black popular cultures and the Diasporan routes of the Black Atlantic.[3] This text foregrounds that work as we recognize that his literary canon continues to argue for the conscientized re-reading of the Christian tradition in light of Black Diasporan existential experience for the ultimate purposes of liberation and systemic, social transformation.

Conversely, we have decided not to foreground Beckford's documentary work as we feel that not all of it can be necessarily understood as Black theology. Whilst some of that work (*Black Messiah*) can be construed to be Black theological work, others (*The Real Patron Saints*) cannot. We are not seeking to make any value judgements on the efficacy of this work—rather, we are simply trying to be consistent in our criteria for determining what works are featured in this text and those which should be omitted.

In terms of his literary canon, Beckford has written five influential texts to date. These are *Jesus Is Dread*,[4] *Dread and Pentecostal: A Political Theology for the Black Church in Britain*,[5] *God of the Rahtid: Redeeming Rage*,[6] *God and the Gangs*[7] and his latest book *Jesus Dub: Theology, Music and Social Change*.[8]

The editors have chosen sections from each book, which, we believe, contain important insights into the development of Black theology as a whole in the UK, in addition to shedding light upon the nature of his work in particular.

Having read every one of his books, the authors assert that Beckford's work occupies the dialectical nexus between normative Caribbean British Pentecostalism and the so-called mainstream of White theological liberalism. This can be seen, particularly in such texts as *Jesus Is Dread, Dread and Pentecostal* and *Jesus Dub*. In these books, Beckford juxtaposes Black Caribbean theological reflections on British Pentecostalism alongside the liberal theological methods of the likes of Paul Tillich[9] and David Tracy.[10]

It is the juxtaposition of these two sources and norms for undertaking theological reflection which make Robert Beckford the dominant Black Pentecostal theologian in Britain and the most well-known Black theologian in this country. Beckford has an unerring ability to juxtapose and 'correlate' seemingly disparate, almost oppositional, phenomenon in his constructive theological task. No one but Beckford would correlate Marley with theology, the Rasta concept of 'Dread' with Pentecostal or Jesus with Dub.

It is the very juxtaposition of these terms and concepts that renders Beckford's work continuously fascinating, even if the reader finds such forms of theological construction aberrant or simply misguided.

This Reader celebrates the landmark and pioneering work of Robert S. Beckford. He remains the most visible Black theologian in Britain.

'Jah would never give the Power to a Baldhead': Bob Marley as a Black Liberation Theologian

[This extract is taken from Robert Beckford's first book, *Jesus Is Dread: Black Theology and Black Culture in Britain* (London: Darton, Longman and Todd, 1998), 115–27. It is the contention of the editors that *Jesus Is Dread* is the first fully articulated Black theology text in the UK. Although it was preceded by edited works by the likes of Patel and Grant (see opening chapter for further details on these texts) Beckford's first, epoch-making text remains a definitive landmark in the evolution of Black theology in Britain. Beckford, using the correlative theological method of Paul Tillich, seeks to develop the contextual sources and norms for a Pentecostal inspired approach to Black British theology.]

The children in my family were not allowed to listen to reggae music in our house. My parents were members of the Wesleyan Holiness Church, and in the late 1970s most Wesleyans discouraged their children from listening to secular music. My parents kept strictly to this rule, and I remember many occasions when they roughly removed a reggae record which, owing to bad timing, happened to be playing on the family's stereo as they entered the living room. My parents' dislike of secular music in general, and reggae in particular, only fed my desire for this forbidden genre. What they failed to realize was that for me as for many of my generation, reggae music was a primary source of historical, political and social information from Jamaica about Black history, Black culture and the state of the African diaspora. However, despite valuing reggae music, I was suspicious towards Rastafari.

Black Christianity, in the form which I experienced it, was also strongly anti-Rasta. Not only were we not allowed to listen to reggae, but we were also taught to see Rastafari as un-Christian and evil. For much of my teenage life, I 'bought into' the anti-Rasta critique of the Black Christian elders in my community; indeed, on many occasions, I publicly denounced

Rastafari despite having consumed reggae music whenever possible. Like many Christians, I was able to hold in tension, without any awareness of contradiction, a love of reggae and a dislike of Rastafari.

Today things are very different. Not only do I continue to appreciate reggae music but I am more acutely aware of its political and religious significance in Britain. In light of this, I want to suggest that a critical appropriation of Rastafari has much to offer the Black Church in Britain today. Reggae music offers an important theological resource for a critical reflection on Black Christianity. To support this theory, I want to explore the lyrics of Bob Marley—the canon found in his albums from 1973 to 1983—as theological literature.

Bob Marley (1945–1981) has many titles: international reggae star, global icon for Rastafari and Jamaican musical legend. Dare we also add to this list, Bob Marley, the theologian? This depends on what we mean by theology. Paul Tillich suggests that, theology is the use of a 'method' to interpret the Christian faith.[11] So if we can show that Marley has a method for evaluating the Christian faith, then he is a theologian. I also want to ask two additional questions.

1. 'Is Bob Marley a Black liberation theologian?' To be a liberation theologian, one has to be concerned with using this aforementioned 'method' to interpret the Christian faith in the light of an oppressed community.
2. If Marley is a Black liberation theologian, what can theologians and Christians in Britain learn from him?

To answer these questions, I will begin by identifying aspects of what I consider to be Marley's method, after which I will explore the way in which his method evaluates Christianity. I will conclude by identifying ways in which Marley's theology can impact on the theology of the Black Church in Britain.

Marley's Method
What, then, is Marley's theological method? I want to suggest two significant uses: the first concerns the way he validates truth, that is, his system of knowing. The second concerns the way in which he interprets the Bible. We begin with his system of knowing.

Marley's knowledge-system
Naturally, Marley does not use the traditional theological methods found in your average systematic theology textbook. Instead, he draws upon three Jamaican traditions. The first is the use of experience, the second is a commitment to radical social change, and the third is the nature of the discourse, reggae music. Let us begin with experience.

For Bob Marley, experience is the basis for interpreting the social world. Consequently, he rejects the knowledge validation processes used in the classrooms of traditional education. For Marley, traditional education is a false consciousness which maintains the subservient position of Black people. [...]

The *second* aspect of Marley's method is commitment to radical social change. There are two areas of concern in his music. First, the destruction of Babylon and second, the emancipation of the poor. [...]

The *third* aspect of Marley's method is the nature of his discourse, that is, reggae music. Reggae music emerges from the urban proletariat in Jamaica. It is the descendent of slave music, containing the survivals of slave rhythms and songs. Marley's use of reggae shows how the medium in which theology is communicated is important for expressing the meaning of God in the world. A similar use of song occurs in Black Churches; song is a valid means of communicating divine truth—indeed, Black Pentecostals believe that God is present in songs and music. When the presence of God's Spirit is felt in the song, Black Pentecostals talk about the music and song being 'anointed'.

In a similar fashion, I am suggesting that God (Jah) may be present in the rhythms of reggae music, which expresses the aspirations of oppressed people. However, it is important to note that not all reggae is Rastafarian worship music. But our primary concern here is with 'churchical' or worship music in Rastafari.

In summary, Marley's system of knowing consists of three tools: experience, a commitment to radical social change and reggae music. Our next task is to show how theological method interacts with the Bible. We turn to Marley's method on interpretation.

Marley's biblical interpretation

Marley's interpretive method is best understood as a process. It begins with 'inner revelation'—truth which emerges from personal experience. In other words, when Marley says, 'So Jah seh' he refers to revelation, which has come directly from Jah. Once revelation emerges, Bible must confirm it. Guidance means finding correspondence between revelation and a biblical event, symbol or word. This exploration of the text might take place individually or communally. Reasoning with Jah is sometimes assisted by burning incense in the temple of God, that is, smoking 'ganja' (cannabis).

This hermeneutic is witnessed in the development of key doctrines. For example, the founding fathers of Rastafari believed in the deity of Haile Selassie (1892–1975—former Emperor of Ethiopia), in Black repatriation to Africa, and that the Western world, including Jamaica, was evil. They found support for these beliefs in the Bible and used biblical images to signify a range of correspondences with these revelations. Hence in the lyrics of Marley we discover that Selassie signifies Jah Rastafari, Africa corresponds with the Promised Land or Zion, and Jamaica is synonymous with evil or Babylon. Marley uses this hermeneutic to interpret the contents of the Bible. I would like to demonstrate this by focusing on two of his theological hallmarks: the Second Advent of the Messiah and Africa as the land of liberation.

The Second Advent is declared in 'Get Up Stand Up' on the *Burnin'* album. Marley and the Wailers confess, 'We know and we understand, The Mighty God Is a living man.' Here, the 'Mighty God' is Haile Selassie. He is the Black God who has returned to save Black people. The proof of his divinity lies in Rasta's personal revelation and also biblical proof. For instance, in 'Blackman Redemption' on the *Confrontation* album Selassie's genealogy is used as proof of his divinity: as Emperor of Ethiopia, Selassie (like Christ) is 'from the root of David, through the line of Solomon'. So, just as Christians declare Jesus divine because of revelation and biblical confirmation, Marley, as a Rasta, declares Selassie divine. However, this interpretation is problematic for two reasons. First, it reveals an uncritical approach to the text. Second, it relies heavily upon an idealized and romanticized view of African history.

The second theological hallmark of Bob Marley's songs is the belief that Africa—in particular, Ethiopia—is the land of liberation for Blacks. Old Testament references to Ethiopia such as 'Let bronze be brought from Egypt, let Ethiopia hasten to stretch out her hands to God' (Ps. 63:31) are Rastafarian proof texts which support the belief that Africa plays a central role in God's plan for Black redemption. [...]

Is Marley a Black Liberation Theologian?
First, we must answer a more general question: is Marley a theologian at all? As we have seen above, Bob Marley has a theological method and applies it to the Christian Scriptures in order to produce a theology. In my opinion, Marley is a theologian—not necessarily a traditional Christian theologian but definitely a Rastafarian theologian. However, despite speaking on behalf of the marginalized and being of working-class origins, on another level, Marley must be seen as a wealthy musician who maintained physical and political links with the Jamaican proletariat. In short, his perspectives, as a Rastafarian theologian, emerge from a position of relative privilege in the Jamaican context.

Second, I would contend that Marley is a Black Liberation theologian, because his theology is totally concerned with the liberation of the oppressed.

What can we learn from Marley the theologian?
We turn to our next question. If we take Marley seriously as a Black liberation theologian, what can we learn from him? I would like to outline

an area in which Marley's theology speaks into our contemporary context in Britain.

Theology as ideology. First, he informs us that theology is an ideological project—it is never neutral or 'value free'. Like Marx, Marley believes that religion reflects human interests. In this case, Marley's ideology bespeaks local and global resistance against racialized oppression. As far as Marley is concerned, to refuse to stand up for the rights of the disenfranchised is to show a flagrant disregard for the value of human life. For example, in 'Get Up Stand Up' on the *Burnin'* album, Marley declares to Christian people: 'If you knew what life was worth, you would fight for yours on earth'. Importantly, Marley formulates his understanding of God in the oppressed community, seeing God in the faces of the Black dispossessed. [...]

However, we must recognize the negative ideologies in Marley's canon. Black feminist Patricia Hill Collins encourages Black thinkers to look at the lives of those people whom we deem important figures in Black communities, in order to see if their personal lives match up to their ideas. Marley's personal life raises questions for Black women, suggesting that he did not have a lot of respect for them.[12] His promiscuous lifestyle, and his general failure to honour Black women in his music, reminds those of us concerned with using Marley as a source for our theology that any theological enterprise concerned with Black liberation in Britain must take seriously the multi-dimensional nature of oppression. That is, we must be not only concerned with racism but also with sexism. Given the race, class and gender exploitation of Black British women, any theology of liberation must be a theology that empowers Black women.

The African Heritage

Despite Marley's highly romanticized and uncritical appropriation of Africa, there is much to gain from his focus on Africa as an area of biblical significance. Marley's Afrocentrism challenges the thrust of any Black British theology. His method suggests that our religious and cultural African roots are as important as the historical and cultural routes that make many of us a diasporan people. This point is vitally important, especially when we consider the cultural, social, political and religious ignorance of many Black Christians in Britain concerning their African heritage. Furthermore, Marley's orientation inspires a healthy political suspicion of all theological studies and approaches which are patronising and negatively biased against Africa and Africans both continental and diasporan. This is a real issue in theological education where Africa and Africans are ignored in biblical studies. Only in recent years through the efforts of Afrocentric biblical scholars and popularist writers have Black biblical studies crept on to the syllabus of a few British theological institutions with the vision and courage to take Black perspectives seriously. It has been interesting to note those biblical scholars who go out of their way to denigrate Black approaches to the text, despite not having read work by Afrocentric biblical scholars.[13]

Liberation Theological Praxis (LTP)

[This extract is taken from *Dread and Pentecostal: A Political Theology for the Black Church in Britain* (London: SPCK, 2000), 150–55. *Dread and Pentecostal* was Robert Beckford's second book and was adapted from his PhD. In many respects, it is the most systematic and 'traditional' work in the Beckford canon to date. In it, he outlines, in very methodological terms, the sources, norms and theological method for a radical approach to constructing a Black Liberation theology for the British context. Like his first book, he continues to mine African Diasporan sources in order to correlate 'Dread' (incorporating a 'Rasta hermeneutic') with Black British Pentecostalism. This text plays particular attention to theological method and offered the first substantive, delineated model for a Black theology of Liberation in Britain.]

A Theological Method for LTP (Liberation Theological Praxis)

LTP requires a particular theological method that takes into serious consideration liberation, praxis, revelation and history. In terms of theological methodology the action–reflection dynamic best expresses the central thrust of this model (see Fig. 1).

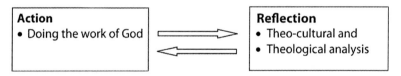

Action	Reflection
• Doing the work of God	• Theo-cultural and
	• Theological analysis

Figure 1. *Action–Reflection Model*

The action–reflection method prioritizes creative transformation of the social context through action. By bringing together the action–reflection model with my earlier discussions on epistemology, analysis and theology it would be consistent to suggest that action must be reflected upon through theo-cultural analysis and through theological reflection—what the Bible has to say about a given situation. This is a dynamic process that results in more action.[14] Here, I will conflate the action–reflection model in LTP into three distinct phases for LTP theological method. These are *experience, analysis* and *action* (see Fig. 2). These elements require a brief explanation.

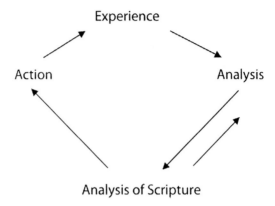

Figure 2. *Analysis of Scripture*

Taking the concrete experience seriously as a starting point: whereas for Cone, the primary concern was the elimination of racism, other Black theologians have suggested alternative starting points. [...] Similarly, other theologians have made class and sexuality other existential starting points.[15] What this means for me is that the experience of being Black in England is a legitimate starting point for theological inquiry. Because Blackness is multiple, this multi-dimensional approach to experience means that the liberation strategies will not all be the same because experience is not singular.

My focus on analysis as theo-cultural provides a greater understanding of oppression, particularly race, class and gender concerns within the British context. Furthermore, the theological dimensions of analysis ensure that a holistic approach is normative.

Analysis also involves biblical reflection, that is, what the Bible has to say about our analysis of a situation. As demonstrated above, Cone and Williams have shown that there are ideological issues of justice, oppression and resistance within the biblical text that must be explored. Hence, as well as asking what the Bible has to say about a particular experience, I must also enable a dialogue between analysis and scripture in order to discern African-centred and theo-cultural themes within scripture. Hence, there is a two-way action between analysis and analysis of scripture represented with two arrows in Fig. 2.

Finally, these new insights must result in action which transforms the experience that began the first movement. For example, if the starting point or experience is responding to a racist attack then the final movement must be action that makes sense of and deals with the attack. Transformation must be related to the theo-cultural analysis and theological reflection so that praxis is holistic, challenging and changing the social world as well as the hearts and minds of the individuals within it.

The strength of this method is that it ensures that theology takes seriously Black experience and also the Black Church's centralization of the Bible. In essence, experience is held as equally valid a tool for theology as Scripture. However, the danger with this method is whether it can ensure that radical praxis is the regular outcome of theological analysis or an illusion to be pursued but never arrived at. Bearing this in mind, I want to end this chapter by exploring the utility of LTP through an analysis of the Black Theology Support Group (BTSG) in Birmingham.

The Black Theology Support Group

In my opinion the BTSG represents the most advanced Black theological centre in the UK context. There is no other location where Black theologians 'do theology'. Therefore, applying the method found within LTP provides insight into BTSG and also the theological content for LTP. As stated in the introduction, illustrative material is used to ground theory. In this case the material is derived from my participation within the BTSG over a two-year period. During this time, as a member of the BTSG, I was able to address and explore the issue of praxis raised above.

In addition, a search for a LTP should also include an exploration outside of the confines of traditional worship and church services to locate evidence of a LTP. This is possible because defining the Church as an expressive, urban social movement enables a search for similar patterns of organization outside the perimeters of the 'Black Church'. The idea of 'church' outside of Church is not a new concept in Black African Caribbean Christian circles. Black Pentecostals often say that they have 'had church' when the presence and the power of the Spirit are experienced. Such a pan-location pneumatology enables 'church' to occur in any space: 'wherever the twos or threes are gathered'.

The Black Theology Support Group (BTSG) was established in 1995 by a group of Black theologians and Black church leaders in Birmingham. Meetings occur roughly every six weeks at the Centre for Black and White Christian Partnership in Selly Oak, Birmingham. Although based in Birmingham, it has a national perspective: its participants come from the Southeast and the North of England as well as the Midlands area. Initially, the group was concerned with providing mutual support and encouragement. Hence, each session begins with greetings, sharing of information, a presentation and fellowship. However, the need for analysis of the social context and the intellectual prowess of the group resulted in writing of papers, essays and the emergence of a *Journal of Black British Theology*.

My task here is to make a brief assessment of the BTSG in light of my previous discussion on LTP. There are two areas of concern. First, I will explore the 'experience' of the BTSG through an evaluation of it as an ecumenical group. This is because its Black ecumenism encompasses several features that constitute and shape the self-understanding of the group. Second, I will analyse its approach to analysis and action. These categories are important because, as demonstrated above, they are central to LTP.

In terms of analysing the BTSG from the perspective of LTP it is important to unlock its central concerns. While not being a worshipping community, the BTSG provides an important theological and experiential function for its participants as an ecumenical group. As an ecumenical group of Black Christians, the BTSG represents a paradigm of Black ecumenism. There are three points of importance.

First, it encourages participation from Black men and women. The group has nurtured the emergence of a second generation of womanist theologians[16] by providing a space for the development and articulation of a British womanist theology. However, despite the participation of women, the 'unofficial' leadership of the group continues to be male dominated. Hence, while there is an inclusive thrust, male leadership still prevails.

Second, the BTSG experiences a particular understanding of ethnicity and identity. Regarding the former, the mode of Blackness present at the group incorporates African Caribbean, African and Asian identities. In other words, while 'Black' is used as a signifier of non-White interests and experiences within the group, there is also recognition of Black diversity and multiplicity. For example, Pradip Sudhra, an Asian church leader, said on one occasion to the author that: 'It is important to remember that "Black" includes Asians Christians as well—and that Asian Christians engage and develop Black theology'. This view of Blackness is not true for all Asians. However, here it suggests that Blackness is organically related to Christian identities. That is to say, in contrast to the analysis of Toulis, here, Black identities are held in a diunital (both/and) and dialogical (relational) coalition with Christian identities (see Fig. 3), rather than Christian identity overwhelming ethnicity.

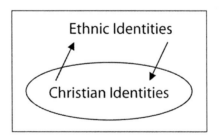

Figure 3. *Ethnic Identity and Christian Identities*

Ideologically, the group are explicit about the need for a deconstruction of White hegemony, in particular its effects upon Christian and ethnic identity. For example, in one paper, Anthony Reddie, a PhD student at Birmingham University, argues for the use of Black oral history as a tool for developing an alternative epistemology. Hence, in contrast to Black Churches, the BTSG articulates an explicit Black identity and Black politics as part of its commitment to transformation.

Finally, as an ecumenical group, the BTSG articulates a new relationship between spirituality and political engagement. The BTSG makes political analysis an integral dimension of their spirituality. For example, Lorraine Dixon, a BD student and Anglican priest in training, stated in an analysis of the praxis of gospel singer Mahalia Jackson that it is impossible to ignore the political dimensions of Black faith in a context of racial subordination.[17]

However, as the BTSG is not a worshipping community, it has greater freedom to explore and be explicit about political liturgy as an integral function of the support group. A critical question, however, is to what extent is spirituality ignored or undervalued at the expense of political prowess. I want to suggest that the implicit spirituality in the explicit politics of the BTSG is an *inversion* of the implicit politics within the explicit spirituality of Black Churches. Neither approach creates a healthy relationship between spirituality and political action. This is because neither approach defines a space for a creative and explicit spirituality of liberation.

What kind of analysis is produced as a result of the experience of gender, ethnicity and politics? Regarding analysis, the BTSG has developed expertise in analysing Black British experience. Numerous papers have been presented that analyse the experiences of Black people. For example, themes have included Womanist Theology, Black Male Education, The Black Christ, Blacks in White Majority Churches, The Death of Diana and Black People, Black Oral History and Methods for a Black British Theology. These papers and discussions have revealed a willingness to engage with a socio-cultural and theological analysis of Black British experience. However, during my visits and participation in the group there was an under-representation of theological analysis. As a consequence, although there is an awareness of the socio-cultural issues within the Bible, most explorations made little reference to scripture. Instead the emphasis was upon the socio-political analysis of Black experience. Such an imbalance fails to address the centrality of the Bible in the Black Church.

There are two possible reasons for this situation. First, there is a structural issue. There are few Black British theologians. Furthermore most are still in the process of gaining higher degrees. Second, very few, if any, participants in the group are engaged in biblical studies; instead there is a bias towards pastoral and systematic theology. This situation mirrors the professional development amongst first and second generation Black British who tended to enter professions that most readily assisted with the social needs of Black people. Hence, pastoral studies and systematic theology provide bridgeheads into the White dominated world of academic theology. In sum, from the perspective of LTP the BTSG needs to mobilize the Bible in order to avoid the danger of developing a socio-cultural gospel that lacks theological reflection. A similar concern emerges over the issue of action.

Regarding action, the theological method employed at the BTSG is primarily intellectual—the production of texts and journals. As we have seen above from our analysis of culture, the creation of intellectual ideas has material force in the world and can challenge the status quo. In this sense, the collective praxis of the BTSG is that of 'organic intellectuals'. Organic intellectuals express the interests of a class without necessarily belonging to that class. Their task is to produce ideas that challenge received knowledge and systems of understanding. Organic intellectuals contrast with traditional intellectuals who maintain continuity.[18]

However, while organic intellectualism offers a cognitive challenge it must be accompanied by a structural challenge. Structural challenge is concerned with making concrete the principles of justice and equality envisioned within the social context and integral to 'action' within LTP. While the intellectual challenge will ensure the development of a class of Black theological intellectuals, without structural challenge the group will have a weakened effect on the academic and social life in Birmingham.

Therefore, in terms of LTP, the BTSG offers limited liberation praxis. Whereas Mile End represented *passive active radicalism* and Ruach, *reactive active radicalism*, from my perspective the BTSG represents a *cognitive active radicalism*. That is to say its focus is primarily intellectual radicalism. However, intellectual development by itself is only limited challenge. I argue that *cognitive active radicalism* is synonymous to the survival tradition in Black faith. Survival is a space for nurturing holistic liberation, similarly *cognitive active radicalism* nurtures full *active radicalism*. Hence, in many ways the BTSG has not moved beyond the limitations of passive radicalism within the Black Church. Instead it has reconfigured the weaknesses of passive radicalism in academic clothes.

Kingdom of God and God of the Rahtid

[This extract is taken from *God of the Rahtid* (London: Darton, Longman and Todd, 2001), 41–47. It was the third in the early triumvirate of groundbreaking works by Beckford. In this text, Beckford draws upon Black theological insights concerned with the nature of the Economy of God, and argues that our understanding of God's reign provides the necessary tools and resources for a redeeming construct of Black rage. Redemptive vengeance, argues Beckford, can be found within the notion of a realized eschatology, in which the agency of God, incarnated within the ministry of Jesus, provides the focus for harnessing the emotive power of Black anger. In the Beckford canon, this is our favourite piece of work. In it, Beckford harnesses the 'righteous anger' of the marginalized and the oppressed and, taking Steve Biko's dictum to heart, writes what he likes!]

I want to ground the concept of a God of the rahtid in Jesus' teachings of the Kingdom of God. The Kingdom symbolizes the rule of God here and now and provides a space of radical transformation where boundaries, insecurities and impossibilities are overcome. In Black churches all over the country we sing and shout about the joy of living in the Kingdom of God because it is an exciting place for the marginalized, downtrodden and abused to find 'somebodyness', uplift and status. Black rage when placed within the Kingdom is refocused and redirected—Kingdom theology reformulates and reconfigures the concept of a God of the rahtid so that it becomes aligned to both spiritual renewal and socio-political transformation. In order to demonstrate how the Kingdom challenges the God of the rahtid, I will explore in brief views in the Black Church and Black theological perspectives on the place of justice in the Kingdom now and in the future.

Black Theology and the Kingdom of God—Realized Eschatology

It is well documented in New Testament scholarship that there were many angry groups often subsumed under the heading of Zealots who desired vengeance against the Roman colonizers. The critical question is did Jesus share their vengeful desires? In the Black British Church tradition opinion is split over this matter.

On the one hand, there are traditionalists within Black churches who argue that divine retribution in the teachings of Jesus was for the end of the age. In the meantime, divine rule meant rule over the *hearts* of men and women.[19] Therefore, a distinction was to be made between the present spiritual and the future political. However, this myopic gaze does not explore the teachings of Jesus concerned with holistic transformation in the present. In essence, the kingdom being 'at hand' implies that change is taking place now.

On the other hand, there is a small radical group of academic theologians in the Black Church that view Jesus' proclamation of the arrival of the Kingdom as political. For this second camp, Jesus' announcement of divine rule was a direct challenge to Roman political authority. Therefore, today humans must participate with God in socio-political change consistent with the ethics of the Kingdom. The main difficulty with this realized eschatological camp is that they neglect the apocalyptic dimensions of Jesus' teachings and consequently reduce a fluid concept to a static one. However, it is possible to opt for a view of the Kingdom of God in Black thought where the future vision of the Kingdom has a transformative effect in the present. Two examples from the 'old' and 'new' schools of Black theology in the USA reveal how this can happen.

Old and New School Views on the Kingdom of God

From the 'old school' of the 1960s and 70s, African American theologian James Cone argues that the Kingdom ushers in a new age for Black people. Because the Kingdom is at hand, oppressed men and women are compelled to deal with evil in the world rather than fixing their attention on the eschaton:

> If eschatology means that one believes that God is totally uninvolved in the suffering of men because he is preparing them for another world, then Black theology is an earthy theology! It is not concerned with the 'last Things' but with the 'White thing'. Black theology like Black Power believes that the self-determination of Black people must be emphasized at all costs, recognising that there is only one question about reality for Blacks: What must we do about White racism?[20]

However, despite Cone's emphasis on the immanent nature of liberation, elsewhere he accepts that liberation is *also* transcendent over history:

> It is important to note that Black theology, while taking history with utmost seriousness, does not limit liberation to history. When people are bound to history, they are enslaved to what the New Testament calls the law of death...if the oppressed, while living in history, can nonetheless see beyond it, if they can visualize an eschatological future beyond the history of their humiliation, then 'the sigh of the oppressed', to use Marx's phrase, can become a cry of revolution against the established order.[21]

Here Cone accepts the power of the 'not yet', but only as a motivating force in the liberation struggle in the now. In other words, viewing liberation as a future event can have a powerful effect on the struggle in the present. What Cone provides for us is an image of how it is possible for an otherworldly eschatology to secure participation in liberation praxis in the present.[22] Even so, there are several difficulties with Cone's early views; in particular, his realized eschatology failed to take seriously the internal liberation within Black communities. Women, the disabled, gay and lesbian Blacks were not part of his vision of the Kingdom on earth. As a man of his time and dealing with pressing social conditions pertaining to racial advancement, Cone was not in a position to consider a multi-dimensional view of emancipation concerned with liberation for the environment and for healing between ethnic groups, or the rich and poor.

In contrast, the 'new school' of the 80s and 90s has attempted to redefine eschatology for second and third generation Black and womanist theologians living in the post-civil rights, consumerist cultures of North America and the domestic neo-colonial cultures of Europe.

For example, womanist theologian Karen Baker-Fletcher provides a wider scope in her realized eschatology. She demands a vision of a society concerned with social and environmental renewal.[23] Most significantly, Baker-Fletcher suggests that Black eschatologies draw from holistic African worldviews where past, present and future are intertwined. That is 'past, present and future are held together within a spiritual reality that is both immanent and transcendent'.[24] Therefore, God stands outside and inside of time, as an empowering Spirit seeking harmony and wholeness for humanity and creation.[25] Here, human beings participate in the growth of the Kingdom, and are able to risk all because the future is secure. This view from the new school provides a broader and more complex eschatology where justice, love and wholeness are central to the coming of the Kingdom.

The Challenge of the Kingdom of God to the God of the Rahtid

Returning to the concerns of this chapter, the second generations' eschatological vision raises questions about the nature and practice of Black rage concealed within the concept of the God of the rahtid. This requires two points of clarification that can be summarized under the headings of compatibility and challenge.

Compatibility

First, I want to affirm compatibility between the God of the rahtid and the Kingdom of God. The God of the rahtid can be located within the thrust of the Kingdom of God only because the Kingdom is concerned with a non-oppressive future breaking into the present. Where there is a quest for justice there is space for rage. However, the type of rage validated by the Kingdom is righteous rage. Righteous rage is the rage geared towards seeking wholeness. Righteous rage demands a broader analysis and a response to injustice, which seeks to do more than redress or compensate. Instead righteous rage seeks to build a new order that makes injustices less likely. This kind of rage can be distinguished from unrighteous rage, which is geared towards petty revenge, as the— 'eye for an eye, tooth for a tooth' became.

Righteous Black rage is a dimension of the Kingdom of God. This means that Black people struggling with vexation and seeking restitution can find a home within the teachings of Jesus on the Kingdom. There has long been

a common sense argument that Black theological thought cannot provide
answers for 'street level' debates about Black rage. Against this, we can
say that Jesus, as a God of the rahtid, 'prepares a table in the presence of
our enemies' so that we are able to find strength, guidance and power to
overcome.

Finally, the fact that a God of the rahtid affirms Black rage nurtures a
hermeneutic of suspicion towards those who encourage us to surrender
our rage. As mentioned above, inner-city comprehensive education
encouraged me to repress my rage rather than find a positive articulation.
Today the temptation to sacrifice black rage is just as strong. This is because
the 'rewards' for remaining silent are so great. bell hooks in *Killing Rage*
articulates the complicity of silence:

> By demanding that Black people repress and annihilate our rage to assimi-
> late, to reap the benefits of material privilege in White supremacist patri-
> archal culture, White folks urge us to remain complicit with their efforts
> to colonize, oppress and exploit. Those of us Black people who have the
> opportunity to further our economic status willingly surrender our rage.
> Many of us have no rage.[26]

Challenge

Second, also important is the challenge of the Kingdom to aspects of the
God of the rahtid. In sum, Kingdom theology requires a use of Black rage
that provides 'revolutionary hope' and healing for the whole community.
In order to provide revolutionary hope, the God of the rahtid *cannot* advocate orientations which are nihilistic. As shown in my experience outlined
earlier, all too often, Black rage leads to neurotic or psychotic episodes
which, while providing short-term relief, do not deal with the underlying
or long-term issues that must be alleviated. On the contrary, revolutionary
hope provides a pathway for new ways of being and doing. Revolutionary
hope provides the 'ways and means' for social transformation. Therefore a
God of the rahtid is constructive rather than destructive and provides faith
rather than despair. Under these conditions there is always the potential
for Black rage to become focused, organized and compelling. bell hooks
affirms this point in *Killing Rage*. She states:

> Confronting my rage, witnessing the way it moved me to grow and change,
> I understood intimately that it had the potential not only to destroy but also
> to construct. Then and now I understand rage to be a necessary aspect of
> resistance struggle. Rage can be a catalyst inspiring courageous action.[27]

Kingdom theology also challenges the God of the rahtid to provide healing.
To talk of healing in the context of Black Britain is to be concerned not only
with freedom and liberation but also with reconciliation. In other words,
as well as being concerned with setting our selves free from the tyranny of
racism, sexism and classism it is also important to move beyond freedom

to love. Moving towards love means taking seriously the need for reconciliation. Later, I will show that this is a complex process that must take into consideration the ways in which Black people are often 'conned' into bypassing freedom for the sake of a *weak reconciliation*.

Weak reconciliation is restitution without justice. It pays no attention to the past and focuses on the future. Therefore, past injustices are not corrected. Also, weak reconciliation makes no demands from the victimizer; instead it is the victim who has to cover most ground by forgiving the most and receiving the least. In contrast, *strong reconciliation* views justice as an integral component of reconciliation. In addition, strong reconciliation is concerned with past, present and future. This is because it is concerned with redeeming the past in order to secure peace and justice today and tomorrow.

Strong reconciliation is hard to find, especially within the British context. Take, for example, the need to make restitution for slavery. Even the most 'Black friendly' government in the post-war period has found itself incapable of apologising for the nation's complicity with slavery. There is still not Remembrance Day for the millions of Africans killed as a result of the English slave trade. Strong reconciliation makes demands on both the victim and victimizer. Both have to make amends for the past in order to secure peace and love in the present and beyond.

So far in this chapter, I have made an existential connection between Black rage and the rahtid and Kingdom theology. I have suggested that within the Kingdom of God, Black rage becomes a healing force that is able to save both victim and victimizer alike. In other words, Kingdom theology transforms the God of the rahtid into a *redemptive vengeance*.

Whiteness

[This extract is taken from Beckford's fourth book, *God and the Gangs* (London: Darton, Longman and Todd, 2004), 74–78. It is in many ways his most accessible work. The accessibility of the book is very apparent. Beckford makes concerted and very real attempts to decipher the often complex nature of academic biblical and theological discourse in order that ordinary Black Christians can begin to engage with the necessary forms of systemic analysis. These forms of analysis are ones that can assist in bringing an authentic radical Christian presence to bear upon a major contemporary social problem of our time.

As we can deduce from the following extract, Beckford, a far-sighted prophet as always, was the first to take on James Cone's rallying cry, in a lecture given at the Queen's Foundation in 1997, that Black people should begin to study White people. Beckford offers the first significant analysis of Whiteness from a Black British theologian.]

Whiteness is difficult to define because its essential meaning will vary from context to context and from situation to situation. When most of us think about whiteness, it refers to skin colour. But whiteness is about more than just the epidermis, it is also about behavioural characteristics, social location and world-view. Ironically, many black urban cultures have created urban myths about whiteness that hint at a perceived superior intellectual and moral character. During talks I have given in inner-city schools on the virtues of higher education, I've heard black kids in school use the phrase, 'acting white' to describe performing well at school or playing what are perceived as elitist sports such as polo or croquet! Similarly, I've listened to conversations where whiteness is associated with correct moral behaviour as expressed in the phrase 'act the white man'.

What I am suggesting here is that whiteness is the way in which ideas, myths and language are used to ensure that white skin colour is represented in a particular, superior way. Now, we know that not all white people are the same and that the issues of ethnicity, class, gender and even sexuality impact upon how one is treated. Decades of feminist scholarship have made clear that gender plays a role in the workplace, home and also the Church! Therefore white men and white women do not always have the same social standing. Likewise, the negative experience of some Eastern European refugees in inner cities informs us that class and nationality also distinguish white people.

I often joke with white asylum seekers I have befriended that if they 'play their cards right', within a generation they will become fully white! What I mean by this is that whiteness as a form of social advantage is not a closed door, as you can become white or gain admittance to the club. This is also a truism for a select group of black people. No one would doubt that General Colin Powell, who at the time of writing was the United States Secretary of State, has ascended to the lofty heights of white privilege in America.

What, then, are some of the characteristics of whiteness in the contemporary urban situation? How does whiteness work?

Invisibility
The first point to note about whiteness is that it is an invisible norm. We tend not to see it as part of the cultural mix. This is why the coroner was able to present multi-culture in Birmingham, as a collection of Asian and African Caribbean communities. We don't generally place white people (whether English, Irish, Welsh or Scottish) within the multi-cultural mix. Consequently, multi or inter-cultural issues are often seen as just the preserve and concern of non-whites.

Because whiteness is unmarked racially, some white people tend not to see it in operation in everyday life. For example, when I ask my predominantly white undergraduate students to tell me five things about being white, they freeze and have no answers. Comparatively, if I ask my predominantly black group of post-graduates they are full of suggestions! The latter outsider group seem to be more aware of the subject matter than the former insider group. However, it is also evident that white students who have lived in minority white situations tend to be more aware of debates and issues concerning being white.

There is an important point to be made here, because whiteness and white people are not 'racialized' in the same way as other groups; whiteness is able to function as an ethnically neutral category that can go unexplored and unchallenged as the standard of expectation and evaluation. As mentioned in the discussions on Afrocentricity, white standards of intelligence and beauty are still invisible norms that operate in contemporary culture and politics. Hence, for many black people in Britain today, to be accepted as 'normal' in white dominated circles of power and influence requires a sacrifice of aspects of black identity and culture.[28]

Economic advantage

As well as being invisible, whiteness is also a place or location associated with privilege. In the summer of 2002, the BBC screened a documentary entitled 'Trading Races'. Within this series a black African Caribbean man and a white English woman and man were cosmetically transformed to take on the features of another ethnic group. Morphed into a white person, the black man was able to march with the far right British National Party and also attend dog races—two activities that he would never have been able to participate in before! It was interesting to note that, time and time again, the black man expressed how differently people treated him when he appeared as a white man. All of which indicates the way in which being white, even in working-class settings such as a greyhound track, had certain advantages.

Tragically, in the real world, whiteness as structural advantage is played-out to the detriment of black people in our nation's classrooms, employment statistics, promotional opportunities and health provision. Whiteness is for most white people a place of economic advantage, even in an age of 'equal opportunities' and community cohesion.[29]

Discourse(s)

The most interesting aspect of whiteness for me is that it gains strength by drawing from other discourses or particular representation of bodies of knowledge. A good and relevant example of this process for us as Christians is the way in which whiteness is still synonymous in Western theology with goodness and the presence of the divine. God is still thought of as an old white man and Jesus depicted as an Aryan in most city churches. The repercussions of this logic have a public expression, hence in civic life it becomes natural to associate whiteness with correct moral behaviour and blackness with deviance. As a black professional, I experience the negative outcome of the interface between whiteness and intelligence on occasions when, away from the university, I have to present or introduce myself by my professional title. On one occasion a secretary working for the BBC came looking for me in the lobby of a BBC building in London. I sat in my suit waiting next to a white motorcycle courier who was clad in black leathers. There were only two of us waiting at that time. Intriguingly, the secretary approached the cyclist before me and asked, 'Are you Dr Beckford?'

Terror

When discussing whiteness we cannot forget that for many people in the urban context, whiteness is still associated with racial terror. There is a perception that when senior white politicians make negative statements about the ethnicity of black people, whether a comment about crime or asylum, there is a fear that on the ground the lives of minority ethnic people are put in real danger. The steady rise of racial attacks and the failure to eliminate discrimination against black people clearly shows that racial terror is still a feature of contemporary British life.[30]

Appropriation

Another dimension of whiteness is the way in which it is put together or constructed through an appropriation of aspects of other cultures.[31] This is particularly visible in youth culture in Birmingham and other towns and cities in the UK. As I walk through the library area of Birmingham on Saturday afternoons, I am confronted with young white kids wearing clothing originating within black urban cultures of the Caribbean and North America. This cultural borrowing is not new; those old enough to remember the 60s or 70s 'mods' will remember that in both incarnations this youth culture was deeply associated with the soul music and style of inner-city Detroit, New York and Chicago. For some time now, white youths have borrowed black style and language, but as mentioned above, often, credit and material reward for black cultural innovation is not given to the black community.

Anti-racism

Finally, I believe that whiteness is at its most significant when it is associated with anti-racism. There has been a long, if often hidden, tradition of whiteness as being a part of a symbol of the struggle for justice. Sadly, even our churches have not fully recognized and celebrated white men and women who fought to free slaves, marched against fascists in the East End of London, stood in solidarity with Ghandi or marched and died with Dr Martin Luther King.

Dub, Signification and the Trickster Motif

[This extract is taken from *Jesus Dub: Theology, Music and Social Change* (London: Routledge, 2006), 74–80. *Jesus Dub* is Robert Beckford's fifth book. No other Black theologian in Britain has achieved the visibility or the overarching influence of Beckford, and in this, his latest book, the author continues in his radical juxtaposing of Black religion (African Caribbean Pentecostal Christianity) and Black popular culture. In this text, in many respects a long-awaited thematic sequel to his now iconic *Jesus Is Dread*, Beckford juxtaposes the 'Church hall' and the 'Dance hall' in order to re-work the theo-political dimensions of Black aesthetics, space and religio-cultural positionality in terms of Black peoples' postcolonial subjectivities and identities in twenty-first century Britain. This extract outlines his approach to the issues of 'dub' and 'signification'.]

Signification is a term used in cultural criticism to describe how signs function. Signs are sounds, words, objects or images and consist of two parts: a signifier, the sound, word, object or image—and the signified, the concepts which the sound, word, object or image represents. 'Signifying', therefore, describes the act of producing and projecting signs.

However, signifying is not always a clear-cut process because the relationship between signifier and signified is not at all times transparent and we must rely on context, association and other codes to help us make sense of a sign.[32]

Signifying is an important aspect of Black cultures. A groundbreaking study in this field is Henry Louis Gates's *Signifying Monkey*. This text examines the coded language of African American writers and their meanings, in a highly racialized society. Drawing on West African traditions of the double voice, Gates concluded from his study of African America literature that Black signification is arriving at 'direction through indirection'.[33] The best way of explaining signification in Caribbean cultures is to refer to the mythic spider Anancy.

Anancy, the spider trickster, is prominent in the folklore of the Akan group of Twi-speaking people including the Ashanti. Akan peoples were transported in large numbers as slaves to Jamaica (1730–90) and their numerical superiority enabled their stories and language to endure and leave an imprint. The Jamaican Anancy tales were reshaped in their slave context, but the aim remained the same: to 'gain direction through indirection', that is, enabling the weak to outwit the power structures by a host of tactics such as evasion and manipulation. The genius of the Anancy story is not only in its content but also how it is told; both aspects signify!

> Anancy's realm is the realm of the polymorphous perverse, of endless deviation, deflection, and switching of roles, and the storyteller's art is like-wise one of subterfuge and multiple meanings, so that any Anancy story operates polysemetically, with one meaning, say for children, another for adults 'in the know', and another still for outsiders, particularly outsiders who are White.[34]

To succeed, in every story Anancy breaches rules, inverts conventions and demonstrates the 're-creative power' in social life.[35] Put simply, Anancy accomplishes his ends by *playing* the trickster; he uses the double-voice— that is, saying one thing and meaning another.[36]

What I want to suggest here is that in addition to understanding dub as deconstruction with its incumbent folk religious sensibilities, we also view the actions of the studio engineer, reworking, remixing and recoding a track as a process of signification. The engineer is on one level, as a trickster character that mixes and plays with the rules of sound and recreates so that each dub has many voices or many levels of meaning. After all, dub's aesthetic power lies in this playing of tricks on the listener's memory:

> Because it's often applied to an already-familiar song or rhythm track, dub has a uniquely poignant quality: memories are revived, but rather than being simply duplicated (as when we hear a 'golden oldie' from our youth on the radio) they are given subtle twists. Memory is teased rather than dragged up, and is thereby heightened.[37]

Let me restate the argument thus far. The origins of dub emerge from a sound system culture in Jamaica. It is the creation of studio engineers and the product of experimentation with new recording technology. Dub has gone through various stages of development before evolving into a distinct genre. I have theorized dub as a form of deconstruction and signification. The penultimate task of this chapter is to connect dub in a more meaning-ful way to the spoken word.

The connection between dub and the spoken word is organic, as DJ lyri-cism relies heavily upon dub tracks as background material. But it is with the emergence of 'dub poetry' that we have a more intimate connection between the dub technique on vinyl and the spoken word.

Dub Poetry

As outlined in the previous chapter, running concurrently with the new forms of racialized oppression within post-war Britain is cultural resistance. As sociologist David Brain explains, cultural production enables us not only to make sense of our lives, but also to resist structural oppression.[38]

In a similar vein, successive generations of African Caribbean youth have utilized cultural production as a political weapon and this is also the case with the dub poets.

Dub poetry in Britain and the Caribbean emerges from the toasting scene inspired by dub. It was a politically *ghettocentric* art form,[39] influenced by Black Nationalism, Rastafari and Leftist political struggles. The first 'dub poets' appeared in the latter part of the 1970s and the Jamaican dub poet Oku Onuora coined the term in 1978. Arguably, the pioneer of dub poetry was Linton Kwesi Johnson. His debut album, *Dread Beat and Blood* (1978), introduced a unique style of poetry performed in Jamaican patois to a one drop reggae beat. Johnson opened the door for a new generation of artists and Onuora further developed the genre through the establishment of the 'Prugresiv Aatis Muvmant' in 1979.

Dub poetry gained notoriety not only because of its musical innovation but also because of its social and political subject matter. Even today, dub poetry is still associated with political consciousness and social criticism. While no longer the dominant form of performance poetry in Black communities, dub poetry laid the foundation for 'slam' and 'conscious poets' of the present age. Three performural qualities of dub poetry are important to this exploration.

In dub poetry there is the interplay between word and sound. Dub poetry makes words into the 'riddim' driving the sound and structure of the poem. So hearing dub poets in a cappella, the rhythm of the music is structured into the sound and arrangement of the spoken poem.[40] Building in rhythm from the beginning is a creative process, ensuring that the new and original backing tracks are created for the performance, rather than simply utilizing already existing vinyl.

Acoustemologically, in dub poetry 'dub' takes on a new life; it signifies a *playful deconstruction of words* guided by a particular ideological framework, so that these 'word-sounds' are 'infused with cultural values'.[41]

Word Dub

What I want to propose is that dub poetry introduces 'word dub', where words are deconstructed and signify. As a result, word-sounds contest reality, and have a combative *power*. For instance, in the dub poem 'Liesense fi kill', Linton Kwesi Johnson 'plays' with the word 'licence'. Removing the letter 'c' and adding 's' after the first 'e' he communicates a sense of corruption and disreputable activity in the police. It now means to 'cover-up', that is, 'lie', 'sense'. Similarly, Birmingham-based dub poet Kukumo plays with the word 'diaspora', re-interpreting the word in light of Caribbean economic struggle in Britain to coin the term 'die-as-poor-ya'.

Word-sound-power provides us with a model of how dub signifies. The act of deconstruction is influenced and informed by socio-political aspirations and concerns, and these concerns guide the reworking of words and their meanings. The signifying that occurs in dub poetry builds on the trickster motif of the studio engineer. While the engineer mixes the music to create a new encoded narrative, so the dub poet reconstructs words so that they portray political realities. I want to end this chapter by making a connection between dub as word-sound-power and Pentecostal faith in Britain. [...] Dub is a form of deconstruction. So it is my intention here to bring this understanding of dub to the context of the church.

As stated in the title of this chapter, dub is a gospel, that is, 'good news'. So how is dub good news from the context of African Caribbean Christianity?

Word-Sound-Power and Black Pentecostal Faith

Its important to begin this section by noting that word and sound has always been important in the church. African Caribbean Christians believe in the creative power of God's word. God creates with words (Genesis 1.2ff.), and human beings made in the image of God have the capacity to transform their lives and the world around them with words (Proverbs 12:19). Thus, the spiritual power of words, whether in testimony, sermon or song, is never under-estimated. (This is one of the reasons why the oneness or Apostolic Pentecostal tradition places a high emphasis on the power in the 'name of Jesus' in their baptismal formulae and theological orientation.)

What I am stating is that in these congregations believers participate in the ongoing creative work of God in-and-through the use of words and sounds. Therefore, they too, as believers, have the ability to use words creatively and with spiritual force.

For instance, during worship in African Caribbean churches, there is a belief that as believers praise, God 'inhabits their praises'; in other words, there is a sense of the divine or spirituality in the sonic field. This is why so often churches make a sharp distinction between *ministry* (singing and praising in sync with the Spirit of God) and *minstrelsy* (singing and praising out of sync with the Spirit and therefore a promotion of the individual rather than God).

I believe that the 'word dub' practice of the dub poets offers the church a method for an explicit politicization of sound. Specifically, the word-sound-power tradition in dub and dub poetry provides a model for encoding and transforming the word-sound-spirituality of the church.

A way of explaining the nature of this proposal is through the literary device, collocation. A collocation is the process by which words influence the other words, which are part of a sequence:

> The term collocation...refers to sequences of lexical items which habitually co-occur, but which are nonetheless fully transparent in the sense that each lexical constituent is also a semantic constituent. Such expressions

as…*fine weather, torrential rain…are examples of* c̠ollocations… [T]he semantic integrity or cohesion of a collocation is the more marked if the meaning carried by one of its constituent elements is highly restricted contextually, and different from its meaning in more neutral contexts.[42]

So, in my case, the pairing of the word 'dub' with Christian terms such 'Jesus' or 'Holy Spirit' can produce a new way of understanding how these Christian terms function and what they mean. Therefore to 'Dub Jesus' or the 'Spirit', once transparent, provides a new approach to the study of Jesus and the Spirit respectively.[43] Likewise, to imply a 'Jesus Dub' or 'Spirit Dub' is to speak of the work of Jesus and the Spirit as deconstructive work with an active socio-political agenda. It is this later reading that is the focus of this book.

Introducing dub as a collocation into the vocabulary of church life offers new theological opportunities. As mentioned in the introduction, language produces new possibilities for Christian action. This is the reason why African American New Testament scholar, Brian Blount, suggests that by scrutinizing language in the church one identifies theological orientation and action.[44] Taking Blount seriously, by introducing the concept and word 'dub' into African Caribbean Christian vocabulary, provides new ways of hearing, feeling and interpreting aspects of church life.

The critical question that confronts us now is what can dub transform in order to produce new action in the church? In the next chapter, I want to infuse the meaning of dub with particular theological sensibilities that parallel the politicization of word-sounds in dub poetry. Dub deconstruction will be allied to African Caribbean emancipatory theology.

In conclusion, let me recap my central arguments. I have explored the social context in Jamaica from which the concept and practice of dub emerged. Dub developed by studio engineers has undergone several recreations on its way to becoming a genre within reggae and other forms of popular music. Dub is more than musical backdrop; it is a perspective; it concerns the taking apart and reconstruction of reality from a particular vantage point. Consequently, to 'dub' something is to recreate the way it is heard, understood or practised.

It is in dub poetry that dub is recreated in word. Through a creative play of written and spoken words, dub poets introduce the dubbing of words so that they signify in new ways. The central focus of this book is to take the word 'dub' and imbue it with particular theological meanings so that when it is attached to words, ideas and practices in the church, these words, ideas and practices take on a whole new meaning!

Given the harsh realities of black urban life in Britain, there is a need for a theological method that takes things apart, and puts them back together. This method, arising out of popular culture, is not afraid of the political world, but, instead, embraces it. Rapper Kanye West tells us that 'Jesus walks' with those on the margins of society. The phrase describes God's omnipresence amongst the socially marginalized. In Jesus Dub, I want to go further than Mr West. When 'Jesus dubs', those on the margins are enabled to tear down the walls that exclude and rebuild and refashion things so that all people are free from the ravages of oppression.

5 What are the Sistas Saying?

Christianity is undoubtedly a patriarchal and androcentric religion. I say undoubtedly, aware that there are many who will contest this (at least to our minds) incontrovertible fact. Feminist scholars of the ilk of Mary Daly[1] and Daphne Hampson[2] have long argued against the male centred and male privileged character of Christianity in their feminist writings. In the British context, whilst not seeking to align her work with the aforementioned, Elaine Foster's M.Phil thesis[3] on Black women in Black-led churches proved an important milestone in charting the patriarchal nature of Black Christianity in Britain.

In constructing this text the editors have been mindful of an ongoing dialectic in the development of Black Christianity in Britain, from which Black theology has emerged. Namely, that much of what can be construed as Black Christianity is tinged with (or even soaked in, if you prefer a more dramatic analogy) sexism and patriarchy and yet neither the Black church (in whatever guise) nor Black theology, for that matter, could survive without the women.

As two male scholars, we have attempted to both acknowledge our own myopic thinking on occasions, in addition to identifying ways in which we can deconstruct the male supremacist leanings of Black Christian faith in Britain. In order to assert the latter whilst challenging the former, we have identified (to our minds at least) some of the most important Black theological work by Black women in Britain and have produced extracts of it in this chapter. Given the ways in which Black women have been marginalized within Historic and Black-led churches, and in order to assert an anti-hegemonic and anti-androcentric framework for this text, we have included additional extracts in this chapter, so making it the biggest of all the chapters in the Reader. We have taken this decision, not as a cringe-making attempt to placate Black women, but rather, as an act of radical solidarity in the knowledge that it was almost impossible to choose between the claims of the brilliant women writers on show within the Black theology in Britain movement.

As we have detailed in the first chapter we have made a distinction between work that can be seen as Black theology and that which is theological work done by people who are Black. The former is consonant with the theological intent and method of this text, namely the foregrounding of Black experience and reality as a means of undertaking theological reflection and re-articulating the meaning of God revealed in Jesus Christ as depicted in the Scriptures. We have not included Foster's work, for example, because as fine a piece of scholarship as it is, it is best understood as theological work by a Black woman and not Black theological work per se.

This chapter highlights the work of a number of stalwarts in the development of Black theology in Britain. One of the challenges we have faced in constructing this chapter has been to identify the appropriate nomenclature for Black British women's theological output. Reddie has attempted this work to much greater effect in one of his previous publications.[4] In the US context, the term 'Womanist' has become the designation of choice for many African American women within the theological academy. In Britain, the scene is much more varied and complex as befits our migratory travels across the Black Atlantic and the hybrid nature of our postcolonial subjectivities. We have taken the view that it is not the place of two male authors to seek to define Black women's theological writings. Instead, we have sought to document but not interpret the work of our Black British sisters.

This chapter contains the work of Valentina Alexander, Kate Coleman and Lorraine Dixon (three of the most important of the early Black women theologians in Britain), plus a more recent and hugely promising voice, Maxine Howell Baker. All these contributions illustrate the articulate, challenging and varied voices of Black women in Britain and their highly creative and innovative approaches to the task of doing theology in light of their existential experiences. This is an important chapter and contribution to the overall narrative of Black theology in Britain.

Black Theology and Black Liberation: A Womanist Perspective

Kate Coleman

[This essay is one of the earliest by a Black British woman theologian. Here, Kate Coleman uses aspects of her personal narrative of 'conversion' and the relationship to her journey towards a liberating consciousness and the significant place of Womanist discourse and experiences in this process. This essay was originally published in *Black Theology in Britain* 1 (1998), 56–59.]

Journey Toward a Liberating Consciousness

My Christian experience of Black liberation and Black theology has been one that can only be described as a journey toward a liberating consciousness. As such I will begin this paper at the point when I first became aware of the liberating impulses that had largely lain dormant within me until they were triggered off specifically by a number of personal life crises.

In 1984, a few months after I had made a 'commitment' to faith in Jesus, I developed a strong conviction that I was being called to 'missionary' work. My understanding of 'missionary' work was fairly limited at that time and my exposure to Christianity thus far had led me to think of it almost exclusively as a call to some kind of evangelistic and proclamatory activity that would take place in some location other than the one in which I was currently situated. However, since it seemed in some ways a rather nebulous and distant prospect I held the whole thing on ice and proceeded as per usual with my life.

Two years later, after I had finished university, I went to Scotland for three weeks with the express intention of praying, 'seeking God' and discovering exactly what I was to do with the rest of my life, since my own plans no longer seemed viable. While I was there I received the clearest piece of 'guidance' I think I have ever had. It seemed to be a clear call to Christian leadership and to the task of caring for others. If I had literally witnessed writing on a wall things could not have been clearer. However, rather than this bringing me the clarity I felt I had needed, I found myself feeling more confused than ever. One of the main reasons for this was that I had 'converted' to Christianity in a context that verged on fundamentalism in its religious and Christian expression. Consequently I was already indoctrinated with the view that women could serve in every capacity other than that of Christian leadership. This was so in spite of the fact that I attended a Baptist Church that claimed to adhere to the doctrine of the priesthood of all believers. Even now Baptists in Britain still have one of the worst records of any denominational grouping in terms of ordained women ministers (less than 3 per cent). In addition to this, at the last count there were approximately 15 Black Baptist ministers out of the 300 or so presently serving in London where one of the largest concentrations of Black Baptists worship.

To add to my confusion I knew that my then Pastor was also wholly opposed to the idea of women in leadership. Indeed I had thought that I was opposed to the idea of women in leadership; fortunately I was unable to shake off the conviction that my future work and ministry would involve the responsibility of leadership. In retrospect it is probably just as well that I was alone at the time I received my 'calling'. Had I shared it with any of the Christians from my home church I would have almost certainly been talked out of the conviction and it would doubtless have been reinterpreted to tow the official line—so I kept my thoughts to myself and committed everything to God's keeping.

A year or so later, quite unexpectedly, I found myself to be the only full-time church worker effectively leading the church as the then pastor prepared to move on. While no official title was attached to my leadership activity, everyone was prepared to overlook the obvious and were really quite supportive. I suspect that they were relieved that I was willing to serve the church in any capacity at all during very difficult circumstances. However, when the church overseers proposed that one of the three new elders should be me it all became quite a different matter. The phrase 'all hell broke loose' springs all too readily to mind.

Crisis of Validity

The objections to the proposal came thick and fast. The reason? Supposedly doctrine. Incidentally, this amounted to an appeal to a doctrinal position that ensured the perpetuation of the domination of those already powerless and exploited. The objection was thus related to the inappropriateness of my gender for such a task. The fact that I had already been exercising the role was conveniently side-stepped by those whose beliefs ran contrary to the actual facts. Looking back I can also see the role that unuttered racial politics played in the whole process. This was the occasion of one of the most significant crises of my life. I refer to this experience as 'my crisis of validity'.

It soon became apparent to me just how women and black people were really viewed in the wider church—the very church being one claiming to preach a gospel of equality, liberation and affirmation. One that so easily, at least in theory, laid claim to the words and works of Jesus as authoritative and directive but that had lost its ability to recognize its own duplicity. It was in this same place that an active process of invalidation was taking place. I began to notice the way that women and black people were demeaned and devalued through phrases like: 'There are just a few old women left at that church'. I began to get suspicious of questions such as: 'Is your church a black church then?' which could be interpreted as 'I suppose that only black people (the inference being not real people) go to your church'. Questions like: 'Are there many men in your church?' interpret this to mean any of the following 'Aren't there any real men who can lead?' 'I suppose only women go to your church?' (see above), 'I wouldn't want to be led by a woman, risky business!' There were questions including: 'How does it feel to be a black woman in leadership?', interpreting this to mean the more benign, 'How does it feel to be part of a minority?' or the more idiotic 'How does it feel to be a black woman?' or the more insulting 'It's very unusual for black women to exercise leadership isn't it?'[5] Some may want to describe this emerging awareness as a persecution complex. I prefer to view it as an emerging womanist consciousness, for I was beginning to see and hear things that I had previously overlooked, ignored, denied or excused.

Crisis of Invisibility

Add to this the (my) experience of theological training, where the only 'relevant' theologians cited were European or American. In that training setting the only 'valid' theology presented was patriarchal and invariably Euro-American. There, significant biblical characters and contributors to early church history were presented as being very male and, in addition, remarkably white. The assertions of African or Caribbean theologians were seldom referred to and the theological voices of significant Black British men and women were never heard. For example, I was astounded that the theological arguments against slavery and slavers made by the Black abolitionist, Olaudah Equiano, were never raised in related debates:

Consider this piece from Equiano's writing:

> Recollect Sir that you are told in the 17th verse of the 19th chapter of Leviticus, 'You shall not suffer sin upon your neighbours' and you will not I am sure, escape the upbraidings of your conscience, unless you are fortunate enough to have none, and remember also that the oppressor and oppressed are in the hands of the just and awful God who says 'Vengeance is mine and I will repay', repay the oppressor the justifier of the oppression. How dreadful then will your fate be?... I have the fullest confidence many of the sable race to the joys of heaven and cast the oppressive white to that doleful place where he will cry, but will cry in vain, for a drop of water.[6]

This experience of theological training was the site of another major personal crisis. I refer to this as 'my crisis of invisibility'. I had developed my theological understanding in a context that insisted that the colour of Jesus/God was unimportant unless he was depicted as Black and where God was most definitely Spirit unless he was referred to as she. To be a Black woman in such a context is to reflect the antithesis, in fact the polar opposite, of what has long been agreed by both the dominant culture and the dominant theology as being normative.

This reminds me of a 'joke' I used to hear in primary school. I remember that I would laugh at it like everyone else. Had I grasped the point of it I might have thought better of laughing. However, I did eventually get the point a few years ago whilst in the throes of resisting both invalidation and invisibility. I saw the joke again, this time quoted by Constance M. Carroll in the book *But Some of us are Brave*:

> I saw God last night
> Really? What's he like?
> Well, he's a woman and she's black.[7]

The point being made here is the absurdity of the notion that God could possibly be either. In the dominant culture and, according to the dominant theology, the lived realities and theological perspectives of black women are at worst viewed as 'deviations from the norm' and at best as 'exotic' or 'interesting' alternatives. The dominant theology, in its presumptions and assertions, actively displaces us from any position of centrality and in universalizing its theological claims denies us a theological voice. [...]

A womanist, according to Alice Walker who coined the phrase in her 1983 text, *In Search of Our Mother's Gardens*, is someone who is committed to the survival and wholeness of entire people, male and female. A womanist is not a separatist, except periodically, for health. A womanist is also 'Responsible. In charge. Serious'.[8]

The term has its origins in the black folk expression of mothers to female children, 'you acting womanish', that is like a woman, usually referring to outrageous, audacious, courageous or wilful behaviour, wanting to know more and in greater depth than is considered 'good' for one. 'A womanist', she adds, 'Loves music. Loves dance. Loves the moon. Loves the spirit. Loves love and food and roundness. Loves struggle. Loves the folk. Loves herself regardless.'[9] As Cheryl J. Sanders suggests:

> Its usage has now gone beyond her [Walker's] definition. African American women have adopted the term as a symbol of their experience. 'Womanist', they write, 'signals an appreciation for the black and female in a society that is hostile to both blackness and womanhood.'[10]

Mary Seacole responds to her crisis of invisibility by courageously and, I might add, audaciously challenging the assumption of her externally imposed invisibility through her very decision to pursue what she had come to believe was her God-inspired vision. Through subversive action she ensured both her validation and her visibility. The Black church women although at one level rejecting the right to validity for themselves effectively lay claim to that right for the whole Black community by rejecting the notion that their bondage may have been sanctioned by God. This theme of self-validation is expressed best in Walker's assertion that a womanist 'Loves herself regardless'.

Womanist theology has been defined by Debra Washington as being 'primarily concerned with the liberation of black women and black people from white oppression, the liberation of white oppressors from themselves and the reconciliation of humanity'. She goes on to describe what womanist theology is not.[11] She states that it is not a new consciousness in the sense that it has existed prior to its being recorded and developed. Neither is it simply another term for feminist theology that is primarily preoccupied with the critique of the patriarchal bias of traditional theology. However, it does include this critique after it has been divorced from its Eurocentric entrapment. For womanist, Walker writes, 'is to feminist as purple is to lavender'.[12] Moreover, Washington outlines what she believes womanist theology to be. It is 'a theological window which makes visible the perspectives of black women'.[13] It is the self-defined theology of Black women. In other words, it assures agency. Black women are at the centre of womanist theology. This being the case, womanist theology not only provides a critique of the universalizing tendencies of Eurocentric male theologies, it also interrogates Eurocentric feminist theologies and other Third World liberation theologies. In the words of African-American womanist theologian, Jacqueline Grant:

> Ironically the criticism that Liberation Theology makes against classical theology has been turned against liberation theology itself. Just as most European and American theologians have acquiesced in the oppression of the west for which they have been taken to task by liberation theologians, some liberation theologians have acquiesced in one or more oppressive aspects of the liberation struggle itself. Where racism is rejected, sexism has been embraced. Where Classism is called into question, racism and sexism have been tolerated. And where sexism is repudiated, racism and Classism are often ignored.[14]

At this point in my journey I am inspired by two things. The first is a vision of Jesus as liberator, the one who is our 'Shalom'; the second is a vision of the wholeness of entire peoples, male and female. Black British womanist perspectives provide the necessary incentive toward this goal. Therefore Black British women's concerns must also be placed on the agenda of liberation. Let me end with these words from Alice Walker:

> I believe that the truth about any subject only comes when all sides of the story are put together and all their different meanings make one new one. Each writer writes the missing parts to the other writer's story. And the whole story is what I'm after.[15]

Black British Christian Women, *'We too have a story to tell'*.

Black Women and Theology

Kate Coleman

[This next extract is taken from an article by Kate Coleman, in which she delves deeper into the significance and implications of womanism for Black British women and Black theology. In the context of Black theology in Britain, particularly Womanist theology, Coleman was a key early voice for a mature articulation of Black British Womanist theology. This article originally appeared in *Black Theology in Britain* 3 (1999), 51–65.]

The Origins of Womanism

It has been said that: 'The lake one decides to fish in predetermines the kind of fish one will catch'.[16] This is no less true in the practice of theologizing than it is in any other scholarly discipline. What I intend to do in this brief article is to outline some of the major developments and themes that have led to the emergence and development of Womanist theology and hence the particular lake that many black women theologians (African-Americans in particular) have decided to fish in!

It is therefore necessary to commence by establishing the origins of Womanism itself. The outline themes of Womanism are drawn from Alice Walker's 1983 text *In Search of Our Mother's Gardens*:

> From womanish (opposite of girlish i.e., frivolous, irresponsible, not serious). A black feminist or feminist of color. From the black folk expression of mothers to female children, 'You acting womanish', i.e., like a woman. Usually referring to outrageous, audacious, courageous, or wilful behavior. Wanting to know more and in greater depth than is considered 'good' for one. Interested in grown-up doing. Acting grown up. Being grown up. Interchangeable with another black folk expression: 'You trying to be grown'. Responsible. In charge. Serious.

> A woman who loves other women, sexually and/or non sexually. Appreciates and prefers women's culture, women's emotional flexibility (values tears as natural counterbalance of laughter), and women's strength. Committed to the survival and wholeness of entire people, male and female. Not a separatist except periodically for health. Traditionally a universalist, as in: 'Mama, why are we brown, pink, and yellow, and black?' Ans.: 'Well, you know the colored race is just like a flower garden, with every color flower represented'. Traditionally capable, as in: 'Mama, I'm walking to Canada and I'm taking you and a bunch of other slaves with me'. Reply: 'It wouldn't be the first time'.

> Loves music, loves dance. Loves the moon. Loves the Spirit. Loves love and food and roundness. Loves struggle. Loves the Folk. Loves her self. Regardless.[17]

It is said that Alice Walker, who coined the phrase Womanist, had grown weary of having to use qualifying words whenever she described herself as a feminist, such as 'Well, I'm a Black Feminist', and then having to explain what she did and did not mean by that. This has often been the case for many black women who have wanted to express allegiance to certain feminist themes without necessarily having to identify themselves with it in its entirety. In addition to this there are many black women who, perceiving feminism as anti-black and anti-men, have not wanted to become identified with it at all. Alice Walker therefore 'offered' black women a term that would first and foremost illustrate the concern of black women like herself to name the different nature of their experience.

The Need for a Womanist Perspective: Theological Developments

Since the 1960s, theologians have witnessed some major landmarks. During this period, theologians located primarily within the context of struggles for liberation began to articulate their theological perspectives. These reflections represented a departure from traditional Christian theology, effectively challenging Western theological assumptions, notably their claims to universalism.

These 'Third World' theologians raised questions about the normative use of Scripture, tradition and experience in Christian theology. They maintained that the dominant theology had simply served to sanction and perpetuate the status of the oppressors over the oppressed. Initially, it was through the particular insights of Latin American theologians such as Gustavo Gutierrez and Leonardo and Clodovis Boff that theological categories were recognized as being related to the socio-economic and political realities of human existence.[18] These voices were followed by Third World theologians from Asia, Africa and North America who proceeded to introduce further categories of oppression arising out of their own unique contexts. In recognition of these they went on to propose analytical approaches that emphasized the relevance of specific socio-historical features, such as religious pluralism, indigenization and the analysis of race.

The influence of both the human subject and the socio-historical context on the assumptions and outcomes of the theological process has been summarized by African-American theologian James Cone (often referred to as the Father of Black theology) as follows:

> Because Christian theology is human speech about God, it is always related to historical situations and thus all of its assertions are culturally limited... Although God, the subject of theology is eternal, theology itself is, like those who articulate it, limited by history and time... [Our image of God] is finite image, limited by the temporality and particularity of our existence. Theology is not universal language, it is interested language and thus is always a reflection of the goals and aspirations of a particular people in a definite social setting.[19]

The 1960s also heralded the rising influence of the women's movement, particularly in North America. This development led to the articulation of feminist perspectives on theology. The observation made by black theologians that all theology is subjective and is contextually produced had also been recognized by feminist theologians. However, both having stated these assertions they ironically fell into the same universalizing trap in relation to black and other 'Third World' women. White feminists were thus also found guilty of a similar oversight to white male scholars. Having rejected the universalizing tendencies of 'traditional' male patriarchal ideologies, they had succumbed to the temptation of universalizing the Eurocentric middle-class values and experiences of a defined and limited group of mainly white, female academics. [...]

Some Distinctive Features: White Feminists/ Black Womanists

White feminist academics historically have formulated theories grounded in notions of a universal female powerlessness in relation to men, experiences in which race and class are not felt as oppressive elements in their lives.

When theorizing the so-called 'natural' division of gender, for example, themes such as 'family' and 'patriarchy',[20] terms central to feminist theory, assume different configurations within the discourses of feminists and womanists.

Family

When utilized in a middle-class, white feminist context the 'family' is often named as a major source of oppression for white women who are 'relegated' to the career of homemaking. In feminist discourses this has often become identified with vivid imagery of stagnant regimes of child rearing, keeping house, servicing men and being caught up in a debilitating dependence and thus closure. Motherhood and domesticity has been constructed as central to national identity such that when white women were eventually granted entry into the work force it was under the general understanding that the 'family' would continue to be prioritized and therefore not exposed to the harm of neglect. [...]

Patriarchy

The ideology of 'dependency' is also problematized for black women who may be actual heads of households, or where, because of an economic system which structures high black male unemployment, are not necessarily financially dependent upon black men. There is therefore a high incidence of black female economic activity. Despite increasing numbers of black women acquiring high academic and professional qualifications they are more likely than their white counterparts to be employed in jobs for which they are over qualified. They therefore continue to be located at the bottom of their respective career ladders and continue to be the last hired, often to do work that white men, white women and black men refuse to do, work that is often detrimental to their health and is by far the most underpaid. How then can it be asserted that the concept of patriarchy operates in the same way for black women and white women? Black male dominance cannot and does not exist in the same forms as white male dominance for the simple reason that black males have not enjoyed the benefits of white patriarchy. Similarly, black women have not had the 'privilege' of protection from white male power in the way that white women have enjoyed such 'protection' from black men. This is not to deny the presence of patriarchal relations between black men and black women. It is simply to state that men of different 'colours' have dominated black women 'patriarchally' in different ways.

Racist ideology has therefore been instrumental in shaping black men's relationship with black women, the black community and white society. The struggle for black women has been the struggle to survive in two contradictory worlds simultaneously, 'one white privileged and oppressive, the other black, exploited and oppressed'. Patriarchy may well describe the relationship between many white women to their fathers, brothers and other dominant males governing their world. However, it proves to be an inadequate term when seeking to describe black women's relation to the dominant socio-economic system which is often manipulated by both white men and white women in ways that maintain white privilege and power.

Katie Cannon employs some of these points in her text *Black Womanist Ethics*. Here, in constructing the black woman as the moral agent, she writes:

> I discovered that the assumptions of the dominant ethical systems implied that the doing of Christian ethics in the Black community was either immoral or amoral. The cherished ethical ideas predicated upon the existence of freedom and a wide range of choices proved null and void in situations of oppression. The real-lived texture of Black life requires moral agency that may run contrary to the ethical boundaries of mainline Protestantism.[21]

She continues by stating that the dominant ethics which makes a virtue of qualities that lead to economic success is assumed to be possible for anyone who makes the attempt. It presupposes that a moral agent is to a considerable degree able to choose whether to make suffering a desirable norm or whether to make a particular sacrifice. However, the contrary is normative for black people for whom suffering and sacrifice is the normal state of affairs. Forced to the lowest echelons of society black existence is often deliberately and openly controlled. Black and white women and men, then, operate within very different scopes of freedom; and liberty, in the traditional sense, is not an option. [...]

Delores Williams employs the biblical story of Hagar, the African slave of the Hebrew woman Sarah, who is referred to in Gen. 16.1-16 and 21.9-21. Hagar, she says, is a figure who appears regularly throughout the deposits of African-American cultural resources. She demonstrates through her book *Sisters in the Wilderness*[22] the way in which Hagar's story bears specific social, historical, religious and personal significance for the African-American community:

> I reasoned that her story must be the community's analogue for African-American women's historic experience. My reasoning was supported, I thought, by the striking similarities between Hagar's story and African-American women's history in North America.[23]

Hagar was brutalized by her slave owner Sarah largely out of her own frustrations—a parallel of many of the white women who brutalized their African slaves out of personal frustrations, jealousies and fears.

As a chattel Hagar's body was not her own and she was subjected to an unsolicited sexual relationship with her slave master Abraham for the sole purpose of surrogacy. African-American slave women were also owned by their masters and were often raped by owners unconcerned about curbing their lustful and oppressive tendencies. In addition they were forced to submit sexually to black males for the sole purposes of reproduction at the command of their slave owner's intent on increasing their slave stock.

A child Ishmael was born and mother and child were eventually cast out without resources for survival. Slave women often bore children that their masters seldom claimed and in fact would often cast out or sell them to other slaveholders. Hagar resisted the brutalities of slavery by running away. Running away has long been a form of resistance for African-American slave women. Hagar's experiences are interspersed with personal encounters with God that prove to be salvific, equipping her with new vision to see survival resources where she had seen none before. Many black women testify that 'God helped them to make a way out of no way'. Cheryl J. Sanders also explores the relevance of the paradigm that Hagar presents to the Womanist theologian.

> The contemporary vantagepoint of living the intersection of black female identity brings a peculiar dynamic to bear upon the reading and appro-priation of biblical texts. The interpreter becomes attentive to: (1) resist-ance to evil by employment of bold or unusual strategies, (2) affirmation of the good in terms of identity, loyalty, and values, and (3) empowerment as the manifestation of divine and human intervention in the life situations of women of African descent.[24]

Jacqueline Grant traces an independent development in regard to the Christological theologizing of African-American women and captures this within the title of her text on the subject *White Women's Christ and Black Women's Jesus: Feminist Christology and Womanist Response*.[25] Delores Williams outlines the ways in which traditional, Eurocentric theologians have constructed the central theme of Christology and contrasts this with the liberative view of Jesus in the spirituality of black women:

> Black women are, then, more apt to see Jesus/Christ as spirit sustaining sur-vival and liberation efforts of the black community. Thus black women's questions about Jesus Christ are not about the relation of his humanity to his divinity or about the relation of the historical Jesus to the Christ of Faith… Jesus is their mother, their father, their sister and their brother. Jesus is who-ever Jesus has to be to function in a supportive way in the struggle.[26]

Considering that the experiences of black women differ substantially from those of white women it cannot be assumed that black women and white women will express the same things in their theologizing any more than they would in terms of their 'female' reality. The same kind of theoretical framework can also be applied to black women's distinctive experience in relation to that of black men. It should not be assumed that black women will relate to either feminist thought that may be effectively racist or to black nationalist thought that may be effectively sexist simply because she is a woman or indeed black. It is clear then that black women cannot simply be subsumed within the category 'Women' or 'Black' as if they were flat unproblematic categories. [...]

The Nature of Womanism

Alice Walker took the word 'Womanish' that emerged organically from within the African-American working poor community and politicized it by calling it *Womanist*. Womanism has subsequently emerged in the North American context as a movement. Having initially emerged as a political category within the academy it thus continues to exert most of its influence there and is also beginning to become incorporated within the major disciplines of the social sciences and natural sciences in the US. However, it is as yet not generally to be found in popular usage or in street vernacular.

Womanism utilizes liberation praxis and in this sense is organically related to both male liberation theology and feminist theology in all its various expressions.[27] Womanism is contextual; it is concerned with liberative and emancipatory themes; it is preoccupied with the oppressed and the marginalized and offers a critique of traditional theology. Womanism is interdisciplinary, requiring the insights of historians, anthropologists, sociologists and ordinary black women; it offers a critique of feminism, patriarchy and class privilege and it prioritizes the welfare of the whole people group—men, women and children. It also recognizes the importance of relatedness of all women of colour; it recognizes that knowledge production is a community endeavour that is multidialogical; it discounts homophobia; it emphasizes black women's culture and love of the spirit.

This outlines the essence of the secular term. When transferred to the arena of theology the aim is to bring black women's history, culture and religious experience into the interpretative cycle of Christian theology and into the liturgical cycle of the church. African feminist scholar, Mercy Amba Oduyoye, explains how this affects the process of theologizing:

> In the same way as most accepted traditional Western theological categories went without question until they were examined in the light of the peculiar contexts of the Third World, so Christian women have begun to see that from their experience they cannot confess the same sins or affirm the same reading of the Christian faith. Is this not what liberating theology is about, a hermeneutic that enables us to get the most out of the confrontation of texts and contexts as well as their interaction?[28]

Some Sources for Womanism

In order to help construct the themes and characteristics that more accurately reflect the lived experiences of black women it is necessary to determine some of their cultural sources. These realities influence black women's responses to theological questions such as 'who is God' and 'what is God like'. Christian Womanists seek to construct their theological assertions while embedded within the culture of black women. It is therefore possible to extract some of these 'cultural' characteristics by exploration of a number of key subjects. [...]

In conclusion, Womanism enables black women to name and describe their experiences, to reclaim their voice and thus their agency. It enables black women to validate their knowledge claims and to present a unique perspective. The task of describing the specific contextual and thus theological paradigms that might best fit the black British woman's experiences is still effectively in its infancy.[29] Black British women's contextual issues are problematized by the particularly complex interactions of their historical, social, cultural, linguistic and ethnic traditions that continue to be practised, reproduced and transformed within the British social structure. These and other distinctive features affect the theoretical considerations involved in such an assignment. The difficulty and necessity of the task of theologizing from and in relation to the specific location of the Christian church is expressed by Valentina Alexander:

> In reality, the British Christian Black woman is extremely difficult to generalise about. Just when you feel that you have understood her most essential characteristics, a new dimension emerges from the depth of her experiences.[30]

Further exploration and investigation of this particular 'lake' is necessary if black British women are to do more than continue to catch everyone else's fish.

bell hooks: Teller of Truth and Dreamer of Dreams

Lorraine Dixon

[Arguably, Lorraine Dixon is one of the sharpest voices among Black British women theologians with the particular gift of making theological discourse 'plain' and accessible to the whole people of God. This essay is an insightful piece into the significance of bell hooks' articulation for Dixon's journey with wider implications for Black theological discourse. It is taken from Anthony Reddie (ed.), *Legacy: Anthology in Memory of Jillian Brown* (Peterborough: Methodist Publishing House, 2000), 129–35).]

bell hooks has been a significant force in my life since my early 20s. Let me tell you why. By the time I was in my mid-teens, I had become aware of how racism affected not only my life as a young Black woman growing up in Britain but how it shapes the whole society. I had learned this lesson from the Anglican church that I attended, from school and from being a consumer of television and cinema. Our lives as Black people were rendered unimportant by invisibility. Blackness only became visible when it was denigrated either in personal and institutional abuse or by media distortion. Gender awareness was also coming to the fore, as I began to become aware of the models presented by my mother and father and their peers. I realized then that many women function as the servants of men, and that my mother was grooming my sister and I to follow in a similar vein. My growing alertness to sexist practice in the home and the wider community was channelled into the fight for the ordination of women as Anglican priests.

At 21 years of age, I began to train as a Church Army Officer[31] at the Wilson Carlisle College of Evangelism in London. Being in the big city, I joined up with numerous women's groups including amongst others the Spare Rib Collective, War on Rape and a prostitutes' collective. Subsequently I joined 'Men, Women and God', an organization for Christian women and men who wanted to engage in the struggle against sexism. Yet I felt ill at ease. I could not name what was troubling me, until bell hooks came into my life with her seminal book, *Ain't I a Woman*.[32] In the book she posits that feminism does not connect with Black women's experiences properly because it is racist. Women's experiences are the primary source for feminist discourse. However, these experiences are often predominantly White and middle class. When the word 'woman' is used there is an unspoken assumption that 'they' are White. Although Black and White women share similar experiences of discrimination on the basis of their gender, these similarities may be outweighed by contrasting radically different life experiences. hooks explores how slavery and/or colonialism, followed by the ongoing legacy of racism, has made our experiences as Black and White women different. Feminism universalizes the experience of White, middle-class women as the experience of all women. Consequently, sexism became the only point of political engagement, which alienated possible allies in Black women who may have shared related concerns. Feminism becomes racist because of its silence, and thus agreement by default with the inequalities and discrimination that affect women's lives other than sexism.

Privileged White women benefited from slavery and colonialism. Some White women of privilege involved themselves in the Abolitionist movement and various freedom movements, seeing the freedom of Black peoples as linked to their own as women. However, the majority of privileged White women stood by as Black women and men were brutalized by their menfolk or they engaged in the mistreatment themselves.

Today, White middle-class women, although sexism can and does blight their lives, still benefit from the racist society and churches we inhabit.

White middle-class women are open to more life and career choices than Black or working-class women, who are often dealing with survival rather than fulfilment issues, as a result of racism and classism. The discussion in various White feminist groups I attended, for example, was often about whether if you had a child you would stay at home or go out to work. Looking at the life of my own mother, and the lives of the majority of Black women I knew, this choice was not a present reality. They had low-paid, demeaning jobs that they hated, but in which they had to remain, in order to keep a roof over our heads, clothes on our backs and food on the table. The choice of stay home or go out to work was a middle-class choice. Choice of career was also a major discussion point. Yet, drawing on my own experience, I saw that the choices of most Black women were limited not only on the basis of their gender, but, like Black men, by their ethnicity, and alongside working-class White folk, often by their class.

In recent years, helped by the analytical insight of hooks, my concerns have found a home in Womanist and Black theologies. Womanist theology owes its holistic agenda to such Black feminists as bell hooks. Jacqueline Grant in her book, *White Women's Christ and Black Women's Jesus* (1989), acknowledges this. In her books, hooks constantly challenges the White feminist movement for equality as well as the Black liberationist struggle against White supremacy to broaden their agenda to include rather than exclude Black women and other marginalized groups. This challenge has fed Womanist theology, connecting it to these and other liberation struggles. I have been able to identify with Womanist theology because it probes Black women's experience to reflect on their particular oppression as Black women. This has a multidimensional landscape relating not only to 'race' but to its interaction with gender, class and so on. hooks and other Black feminists such as Angela Davis engage in a tri-dimensional analysis of Black women's lives, which explores how racism, sexism and classism can form a web that entangles and thus limits them. Such thinking has enabled Womanist theology to engage in attempts to affirm

> Black women's resolute efforts to survive and be free from that oppression. It also affirms Black women's faith that God supports them in their fight for survival and liberation.[33]

hooks has provided a means for Black women's lives to be brought from the shadows of invisibility and the margins to the centre. However, her concern has never rested solely with Black women. She seeks the wholeness of all peoples of colour. I think of all her 18 books *Killing Rage: Ending Racism* has had the greatest impact on my theological thinking.

In *Killing Rage*, hooks dreams of a world without racism: Martin Luther King's idea of a beloved community. She begins her book with an incident involving the harassment of Black women on an airline on which she is travelling. The incident concerns a Black woman who has the right ticket for first class but who is assumed to be a second-class traveller, and is subsequently told to move. She contrasts this with the White men who have not been shouted at, or told to remove themselves from the wrong chairs, or called to the front of the plane and 'shamed' as was hooks's friend. What resonated with me was hooks speaking of her 'inner voice' which urges her 'not to make a fuss, not to complain and possibly make life more difficult for other black folks...'[34] She manages to override this inner voice to challenge the racism to which she and her friend are subjected. She says:

> I was compelled to complain because I feel that the vast majority of black folks who are subjected daily to forms of racial harassment have accepted this as one of the social conditions of our life in white supremacist patriarchy that we cannot change. This acceptance is a form of complicity.[35]

hooks brings to voice the everyday reality of many Black people who swallow down and suppress their rage at racist discrimination that encompasses their life. This occurs, often, because White people choose not to listen or are unbelieving. Black people still have to explain rage, says hooks. This caused me to reflect on Ephesians 4:25, which states: 'Then have done with falsehood and speak the truth to each other, for we belong to one another as parts of one body.'

hooks is a truth teller trying to enable White and Black people to acknowledge the truth of our society, to, as it were, 'SPEAK THE TRUTH AND DROP THE MASK'.

I believe with hooks that we often do not speak the truth about racism. Many white people deny its reality, demanding that Black and Asian people 'spill their guts' and tell stories, but even then they may not be believed. Some Black and Asian people, too, are in denial about racism, often saying it does not exist, in order that they are not made uncomfortable, whether out of a sense of fear or because they do not wish to rock the boat. However, racism is an ever-present evil that affects the lives of Black and Asian people, denying them access to equal opportunities and a level playing field, not only in society in general, but within White majority churches in particular.

It struck me, reading hooks's *Killing Rage*, that racism will never change or be destroyed, until we start speaking the truth and dropping the mask. We have to speak the truth about the reality of racism and drop the mask that says everything is all right in our community and in our churches. Racism is a reality. It is not political correctness gone mad or the imaginative speculations of society's losers or even Black and Asian people whining because they like to complain. Racism is a reality which can have devastating consequences.

bell hooks discusses how the reality of racism is denied in our society. She explores how rage can bring clarity of mind. In my own experience I have found this to be true. Confronting my anger about the Church brought a realization that injustice exists there too. However, it is here that sometimes the greatest denial concerning racism takes place. Good, White Christian folks often cannot believe how racism and other forms of oppression can limit the experiences of many within the Church or how they continue to benefit from an unjust institution. In many predominantly White churches, it is said 'We do not have a problem here as we do not have any Black people here.' However, this creates a number of difficulties. Firstly, it contends that Black people are the problem and not White racism. Secondly, it highlights how the Black and Asian presence is often overlooked or ignored in particular churches. Consequently, Black and Asian people in these faith communities are isolated. Again, I have often heard in various places people saying, 'Everything is fine at our church. We smile at one another and get on. We are a family. A multicoloured family. There is no racism here.' Then I am told that they have a Black or Asian church warden/church steward, Black and/or Asian people who read the lessons, do the intercessions, help distribute the Communion and so on. I say that is good, but this is not the end of the struggle for racial justice.

The reality of racism is not just about calling Black and Asian folks names. It is about looking in truth at the Church institution and the subtle and not so subtle ways that people are excluded from positions of authority. It is about highlighting how Black and Asian church members are made invisible in our churches and kept on the margins. It is also about looking honestly at how our spirituality and theology can be tools that maintain the racist status quo in many of our churches. Finding one's place as a person of colour in one of the mainstream Churches in Britain can be a difficult process. The structures that continue to make us invisible in our own churches are the results of history and White supremacist practices that promote Black inferiority.

hooks holds to the dream of a community where White supremacy is unlearned by divesting of White privilege if one is White or the vestiges of internalized racism if one is Black. This is a community joined together by a shared concern for equality and true freedom for all. Breaking through our denial is a first step on this shared road of struggle: speaking the truth and dropping the mask. However, speaking truthfully about racism makes demands on us and our institutions. Fear and guilt often stalk White people when they begin to look at these issues: fear of being called a racist or guilt at discovering the extent of the racism in their interactions with people of colour. So some prefer to bury their heads in the sand or belittle this reality, whilst continuing to benefit from the oppressive system. For Black and Asian peoples, there may be fear of rocking the boat, or colluding with the system because it is the easiest road. But we are not called to fear and guilt but to speak truth. For, as scripture says, the truth will set us free. We will then be free to be truly society, truly church. We can then be a *'beloved community...seeking* to live in an anti-racist world'.[36]

Are Vashti and Esther our Sistas?[37] The Stories of Two Biblical Women as Paradigmatic of Black Women's Resistance in Slavery

Lorraine Dixon

[In this essay Dixon uses the historical lens of slavery (African-Caribbean) to re-read the narratives of Vashti and Esther. It is also taken from *Legacy: Anthony Reddie (ed.), Anthology in Memory of Jillian Brown* (Peterborough: Methodist Publishing House, 2000), 97–108.]

Introduction

I thought before we got into the meat of this particular biblical text that I might talk about my use of Esther, to reveal my cultural bias as it were. I think one of my major influences has been African-American Black theology, which constantly refers back to slavery as a way to explore theology and Black life in the present. I too see this as an important way to examine Black experience in the present British context—a way of exploring issues and concerns.

One of my favourite writers is Iyanla Vanzant. In her book *The Value in the Valley*[38] Vanzant talks about using the valleys of our lives—the sorrows, the low points, the struggles, etc.—as times from which lessons can be learnt, as points of value. I am sure many of us would agree that slavery and colonialism have been harsh valleys in many of our ancestral stories as Black peoples, valleys that have continued to shape our lives in terms of neo-colonial experiences in our churches and wider contexts.

I am aware, however, that there are some of us for whom slavery and/ or colonialism has not been a trope in our historical narratives. Perhaps migration might be nearer to your experience. What I would say is that although I will be speaking from a particular cultural perspective—that is, I am African-Caribbean in heritage, born in Britain—I would invite us all to read Esther out of our own experience of movement, travel, diaspora, exile. Make the story our own.

As I read the book of Esther, the two main women characters seemed to remind me of the Black women who were involved in resistance to slavery. So many elements in the biblical narrative seemed to ring bells in relation to slave discourse. This was further confirmed as I read Stella Dadzie's 'Searching for the Invisible Woman: Slavery and Resistance in Jamaica' and Barbara Bush's *Slave Women in Caribbean Society 1650–1838*.[39] Black women are often not included in our stories of liberation. The two texts just mentioned seek to correct this gender-biased omission.

Womanist Hebrew biblical scholars, however, such as Renita Weems and Koala Jones-Warsaw along with other Womanist thinkers, have argued that patriarchy is often not the only perspective influencing the lives of many women of colour. It is compounded and shaped by racism, class and economics. These perspectives have to be brought to bear on the biblical texts when minority ethnic communities read them, if it is to have any meaning for our life experience at all. Therefore, I wish to look at these socio-political dynamics in the context of exploring Vashti's and Esther's strategies of resistance as reminiscent of the strategies employed by Black women during slavery.

Esther 1:1-11

The opening verses of Esther set the scene regarding the power relations that colour the relationships and interactions in the book. We are left in no doubt as to who has the power in this narrative: King Ahasuerus. The Persian King's empire is said to stretch from India to Africa. All of a sudden Esther's story includes our stories and these diverse threads are weaved into one particular narrative. It can be assumed that the King maintains his wealth and dominance through the colonization of others. He entertains his male allies and cohorts to impress his authority on them. The use of rich textiles of blue and purple and white cotton, plus the decorative utilization of precious stones and metals, further enhances King Ahasuerus' might. The King's power seems to be based on colonialism, which produces the wealth of this nation through tribute and slaves. The presence of a harem and eunuchs gives a small clue to what is occurring. As Itumeleng J. Mosala says in his essay on Esther in *Voices from the Margin*,[40] we have to assume this from what is 'not said' in the text.

King Ahasuerus and his noble supporters are rich and powerful because others are exploited, oppressed and kept in poverty. Why is the text silent on this issue? Is it because the cause of the powerful and dominant are privileged in this book? Or does it present the reality of the common experience of the oppressed as marginalized or silenced? In the Esther narrative, oppression is multi-dimensional and takes on diverse forms. The system is maintained by a matrix of domination that incorporates issues of gender, ethnicity and economics.

The social order as set out in the book of Esther is reminiscent of the complex organization of the Triangular trade or the Slave trade. Its triangular nature reveals that the financial and economic rewards were shared by the rich and powerful in Europe, Africa and the so-called New World. The trade, involving the sale of Africans by slave traders, began in the sixteenth and seventeenth centuries. Its genesis comes out of 'explorations' in Africa in search of gold. They found gold in two forms, one was the precious metal and the other was Black gold, in the form of African slaves. The trade in Black flesh, used to provide virtually free labour on the plantations in the Americas and Caribbean, proved to be very profitable. Moreover, the Kings of West Africa colluded with the trade, by selling their prisoners of war for arms and manufactured goods. The goods and capital gained by these rulers ensured that they engaged in more frequent wars against neighbouring communities. European slave traders sought to encourage these wars in order to maintain their wealth.

The plantation system in the Americas produced raw materials such as cotton, sugar and tobacco. These helped to finance the Industrial Revolution occurring in Europe: 'a revolution which laid the basis for Europe's subsequent domination and monopoly of the world's resources'.[41] Factory owners and their families made their fortunes working in industries associated with the slave trade, such as providing the shackles to keep the slaves in chains. Seaports grew rich from investment in ships and 'Lloyds of London' became strong through the insuring of slaves, ships and plantations. In fact the impact of the slave trade on the economic and hegemonic well-being of some European countries is beyond measure. So it was in the interest of all the major economic players that they kept the system going.

Esther 1:12-22

The maintenance of the social order is a perspective that can be drawn out of the biblical narrative in question. An overriding societal bias is patriarchy. This shapes the lives and the experiences of Vashti and Esther. Other issues are brought to the fore as the story unfolds, including the dimension of ethnicity, and the importance of a socio-economic and political structure to maintain the power of the ruling classes. The figure of Vashti is fascinating, even more so because the author of the text did not consider giving much time or space to developing her character or informing us of her ultimate fate. Is this because the author does not consider her behaviour becoming for a woman?

What little we are told is that Queen Vashti gives a banquet for the palace women. There is a sense that these women's lives and destinies are not their own. Their bodies are certainly not their own either. This is emphasized by the King's request to have Vashti display herself in front of him and his nobles. But here is the rub! Vashti refuses outright. What is she refusing to do? There appears to be a difference of opinion among scholars. Andre LaCocque, for instance, is of the opinion that she was being asked to come naked before the King and his friends to act like a concubine rather than a queen. She refuses, and her status is demoted from Queen to concubine effectively. (LaCocque is influenced by rabbinical thought in his conclusions.[42])

David Clines does not agree with this reasoning, but thinks that

> her resistance lies in the very absence of a reason for refusing his demand. She doesn't need to have a reason, for she is under no obligation. Her power lies in her freedom to choose for herself.[43]

Clines concludes by suggesting that she has not broken any laws and so the King and his advisors cannot punish her 'according to the law'. Instead, they punish her by not allowing her to come before the King, the very thing she did not want to do anyway (Clines). Whatever is the likely reason for her action, Vashti subverts the patriarchal system in place by her resistance. She is seen as a dangerous and troublesome woman. Vashti is seen as someone who will give other women ideas, and thus is punished for crimes against the system. Is this the purpose for telling the story? Is it to serve as a warning to other women who go against what is perceived as societal norms? Perhaps there is a suggestion that a woman's place and status may be vulnerable in a context of institutionalized and intimate domination. Still, there is something empowering about the action of this woman who says *no!*

The triangular slave trade was a horrific and brutal system. On the slave ships, women and men were chained up and kept in very dirty, restrictive spaces that frustrated any attempts to move freely. Malnutrition and disease were part of the life of the slaves on these ships. As well as the cruelty of beatings, these African women also faced the outrage of rape and sexual abuse. However, the narratives by and about enslaved African women tell of these Vashti-like 'troublesome' women who sought to resist and destroy the evil. Their resistance, their 'no' to slavery, started even before they arrived in the Americas.

Many defiant and desperate women jumped overboard and drowned rather than accept the indignity of this dehumanizing experience. Others planned and took part in slave ship insurrections. Their bones litter the bottom of the ocean,[44] because of the punishments they received upon discovery. Narratives tell of the mutilations of these women that were to serve as a warning to others who might want to subvert the system.

Most of the slaves were taken to the Caribbean. They were either kept on the islands or dispatched eventually to other parts of the Americas. Slavery, especially as manifested on the plantations, attempted to deny Black people their humanity or place in the world, aside from a subordinate one. The social construct of racism and flawed theological reflection were used as an apologetic to maintain the economic interests of slavery. Legislation and political will further institutionalized and legitimated the system.

Tribal and kinship affiliations were denied to slaves. African 'ways' were beaten out of them, including their original names, language and customs. Beatings, rapes and other forms of brutality were used to ensure that the Africans settled into the life of plantation work. Family life for the slave was non-existent or temporary. The latter, depending upon which slave or slaves the master wanted to sell off, or conversely, which men or women should be used to mate with one another or with himself. Women's bodies were seen as belonging to the master, possession of which allowed him to do as he so wished.

On the plantations, as on the ships, women's resistance did not cease. They were even perceived as more troublesome than the men. In the journals kept by plantation owners, many complaints are recorded in relation to Black women feigning illness to be released from work. Others refused to work and proved uncooperative, abusive and awkward. Yet other women deliberately did their tasks in a shoddy or improper manner. Even threats of punishment or death did not affect them, as what could be worse than their current situation? Some even resorted to running away to gain their freedom, perhaps joining up with maroons (runaway slaves).

The Black woman was perceived not only as a labourer alongside men (without any concessions because of her gender), but as a breeder of more workers for the slave economy. She was expected to produce many slaves and only given a short time to recover after the birth before she had to return to her work. Her body was mistreated due to rape, abuse and lack of space between pregnancies. Often the women were separated from their children and suffered from grief as well as the discomfort of being unable to nurse their child. Yet as Vashti decided to take control of her own body and dent the forces of oppression, Black women also engaged in resistance to 'massa' in the area of intimacy. These women knew that if they could limit the numbers of children they gave birth to, they would hit the pockets of the plantation owner. There was the added incentive of not wanting to bring children into the world only to have them suffer the heinous institution of slavery. Knowledge of herbs and herbal medicines were brought from Africa by the women and passed down from mother to daughter. Such knowledge included treatments (e.g. 'wild cassava'[45] and 'salt, green mangoes and lime juice'[46]) to induce abortions or miscarriages. Others resorted to natural contraceptives (e.g. 'pineapple juice and frangipani juice [were] used as spermicides'[47]). It was also common knowledge that breast feeding one's child offered some contraceptive protection. This enabled a woman to attempt to space her pregnancies. There is evidence that other Black women employed more drastic measures:

> Sabrina Park, a slave woman who was tried for the murder of her three-month-old child…testified that she had worked enough for buckra already and would not be plagued to raise the child to work for white people.[48]

The Black women's use of methods to limit their fertility or to limit the numbers of babies going to full term have to be viewed in the context of slavery as

> the conscious decision made by countless black women to undermine the system by exploiting the most effective weapon they possessed.[49]

The strategy that Vashti employed can be seen as one type of resistance to domination, a more direct strategy. As can be seen from the biblical narrative and from the lives of Black women slaves, it could be quite costly in terms of position, risk of punishment or execution. It seems that direct action by a lone woman of low status, who confronted the oppressive structure that oppressed her and/or others, incurred the violent wrath of those who were in power. Hence, other more subtle strategies were employed by slave women to protect themselves from the white heat of hegemonic rage. These methods, however, also played their part in frustrating the slave economy, methods not too unlike those employed by the other main female character in the biblical story, Esther.

Esther 2:5-28

Esther is described by both Clines and LaCoque as a beauty queen, someone who uses her looks and sexuality to get what she wants. However, this perspective is too simplistic and does not take on board the structural nature of oppression that might limit the strategies and paths open to women in such a patriarchal system. The fact that she uses her role as Queen to great effect later on in the narrative should alert one to this fact. Esther wins the favour first of Hegai and then King Ahasuerus. Her power and influence is mediated through the men around her. She knows her position is circumscribed but will seek to use it to her advantage later on. Following the counsel of Mordecai she hides her Jewish identity, whereas Mordecai is identified as Jewish. Why is this? Is it because having a particular ethnicity in this context is a dangerous thing? Could it be that even more than her gender and despite her social climbing, her ethnicity will shape her life at court?

Esther and Mordecai are sucked into the system in order to survive. Esther submits to the process to choose a new queen. Through her humility and adaptability to her new situation she is both acceptable to and accepted by her colonial master, the King. Then there is Mordecai, who acts as an informer when he hears of a plot against King Ahasuerus. He becomes an official at court and by the end of the book has become even more powerful, second only to the King. As Itumeleng J. Mosala suggests, they 'have bought into the dominant ideology in order that their survival struggle should find approval'.[50]

Both Esther and Mordecai are implicated within the system and are problematized. Moreover, it could be said that the colonialist system produces this type of perverse behaviour, with the colonized identifying with their colonizers and their own oppression. They survive, but at what cost?

Esther 4:1, 4-17

In the third chapter of the book, we hear of Haman's threat to the Jewish people. This radicalizes Mordecai into action and (in chapter 4) he asks Esther to put her status and her life on the line. She is entreated to get involved in the struggle, to take on her Jewish identity in the open rather than in secret and to plead for mercy to the King. Mordecai reminds Esther, when she hesitates, that even though she is in the palace, she will not escape the fate that awaits her people. Her position in the master's (massa's) house gives her some influence as well as access to the King.

Esther reconnects with her people through solidarity in tribulation and religious expression. This connection provides her with the strength to do what is necessary. Her actions, however, are not direct, but take on an indirect and subversive nature. She hosts two dinner parties for the King and Haman. The result of this diplomatic activity is that the King is more amenable to Esther's request and Haman is set up to fall from his pedestal. Queen Esther saves both herself and her people, and enables Jewish communities throughout the Persian empire to protect themselves from Haman's edict.

Everything ends well, and then the story changes from the middle of chapter eight. The author de-centres the role of Esther as her people's deliverer and Mordecai is given that role. Esther disappears into the background as nothing more than the adopted daughter of Mordecai and the wife of a dictator king. What is the author saying? Perhaps he (if it is a he) is trying to re-configure patriarchy as the social norm? It is indeed strange that the story changes direction and focus at the point it does. Esther's role in Jewish salvation history is an important one, if seemingly obscured, perhaps to make it easier to add the text to the canon. It is certainly not very different from the invisibility of Black women in slave resistance history. There has been until very recently an emphasis on male resistance and the rebellions led by men. Scholars such as Stella Dadzie and Barbara Bush have begun to correct this neglect.

Esther's use of wit and cunning has its equivalent among Black women who were slaves. One such figure is that of Quasheba.[51] There is a Jamaican proverb that states that 'you play fool to catch wise'. This was Quasheba's strategy, as she took up her role in the big house, the massa's house. There is no evidence to suggest that domestic slave women were any more contented and obedient than field slaves (despite the 'mammy' figure of Hollywood myth). Due to their proximity to the plantation owners, however, their methods of resistance had to be subtle and indirect. Bush states:

Of all slaves, domestics probably exhibited the greatest degree of duality
of behaviour. Outwardly they conformed and adopted white culture to a
greater degree than the more autonomous field slaves, while covertly they
rejected the system.[52]

These slaves also found ingenious ways to avoid work. Washerwomen,
especially, proved to be very troublesome in this respect according to
Bush. Other Quashebas used their enforced intimate roles as massa's sex
slave or wet nurse for the mistress's children to get information. This information often aided the resistance struggle. In fact domestic slaves were
often involved in such struggle. Just as Esther connected with other Jewish
people in order to strengthen her resolve, equally this connection was a
characteristic of effective Black resistance and the numerous slave revolts.
It gives truth to the sentiment that one person cannot succeed but one of
many—that is a different matter.

So to conclude, I ask again, 'Are Vashti and Esther our sistas?' I would
say yes. The story contained within the book of Esther seeks to interrogate
the dilemmas and complexities of the diasporan condition in the context of
slavery or colonialism. The idea of a dual heritage in terms of one's current
residence as well as commitment to 'home', one's motherland, such as
Israel in this case, is explored as a resource for survival and the struggle for
freedom. There is an attempt in the book to look at the way one works out
identity in an oppressive environment that seeks to annihilate a people and
their sense of personhood. It is a discussion that resonates with the situation of those taken from Africa to service the needs of European colonies in
the so-called 'New World', as well as their descendants.

Esther and Vashti made choices about how they were going to deal with
their repressive situations and acted on them. Although Vashti's ethnicity
does not appear to be an issue, I believe that both women are sistas in
the struggle, although patriarchy separated them from coming together in
common concern. Nevertheless, these two women serve as paradigms of
Black women's struggle in slavery as well as the continuing struggle for liberation and visibility by minority ethnic women and men in Britain today.

Robert Beckford, in his book *Jesus Is Dread,* uses Sivanandan's idea of
'neo-colonial' to describe the condition of mainline churches in relation to
'race' politics and dynamics.

Like Esther, many of us are part of the system by nature of our work.
We are deeply committed to where we are located, even though for many
of us as Black people it is hard to continue or remain in these settings. In
these churches, we need to assert ourselves as significant and equal partners in our faith communities. We need, constantly, to commit ourselves
to the expulsion of the attitudes, practices and structures that maintain
our marginalization and colonization within the Churches. Black people in

the mainline Churches belong to a racist, patriarchal and elitist institution whose traditions we have adopted. Like Esther, one can get mystified by the system and blunted from radical action. We need to continue in the struggle for a new kind of Church where all people are valued. This is an ongoing programme of de-colonization.

Afrocentric and Black Christian Consciousness: Towards an Honest Intersection

Valentina Alexander

[The following piece is an extract from an article written by Valentina Alexander in the first issue of *Black Theology in Britain* 1 (1998), 11–18. Alexander's work is crucial to the development of Black British women's theology for the pioneering role she has played within the movement in the UK.]

In a contribution to a conference at Queen's College, Birmingham, in 1994 I read a paper entitled 'A Black Woman Moves Towards an Understanding of her Spiritual Rites'. In that paper I attempted to tease out my changing relationship to both black and white Christian tradition and later Afrocentric identity here in Britain. In this present paper I wish, partially at least, to continue from where I left off in 1994, in that I want to explore how, as a Black woman in British society, I am able to make sense of and gain meaning out of two very important influences on my life, namely, African-centredness and Black Christian tradition.

I feel the task is an important one for several reasons. First, because I continue to believe that both of these ideological systems have powerful things to say to Black people, as indeed all struggling people, about holistic pathways to liberation and self-redemption. Secondly, that, in spite of each philosophy's insistence on their separateness from the other, I have found that in reality, as well as sharing similar strengths they have also, in places, fallen victim to similar weaknesses. Finally, and in summary of the first two points, I feel it is vital that dialogue be actively pursued between the two identities so that they can both more effectively respond to the very tangible and audible calls in our society for support, for recognition and for spiritual, mental and physical salvation.

Afrocentricity

To begin this second explorative journey it is probably most helpful to clarify the terms used to describe these two focal identities. The first, African-centredness, is most usually articulated as *Afro-* or *Africentrity*. The latter term is sometimes employed by those wishing to retain closer affiliation to the concept of Africa as the focal point for centredness.[53] In either case the term symbolizes, as Cheryl Townsend Gilkes has observed, 'a commitment to standing in the middle of the black experience...and starting one's thinking there'.[54] In academic terms the Afro-centric movement is most often connected with those American scholars such as Maulana Karenga, Dr Leonard Jeffries, Patricia Newton, and perhaps most notoriously, Molefi Kete Asante, writing and lecturing on the significance and essential relevance of African civilizations and cultures to the rest of the world. Socially it is most often symbolized by a refamiliarization, recreation and neo-expression of African spiritual and cultural forms by Africa's descendants in the West. It is recognized as their attempt to both reconnect with an Africa of the past and present and also to resist the cultural, spiritual and political impositions of their European and American realities. The most lucid illustration of this is Karenga's *Kwanzaa* celebration with its associated seven principles (the Nguzo Saba), which is marked by a growing number of Americans and Britons, from the week beginning 26 December each year.

Afrocentricity, however, is not purely an American invention. Its current manifestation in the conferences, organizations and neo-spiritual developments in Britain has been nurtured by the long-established and ubiquitous traditions of African-centredness carried across to Britain by migrants from the Caribbean and reinvented here by their children. Most popularly this has been in the form of Rastafarianism, but it has also been represented by a broad range of pan-African and Black nationalist identities. Within this wide interchange of ideas, unavoidably then, Afrocentricity has come to mean different things to different people. Within this context, it is perhaps best defined as a historical and diasporic movement founded on ideological principles that attempt to draw upon a range of African inspired worldviews and epistemologies in order to counteract the perceived corruptions inherent within dominant Eurocentric lifestyles.

Black Christian Consciousness

The second term, Black Christian consciousness, is equally as diverse as the former in terms of its historical and diasporic roots. It is used here to denote a development of African-influenced spiritual and theological heritage, established, as an act of protest and survival, under the backdrop of Caribbean slave society and nurtured through subsequent centuries and locations to serve the needs of Black communities seeking to integrate their religious identities with their political realities. The 'Christian' within Black Christian consciousness seems to place the ideology, more securely than the first, within a European continuum of cultural expression. However, the addition of the adjective 'Black' draws a question mark around this assumption and suggests instead a consciousness that seeks to understand, explore and respond to the Christian world-view—like Afrocentricity—through an epistemology that challenges whiteness.

Like Afrocentricity, Black Christian consciousness has many expressions and levels of intensity. These have ranged from those formalized theologies of James Cone, Kortright Davis, Renita Weems and others, to the very informal and even subconscious expressions of contextualized faith manifested by members of Black congregations. Within the British context I have, elsewhere, referred to it as African Caribbean Christian expression.[55] It is meant, in this present context, to represent those who have both passively and actively accommodated their Blackness within the manifestation and articulation of their Christianity, whether this be within the context of historic European or Black-led churches, or indeed, within any church tradition at all.

Afrocentricity and Black Christian Consciousness: Contributions to Struggle and Liberation

In the paper on 'spiritual rites' referred to earlier, I examined the ways in which my exposure to both Afrocentric and Black Christian consciousness had contributed greatly to my own spiritual development and liberation. This power to liberate has not been experienced by myself alone but rather—I feel it is not too bold to argue—it has undergirded the very experience of liberation, of self and community redemption throughout the Black historical experience of slavery, colonialism, racism and oppression. I want now to pursue this idea by focusing on both identities as they express themselves within contemporary struggling communities in Britain.

When I first became aware of philosophies of resistance represented within Afrocentric and Black theological ideas it was like looking into a mirror and seeing my own image reflected. Now this may not appear a particularly extraordinary reaction; after all one expects to see one's own reflection when looking into a mirror. However, it is only when you begin to realize that for all of your life you have been looking into that mirror and not seeing yourself at all, but rather seeing everything and everyone else apart from who you are, that you begin to realize the real significance, the real impact of the discovery. Afrocentric consciousness, argue Herbert Ekwe-Ekwe and Femi Nzegwu, 'is the totalising focus on the African person and their interests as the fulcrum [the lever, the pivot] to our understanding and explication of reality'.[56] It liberates, therefore, by breaking down the centredness of whiteness and by revealing ourselves to ourselves and in the process allowing us to reject those other images of reality that we have taken to be our own simply because we were not aware that anything else existed. Once this discovery is made, a huge and liberating potential is unleashed, first in the individual and then, through what Asante has termed the 'collective conscious will',[57] in the wider community.

In a world in which Blackness is either a commodity, a danger or simply an irrelevance, I discovered, in the Black church gathering as well as in the Kwanzaa celebration, an opportunity to centre myself and to become both visible and valued. It is ironic, therefore, that so often while in the discussion forums of both Afrocentric and Christian supporters I have witnessed a pernicious and counter-productive mistrust of the other. In the one camp, the Afrocentric scoffs at the Christian for his naive allegiance to all things European, his seeming inability to let loose the chains of mental slavery and encompass wholeheartedly the African way of living and believing. In the other camp the Christian pours scorn on the Afrocentric's dependency on narrow and material concerns of colour and culture, his apparent opposition to everything European and his inability to place Christ at the centre of his consciousness. Consequently, in spite of the fact that from both of these philosophies has emerged a most significant impetus for revealing Blackness and decentring white hegemony, they continue to maintain an often critical and judgmental distance from each other.

However, their mutual mistrust does nothing to undermine the common liberational heritage shared and utilized by both, albeit in different ways. In fact, it can be argued that at the heart of the Black Christian consciousness is an African-centred epistemology that recognizes and imposes limitations upon the imposed universality of both religious and secular Whiteness and seeks in its place to promote, maintain and, as bell hooks has argued, to love Blackness as political resistance.[58]

Evidence of this inextricable connection between African-centred identity and Black Christian consciousness is provided from several sources. It is there, for example, in George Mulrain's description of the seven attributes of African spiritual world-views, which were transferred and translated into the Caribbean religious context and through this to the context of Black Christianity in Britain.[59] It is also there in Patricia Hill's description of Afrocentric and feminist ways of knowing, which organize themselves around principles of community accountability, responsibility and mutual support. It is also represented in Ekwe-Ekwe and Nzegwu's[60] analysis of the eight central organizational characteristics of African societies that include: the family as a vital reference point for identity, the promotion of wholesome human relations among peoples manifested through an 'altruistic and community ethic, the principle of communal ownership, the respect for elders, and a generosity and hospitality in terms of the visitor and stranger'. Each of the traits described within this context can be demonstrated, in some way, by communities of Black Christian believers, although they are most clearly and explicitly manifested through the organizational structures of the Black-led church.[61]

It is the Black-led church that has demonstrated, for example, an ongoing commitment to the ethos of mutual care and responsibility. This has been demonstrated not only in internal structures of support, but also increasingly by external services and social projects offered to the unchurched Black community. In these ways the tenets of an Afrocentric value system—self-awareness, self-love and self-help—have been combined with the structures of a Black Christian consciousness to promote a programme that serves to effect both practical and spiritual liberational change in communities up and down Britain. Similarly, it is very often the organizational structures, commitment and collective discipline of the churches that serve as model and inspiration for the small African-centred Saturday schools, community groups and organizations. Clearly some degree of reciprocity exists between the two philosophies, which itself originates from an African source.

Barriers to Liberation

Afrocentricity and Black Christian consciousness, then, share in common a significant contribution to Black liberational methods, structures and ideologies in Britain. They also, however, share two fundamental weaknesses that can serve to limit, and in some cases obstruct, liberational progress and it is to these more problematic similarities that I now wish to turn.

First, both ideologies have what at best can be described as an ambiguous relationship to broader contexts of oppression. This is particularly, although not exclusively, apparent when examining the role of women in Afrocentric and Black Christian consciousness. Afrocentricity, in its formalized and contemporary version, has been severely criticized for its tendency to either ignore or pedestalize women in its attempt to create and promote a cultural ideal. Molefi Asante has, perhaps more than any of his contemporaries, been attacked for the limited role he allows for Black women, either as Black power style superwomen fulfilling unrealistic, almost fantasy, expectations, or as simply absent from his analysis of the creative foundations of the movement.[62]

Within the structures of Black Christian consciousness the limitations of allocated roles for Black women continue. Here, as in the formal meeting places for Afrocentricity, women are allowed to be carers and supporters and sacrificers for the cause. They are permitted to be superwomen for the cause, keeping buildings clean and collection plates full, raising children and being a shoulder for their men-folk. However, in either case, their mainstream contributions to the very creation and sustenance of the movements are most often ignored, underestimated and undervalued. Nor are they often afforded positions of headship over men within their organizations. In this way limitations to liberation are imposed upon ideologies that are otherwise designed to remove all such barriers to liberation.

The second area in which the two philosophies share similar difficulties is with their very exclusivist and narrow interpretations of their own identities. In the case of Afrocentricity, this has sometimes been referred to as the problem of essentializing Blackness, while in the context of Black Christian consciousness it is most often described in terms of allegiance to fundamentalism. Ironically, in both situations, it is this devotion to ideological dogma that has most often led to the levels of mistrust mentioned earlier, since they both insist on qualifying others by a very specifically defined set of criteria. For the one it is whether a person is sufficiently African in their outlook on life that will determine his or her suitability for membership, while with the other it is whether they are sufficiently Christian. In both cases admittance to full and accepted membership is governed meticulously by the gate-keepers of enshrined and essentialist values. In both cases too, this dogged insistence on policing Black and Christian identity can often lead to Pharisaic tendencies, where the truly essential and, indeed, the truly liberational qualities of the ideology, are lost amid an unnecessary and destructive sea of barriers which prohibit meaningful liberation with prescriptive and enforced definitions.

A Black Woman in Britain Moves Towards an Understanding of her Spiritual Rites

Valentina Alexander

[Alexander's essay is a personal exploration into the spiritual identity of a Black Woman that highlights the joys and challenges of articulating a spirituality that challenges the patriarchy of the Black-led Church context. For Alexander, Black theology, in this process, becomes an essential life breath as she seeks to make sense of herself and the world. The ability to draw from a wealth of Black and non-Black traditions has been helpful in the process. This essay is taken from Anthony Reddie (ed.), *Legacy: Anthology in Memory of Jillian Brown* (Peterborough: Methodist Publishing House, 2000), 119–25.]

The subject of spiritual paths is one with which I have become well acquainted. If I had known all those years ago that leaving behind the incompatibilities of British evangelical Christianity would have plunged me into such a complex and seemingly unending web of discovery and re-evaluation I may have been tempted to cancel my journey. If my years of spiritual wandering, however, have taught me anything, they have taught me that the way to go is always forward. I have learned that you cannot really ever return to a faith, you can only begin, again, to live *in* faith, allowing the challenges and transformations of life's experiences to guide and enhance that renewed reality. It is a bit like the old joke about lightning never striking the same place twice because a place is never the same once lightning has struck it.

Sometimes I am frustrated at the ambiguity of my spiritual convictions and long for the comforting familiarity of the old spiritual me. I know, nonetheless, that really what I must do is to allow the complexities of my present experiences to guide me on to an ultimately more fulfilling spiritual reality, grounded firmly in the ever-expanding knowledge of self that I have strived so diligently to develop.

Over the past decade I have experienced a spiritual journeying that has enabled me, amongst other things, to begin to scale the breadth of Black faith and philosophy. Like most journeying, the process has been simultaneously stimulating, challenging, difficult and rewarding. I have felt weary and exhilarated, overjoyed and disappointed, but most of all, I have felt as though I have developed as a human being into a greater awareness of my spiritual self. My journeying, I feel, has taken me through some necessary rites, and it is sometimes only in pausing to reflect on them that I realize how far I have come as well as how much farther I have to go.

Without a doubt my first significant rite of recent years was my physical and ideological move out of the assumptions of British fundamentalist religion, and into a commitment to nurture a spirituality that would allow me to explore, know and love myself, as it were, in full colour. I needed to reject the confines of charismatic evangelicalism that told me God's Kingdom was in heaven, and that I needed to concentrate exclusively on a narrowly defined brand of holy living and evangelical mission in order to find my true place in life. That encouraged me to deny myself material and ideological rights due me, for the sake of the gospel. Conversely, this perspective actively or inactively supported/endorsed structures and systems of power that acted against my interests. My first challenge, therefore, was to recognize the harmful implications of a gospel that ran contrary to my material, emotional and spiritual needs as a Black person living in a materially, emotionally and spiritually oppressive society.

I emerged ready to pursue a new spiritual path, one which did not try to negate my needs, and was open to the material and spiritual concerns which should and did affect me. I required a conscious and uncamouflaged perspective on racism and injustice, both within and outside of the Church context. I needed to have guidance and direction from a spiritual source that could comfortably and unaffectedly address itself to my cultural placing. I had developed a new sensitivity to culturally-relevant spiritual contexts, and the best and most obvious place to nurture this seemed, for me, to be the Black-led Church.

Making a place for myself within the Black-led Church felt like coming home to a familiar and safe tradition. I could have positive directives from a Black source. I could receive support and edification from a Spirit-filled family of believers. There was potential for growth and development within a culturally relevant environment. The Church held so much capacity for my development that I felt the need to commence my second rite, which was to end three years later with my doctoral study of the Church's response to issues of oppression in Britain.

During the research process I was to discover a certain ambiguity in the attitude of this Black-led spiritual institution. The Church had within it the seedbed of resistance but never seemed to allow this potential to grow to fruition. It was faced with the dilemma of having a Black culturally-specific spirituality stuck inside a Europeanized theology that was even more pedantic in its adherence to a colourless/cultureless gospel than was its originators. This, as I was to discover, then affected the extent to which the Church was willing and able to involve itself in the material advancement of its people as they battled against the various injustices encountered in Britain.

My appetite for a spiritual identity that spoke to holistic needs and aspirations required a different experience for its fulfilment. My third rite was accessed initially through the literature of Black Liberation Theologies. Reading Cone and Wilmore I was able to discover a direct lifeline between the Black spirituality that I had grown to love and respect, and an urgently needed Black theological exegesis that was able to apply itself explicitly to the material realities of Black people. When I encountered the work of Kortright Davis I was able to find a Caribbean interpretation of that same basic theology. I discovered that it was not necessary for me to throw out the baby of basic Christian theology with the bath water but that it was both possible and necessary to come into an awareness of the political and even physical Blackness of Christ in order to experience the wholeness of his liberation in my life.

Whilst the theory of Black Liberation Theology was able to stimulate and satisfy my intellectual needs, the absence of its manifestation in the Black Church experience of Britain meant that it was unable to end my search for an active, culturally-relevant spiritual reality. Whilst not abandoning the reasonings of this tradition, what I was able to pursue and explore more thoroughly within the British context was the development of the Afrocentric movement. This movement was being promoted through the various conferences, liberation days, seminars and lecture tours up and down the major Black population centres of the country.

Afrocentricity opened me up to a universe of self-knowledge, self-esteem and self-love, the scale of which I had not previously encountered. From exploring the contemporary implications of the glories of Africa to examining the value of the philosophies of Malcolm X and Marcus Garvey, Afrocentricity gave me a social and historical context from which I could continue my search for self-knowledge, with confidence and purpose. Most of all, it provided an active scope for my desire for personal and community development by heightening my love for education. Moreover, I now had a specific context from which to pursue and pass on knowledge that promoted my experiences and aspirations. The pinnacle of this discovery was represented, above all things, in the 'Rites of Passage' educational programme brought to my attention some years ago through a conference based on the education of the Black child.

Whilst the concept of cultural education for Black children was familiar to me through my years of Saturday School work, 'Rites of Passage' opened up a completely fresh perspective on the need for holistic education and life skills for our children at the various stages of their development. It pointed out the need to guide them into adolescence and adulthood rather than leave their development to wider hostile influences, whether they emerge from European or Black cultural sources. It offered a two-pronged focus: the first one provided the means of arming the child against the attacks of European racism and miseducation, whilst the other initiated the child into a world of history, culture and lifestyle that emanates from an Africa-centred world-view.

Moreover, in being holistic, it carried with it, in fact it was centred upon, a spiritual philosophy that rejected the narrow confines of formal religion, be it the mosque or the church. Alternatively, it allowed the child to focus on the essence of spirituality rather than the dogma of alien value systems. It provided, too, a structure for practical application in the form of the seven guiding principles of the Nguso Saba: a life-enhancing manifesto for self-determination, creativity, purpose, faith, co-operative economic and collective work and responsibility.

It was the spiritual context of the 'Rites of Passage' educational movement that led me to enter into my fourth rite, and confront a world of African spiritual values that had formerly been tabooed in my mind by my traditional evangelical upbringing. Commencing with a study group on the Metu Netu and moving on to a general perusal of West African, in particular Yoruban, traditions, my rite into traditional African spiritualities was perhaps the most challenging and stimulating of all my recent wanderings.

Whilst I have been selective about my embracing of these ancient traditions and philosophies, undoubtedly my brief foray into the meaning of Egyptian metaphysics and West African belief systems has greatly enhanced my vision of the spiritual world. I have always believed in a mammoth sized God and yet I find 'him' now to be enlarged to even higher magnitudes. African spirituality taught me about the huge complexity of God and the spirit realm. It made me more aware of the significance of tradition and ritual. It heightened my respect for community elders, and for the contribution of former generations. It enabled me to tap into aspects of my inner self, my mind, my spirit, my consciousness, which had been left unexplored by my conventional Christian upbringing. It helped me also to bring those formative experiences into perspective, thereby examining the root connections between those traditions, helping to bring them into focus.

My spiritual journey thus far had largely been a matter of discovery, recognition and further exploration. The paths I have most recently travelled, however, have been causing me to begin to confront my influences in the light of their impact on my own personal development. Most recently, I am discovering the extent of my closeness to and distance from all of the spiritual philosophies that have been a part of my experience over the past years.

The closeness has to do with my love for the many expressions of Blackness, and particularly of Black spirituality with its enthusiasm, its energy and its naturalness. The distance that has emerged has emanated from my own awareness of myself as not only Black but also female, and not only female but having particular life experiences that would make me perhaps different from other Black women.

In this light, my fifth rite of passage has involved me becoming conscious of the need for a critique of systems of spirituality and philosophy that in any way revolve around the needs and dictates of maleness or which cleave hold of images of a majority, thereby leaving little space for otherness and difference. This reality is something that disturbs me on many levels. It is something that has proved an obstacle to development in many instances. For example, do men of the Church attempt to transfer their temporal powerlessness to a dominating power of control over women, supported by convenient doctrine? Do Black theologians focus on one form of oppression at the expense of others, and in so doing, perpetuate the very injustices they seek to eliminate? Do Black women allow themselves to be marginalized within Afrocentric programmes, so that they place all other needs above their own, satisfying themselves with convenient myths about the strength, togetherness and self-reliance of their gender?

The implications of such questions were such that I could not rest easily in any spiritual tradition, until I had at least placed myself on the road to getting answers for them. Constructive analysis was crucial, because I did not want to substantially alter my journey from one of self-development to one of cynical development. I needed room for evaluation that did not impinge on room for growth. The fact remained, however, that I was encountering very tangible ways in which these spiritual paths of liberation were frequently made awkward and even impossible by those who claimed to be rooted in an emancipatory tradition. Very often, the problem was caused by the oversimplification of complex behavioural patterns and relationships, the creation of boxes into which all actors must be relegated.

At other times, marginalization was caused by the insistence on roles that the actors are expected to play.

The problem arises when these enforced value systems act as a censor to creative development and thinking. If I must restrict my dress code, put aside my self-assertion and deny my potential for headship because I am a woman in a Church run by male values, then I am suppressing my ability to develop holistically and to experience liberation. If I must compromise or reduce the significance of my own need for self-improvement and relationship building with other women, in order that I can prioritize the need for male development and assertiveness then, similarly, I am not giving myself the necessary space to grow. Furthermore, I will have come full circle from my earlier spiritual experiences and, once again, be trapped in a pathway of denial of the significance of self.

This rite leads naturally on to my most current spiritual path. This most certainly involves the most significant lessons. I have discovered through my explorations that questioning is in itself an essential rite of passage. Amidst all of the buzz-words from the various spiritual traditions encountered, the one that has become most meaningful is Maat, the pursuit of truth, equilibrium and harmony. Whilst I still sometimes long for the security of one faith, I have come to understand that the power of Maat will never be contained in one experience, and will always require a commitment to its pursuit. This does not mean that I am doomed to the life of an eternal wanderer, never quite satisfying myself with one tradition. For me, in fact, it has come to mean the exact opposite.

My spiritual wanderings have confirmed me in the knowledge of several things. Firstly, Maat is a spiritual energy, released when the individual commits herself to holistic self-development. Not just of the intellect, but of the body and the spirit. Secondly, self-development must involve a resolution to self-love, and whilst this rightly includes an element of self-interest, real self-love extends beyond this to the needs and interests of others. Thirdly, spirituality as lived out within a material context is best understood and experienced when given a cultural-historical placing. Therefore, a Black theology is an essential life breath for me as I seek to make sense of myself and the world.

Ultimately, as my spiritual journey continues, I am aware that each new rite I enter into involves a greater commitment to my holistic and integrated self. When these basic concepts are grasped, I need not run away from any truth in whatever form it is presented. When I am committed to an active spiritual experience, I am able to ground myself in the knowledge of Spirit and draw from a wealth of Black and non-Black traditions to inspire and inform me. The option is not necessarily an easy one, but for me it is a truthful one. The reality I have found, then, means that I can draw from the very best of the traditions that have been an influence in my life without any fear of inconsistency of not choosing one over another. This spiritual path is both stimulating and challenging, and if I remain within its discipline, then I will be ready for my next rite when and as it arrives.

Towards a Womanist Pneumatological Pedagogy

Maxine Howell-Baker

[This extract is taken from a longer essay in *Black Theology: An International Journal* 3 (2005), 32–54, that offers a critical introduction to the practice and study of theology and education. Its characteristic feature is that it adopts a womanist theological approach to this growing field, which rarely utilizes the religious experience, history and cultures of Black women as a resource for addressing complex issues in contemporary society. The essential aim is to offer an introduction to what is considered a more holistic approach to theology and education in the global context which celebrates Black Christian women's ethics. It also aims at providing a resource for teaching practitioners in a wide range of educational settings.]

I am a British Black Christian woman and educator conscious that the realities of *my* existence illuminated by *my* faith are as Womanist Stephanie Y. Mitchem states:

> …powerful motivations to step into the streams of womanist thought. The continued marginalization of black women with personal experience of oppression is a powerful incentive to think about God's action in daily life.[63]

Several experiences have shaped my educational, cultural and spiritual perspective as well as sustained my professional quest to find an educational approach that is liberative. Presented in narrative form, these experiences allow others in the church and community to access and test the authenticity of my claims.[64] In short, as Black, feminist and narrative theologians acknowledge about life stories, my personal experiences mould and drive my theological and pedagogical praxis.

Educational Formation

My experience of the British education system, like a significant number of Black working-class women, has been one of great achievement, worthy of praise and celebration.[65] This means I have strong resources to draw upon in order to illuminate the nature of a liberative approach to education and an engagement in its praxis. These resources or sources, as Cone[66] terms them, are legitimate and fundamental tools for authenticating theological enquiries, such as this one, that have the liberation of the oppressed at their heart. Some of these resources are presented now in order to identify the key question, as I perceive it—*Can the education system be liberative?*

In 1982 I left secondary school with the equivalent of six GCSE A–C passes including History and English Language at grade A,[67] and later university with standards of attainment that even exceeded my mainstream counterparts, let alone the standard expectations for the oppressed. I was, thereby, contradicting many theories about achievement and underachievement prevalent today and at the time, which anticipate pupils like myself to leave school unqualified, unmarried and raising a family all by ourselves.[68] *As a result, my view on education is that any child, regardless of any perceived disadvantages within the system and society, can achieve!*

As a professional educator, for over two decades I have worked in inner-city education (school, church and community), striving to ensure the educational achievement of all pupils, especially the subordinated. Such activities brought me a phenomenal amount of attention from fellow educators, locally, nationally, in Europe and Africa, when I obtained funding from the Teacher Training Agency (TTA) to investigate a pedagogical approach that intrinsically links geography with literacy.

The work was grounded in my own experience of reading, which was wrenched from a road to illiteracy when I discovered Ladybird History books and was inquisitive about the lives of real people like Henry VIII.[69] I was driven to read by curiosity rather than mere ambition to jump through the hoops (stages) of the reading scheme that at seven I had already learnt were designed to topple me.

The research, therefore, represented a concerted effort on my part to refuse[70] the excesses of the National Literacy Strategy (NLS), which I feared would alienate rather than liberate pupils, because it took literacy out of any real and meaningful context, and with its links to Standard Attainment Targets (SATs) posed a threat rather than an opportunity to develop intelligently.[71] In stark contrast the literacy involved in the project was connected to a relevant child-centred enquiry.[72] Indeed one pupil who lived miles from the school was so engaged by the project that she took it upon herself to write to the Prime Minister and demand he support the campaign to restore the park's play area to its former splendour, which after several letters he complied!

My experience of achievement clearly shows I was no ordinary learner or teacher, yet the crisis of Black underachievement clearly demonstrates a need for an approach that is free of this alien, abstract and meaningless (except in terms of passing tests) approach to learning that permeates the National Curriculum.[73] An approach to learning that, despite major reform over the past fifty years to ensure equal opportunity for all, continues to fail our children. Out of this experience the more refined question arises—*Can the education system be liberative by nature not default?*

Cultural Formation

Achieving, along with my brothers and sister, within a single female-headed impoverished household, in which my mother was critically ill for most of her reign, has equipped me with a 'hermeneutic of suspicion'[74] regarding, amongst other things, the thinking that links such a family structure to Black underachievement. Far from seeing my cultural background deficient and at odds with educational achievement unlike the western, bourgeois and male-centred culture that is usually heralded, I believe it is, despite its limitations, culturally rich (as much by what is absent as well as what is present) and empowering, offering a great resource for resisting the excesses of the dominant oppressive culture.[75]

The Bible, for instance, was held in the highest esteem and was central to many practices. From being the centre of worship at church, to being the key method of protecting our family members (it was always laid open in the cot above a baby sibling's head), to being simultaneously the key fiction and non-fiction text. My mother, especially, read stories to us from it, making it clear that these stories were to be understood as truths that we should live by and not dismissed as a form of escapism.[76] In this way she passed on the value of active not passive interaction with text and life. Additionally, she inculcated the belief that the wisdom that comes from God is central to meaningful knowledge that fulfils and transforms.

Similarly when she purchased the encyclopaedia, from a door-to-door salesman, by paying him a small amount each week for many years, she knew (like Alice Walker recognized in her mother when she presented her with a library card) the insurmountable wealth of a liberated mind.[77] Thus in such a cultural context *The Sun* newspaper (Britain's leading, right-wing leaning, tabloid newspaper) was understood purely for what it was, escapism, which taught me the need for acumen and 'respite'.[78] What she did was to support my learning radically, and consequently, to encourage me to use what limited material resources I had at my disposal, plus the unlimited resources God provides, to solve real-life problems in order to survive and overcome the harsh consequences of class, 'race' and gender disadvantages.

My father, despite not living with us, instilled from an early age my purpose for being in school—to learn without being disrespectful. He also, like so many first mass wave African-Caribbeans to Britain, emphasized the liberating effect of a good education in terms of greater economic and social freedom, as he pressed me to do better in school, even when I scored As![79]

Furthermore, and what I believe significantly contributed to my outstanding performance, was what my mother did not do. She did not discourage me from my love of learning. Nor did she encourage me to learn what the school said I should learn. My mother, along with her peers, did not understand or approve of my perpetual reading, but despite perceiving my passion as excessive and unhealthy (she often said studying makes you mad)[80] she did not go out of her way to stop me.

By not discouraging me from real learning yet fostering the value of a formal education, my family (especially my single mother) and community provided me with a culturally rich learning environment that was free of fear and failure and conscious of a God who has the power and strength to transform life.[81] On the contrary my mother enabled me by her disinterest to engage in the real intelligent learning Holt describes when he writes:

> The intelligent person, young or old, meeting a new situation or problem, opens himself up to it, he tries to take in with mind and senses everything he can about it, he thinks about it, instead of about himself or what it might cause to happen to him, he grapples with it boldly, imaginatively, resourcefully, and if not confidently at least hopefully, if he fails to master it, he looks without shame or fear at his mistakes and learns what he can from them. This is intelligence.[82]

Consequently I am suspicious of the thinking that underpins cultural and social deficit arguments[83] popular in the 1960s and 1970s that identify raising self-esteem levels, through compensatory education, as the key strategy needed to tackle Black underachievement. For example, Maureen Stone's review of educational policy regarding the Black child identified the 'Plowden Report' of 1967 and the 'Newsom Report' of 1963 in this camp when they both set social and psychological as opposed to educational goals for poor/black and underachieving pupils. The former labelled Black children and their parents deprived of the culture needed to support the children academically, such as taking an active interest in their child's schooling, and fostering high self-esteem.

The latter in a similar vein identified 'inadequate powers of speech and poor home backgrounds' as main indicators of this deprivation.[84] Yet Black children attain average if not high scores in self-concept tests, and there is an established trend of achievement amongst Black girls, especially when compared to their Black male and White female counterparts, which these arguments ignore.[85]

Curiously, as Mirza[86] points out, even when Black female achievement is acknowledged, arguments for tackling Black male underachievement is still underpinned by masculinist notions of the pathological female headed family structure which marginalizes the Black male and thereby ensures his underachievement.[87] Whether Christian or Afrocentric, the masculinist thinking is the same, namely that Black male adults must target Black male children so that the negative impact of female-headed families can be reduced and eventually removed.[88]

Nevertheless, there is evidence which demonstrates that female-headed households are no more likely to disadvantage a child academically than a nuclear or single male-headed household. Indeed they can be seen as giving their children a distinct advantage.[89]

Those same female-headed households raise children who outperform their White and Asian counterparts[90] and are often behind the supplementary schooling initiatives, which have made a positive difference to the school-leaving performance of many Black children. As Mirza demonstrates, Black women often use their success within education to resist and challenge the institutionalized racist practices that discriminate against their children—male and female.[91] Given, then, the church's apparent masculinist perspective regarding education and Black (under)achievement, the question arises *Is there a home for Black feminism within the church?*

Spiritual Formation

My earliest experience of apparent ecstatic glossolalia/charismata pneumatic (signs/gifts of Spirit baptism)[92] was as an infant when my mother's friend had such a frenzied attack of the 'spirit' that she stepped on my toes. The pain was so excruciating that for one moment onlookers believed I too was in the 'spirit', but this was soon dismissed when they saw the look of disgust and pain on my young face. Why would the Holy Spirit let her hurt me in that way, I deliberated? Moreover, this seed of doubt about what 'spirit' actually entered her diminished when I observed her wild party lifestyle and hunger for gossip on the other days of the week.

The notion of many spirits was further diminished by my mother's frequent reply to my question (always from a very safe distance) 'why Sister so and so was acting the way she was in church?'—(reply) 'The devil a jook ar'. Her reply shaped my spiritual perspective that not all signs of the 'spirit' are of the Holy Spirit, and that we are constantly engaged in spiritual warfare, and as such, must put on the full armour of God. Little did I know that twenty-five years later my teaching experience in schools would deepen my understanding of spiritual warfare!

Both (mine and my mother's) suspicions have credence within Womanist and core Pentecostal pneumatological thinking that believes in the necessity of spiritual discernment. Baker-Fletcher,[93] for example, recognizes that 'Sometimes the pastor or deacon is so moved by the Spirit during church service he returns home to beat his wife'. MacRobert,[94] writing on the British Black Pentecostal church movement, spotlights its acknowledgement that '*tongues can be counterfeited by the devil*'.

Biblically, this pneumatological thinking is verified. Karkkainen,[95] in his survey of current debates on the Holy Spirit, draws our attention to the New Testament focus on spirits, which indicates 'It [the early church] recognizes the reality of battle between the kingdom of God and evil spirits'[96] and the need to take counter measures against it.

The apostle Paul was earnest in his endeavours to keep glossolalia in check without hindering manifestations of the Holy Spirit by stressing the gifts that edified the church community but not the individual.[97] Yet time and time again, I would witness individuals, unchecked by the church, 'get in the spirit' with no other purpose but to edify self.

As I matured and became passionate about social justice, my suspicion centred on the question 'Why does Sister **** only get in the spirit at convenient moments in the service and never whilst trying to evangelize to warring gangs?' Later this question became extended for two main reasons, to 'why doesn't the Black church use its access to the most powerful force to fight social injustice?'

Firstly, the TTA research project also brought me a phenomenal amount of negative attention from my White, middle-class, mostly female colleagues at school, which intensified when I proclaimed in faith, Jesus Christ as my role model and rejected the suffocating curiosity of the specialist they offered me. Secondly, the local pastor, hailed up as a British Martin Luther King, advised me to 'leave the school and leave quietly or they (the educational establishment) would see to it I never work again'.

These questions relating to the role of the Spirit in church life are even more pertinent for me today in my conscious determination to provide a liberative education for all the youth and their educators that began with the TTA project. A quest that is fuelled by a political pneumatology[98] that believes God can and will make a way out of no way, and so long as I have faith in Him/Her I, my pupils and fellow subordinated colleagues can and will achieve anything. Given the obvious limitations of spiritual love and power (which William J. Seymour identified as necessary evidence of Spirit baptism),[99] in the church, the question that I must next pursue is *what does the Christian faith say about the centrality of the spirit in a liberative approach to education?*

The Case for a Womanist Pneumatological Pedagogy

When the experience of Black women pivot the White male bourgeois bias in education and church, as has been demonstrated above, a new set of issues arise regarding the nature of justice/liberation. Notably, can societies be liberative beyond breaking the external chains of the socio-political and religio-cultural processes that oppress the poor and marginalized? Or rather, can societies be liberative from inception? In other words, can the very thought structures of the liberationist break the internal chains of the thought processes that created the oppressive systems s/he fights to eradicate? The implication within the study, thus far, is that subjugated epistemologies can break these chains, so long as each liberationist is conscious of their alternative way of knowing, and shrewd enough to employ this epistemology so that it does not decentre other epistemologies nor let them dominate.

Put briefly here, the character of Womanist pneumatological pedagogy (WPP) is Womanist because of its primary focus on ordinary Black women and their love of self, others and the Spirit, as well as its multi-dialogical and didactic intents.[100] It is pneumatological because of its love of the Spirit and its awareness that spiritual dynamics demand two key things: firstly, a priestly approach to matters concerning all aspects of life and secondly, a willingness to learn from and be led by the Spirit in all that you do.[101]

In other words, WPP is conscious of the necessity to harness the power of the Holy Spirit to ensure effective and sustainable transformation of the social realities of the poor according to the liberation message contained within the gospel.[102] Finally WPP is pedagogical because of its consciousness-raising intent. That is, its concern with utilizing the experiences of Black Atlantic[103] women in church and society, to produce a teaching and learning heuristic for the marginalized, driven by love of self, others and the Holy Spirit.

6 Interpreting Texts

It is an undeniable truth that Black Christianity the world over, not least in the UK, is a phenomenon that is governed, overwhelmingly, by one dominant material artefact, namely the Bible. 'Holy Scripture' has become part of the essential template of Diasporan African spirituality since the middle to late nineteenth century. It might well be argued that the development of Black Christian faith in the eighteenth century featured a complex dialectic between the text of scripture and the context of Black experience.[1] The rise of the holiness culture towards the end of the nineteenth century marked a pivotal shift in that dialectic. The movement from the complex balance between text and context/experience towards text plus context/experience has been explored by a number of scholars.[2] Whilst there are undoubted positive and negative theological dimensions and interpretations to this developmental movement there can be no doubting the reality of many Black Christians' adherence to the one book.

This chapter contains extracts from a number of Black theologians in Britain whose work offers interesting and challenging ways in which the biblical text has been re-contextualized and reassessed in order to explicate the central theological norm of liberation, from within the contexts of Black existential experience. The theological method of Black theology operates from the mandate that asserts the inviolability of the Black self and seeks to plumb the depths of religious tradition, most usually Christianity and the Bible, in order to locate resources and themes that attest to Black existential liberation.

Taking its cue from the indefatigable work of Black slaves during the seventeenth and eighteenth centuries (as demonstrated in previous chapters) through to the iconoclastic work of James Cone in such landmarks texts as *God of the Oppressed*,[3] Black theologians have continued to engage with and prioritize the Bible in their theological method. Whilst Black theologians from alternative 'schools of thought' have critiqued the normativity of utilizing Christian notions of revelation and the self-referential modality of biblical witness as the non-foundational ground for talking about liberation,[4] the editors of this text, nonetheless, recognize and affirm the basis for this particular approach to Black theology. As Reddie has stated on at least one previous occasion, Black people are not going to let go of the Bible any time soon.[5]

Black theology in Britain has never let go of the Bible. For many Black Christians in Britain, to argue for the relevance of the Bible to Black life is to indulge in tautological semantics. By virtue of the fact that the Bible is the 'Word of God' renders its relevance as self evident, and not worthy of idle speculation. Black theology in Britain rightly eschews that form of self-evidential normativity, but nevertheless continues to recognize the importance of this text as an essential source for talking about God in the context of history, human life and Black existence.

The essays in this chapter contain work by the likes of Hyacinth Sweeney, Joe Aldred, Mukti Barton, Michael Jagessar, Kate Coleman and Valentina Alexander. It confirms the vibrancy and the creativity with which Black theology in Britain has and continues to engage with biblical texts.[6]

The Bible as a Tool for Growth for Black Women

Hyacinth Sweeney

[In this essay Sweeney makes a case for the significant role of the Bible, in spite of its misuse, as a tool for the development and liberation of Black women by drawing from four approaches of Womanist theologians. The essay is taken from Bishop Joe Aldred (ed.), *Sisters with Power* (London: Continuum, 2000), 114–22.]

The Bible is not a closed book that has already said all that needs to be said. It is a collection of texts that can speak to everyone in many different ways if we take our time to be open to it. It is a text that can speak to us in our present times about things that have gone by, the things of now and the things to come. Throughout the course of biblical studies, black scholars have sought to understand the realities of the Bible for black people. The Bible was used against black people as a means to justify the slave trade and slavery.

It was used against them to keep them submissive and subhuman. Despite this there are many thousands of black people who live according to the Bible and its teachings. It can still be said, even today as we move into the twenty-first century, that most African Caribbean households, in Britain and the Caribbean, still have a Bible somewhere in the house. It may not be used as much today as before, but it is the one book that will be turned to in a time of need.

Within most households you will find that it is the woman who does most of the teaching and nurturing. This is usually due to the fact that they spend most of the time with the children. The mother or grandmother will take the children to church, and be the one who helps them with the memory verse for next week's Sunday School. When the children get to a certain age, usually around teenage, they make a decision whether or not to continue going to church. Their choice depends upon what is going on around them: peer pressure, family and friends. If, however, they choose to reduce their attendance at church, this does not usually mean that they also abandon the teaching that they have received. The Bible is still the book that is turned to when 'trouble comes calling'.

In this paper I will be focusing on the four approaches that are used by womanist theologians to read the Bible. As most of the data comes from the African American contexts, I have used the data gathered from the questionnaires/interviews to get a black British perspective. All of the approaches are based on the hermeneutical method of biblical analysis as it focuses on the experience of the people rather than theory. The main emphasis will be on the Recuperative, Suspicion, Postmodern and Survivalist approaches as tools for growth. I will be using material from Professor Renita Weems, the leading African American womanist biblical scholar's lecture, 'Reading as an Act of Rebellion' (Queen's College, Birmingham, March 1997).

When it comes to the people in the Bible, women as a whole are submissive and black women within the text are invisible. They are camouflaged in terms of country of origin or by their family name, usually their father or husband. This obscurity does not enable the reader to recognize the black women or the black family lineage. With this knowledge, black theologians, male and female, began to approach the Bible using a hermeneutical method. This approach is described by J. S. Croatto as a way of understanding the Bible through the eyes of the oppressed.[7]

If we look at the black experience, our culture and experience shape the way that we worship God and study the Bible. Our traditions were taken from Africa up through Europe and transformed within the Caribbean and America and then distributed all over the world. Therefore our experiences, our culture, our traditions, all go together to help and shape the way we see God. Similarly, European theology was formed out of the experience and culture of the European (mainly white males). Other forms of theological discourse therefore are not a new thing, but an area that has been kept silent and invisible.

Black women began to 'come to voice' and speak out against these continual injustices which others seemed to not see or just ignore. Black theologians seemed to ignore sexism and the white feminist movement failed to address racism. Many African American women[8] began to write about their own experiences and theological analysis. They took on the term 'womanist', coined by the novelist Alice Walker,[9] and began to call themselves womanist theologians. Their work takes seriously the experience of black women and men, focusing on how this experience affects the construction and production of their lives. Experience is the key element within this discourse due to the fact that black women are seen to be suffering from multidimensional oppression, e.g. sexism, classism, racism, heterosexism, homophobia.

The Recuperative Approach

This method sees finding black women within biblical texts as imperative. This approach enables black women to reclaim their historical presence which tradition had either camouflaged or made invisible. It takes the viewpoint that there is evidence of black women within the Bible and we must claim back our heritage. This approach reclaims the role and the identity of black women and black people within the Bible. This is evidenced within various texts, in addition to their heightening contribution through history. The aforementioned can be seen, for example, within the biblical narratives themselves and in their relationship with God, which is manifested in their expressions, experiences, spirituality, and theological portrayal of Jesus.

The Bible is an Eastern document in origin, and is based in a part of the world where the dominant culture is black. For example, within the Bible you have accounts of the Queen of Sheba (near Ethiopia), Moses' Cushite (Ethiopian) wife; Hagar, the Ethiopian slave woman of Sarah and Abraham, to name a few. There are many more black people within the texts that need to be identified.[10] Therefore, this approach can be seen as a positive form because it demystifies the Bible in terms of Eurocentric ideology. It places black women and men within the contexts of the pages; their life, culture and traditions are there to be seen. It is about 'claiming back', and black women need to therefore ask themselves, 'What is it that they need to claim back and how are they going to do it?' It is about gaining historical sources as a background and then moving forward towards liberation and growth.

The Suspicion Approach

This method approaches the Bible objectively and so makes the starting point experience. It allows us to go beyond the face value of Eurocentric biblical hermeneutic to an African-centred form. It has a strong resistance to male domination and bias, or what can be termed as 'anti-women', 'androcentric' in attitude and form. This usually takes the form of misinterpretation, misrepresentation, being seen as or made into a second-class role, if any role or position at all. This in turn points to the Bible as being biased towards men, i.e. it highlights the men more than the women within the text. The fact that the Bible has been written mostly by men encourages the notion of male superiority and female inferiority. This means that the texts therefore enslave women, especially black women, placing them in a multidimensional oppression. This is achieved in many ways: belittling the women by demonizing them, allowing them to remain as unnamed characters, which in turn makes them less obvious to the reader.

If we look at the account in Exodus 2:3-5 about Moses as a baby, four women were very influential in the continuation of his life: 'his mother hid him, he was watched over by his sister, rescued by the daughter of the pharaoh and her maid'. These important historical contributions by women have failed to be recognized by interpreters, or maybe it was a deliberate act to divorce and deny the importance of the role of women. With this approach you learn to re-read the Bible in a new form, as an act of rebellion.

The Postmodernist Approach

Within this method the Bible is rejected as a collection of stories that have successfully kept black women in their place, through maintenance of certain power relationships. Women have looked beyond the male centredness of scriptures and have shown themselves to be approved by God. However, within this approach there are many who have rejected the Bible altogether, as they view it as serving male interests only.[11] These women look for answers outside of the Bible as they see God's relationship with women as an abusive one, as in Hosea 2:10 and Haggai. Also within this approach you would bypass the biblical narratives in order to use experience and modern-day concepts as tools. This approach draws on resources outside the Bible to enhance the plurality and cohesion of the texts along with our life experiences.

Howard Thurman, in his biography, tells the story of his grandmother's listening habits. She was raised in the period of slavery in America, and particularly depended upon memory and listening to grapple with and to interpret the Bible. Thurman writes:

> Two or three times a week I read the Bible aloud to her. I was deeply impressed by the fact that she was most particular about the choice of scriptures. For instance, I might read many of the more devotional psalms, the gospel again and again, but the Pauline Epistles never, except at long intervals, the 13th chapter of 1st Corinthians. With a feeling of great temerity, I asked her one day why it was that she would not let me read any of the Pauline letters. What she told me I shall never forget. During the days of slavery, she said, the master's minister would occasionally hold services for the slaves. Old man McGhee was so mean, he wouldn't let a Negro minister preach to his slaves. Always the white minister used as his text, something from Paul, and at least three or four times he used as his text, 'Slaves be obedient to them that are your master...as unto Christ'. Then he would go on to show how it was God's will that we were slaves and how if we were happy slaves, God would bless us. I promised my maker that if I ever learned to read, and if freedom ever came, I would not read that part of the Bible.[12]

The grandma presumably never learned to read the Bible for herself and needed her grandson to read for her. Because of her aural contact with the Bible, it left her free to criticize and reject those portions and interpretations of the Bible that she felt insulted her innate sense of dignity as an African, a woman, and a human being. Likewise she felt free to cling to those that she viewed as offering her inspiration as an enslaved woman and had portrayed, in her estimation, a God worth believing in. Her experience of reality became the norm for evaluating the contents of the Bible. That grandmother's refusal to have the Pauline portions of the Bible read to her highlights important ways in which the experience of oppression has influenced women's, particularly African American women's, disposition toward reading the Bible.[13]

The Survivalist Approach

This method adopts a 'by any means necessary' approach. The starting point can include any of the above methods as the emphasis is placed on the liberation rather than application. This method incorporates the interpretation of the Bible in such a way as to enable it to come alive in a liberative form. This is accomplished by looking beyond the male-orientated text and the frailty of human beings and seeing God's liberating power for women. This approach esteems the value of womanhood and raises the level at which it is perceived, thereby revealing God as non-partial.[14]

Womanist biblical theologian Delores Williams looks at the story of Hagar and uses her encounter to express the issues of survivalism within the African American women's experience. It is a story familiar and even haunting for African American, Caribbean, and black British female readers. The experience of Thurman's grandmother shows that there is a history of resistance with particular African American women and women in other cultures when reading the Bible.

Professor Weems can be placed within all of the approaches, as her work not only looks at the reclaiming of the black women from within the texts in a liberative form, but also rejects those scriptures that dehumanize and misogynize women. Professor Weems asks how and why contemporary readers from marginalized communities continue to regard the Bible as a significant resource for shaping modern existence. She explores the rationale by which African American women, marginalized by gender, ethnicity and often class, continue to regard the Bible. In her attempt to develop a critical hermeneutical method for dealing with African American women's issues, she provides a model for the way in which other problematic material in the Bible (e.g. slavery, homosexuality, war, racism and classism) can therefore be assessed.[15]

A Black British Perspective

In the interview/questionnaire, I gathered data from people to ascertain their responses on tools for growth within the Bible. I addressed a number of different black women within the church, lay and ordained, at different levels. Most of the respondents agreed that the Bible in itself can be used as a tool for growth. They were all cautious about using only the Bible as a resource, as there are many other tools that can be focused on as well. They all read the Bible in different ways, but mainly as a tool of spiritual growth. They all use caution within their reading, as they see it as a book that has been used as a tool of subjugation and oppression. They see a need for the continual discovery of black women within the text, for the accounts that are popular (as mentioned above) are far and few between. The stories of the women are welcome as a tool for identification and direction, but due to the non-recognition of most of the women within the Bible, many feel angry. They see the accounts as a small oasis in an arid mass, nurturing water splashing on you when you are hot. This, however, is not enough, and they all contend that there needs to be more recognition of women in the texts.

Most felt that women did too much in church and society without recognition. Some felt that many women saw their worth measured by the work that they did, which then becomes problematic for growth. The other side of this 'giving of self' is the model that is shown to their children. Many women will sacrifice a lot for the sake of their children and this can be seen as the testimonies of black women's commitment to growth. However, the one-sidedness of this giving needs to be thoroughly addressed by the black community throughout the world.

As we can see, the approaches used are varied, according to what your experiences and needs are. However, in order to attain tools for growth, black women need to employ approaches that will negate oppressive structures and help to promote empowerment, physically, mentally and spiritually. These tools, I contend, are found within the approaches adopted by womanist theologians as they are drawn from all sections of the community of the African Diaspora.

Liberation and empowerment are words which come to mind when we talk about the tools for growth for many people. Alongside this, you will also need some aids to enable you to achieve the goals that you have set for yourself, or sometimes, ones that have been set for you. For black women over the centuries the path to liberation and freedom has continually been blocked—physically through slavery, or mentally and emotionally by the language used to describe them. Either way, the struggle to shake off the shackles has been difficult and for many a sacrificial choice. One of the main problems is the invisibility and lack of women in ministerial leadership roles, and in the organizations of the Church. The Church is supposed to be the representative of Christ, whose sacrifice was (as Christians believe) for the whole of humanity.

Being Human: A Black British Christian Woman's Perspective

Kate Coleman

[This piece is taken from Coleman's unpublished PhD thesis 'Exploring Metissage: A Theological Anthropology of Black Christian Women's Subjectivities in Postcolonial Britain' (University of Birmingham, 2006). Through analysing the story of creation, Coleman demonstrates the significance of the themes of relationality, truth and difference to anthropological formulations. The knowledge inherent within the creation of humanity is subsequently posited in the terms *differentiation*, *distinctiveness* and *identity*.]

Imago Dei and Genesis 1–3

No single biblical text has been more important in the understanding of theological anthropology than the first three chapters of Genesis, particularly Genesis 1:26-28 (NIV):

> Then God said, 'Let us make humankind in our image, according to our likeness, and let them have dominion over the fish of the sea, and over the birds of the air, and over the cattle, and over all the wild animals of the earth, and over every creeping thing that creeps upon the earth'. So God created humankind in his image, in the image of God he created them, male and female he created them. God blessed them and said to them, 'Be fruitful and multiply, and fill the earth and subdue it, and have dominion over the fish of the sea and over the birds of the air and over every living thing that moves upon the earth'.

The narrative does not purport to be a literal history of origins or a scientific explanation of what is. Rather, the creation narrative confronts humanity, primarily with questions of meaning in relation to God, each other and nature.

Reading Strategies

Those engaged in the task of interpretation acknowledge that reading strategies, rather than texts themselves, tend to be considered authoritative. Brad R. Braxton summarizes this theme succinctly:

> The text is plural, but the achievement of plurality of meaning is not so much an accomplishment of the text. Rather, this plurality is the accomplishment of the various reading communities engaging with texts.[16]

The predominance and legacy of Western reading conventions can thus be partially explained by the pervasive impact and influence of colonial categories. Sugirtharajah reminds us that:

Colonial reading can be summed up as informed by theories concerning the innate superiority of Western culture, the Western male as subject, and the natives, heathens, women, blacks, indigenous people, as the Other, needing to be controlled and subjugated. It is based on the desire for power/domination.[17]

Questions regarding the nature of gender relationships and the socially and ethnically diverse nature of Israelite community and surrounding societies may have contributed to the production of Genesis 2 and 3. However, these questions do not necessarily provide an impetus for societal change. Such questions may be partially responsible for reasons why traditional interpretations have not adequately accounted for difference as an expression of knowledge and truth within this biblical text, where 'Truth is a question not only of what is but of what ought to be…'[18]

A focus on readers in the creation of meaning entails the relative decline of the importance of the author as sole arbiter of what the text really means. Reading strategies are similarly diverse. In outlining the history of biblical studies in the west, Sugirtharajah posits seven reading strategies that elucidate the various, but overlapping, stages of biblical interpretation since the Enlightenment: dissident, resistant, heritagist, nationalist, liberationist, dissentient and postcolonial readings.[19]

Notions of difference and knowledge are a central feature of the narrative when addressed through the general rubric of black women's epistemological concerns. Such an interpretative framework is specifically concerned with how our unique subjectivities as black British Christian women in church leadership shape the task of biblical interpretation. By making this assertion, I anticipate that such a hermeneutic may also prove attractive to black and other marginalized people, regardless of their religious affiliation, gender, country of residence and leadership status.

In utilizing this hermeneutic, I have drawn on historical-critical studies without being limited by the various formulations of authorial intent and original audience reception. Rather than defining my reading strategy, historical-critical methods are secondary to my exegetical approach. This allows the subjective experiences of the reading community of black women to become the determining source and norm in my hermeneutical process. Biblical theologians Robert Morgan and John Barton in their book *Biblical Interpretation* affirm the value of such an approach:

> A literary framework, which includes the results of historical and linguistic research, is today more promising for the study of religion and for theology than the historical framework (which includes literary study) that has dominated New Testament studies since the 1830s… Where the aims of biblical interpretation are religious or theological, it is necessary to consider exactly how historical study is important for this, and to recognize its proper place, which may be a subordinate one.[20]

Foregrounding Phyllis Trible's literary analysis, feminist theologian Ann Clifford elucidates the variety of analytical strategies that may be usefully employed to facilitate the feminist theologian's desire to undermine patriarchal interpretations of the Genesis 1–3 text. With particular reference to the relative usefulness of historical-critical approaches, she writes:

> Scholars who use historical-critical methods of biblical interpretation agree that Gen. 2:4b–3:24 is a very ancient text—part of a tradition that can possibly be traced to the time of Kings David or Solomon (ca. 1000–950 BCE). The narrative is at one and the same time a story of creation and an explanatory myth, or etiology, responding to questions such as why people get married, why women have pain at childbirth, and why serpents lack legs. Knowing the probable historical context in which this text was written and the type of literature it represents is a helpful corrective to simplistic literal interpretations, but this information does not take one very far in remedying the many faulty interpretations of Genesis 2–3 that Trible has highlighted.[21]

By adopting a variety of reading strategies, submerged biblical voices and histories can be unearthed. Subjugated voices ultimately undermine the hegemony of the traditional self-appointed 'guardians' of ancient biblical texts, while affirming previously excluded interpreters.[22]

Rereading Genesis 1–3

The introduction of humankind within the context of the creative process is salutary. Significantly it occurs within a cosmological framework, where the theme of knowledge as interactivity and connection is revealed as being ideologically and pervasively represented, throughout the whole creative process. The creation narratives bear witness to God as the one creating and communicating. Therefore to be made in the image of God is to be created with knowledge claims as inherent expressions of human nature. Indeed, knowledge as interactive experience and concrete engagement is an integral aspect of the human condition. In the words of eco-womanist theologian Karen Baker-Fletcher:

> Dust is a metaphor for our bodily and elemental connection to the earth. Dust includes within it water, sun, and air, which enhance the vitality of its bodiliness and ability to increase life abundantly. So dustiness refers to human connectedness with the rest of creation.[23]

Such assertions are also affirmed by white feminist theologians as demonstrative of specifically female associative ways of knowing. Loren Wilkinson explicates the significance that feminists attach to these ways of knowing:

> Feminism argues that much of our alienation from the earth is the result of the dominance of masculine ideas of exploitation. (Common phrases like 'rape of the land' and 'virgin forest' support the claim.)[24]

Humanity is manifestly a part of the whole of God's natural order, created with an innate relatedness and connectedness. Humanity is 'fully dust'. The relationship between the *human*[25] and all God's creation is thus firmly established. Themes of knowing, differentiation, distinctiveness and diversity are further illustrated by the *human's* acknowledgement of the unique distinctions of all the animals as expressed through the rite of naming.

Naming

In Hebrew society, as in many African societies, naming is less an imposition of identity, than an act of incorporation. It is a recognition of individuality, defining the child's personality, affirming her or his destiny and establishing her or his status in the family. Within these contexts a name shapes one's self-understanding, providing descriptive information about the circumstances of birth or traits emerging in the character of the child, 'proper naming not only acknowledged the child's destiny but also empowered the child to actualize it'.[26] The 'first' *human* 'is neither a particular male person nor a typical human person, but is a combination of dust and the breath of God!'[27] As such, both male and female are represented in the act of naming. However, whereas the animals are named by the human, depicting an act of sovereignty, it is differentiated Adam, who comes to recognize and define, in terms of her being, the differentiated woman. He declares twofold, 'She shall be called "woman" for she was taken out of man' (Gen. 2:23 NIV). This personal identity development is enabled primarily through interaction with the opposite sex. Woman is not 'named' Eve, until after the fall in Gen. 3. At this point, the act of naming essentially establishes her role (as opposed to her being) and future reality, and she does become 'the mother of all the living' (Gen. 3:20 NIV).

Lisa Isherwood and Dorothea McEwan expose the critical ability of naming to regenerate the conditions of human lives, 'The power of naming has been acknowledged as crucial by feminists since it not only expresses and shapes our experience but also gives us the power to transform our reality.'[28]

Through naming, the *human* demonstrates an intimate and familiar 'knowledge' of the reconstituted dust. *Human* acts of naming in Gen. 2 are also reminiscent of God's own act of differentiating and naming the heavens, earth, seas, day and night. In so doing God gives expression to their distinctive roles and specific attributes. In Gen. 1 the world is created through speaking and naming. God's words are both creative and reflective, in that they reveal something of the divine nature. The cosmos subsequently emerges in precipitative fashion from a context described as 'mingled' and chaotic. Each act of creation leads to a 'search' for creative difference and distinction. God as creator promotes the themes of differentiation, distinctiveness and identity, ultimately leading to an orchestrated harmony, depicted as the very opposite of pre-existent chaos. As expressed by Mercy Amba Odoyuye, 'In Genesis, God "delivers" the universe from chaos...'[29] Within the creation discourse, words are both rooted and expressive of materiality. They 'bring life into being', thereby reflecting the emphasis among black feminists and womanists that words should avoid abstraction through a declaration of the identity of the speaker. Indeed, reference to personal journeys and material interests feature prominently in the theological constructions emanating from within marginalized communities. The following words of womanist theologian Delores Williams thus underscore the significance of personal history and social location in the task of theological reflection.

> I have come to believe that theologians, in their attempt to talk to and about religious communities, ought to give readers some sense of their autobiographies. This can help an audience discern what leads the theologian to do the kind of theology she does. What has been the character of her faith journey? What lessons has this journey taught? What kind of faith inspires her to continue writing and rewriting, living and reliving theology in a highly secular white-and-black world paying little or no attention to what theologians are saying?[30]

As such, black women theologians align themselves not simply with good theory, but with discourses that are life affirming, diverse, flexible, inclusive and above all 'good for one's health'.[31] In contrast, however, Eurocentric interpretations of this process emphasize themes of division and separation with tacit endorsement of preference, competition and favoritism.

The themes of differentiation, distinctiveness and diversity introduced earlier are intended to convey mutual interdependence and interrelatedness. As Mercy Amba Oduyoye elucidates, 'Feminist theologians have been critical of the dualistic and hierarchical modes of conceiving and organizing the human community and of its various levels of interaction.'[32] Hermeneutics that foreground black women's epistemological concerns result in an *imago dei* in which emphasis is placed on notions of differentiation, distinctiveness and diversity. [...]

Saming

The *human* experiences a *saming* with the created order that is rooted in materiality, for both are made from the same substance. There is mutuality. In addition, the *human* experiences a *saming* with God. This is revealed through the divine prerogative and notion of *imago dei*, that is, they are made in the image of God. Humanity also experiences a *saming* by virtue of their differentiation; all things express multiplicity and variety. These shared features with creation, God and others are often expressed in human relations in unexpected and diverse ways. Emmanuel Lartey expands upon this theme with regard to human relations:

I have found difference where ethnicity, race, class and gender might have suggested otherwise. I have also found similarity where every possible cultural indicator might have pointed in the opposite direction.[33]

Interconnectedness is further expressed through the notion of relationality.

Relationality

Human life in the creation account is 'shaped' not just through a spoken word, but also through the moulding of the *human* from dust, thereby expressing the tactile relation of potter to clay. The allusion to experiential knowledge and interactive participation is further emphasized in the act of 'breathing' life into the human's nostrils. Kidner writes that 'Breath is warmly personal; with the face-to-face intimacy of a kiss'.[34] God further accentuates the sense of interaction and experiential knowledge by 'walking' where the *human* walks, in the garden.

Human beings are presented as being relational as they interact with diversity in humanity and also with the created order in God-pleasing ways. In addition they are shown to engage with diversity in God. Humanity and creation are thus presented as differentiated, distinctive and diverse, that is, having identity.

To the extent that all humans have the capacity to know, epistemology, as knowledge, is presented as universal, an attribute of all regardless of culture, gender or geography. In the Genesis account, humankind is more than simply acted upon in relational ways; humanity also acts upon the world relationally and in ways that have psychosocial, cultural and political implications. In other words, difference is rooted in materiality, and 'knowledge' is derived directly from these interactions. The means of acquiring knowledge are seen to be basically the same for all humanity, even where they fail to declare it. Differentiation, distinctiveness and diversity in creation suggest that different ethnic groups may put their acquired knowledge to different uses and develop unique approaches to its analysis and expression. Difference, expressed epistemologically, is thus a creative gift, designed to promote holism rather than homogeneity, where each expression of God's creative activity brings back to God some distinctive feature of God's own glory. This is an aspect of human sensibility that is both proposed and endorsed by God. Musimbi Kanyoro explains how such an understanding actually promotes the idea of multiple theologies. She writes: 'This understanding of plurality anticipates that there will be many theologies just as there are many styles of cooking!'[35]

John Parrat explicates that such theological diversity has holistic power in the arena of human expression:

> There must therefore of necessity be a diversity of theologies, and our unity arises because ultimately we all are reflecting on the one divine activity to

set man free from all that enslaves him. There must be a plurality of theologies because we don't all apprehend the transcendent in exactly the same way nor can we be expected to express our experience in the same way.[36]

This underlines the creative intent that difference exists for complementarity rather than competition and exploitation. The personal relationship between God, humanity and creation is further emphasized in Gen. 1:28. God's divine purpose for creation is to be promoted by humanity in cooperation with the divine image within human beings. It is clear from God's creative acts that God's intention is to make humanity responsible for bringing about a flourishing creation in all its diversity. God declares this as 'very good'. Humanity's ability to obey God's command in tending the garden and humanity's own creative space is also borne of a 'knowing', that is, an ability to interpret interactions with a differentiated, distinctive and diverse created order in ways that lead both to its maintenance and cultivation. In other words, the *human's* concerns are to be cosmocentric. Garth Baker-Fletcher elucidates this theme:

> A cosmocentric decision looks toward the entire relationship of the *community* of LIFE rather than toward the private good of an individual human being. To privatize moral choice and decision making would be to violate the fundamental ontology of community that obtains in a wide host of African cultures.[37]

Black women insist that to endorse relationships of mutual support and affirmation within difference is to affirm God's justice and God's original project of differentiation, distinctiveness and diversity. It is to explore and release difference, as opposed to resisting and opposing it. It is also a challenge to differences, that post 'fall', have become demonized, having transgressed God's creative and redemptive parameters for humanity. Taking an inclusive view of creation's differences is in itself redemptive and is an attempt to restore the intended harmony and creative interrelatedness of God's original design. It is to engage in creative acts of revolution that lead to psychosocial healing and liberative praxis in discrete communities.

Hermeneutical Insubordination: Toppling Worldly Kingdom

Mukti Barton

[This essay is taken from Bishop Joe Aldred (ed.), *Sisters with Power* (London: Continuum, 2000), 24–35. Here, Mukti Barton brings fresh insights into the role of women in Church by unearthing some of the biblical female voices during the time of Jesus and the early Church, and then inviting readers to discern and respond to what roles women should play in churches today.]

God's Truth is Making People Free

In the last 50 years Christians have achieved what they failed to gain in the previous 1,950 years. Not only on issues of gender, but on other issues such as that of race and class, Christians have begun to ask some very serious questions. These will have to be answered by the churches. In the last 50 years something unique has been happening in Christian history. It seems as if the prophecy of Joel is being fulfilled:

> I, the Lord, am your God and there is no other. And my people shall never again be put to shame. Then afterward I will pour out my spirit on all flesh, your sons and your daughters shall prophesy, your old men shall dream dreams, and your young men shall see visions. Even on the male and female slaves, in those days, I will pour out my spirit. (Joel 2:27-29)

The Spirit is poured out on the rich and poor, male and female, young and old, so that God's people 'shall never again be put to shame'. Innocent sufferers are especially God's people, since they suffer just for who they are as created in God's own image. Throughout human history non-white people, especially women, have suffered the most. In the last 50 years women and non-white people are the ones who have risen up in an unprecedented way. They are the authors of the prophetic theologies, the theologies of liberation.

The powerless and the oppressed of the world have learnt how to look at their society, their church and their scripture from the perspective not of the powerful, but of the powerless. As a result they discard their false consciousness, the belief that the colour of their skin or their genitalia make them inferior to the others. They claim God's truth, and the truth makes them free to challenge the injustices of the world.

For Christian women, God's truth comes from their own experience of innocent suffering and from the Bible. The primary source for all church doctrines is the Bible. Yet, according to some doctrines, women may be ordained, and according to some others they may not. In some doctrines equal roles are designated to both men and women, while in others only secondary roles are allocated to women. This phenomenon raises the question about how churches which read the same Bible can have such serious discrepancies. The truth is, Christians have read and will always read the Bible differently from each other. They read it from their particular perspective in their own context: there is no other way of reading the Bible or any other books. Therefore, it is natural that different groups of Christians have different doctrines. This is fine, as long as the Bible does not become oppressive to some people. History gives evidence that the Bible has been and is used to oppress various groups of people. In the name of the Bible slavery, racism, colonialism and women's oppression have been sanctioned. Although this has happened, many oppressed Christians are unwilling to blame the Bible itself for their oppression. This is where the whole question of hermeneutics arises. The blame is removed from the Bible and placed where it belongs, on the readers. Gustavo Gutierrez, the father of liberation theology, understands that:

> Human history has been written by a white hand, a male hand, from the dominating social class. The perspective of the defeated in history is different. Attempts have been made to wipe from their minds the memories of their struggles. This is to deprive them of a source of energy, of an historical will to rebellion.[38]

Not only biblical hermeneutics, but all academic disciplines have been affected by the bias of the powerful. In the absence of the voice of the powerless, traditional hermeneutics has often been oppressive to the losers in history. In patriarchal cultures women have been the losers. My argument is, 'If the interpretation of scripture is undertaken only by the powerful in a society, they will consciously, and more frequently unconsciously, continue to legitimize structures of oppression'.[39] Until recently it was assumed that all biblical interpretation must submit itself to the dominant way of interpreting the Bible. The dominant method was believed to be an objective, value-free and scientific method relevant for all people. The challenge to the traditional method has come from 'the recognition that biblical interpretation is not isolated from the social and cultural values and political interests of the interpreter'.[40] Class, race and gender affect people's interpretative context. When churches read the Bible from exclusively male perspectives, women have secondary roles. When women's perspective is respected, eyes are opened to see God's truth in a new way. The truth makes women free from prejudicial treatments. Equilibrium is established and there is the possibility for all people to use their gifts for God.

The Bible was written by men in patriarchal societies, and therefore in the biblical text itself female voices are hidden or even silenced. Certainly these voices are not as obvious as male voices. Here the interpreters can play a part by further silencing the voices of the biblical women. Renita J. Weems raises a question about the interpreters, 'whose voice the scholar-interpreter "hears", recovers, probes, scrutinizes and interprets within the Bible is also a decision about whose voice is not heard'.[41] My hermeneutical aim as a woman scholar is to make these silenced voices heard.

In God's Kingdom the Humble are Lifted Up

The patriarchal Church has always taught women to be humble and subordinated to men. As a result, many women now have low opinions of themselves. They have let men have their way at women's own expense. Some women have brought on their own ruin by giving up their rights. The Bible says:

> Don't underrate yourself. Humility deserves honour and respect, but a low opinion of yourself leads you to sin. Do not let others have their way at your expense, do not bring on your own ruin by giving up your rights According to the Wisdom of Jesus son of Sirach, these lead you to sin (Sir. 4:20-22).

This book of the Bible goes on to say: 'Stand up for what is right, even if it costs your own life, the Lord God will be fighting on your side' (Sir. 4:28).

The biblical good news is not that the humble will be more humbled, but that the humble will be lifted up and the mighty be brought down. Jesus went about putting this good news into practice. God's standard, which Jesus showed, is just the opposite to the standard of the world. The last in the world's standard is first in the eyes of God. Paul, in his letter to the Corinthians, writes:

> But God chose what is foolish in the world to shame the wise; God chose what is weak in the world to shame the strong; God chose what is low and despised in the world, things that are not, to reduce to nothing things that are, so that no one might boast in the presence of God (1 Cor. 1:27-29).

God's standard is reflected in the life of Mary, when 'the Word of God', Jesus, came not through a man, but through a woman, Mary. This is why Mary sang out: 'God has brought down the powerful from their thrones, and lifted up the lowly' (Lk. 1:52). Mary means 'rebel' and her Magnificat was heralding rebellion.[42] Luke records that when baby Jesus was presented in the temple:

> There was...a prophet, Anna... She never left the temple but worshipped there with fasting and prayer night and day. At that moment she came, and began to praise God and to speak about the child to all who were looking for the redemption of Jerusalem (Lk. 2:36-38).

Anna, a woman, spoke about Jesus in the temple. The world's standard is reflected in churches when it is taught that women must not preach the word of God. In his long theological discussion with the Samaritan woman, Jesus, son of a rebel, rebelled against patriarchal customs. He disclosed to her that he was the Messiah. Jesus trusted the Samaritan woman to give testimony to the Samaritans. Her testimony brought the Samaritans to Jesus. She was one of the first missionaries (John 4). Mary of Bethany (another rebel) sat at Jesus' feet listening to Jesus. 'Sitting at somebody's feet' means being a disciple. Together with Mary, Jesus rebelled and taught Mary theology and affirmed her by saying: 'Mary has chosen the better part, which will not be taken away from her' (Lk. 10:42).

Churches have often taken away from women what Jesus affirmed. Martha also broke down stereotypes. Martha headed and owned a household. 'Mar' is Aramaic for lord or master and 'tha' is its feminine ending.[43] Usually church teachings create a division between Martha and Mary, by preaching that Mary chose the better part. However, juxtaposing Luke's and John's versions of Martha–Mary episodes, it becomes clear that Martha was no less a disciple of Jesus. While Mary's voice is hardly heard in the gospels, Martha is vocal.

One of the longest intellectual-spiritual dialogues recorded in the gospels is between Jesus and Martha. Martha recognized Jesus as the Messiah: 'Yes, Lord, I believe that you are the Messiah, the Son of God, the one coming into the world' (Jn 11:27). In order to elevate men, the Church remembered Peter's identical confession: 'You are the Messiah, the Son of the living God' (Mt. 16:16). Martha never received any credit for her confession—the politics of omission in biblical women like Martha, making women silent in churches.

Jesus' own economic, social, political and religious conditions kept women bent double. In the synagogue, women had no right to enter the areas reserved for male religious leaders. Jesus challenged the oppressive patriarchal system by inviting a bent-double woman to trespass into the male areas. Jesus' healing touch made her stand with her head high. Jesus also challenged exclusive male language by referring to the woman as a 'daughter of Abraham' (Lk. 13.16). 'Son of Abraham' was a commonly used term, but 'daughter of Abraham' was unheard of.[44]

According to Mark, a woman anointed Jesus on the head. In ancient Israel, kings were anointed on the head by prophets at the beginning of their reign (1 Sam. 10:1). Christ means 'the anointed one'. It was a woman who performed the task of a prophet and anointed Jesus. Anointing was also a preparation for burial. Jesus' disciple, Judas, involved himself in the plotting to kill him. Peter showed his unwillingness to believe when Jesus spoke about his impending suffering and death (Mt. 16:21-23). The nameless woman in Mark grasped the truth and prepared Jesus for his burial. Appreciating this understanding and support of the woman, Jesus said, 'Truly I tell you, wherever the good news is proclaimed in the whole world, what she has done will be told in remembrance of her' (Mk 14:9). Many churches have suffered amnesia and have not given to this woman the honour that Jesus bestowed on her. Churches have also done a character assassination of her by confusing her with a sinful woman who anointed Jesus' feet. Moreover, for no reason whatsoever the churches have defamed Mary Magdalene by identifying her with the sinful woman. However, the gospels never called Mary Magdalene sinful.[45] Moreover, it is on the testimony of Mary Magdalene and other women that Christianity is standing.

When most, if not all, of the male disciples fled, women walked with Jesus to the cross and remained under the cross. Women were there at his burial and went to anoint Jesus on the Easter morning. For this reason Jesus also honoured women, especially Mary Magdalene, by first appearing to Mary and other women after the resurrection. Jesus sent Mary Magdalene to the apostles with the command 'Go and tell'. Based on the biblical accounts, Mary Magdalene can be called an apostle to the apostles. Neither Jesus, nor the Bible, but the churches silenced women. While the truth of Christianity actually stands upon women's preaching about the resurrection, women are forbidden to preach in some churches.

St Paul sometimes understood the standard of God and sometimes he was influenced by the patriarchal way of thinking. All the gospels give evidence that the risen Christ appeared to women first, but Paul forgot to mention any of the women in his list in 1 Cor. 5:5-8. He mentioned some men and left the others unnamed. Perhaps it is another sign of male amnesia. Women often mark how patriarchy makes some perfectly saintly men forget about women's gifts and contributions. However, in spite of Paul's weaknesses, credit must be given to Paul for many wonderful sayings such as the following: 'There is no longer Jew or Greek, there is no longer slave or free, there is no longer male and female, for all of you are one in Christ Jesus' (Gal. 3:28). All barriers are broken down in Christ. Paul not only spoke about such unity, he and the first Christians worked hard against patriarchy to build up an egalitarian Church.

The Early Church Clothed Women with Greater Honour

Has the Church progressed or regressed? This is the question to ask when I survey more of the New Testament to present a few biblical women's names in the beginning of Christianity.

'Now in Joppa there was a disciple whose name was Tabitha, which in Greek is Dorcas. She was devoted to good works and acts of charity' (Acts 9:36). Here a woman is clearly identified as a disciple. It is like the tip of an iceberg, indicating that there might have been other women disciples who were not clearly identified as such. There are some verses in the Bible which put women together with Jesus' disciples. 'Soon afterwards he [Jesus] went on through cities and villages, proclaiming and bringing the good news of the kingdom of God. The twelve were with him, as well as some women…who provided for them out of their resources' (Lk. 8:1-3).

> …they went to the room upstairs where they were staying, Peter, and John, and James, and Andrew, Philip and Thomas, Bartholomew and Matthew, James son of Alphaeus, and Simon the Zealot, and Judas son of James. All these were constantly devoting themselves to prayer, together with certain women, including Mary the mother of Jesus, as well as his brothers (Acts 1:13-14).

These verses give the impression that women were part of the core group of Jesus' disciples. Women have always heard from their churches that it is natural that men have prominent positions in churches, since Jesus only chose male disciples. However, in the patriarchal society of Jesus' time, God's standard is reflected not so much in the ordinary events of Jesus' choice of his male disciples, but in the extraordinary events of women walking together with the male disciples, women who provided for Jesus' group out of their own resources.

> A certain woman named Lydia, a worshipper of God, was listening to *us*; she was from the city of Thyatira and a dealer in purple cloth. The Lord opened her heart to listen eagerly to what was said by Paul. When she and her household were baptized, she urged us, saying, 'If you have judged me to be faithful to the Lord, come and stay at my home'. And she prevailed upon us (Acts 16:14-15).

Patriarchal standards are turned upside down. Following the lead of a woman, her whole household was baptized. The first churches started in homes like Lydia's.

'There he [Paul] found a Jew named Aquila…with his wife Priscilla' (Acts 18:2). In Romans 16:3-4 more is written about this couple. Paul writes, 'Greet Prisca and Aquila, who work with me in Christ Jesus, and who risked their necks for my life, to whom not only I give thanks, but also all the churches of the Gentiles.' Prisca and Aquila, co-workers of Paul, are mentioned six times in the New Testament (Acts 18:1-3, 18, 24-26; Romans 16:3; 1 Corinthians 16:19; 2 Timothy 4:19). Four out of the six times the woman's name is mentioned before the man's. This is still unusual even today. Priscilla and Aquila taught Apollos, a preacher who had thorough knowledge of the scripture. Here again Priscilla's name is mentioned first (Acts 18:24-26). Most probably Priscilla was a better theology teacher than her husband.

Luke writes in Acts 21:8-9 'we went into the house of Philip the evangelist, one of the seven, and stayed with him. He had four unmarried daughters who had the gift of prophecy'. In Romans 16:7, Paul implores, 'Greet Andronicus and Junia, my relatives who were in prison with me, they are prominent among the apostles, and they were in Christ before I was.' Many scholars now agree that Junia is the name of a woman, a woman apostle.[46] Romans 16:1 reads, 'I commend to you our sister Phoebe, a deacon of the church at Cenchreae, so that you may welcome her in the Lord as is fitting for the saints, and help her in whatever she may require from you, for she has been a benefactor of many and of myself as well.' Paul writes to Timothy, 'I am reminded of your sincere faith, a faith that lived first in your grandmother Lois and your mother Eunice and now, I am sure, lives in you' (2 Tim. 1:5). Here Paul remembered to give credit to two women for Timothy's faith and work.

In the first churches women were not just church cleaners and flower arrangers: they are mentioned as disciples, teachers, prophets, apostles and deacons. It seems it was not stipulated that women should remain single to work for the Church, or that they should only work as partner to their husbands. Some of the early church women were single and some were married. Moreover, the married women were not helpmates to their husbands: they were church workers in their own right.

Hermeneutical Insubordination will Topple Worldly Kingdoms

In the kingdom of the world, men rule and women are kept in subordinate positions. If the same happens in the Church, it is clear that the Church is mirroring the kingdom of the world, rather than the kingdom of God.

For just as the body is one and has many members, and all the members of the body, though many, are one body, so it is with Christ.

> ...the members of the body that seem to be weaker are indispensable, and those members of the body that we think less honourable we clothe with greater honour, and our less respectable members are treated with greater respect, whereas our more respectable members do not need this. But God has so arranged the body, giving the greater honour to the inferior member, that there may be no dissension within the body, but the members may have the same care for one another (1 Cor. 12:12-25).

When women are regarded with less honour in patriarchal societies, in the Church they must be treated with greater respect. Men who have power and authority in the world will not need it in the Church. Although church leaders often confuse their leadership with worldly leadership, Jesus was clear how his followers should behave:

> But Jesus called them to him and said, 'You know that the rulers of the Gentiles lord it over them, and their great ones are tyrants over them. It will not be so among you, but whoever wishes to be great among you must be your servant, and whoever wishes to be first among you must be your slave, just as the Son of Man came not to be served but to serve, and to give his life a ransom for many' (Mt. 20:25-28).

If male church leaders understood their ministry to be one of humble service, exercised in a Christlike manner, there would not be any more room to question whether women are called to do the same or not. Patriarchy and all domination will end when we, the oppressed of the world, continue to search for something available in this (the biblical) canon(s)—something hidden, something familiar, but something eternal—that will inspire us to fight on and sing a newer song. It is our stubborn faith that even our small, uncelebrated, but persistent acts of hermeneutical insubordination will eventually topple kingdoms.[47]

This article is an example of such hermeneutical insubordination and the aim is to topple worldly kingdoms.

Paradigms for a Black Theology in Britain

Joe Aldred

[In this essay, taken from *Black Theology in Britain* 2 (1999), 9–32, Aldred shares biblical and contemporary insights that he perceives as essential tools necessary to understand the contemporary emergence of Black British theology. This excerpt focuses on the two biblical paradigms: Kingdom of God and the exilic life of Israel in Egypt that the author highlights.]

Thy Kingdom Come

Jesus' model prayer (Mt. 6.9-13; Lk. 11.2-4) embraces the hope of the establishment of God's kingdom in the world. The use of the word 'kingdom', a translation of the Greek βασίλείά in the New Testament, conveys the meaning of royalty, rule or realm.[48] This, in the context of the Lord's Prayer, is a plea for God's rule to be appropriated on the earth to the same extent as it is in heaven.

An examination of what the Gospel of Mark has to say about the kingdom of God is instructive. Mark presents it as a mystery to those outside of it (4.11), to whom it is declared through the preaching (1.14) of those chosen for this purpose. It is also declared to be 'at hand' (1.15). Its origin is likened to mustard-seed and its growth is a source of bafflement to natural human perceptions (4.26-32). Some who were alive at the time of Jesus would not die before they saw its powerful appearance (9.1). Anything that might bar one from the kingdom should be sacrificed (9.47). The kingdom is childlike in nature, and its recipients must develop this very quality (10.14). Conversely, the rich would find it hard to enter (10.23). [...]

The kingdom of God, as Jesus proclaimed it, inverted societal norms. Here, the greatest became the servant of all; the meek inherited the earth, for 'he hath scattered the proud in the imagination of their hearts. He hath put down the mighty from their seats, and exalted them of low degree. He hath filled the hungry with good things, and the rich he hath sent empty away' (Lk. 1.51-53).

The *New Dictionary of Theology* (1988) makes the following observations:

(1) The phrase 'the kingdom of God' does not appear in the Old Testament, although notions of God as king and of his kingly rule are pervasive.

(2) In contrast to the Old Testament, the phrase 'the kingdom of God' or 'the kingdom of heaven' occurs frequently in the New Testament, especially in the synoptic gospels where it is the central theme in the proclamation of Jesus.

(3) In the rest of the New Testament, in contrast to the teachings of Jesus, explicit references to the kingdom are relatively infrequent. Stated globally, Jesus preached the kingdom; the apostles preached Jesus as the Christ.[49]

The inhabitants of Palestine at the time of Jesus well understood the workings of earthly kingdoms, with their attendant oppressive structures. Samuel had much earlier given a warning concerning this oppression, in response to Israel's demand for a king:

> This will be the manner of the king that shall reign over you: He will take your sons, and appoint them for himself, for his chariots, and to be his horsemen, and some shall run before his chariots. And he will appoint him captains over thousands, and captains over fifties, and will set them to ear his ground, and to reap his harvest, and to make his instruments of war, and instruments of his chariots. And he will make your daughters to become confectionaries, and to be cooks, and to be bakers. And he will take your fields, and your vineyards, and your oliveyards, even the best of them, and give them to his servants... And he will take your menservants, and your maidservants, and your goodliest young men, and your asses, and put them to his work. He will take the tenth of your sheep: and ye shall be his servants. And ye shall cry out in that day because of your king... (1 Sam. 8.11-14, 16-18 KJV).

Human kingdoms were exploitative in nature. Hence, Jesus' announcement that 'the time [was] fulfilled, and the kingdom of God [was] at hand' (Mk 1.15) was guaranteed a sympathetic hearing among those who 'labour[ed] and [were] heavy laden' (Mt. 11.28). This was particularly so because he offered an alternative where the 'yoke [was] easy, and [the] burden light' (11.30). Now, as then, the poor, oppressed and disadvantaged are the most favourably disposed to the gospel of the kingdom of God. However, while the poor were better disposed to hearing about and receiving the kingdom, it is clear that poverty in and of itself was not the key to the kingdom. From the beginning of their ministry, both John the Baptist and Jesus made it clear that entrance into this kingdom of God was dependent upon repentance (Mk 1.4, 5, 15). The obvious implication was that anyone who could come to repentance was eligible for entry. Raymond Pruitt in *Fundamentals of the Faith* speaks of repentance as:

> not only godly sorrow for sin and a determination to forsake it, but it also involves confession and renunciation of every form of it... Repentance involves the emotions, the intellect, and the will. In each there is a complete change of direction.[50]

Those who occupied the most advantageous positions in the old Mosaic order of 'righteousness by legalism' would have found Jesus' theology of 'entrance by repentance' incomprehensible. So too, apparently, did some rich people. Jesus himself declared 'How hardly shall they that have riches enter into the kingdom of God' (Mk 10.23). Both Matthew's and Luke's Gospels indicate that among the 'violent', that is the heathen and tax-collectors, 'whom the Scribes and Pharisees [thought had] no right to the kingdom of the Messiah'[51] there was an urgent desire to embrace this new concept of divine dominion (Mt. 11.12; Lk. 16.16). Matthew speaks of the violent taking the kingdom by force (11.12) and Luke of multitudes pressing or forcing their way into it (16.16). Mark (12.37) tells us that 'the common people heard him gladly', and Jesus told the religious fraternity in the temple at Jerusalem 'that the publicans and the harlots go into the kingdom of God before' them (Mt. 21.31). There is evidence to suggest that the reason the poor followed Jesus was not entirely spiritually orientated, when in the wake of his call to them to become more involved with him, 'many...went back and walked no more with him' (Jn 6.66).

The gospel of the kingdom of God coming to the earth was, therefore, good news for the underclass who appeared to find repentance less of a problem, having as a result of their condition already lost their pride. It was into this base human material (1 Cor. 1.28) that God had chosen to invest the heavenly treasure (2 Cor. 4.7) of his kingdom—the kingdom whose coming was intended to have a profound impact upon the world. This impact would be the undeniable product of God's power since its human agents would be obviously incapable of the feats which they performed without God. Referring to the immanent manifestation of God's kingdom in the world intended by Jesus, Laurie Green makes the following conclud-ing points on a study of the parable of the biblical kingdom:

> That in Jesus' mind the kingdom of God was of such a quality that its actions and signs would have to do with God's active power and author-ity, that it would be in conflict with and in radical opposition to the activi-ties of the Children of Darkness, that it would be a joyous celebration of the very nature of the Godhead, and that it was even now coming into the world.[52]

Moreover, this New Kingdom which John and Jesus announced was to be entered into by the voluntary act of those who desired it. A kingdom is usually established and enlarged by conquest. As such, if God had chosen to establish his kingdom on this basis it would be no different from earthly kingdoms. He therefore invites volunteer 'subjects' to 'come unto me'. The kingdom of God, then, can be said to consist of those who voluntar-ily come under the Lordship (or kingship) of Christ and are consequently empowered (authorized, privileged) to become children of God (Jn 1.12). Consequently, it becomes the privilege and responsibility of these kingdom citizens to influence the unregenerate world by following a counter-cultural lifestyle of divine love (*agape*) for one another (Jn 13.35). To this end, Christians are called to be the light of the world and the salt of the earth (Mt. 5.13, 14). [...]

My contention is that such a view of the kingdom of God presents us with a paradigm for constructing a Black theology in Britain, which for the sake of righteousness, justice, affirmation and love, sides with the poor. The story of Israel as a people in exile provides another paradigm.

Exiled in Egypt

Genesis chs. 37–50 present the story of how Joseph and his family became exiles in Egypt. This narrative, according to Eric Lowenthal in *The Joseph Narrative in Genesis*, is the longest biblical literary unit, comprising 391 verses.[53] In this story we see how Joseph became the providential bridge between the Patriarch and Moses. We also see the numerical expansion of the 'Children of Israel'. From the 70 entering Egypt they grew to 'about six hundred thousand...beside children' (Exod. 12.37), by the time of the exodus from Rameses, over 400 years later. Comparative points of reference between the descendants of Jacob living in Egypt then, and the African-Caribbean community living in England now, are many and include:

- the underlying factors that brought both to a foreign land promising alleviation from poverty
- the ghettoization of an exiled people
- the exile's unquenchable hope of a return 'home'.

Motivations to Travel to a Foreign Land

During the period of the Genesis narrative, Canaan was already regarded as 'the promised land'. God had appeared to Jacob's father, the Patriarch Abraham—then Abram—and had said to him: 'To your offspring I will give this land' (Gen. 12.7), and again, 'I am the Lord who brought you out of Ur of the Chaldeans to give you this land to take possession of it' (Gen. 15.7). With their original homeland of Ur no more than a distant memory, Abraham's descendants saw Canaan as home, in a similar way that for transplanted Africans the Caribbean Islands became home. However, the manner of first-generation migration in each case was very different.

For the African there was not the sense of a divine call compelling a human response, only the degradation of being rounded up and stacked like sardines into slave ships, bound for an unknown destination. Writing about the fact and effects of this enforced transplantation, Mervyn Alleyne says:

> One issue is the forced extraction of Africans from their homelands. Africans could not prepare themselves psychologically and materially for their departure to the New World, and once aboard the slave ships they had

virtually no contact with their home cultures. Africans were unable to bring with them all the elements necessary to preserve their original cultural traditions and institutions… Finally, their lack of direct ties with Africa meant that they had no access to models or to a higher authority that might have helped and encouraged them to preserve other aspects of their cultures such as religion in a 'pure' form.[54]

The journey into Egyptian exile was also different from Israel's other journeys. Israel's capture and subsequent exilic subjugation are usually portrayed in Scripture as the direct result of their sin against God and his consequential judgment upon, and abandonment of them to the whims of more powerful nations. According to Bruce Birch, Old Testament prophets held the view that 'exile was God's judgement on Israel's own arrogance, injustice and unfaithfulness'.[55] He lists a wide range of evils for which prophetic indictments were enunciated against Israel. These included injustice and unrighteousness, economic issues, socio-political issues, idolatry and their lack of concern for the vulnerable. However, the first biblical account of a Jewish exile pre-dates their later existence as a covenanted nation often given to backsliding. In their pre-nationhood epoch, as Peter Ackroyd points out, 'at no point in the…narrative is it suggested that the people in Egypt were brought into subjugation by reason of their own sinfulness'.[56] In fact we find Joseph asserting, positively, that his own 'unfortunate' entrance into Egypt, the prelude to the entire family following suit, was not as it appeared even to those who betrayed and sold him. He told his brothers, 'it was not you that sent me hither, but God' (Gen. 45.8). We can be quite clear, therefore, that the movement of the 'house of Jacob' from the 'land of their forefathers' sojourn' (Canaan) to an inadvertent exile in Egypt was not due to Divine Judgement upon a sinful people.

The precursor to full emigration was Abraham's incursion into Egypt during a time of famine (Gen. 12.10-20). Here, in spite of certain complications, he and Sarai returned safely to Canaan. When, in later years, subsequent generations might have pointed accusingly at their parents for ensnaring them in slavery, they would have been reminded that their patriarch Abraham had made the same journey in similar circumstances. This linkage has always been important. Louise Spencer-Strachan stresses the dangers of a myopic view of a people's history when she says:

> A people without a historical past has no frame of reference in the planet which we live [resulting in] historical amnesia, feelings of non-existence, alienation and loneliness. Knowledge of accurate history helps to create linkage, ultimately developing better feelings about self as well as the group.[57]

It becomes important, therefore, for African-Caribbean people living in England to know that their presence here, significant since the 1940s and 1950s, was preceded by other Africans centuries before. Dr Selwyn Arnold, discussing the origins of a Black presence in Britain, argues that, 'Black people have been a part of the British society for well over 400 years'.[58] In fact he makes reference to one source which 'claims that a Black presence was prominent in Britain until the Anglo-Saxon invasions of the fifth and sixth centuries'.[59] In more recent history it has been established that some black overseas veterans of the two world wars, but especially the second, remained in Britain after those conflicts. As with Joseph's family expedition into Egypt, so it was with that of African Caribbeans into Britain in the 1950s. Both had antecedents.

Joseph's early life shares characteristics with that of many youngsters in the Caribbean dreaming of a better life, shepherding a small number of animals, carrying and fetching for elders. Many who grew up in the rural areas will identify readily with Joseph getting lost and being found 'wandering around in the fields' in Shechem, or looking for his elder brothers (Gen. 37.15). His privileged life as 'the apple of his father's eye' did not endear him to his brothers, who devised means to get rid of him. They sold him for 20 shekels—about 0.2 kg—of silver to their cousins the Midianites, who sold him again in Egypt. Methods by which funds were scraped together in the Caribbean included borrowing or giving within the family circle, gaining from the sale of the family 'jewels' (usually livestock) or from British companies which sent their representatives to the Islands with the offer of loans (repayable to the companies upon starting work in Britain). Such arrangements left many immigrants feeling 'sold'. Sold and exported they felt they had been exiled to a cold and unwelcoming Britain. Many would compensate, in a retrospective manner, by insisting that Britain has been blessed as a direct consequence of the presence of a God-fearing Black people in the same way that Potiphar's house and field were blessed by the exiled Joseph's presence (Gen. 39.5).

Joseph's apparently unfortunate passage into a foreign land was also the beginning of the realization of his childhood dreams of a superior status in the world and within his family (Gen. 37.5-11). He does not appear to have imagined the dramatic manner in which his dreams would be fulfilled. Bruce Birch illustrates well how it is that the fulfilment of our dreams and hopes of salvation invariably come about through the conduit of bondage:

> In its present context the Joseph story serves a larger purpose in connecting the stories of the promise to the stories of deliverance. It does so, not simply as a matter of geography (how did they end up in Egypt?), but also by preparing us theologically for understanding the experience of bondage which must precede the drama of deliverance.[60]

For Joseph this period or process of 'bondage' continued well beyond his initial selling. There was the wrongful arrest and imprisonment based on the spurious allegations of 'Mrs Potiphar' (Gen. 39.9), and the forgetfulness of his fellow prison inmate which prolonged his imprisonment (Gen. 40.14, 15).

After 13 years, he entered into service in the courts of Pharaoh, King of Egypt. Joseph was a mere 30 years of age, a similar age to that of the majority of African-Caribbean immigrants to Britain during the period being considered. These were young aspirants who dreamed of making money and returning home as soon as possible. They found themselves imprisoned by a socio-economic system that had not been established with their aspirations in mind. Joseph soon settled in Egypt. With a good job and a new identity he probably pondered several times how, when or if he might see his family again. According to John Marshall Holt, people did not regard travel lightly in Joseph's time:

> Travel in the ancient world was hardly a matter of vacationing tourism, seeking out interesting sights for the sake of diversion. If one travelled at all beyond his immediate environments, it was a case of his needing to do so because of war, politics, business or some other pressing concern.[61]

This was also true of the mid-twentieth century Caribbean person. People did, however, make 'necessity travels' to neighbouring Islands, the United States, Canada and then Britain, mainly in response to economic factors and war. Holt reckons that correspondingly, in Abramic times, trips of necessity between the two contemporary cultural and economic focal points of that time, namely Egypt and Mesopotamia, were the prerogative of armies, diplomats, traders and nomads.

By the occasion of the famine which Joseph correctly interpreted from the Pharaoh's dream, the 'dead' Joseph was prospering in Egypt and was about to become the world's saviour through his wise agrarian policy. With Canaan ravaged by drought, an aging Jacob told his sons, 'I have heard that there is corn in Egypt: get down thither, and buy for us from thence that we may live and not die' (42.2). They discovered that what had began as a mission to buy food in Egypt for survival in Canaan was not as simple as it first appeared.

The famine endured and soon it became necessary to 'go back and buy…a little more food' (43.2). In common with many others, this writer's own father returned to Jamaica in 1959, having first left for England in 1955, but found he needed to go back to England due to enduring economic reasons. As with Jacob's sons, this second trip 'to buy food' has proved for many to be the thin edge of a wedge which, when it was fully driven home, brought whole families from their 'Canaan' to 'Egypt'. The twice broken heart of an aged Jacob—first at the disappearance of his favourite son Joseph presumed dead, and then having to let go his 'newly crowned' favourite son Benjamin in order to secure Egyptian food—would find empathy many times over in the Caribbean during the 1950s. Jacob was reunited with them both, of course, but only when they were all in Egypt!

This writer has not met a single African-Caribbean person who had permanent migration in mind at the time of initial entry into Britain. Yet some Black Christians, in retrospect, regard their coming to England as an act of God, who used economic privation as his instrument to achieve his will of having a substantial and permanent Black presence in Britain. Ira V. Brooks, who became a successful pastor in England, gives a classic example of the type of personal situations which God used in bringing him and others to England:

> I lived in Florida long enough to learn that its natural beauty and wealth were reserved for almost anyone—as long as the colour of his skin was not Black. Returning to Jamaica, I resolved to settle down and bring up a family. It was not long afterwards that my pride, patriotism, and sense of freedom gave way to overwhelming economic pressure. So, I said good-bye to my wife and baby daughter, and took ship to England.[62]

Not long after arrival in England, Brooks testifies to receiving a super natural call of God to the ministry. We find that in both Joseph and his family's emigration from Canaan and the African-Caribbean people's emigration from the Caribbean, the human intention was to solve temporary economic embarrassment by temporary migration. In both cases we also find that this led to 'permanent' settlement.

Spinning Texts—Anancy Hermeneutics

Michael Jagessar

[This essay first appeared in *The Journal of the College of Preachers* 117 (July 2004), 41–48. Here the author employs the Caribbean trickster figure, Anancy, as a heuristic means to creatively converse and engage with biblical texts from a multiplicity of angles or optics simultaneously.]

> No one was surprised when Anancy, a genius WORD-smith, gave up politics. She had enough of politics and the politicians. Things were getting from bad to worse on the MOTHER ISLAND... Yet, the whole of Sorrow Hill was shocked when they heard that Anancy had experienced con-version and had joined the OPEN DOOR BIBLE CHURCH on West Street and wanted to be a preacher. Strange words and ideas were working overtime in Anancy's head and she was eager to accept the invitation to spin with a view...

With a View

I like the notion of 'preaching with a view'[63] as preaching involves a 'bringing into view' our take on our convictions about God, God's purposes and God's grace working in human existence.[64] Preaching, like interpreting, is never objective. Preaching is a reflection of the preacher's/hermeneut's view(s). One is in it and deeply involved in the act. Whatever the tools, techniques and scholarship one employs and whatever the role of the Spirit, the sermon and interpretation of a text will reflect the culture, social location and theology (*inter alia*) that have shaped and continue to shape the preacher. This is besides the fact that the biblical texts are culturally and ideologically conditioned.[65] We are cultural beings and as such we all read, interpret, preach and listen with a view, however faithful or orthodox we strive to remain to technique, content and theology. This is especially (not exclusively) the case with Black (Caribbean) preaching. What is significant for Black preachers is the interpretation and connection of their experiences in the light of the biblical witness. God is not a theological dictum for Black people. God is intimately involved in their lives as oppressed people. God is in the thick and thin of every corner of their existence in very specific ways.[66]

As one whose life has been shaped in the Caribbean, my theology, hermeneutics and preaching reflect a Caribbean heritage, especially its colourful rainbow nature with its diversity of peoples, religions, cultures and the ongoing dialogue and interaction in this context. This may be one reason why I find it difficult to preach with 'a' view. My proclivity is to preach with a multiplicity of views in creative and dynamic dialogue. This can be risky, surprising and quite often a counter-*version*.

Spinning a View: Anancy, the Signifying Spider

> *What people did not know were the few voices of serious doubts and contradictions in Anancy's head. Lying suspended on her web-like hammock with one eye closed and the other opened, Anancy's head was spinning like hell and beating like thirsty steel pans as she contemplated. To begin with Anancy was not ready to give up on her culture. Moreover, she still had a lot of questions about the Open Door Bible Church... There were lots of evil dogmatic spirits in God's house. She was tempted to invite sister Kuumba from Cross Street, beyond the Hill, to drive them out and faraway...*

In my theological pilgrimage, I have been led to re-discover Anancy, the patron saint of Caribbean peoples, as a partner in digging deep into texts, lives and the existential contexts of Black people in the Caribbean and beyond. I find in Anancy a creative dialogue partner and an ideal, albeit an ambivalent voice, to use in the form of narrative or story-telling in preaching. In attempting to re-read the biblical texts alongside Caribbean textual sources and lives, I have lifted Anancy from Caribbean folklore and employed him/her as medium to converse and engage with the biblical texts from a multiplicity of angles or optics simultaneously. Anancy, moreover, has been a liberating paradigm in enabling listeners and me in the

Black communities to release some of the biblical texts from their shackles of ideological and cultural captivity.

Anancy (Anansi or Anansi) stories are told throughout the Caribbean. These can be referred to as the Caribbean version of oral wisdom writings. Anancy, the descendant of a West African deity, takes on special significance in the context of Caribbean history. Anancy is hero and villain, loveable and a trickster, wily and stupid, subtle and uncouth, God's mouthpiece and rival, and is known to live by wits. Anancy is often portrayed as shrewd, laid-back and with many of his/her tricks aimed at shaking up or pointing to oppressive situations in all aspects of life. Humour is a key characteristic as the tricks are directed towards turning upside down the systemic oppression and oppressive situations or to hint at situations where such oppression is not overtly evident.

Anancy is the great survivor who wears innumerable masks that represent the behaviour and state of affairs of human beings. Anancy takes different shapes: human form, insect and animal forms. As web-spinner taking refuge in the ceiling, Anancy weaves a calibanesque web and spins a signifying discourse, de-constructing and re-constructing language, texts and stories. Anancy is varied, ambivalent, sometimes a figure of hope, a model of how to survive and a voice of subversion. Dweller at the crossroads, inhabitant of limbo spaces, Anancy is never locked in a prescribed location or enclosure and yet is never outside it. This ambivalence is further attested by the fact that Anancy can be the person named 'peacefulness', as well as the trickster in the form of a politician, business person or preacher!

At the heart of the folklore of oppressed people is 'the ability of the weak to survive through cunning, trickery and sheer deception in an environment of the strong and powerful'.[67] Trickster narratives enable oppressed human beings to survive the overwhelming and uncontrollable agents of death in their lives. Trickster tales are closely linked to the rhetorical practice known as "'signifying' and generally serve satirical or parodic purposes by poking fun at various human behaviours. Trickster figures enjoy stirring up trouble. They are wise and their ability to laugh at the troubles they stir is related to the desire to transform/transcend a situation of hopelessness and contradictions. They have the ability to level the playing field in an instant and bring laughter or playfulness to an oppressed people in an oppressive situation.

The Bible, quintessentially a book of stories and story-telling, is replete with underdog tales and the trickster as subtype of the underdog. The trickster/underdog type, as Susan Niditch observes, 'held special appeal for the Israelite composers who shaped the tales of their ancestral heroes, for throughout its history, Israel has had a peculiar self-image as the underdog and the trickster'.[68] It is in the context of the biblical storytellers' use of trickster as a subtype that I have transposed and translated Anancy into the Christian context of theology, hermeneutics and preaching. I see no reason why members of the Black Caribbean communities cannot re-claim and re-invent the Anancy paradigm to stir the theological imaginations of folks towards *subversive* readings of the biblical stories. Anancy is an ideal dialogue partner in the much-needed exercise of re-telling/telling, re-surfacing of the narratives of Black folks.[69]

Reading/Viewing Habits: Anancy Inculturates Hermeneutics

> *The time was drawing nearer for Anancy to deliver her sermon and God spoke to Anancy: 'See Anancy, today I appoint you to root up and pull down, to shatter and to overthrow—with no weapon, but WORDS. Give them a real version or more precisely a SUB-version. It is time for a RESUR-RECTION in Sorrow Hill!' Well, it was as if Anancy's mind was cracked open. She began to dream of a new earth and new ocean of space. Anancy knew exactly what text she was going to RELEASE in the midst of the gathering…*

What is significant about Anancy's reading/interpreting habits and their relationship to preaching in the context of Black Christian communities in the UK? In a nutshell the reading habits are pragmatic, diverse and contextual. It is unapologetically Caribbean as its frame of reference is the culture, history and the diverse world-views of the region. It is an engagement with the biblical texts alongside and in dialogue with the historical and contemporary contextual experiences of Caribbean people with the purpose of making the message relevant. Throughout their history it is evident that a struggle to survive clearly runs like a thread through the lives of Caribbean people. Yet, in the midst of the scars that mark their constant struggle to survive, one finds grit, humour and a profound religiosity that befuddles the logic of domination.[70] Using Caribbean conceptual frame(s) of reference, Anancy rehearses and brings alive the biblical stories in conversation with the people and such experiences.

The Anancy paradigm allows me to freely draw on the breadth of the historical and socio-cultural context of Caribbean diversity as significant optics.[71] The departure point of Anancy reading habits reflects Caribbean concerns, values, questions and interpretative interests. Of crucial importance is the role of Caribbean cultural identity in the reading habits of Anancy. As a dialogue partner, Anancy helps me, the 'hermeneut', to use Caribbean frame(s) of reference to bring alive and relevantly appropriate a particular text.

> Clearly, the foregoing is a subjective exercise and cannot claim to be otherwise. It is premised on the fact that reading habits are contextual. It is reading from a particular perspective and the specific worldview of the

Caribbean. Consequently, there is the inbuilt recognition that this reading is offering a partial view on the texts under examination and in doing so relates to a particular context outside that of the biblical world and time.

Spinning the Thread of a Sermon—Insights from the Story-Weaver

Anancy got up, limbo in and out of the pulpit and began to weave her message: 'Friends, do I have good news for you? I love you and that is why I must throw the Book at you as Jesus did. God has placed words from Galatians (5:1) on my lips as a reminder of that day on Paradise Island when our ancestors became free people. If I make you uncomfortable, it is because I am God's ventriloquist and partner in releasing these words from the deathly cages of dogmatic absolutes in which we have chained them. I have been sent to remind you that we are called to freedom and a life-style of freeing. Look around and feast your eye-full: evil is crawling in abundance all over the MOTHERland. From Adam and Eve's few limbo hours in paradise to B&B's incursions into Iraq, human beings have never known what to do with freedom—except to gamble it away...'

So what, then, are some of the insights from Anancy/Anancyism for spinning a sermon? For the purpose of this article a few will suffice.

- Preaching is a counter-discourse to the dominant discourse of the world or the daringness to speak in voicing and sustaining an alternative talk.[72] Anancy/Anancy-ism offers one way to plumb this counter-discourse in the context of Black communities. Anancy is able to play a multiplicity of voices, creating the necessary space to enable the voices to be unearthed/surfaced. In the process the voices are liberated to imagine an alternative or counter-discourse geared towards overthrowing the powers. Interpreting/Preaching, like Caribbean stories, becomes an 'emblematic detour' reflected in a system of counter-values or *sub-version*.[73]
- Anancy, the story-weaver, can help us reclaim the central place of story-telling in preaching in Black communities. In engaging the mind and the heart, Anancy points to why something is or is not so in a circumventing way. This is done in a way that re-engages, re-reads and re-visions the biblical stories in the specific context of the experiences of Black people. In the process, the biblical stories are released from the printed texts, and characters, beginnings, endings and futures are invented and re-imagined. Anancy challenges us to trust that God will preserve the integrity of it all!
- Anancy's object is to almost obscure as she reveals. Her style depends on the sheer energy of words, sounds, songs, speeches, rhythm and the dislocation of traditional grammatical structures

for its impact on the listeners. I suggest that the Anancy paradigm is quite suited to release the potential of words, to create new words and semantics, and to imagine words (and worlds) connected to the drama of Black lives. Words and speech enable the community to re-discover the power, depth and intensity of the heart.

- Language as used by Anancy also shifts the focus from inordinate emphasis on the written text, to the faith community in conversation. It invites listening to a multiplicity of voices as the story, alongside past and present stories and history, is remembered and re-told. Meaning is characterized by fluidity and is open to negotiation. In this context, Anancy's speech/language must be a counter-discourse to ensure that it does not become oppressive! Moreover, for children of migrants from the former colonies, language takes on added dimension as they wrestle with the attempt to create identities that defy the border of the modern construct of the western nation/state. In a perpetual state of wandering from one nation to another and where home is elsewhere, language becomes a significant homeland.[74]

Limb-bow Dancing and Rain-bow Preaching

Things were fine in Sorrow Hill until Anancy opened her mouth and heart and all hell broke loose… 'Lest you forget, this freedom that we have in Christ, inside and outside the splintered ship of the Church is a space to become ourselves—a new people, a rainbow people—and not imitations and cloned copies of others.' Because some of us insist on wearing masks, we are using freedom space to shackle our sisters and brothers into poisonous moulds, sucking them dry and then spewing them out like rotten teeth. Take a good look at Sorrow Hill and the surrounding valleys, three limbo feet on either side of Butterfly River. Sorrow Hill needs a resurrection to give its inhabitants and the landscape a ghost of a chance for redemption…

Like a trickster-thief, Anancy borrows from Caribbean heritage and beyond and appropriates to release the biblical texts from bondage. Like a shaman, Anancy stirs in us a sense of mystery, a desire to make the biblical texts 'strange again' and to think of what is not. Like a seamstress, Anancy stitches or weaves together the unusual of the ordinary to release us from our narrowly locked perceptions of life and God in our midst and point towards richer ways of apprehending God and God's purposes for all of creation. Like a liberator, Anancy releases our 'versions of truth' from the neat moulds and rooms we have locked it into—from the neat crisp propositions, to discovering 'truth' in the juicy, earthy and sticky stories of our relational encounters.[75]

Onesimus's Letter to Philemon

Valentina Alexander

[In this essay, taken from *Black Theology in Britain* 4 (2000), 61–65, Valentina Alexander inhabits the psyche of the runaway slave Onesimus (who does not have a voice in the biblical narrative) and seeks to write an imaginative response to his master Philemon in light of Paul's pastoral letter to the latter. Alexander writes on behalf of Onesimus and provides an imaginative response to the slave master, in a manner that is consistent with the liberative praxis of Black theological hermeneutics.]

From Onesimus, one who was once in chains but now, by the mercy and grace of our Lord Jesus Christ, has been set free. To my once master, Philemon and the church that meets in your house, and our sister Apphia and our fellow soldier Archippus. May God our Father and the Lord Jesus Christ grant us all his wisdom and make us all to live in his bountiful light.

Brother Philemon, you are obviously aware that it has been many weeks now since I have been away from you and no doubt you are angry that something which once belonged to you has been stolen away. I am writing you this letter by way of explanation. Not because you are my master but because you are my brother and I want you to understand the huge implications of this great thing that has happened to me. You will have received the letter from Paul. He has been a dear friend and a spiritual father to me. I love him dearly and look to him as the one who gave me the chance to enter into the most wonderful relationship with our Lord and Saviour Jesus Christ. For knowing our Lord has made such a difference to my life and I pray to yours also.

Paul has written to you to plead, on my behalf, for your forgiveness and that you will welcome me back on my return to the church of Colossae. It is with deepest love and yet the strongest of convictions that I must write to you now to contest Paul's request, not that you should welcome me as a brother, but rather that you should still expect me to be your slave.

Paul has suggested that my new-found faith in the Lord should make me more useful to you as a brother and as a slave. Yet as much as I admire, respect and am grateful to him I cannot agree with his opinions in this matter. When I ran away from you all those weeks ago, I felt tired, embittered and a resentful man. It was not that you worked me too hard, or chastened me too harshly, for as masters come you have been a kind one to me. Yet in spite of your kindness I was unhappy and no matter what I tried to do to ignore my unhappiness or come to terms with it, nothing would make it depart from me.

My dearest brother Philemon, the reason I could no longer stay with you was because I could not come to terms with not being a free man. No matter how much kindness that you showed me, something in my heart continually reaffirmed that it was not right that I belong to you and that I did not belong to myself. So I ran away and by God's mercy and impeccable timing I found Paul. As you know it was he that led me to the Lord. I have accepted Christ into my life and I am no longer embittered, resentful or tired. In His great love, Christ has removed my chains and set me free. He has done for me so much more than I could have ever hoped for because now, I have something greater than ever belonging to myself now He has made me His child and I belong to Him.

So you see, my brother, why should I return to you? I can no longer be your slave. What an affront that would be to the Almighty God that He should set me free and you should choose to enslave me again. Such things can never be for those who choose to follow the path of the Mighty Liberator.

Brother Philemon, your love for God and the faith you have in the Lord Jesus is known widely amongst his people. It is my prayer for you that you should come to know this secret truth from our Lord. It is not really a secret because He has made it clear through His life and ministry. It is this, that Christ has come to set us free from our chains. If we understand this truth we cannot let ourselves be enchained again, neither our spirits, nor our bodies, nor our minds.

I wish so much to be reunited with the brothers and sisters and return to continue the Lord's work at home. This is what Paul advises and I would like to follow his advice, but as I have explained, I cannot return without making it clear to you that I should return your brother, free in the body and in the spirit to serve the Lord with you. If this is unacceptable to you in your flesh, then I pray that the Lord will make it acceptable to you by His Spirit. If you deny His Spirit, the chains will be yours and not mine, and in sorrow I shall have to find another place to live out my freedom in the Lord.

So then, my brother, may the Lord speak to your heart and lead you into all the freedom of His truth. I hope to be reconciled with you all soon.

Your brother,
Onesimus.

Several years ago a chance browse through the New Testament saw me drawn to Paul's letter to Philemon. I was familiar with this letter and it had always irked me so that in spite of my greatest efforts I could not come to terms with it. It was something about Paul's normalizing of the state of slavery, his pandering to Philemon's privileged, slave-holder status and his seeming acceptance of Christian faith and enslavement as compatible entities that rubbed me up the wrong way. This time I decided to exorcise my frustrations with Paul by putting myself in Onesimus's place and responding to both Paul and Philemon directly. The result was Onesimus's letter to Philemon that I have enclosed above.

I felt great empathy for Onesimus, an enslaved human being who had decided to demonstrate active resistance, like so many of my own fore fathers and mothers, and make his bid for freedom. I found it extremely cathartic to give a voice to this rebel who otherwise had been given no opportunity to speak for himself, and to challenge those who felt that it was reasonable and 'Christian' to condone his captivity.

Re-reading the text on the eve of a New Year and millennium, it struck me that there was much that we could do well to be reminded of in Onesimus's fabricated response and the scenario that created it. Moreover, although the original piece and my rewriting of it obviously has a Christian context, I feel that there are issues worth considering by all believers from whatever faith tradition, who have experienced oppression and have committed themselves to resisting it within their particular tradition.

First, Onesimus's theoretical response reminds us of the importance of embracing our faith as holistically liberational. His basic instinct was to obtain his freedom and this instinct was enhanced rather than hindered by his faith. Onesimus therefore discovered the centrality of a theology of liberation to his existence as a Christian. He understood that if he was to fully embrace the gospel it needed to have an impact on his spiritual consciousness but also on his social, political and personal context. His faith would not be complete without any one dimension. As people of African, Asian or Caribbean descent, if our faith is to have practical significance for us in the new contexts of struggle that the next millennium may hold, then we too must ensure that we apply it holistically, giving balance to each element of our personal and community lives.

Second, my constructed Onesimus had a finely honed sense of what was good for him. Although his particular context may not have been one of severe brutality and hardship, he was not content to settle for less than he knew God wanted for him. He believed great things of himself in relationship with God and was prepared to follow through on his convictions. He first removed himself from his oppressive context, the environment that he felt rode contrary to his innate sense of humanity. He was not an armchair warrior—a man to stand around and moan about his condition. Having physically removed himself he was then able to set about developing a liberational praxis that would then ensure that when he re-entered his former context it would be on more equal terms.

It is certainly the case that, as proclaimed men and women of faith, it is not enough to take on the veneer of emancipated people without having the conviction or the courage to make our feelings clear in whatever context of oppression we may find ourselves. Moreover it is essential that we remain alert to the ways in which our integrity as unfettered images of the Divine may be compromised by human systems and conventions that consciously or implicitly devalue that status.

Third, Onesimus's engagement in challenging dialogue is a reminder for us to do the same. Having removed himself from his immediate source of oppression—perhaps on his journey he had been able to meet with like-minded brothers and sisters and engage in some life-enhancing fellowship, discussion and strategizing—Onesimus was then able to initiate dialogue with his oppressors. This was significant because up to this point one could argue that Paul and Philemon had been dialoguing with each other about Onesimus without including him in the decisions that would then affect his faith and his life. He was therefore proactive and empowered himself and his cause by making his own representation in the form of the letter. In so doing, while asserting his needs and the cause of truth, he was also able to initiate the possibility of repentance and reconciliation. It is important to note that dialogue for us needs to occur in contexts both internal and external to our faith communities and is ultimately a key vehicle through which holistic theological liberation can take place.

Finally, Onesimus's letter reminds us of the need to apply a critical eye to our faith and to safeguard it from falling prey to our own biases. Onesimus, in my construction, was willing to confront the dominant theology of his day which appeared to suggest that it was acceptable for one believer to exploit another for his own ends simply because the one had a higher social status and significance than the other. Being a victim of oppression himself, Onesimus was able to shake up and challenge the oppressive norms of his faith community. He was a visionary who was committed to having the full revolutionary implications of his faith transform the social fabric of his society and, most importantly, his spiritual community.

If holistic and integrated liberation is the motivating prize of our faith then we must ensure that it is experienced as much by those with whom we journey as ourselves. We should also be open to those voices of dissent that may challenge us to give up our own privileges in order to return to the revolutionary origins of our faith.

As the new millennium confronts us with new and diverse versions of oppression, it is vital that people of faith are empowered with the tools to recognize, confront and redress them. Unfortunately we have no record of Onesimus's own attempt to demonstrate this practical and liberational theology; however, we have every opportunity to ensure that our own contemporary contexts tell a different story and are documented for future generations.

7   Communicating Black Theology: Anthony Reddie's Writing

There is no doubt that Anthony Reddie is the most prolific, creative and committed Black British theologian. To date, his eight volumes, numerous articles, essays and editorial leadership of *Black Theology: An International Journal* reflect the amazing combination of scholar, researcher, teacher and practitioner in Black theological discourse on a still White-dominated theological landscape. This combination affords Reddie the significant need for discerning and cultivating the art of making God-talk, specifically Black God-talk 'plain and real'. While it engages members of the academia, the combination, as reflected in Reddie's *oeuvres*,[1] adeptly unpacks complex theological issues for ordinary readers.

Significantly, Reddie writes from and inhabits a space within one of the mainline Christian traditions in Britain (Methodism). At the same time he is a Black British theologian and part of the Caribbean Diaspora in the UK. Inhabiting a multiplicity of spaces, with the ability to move between and among these, Reddie is able to unearth, give agency to, challenge, articulate, deconstruct and re-construct theological discourse as both an insider and outsider. Hence, his writings challenge Methodism, Black Churches, the largely monochrome British theological establishment and their respective apologists to re-examine their oppressive and myopic lenses through which they read and articulate theological discourse, as well as their proclivity to lock such discourse into fossilized dogmas and exactitudes.

Readers of Reddie's body of work need to be cognizant of the multiplicity of optics that informs his writing. These include the primary hermeneutical optics of 'race', the Black experience within a Diasporan context, insights from Black theology, Womanist theology, and transforming/liberating education. Further, given Reddie's agenda of de-constructing and re-constructing theological discourse on the British landscape, his works (from the inception) draw from a wide range of socio-political and theological tools. In other words, they reflect a critical, creative and constructive interdisciplinary dialogue that draws from cultural studies, Black history, sociology, education, psychology, postcolonial criticism, drama, story-telling and theology.

In suggesting that the interdisciplinary and the practical/contextual approach has always been integral to Reddie's theological articulation does not mean that there is not a development and progression in his *oeuvres*. There is. Hence, what follows in this selection of excerpts of Reddie's writings is indicative of this development.

Here, from his early interactions with both young Black people and Black elders, to his present exploration of drama as a theological tool, three major themes, among others, are ever present. First is the influence of Black theology and its liberating perspective on the Christian faith. Second is the primacy of the Black Caribbean experience as a resource for articulating and doing theology in Britain. Third is the commitment and openness to create frameworks within which Black theology can take place beyond the boundaries of academia. A related theme is that of Reddie's commitment to also explore new language(s) for Black theological discourse.

As noted, Reddie's earliest work[2] was already attempting to put into practice the tenets of this theological perspective. Here, Reddie used experiential exercises, drama and Black history as tools for Christian education in inner-city churches. In this way, young Black people were able to see their own experiences, and those of their forebears, affirmed and celebrated, whilst exploring and participating in the Christian faith. Though Reddie has since widened considerably the remit of his work, this commitment to creating accessible contexts in which God-talk can take place has continued through to his most recent publications, which more explicitly employ drama as a participative method for facilitating theological reflection and discourse. Acting out of the script engenders a participative approach to God-talk and a healthy dialectic between text and performance/performer or player.

To borrow a term from Reddie, there is a *movement*, or more correctly, there are *movements* in his theological articulation. And, it is difficult to 'lock down' or 'to bring closure to *movement*'. This is liberating. It is where Reddie—Black British Yorkshire African Caribbean Jamaican male—is *walking the talk*.

Faith, Stories and the Experience of Black Elders

Anthony Reddie

[This extract is from *Faith, Stories and the Experience of Black Elders* (London and Philadelphia: Jessica Kingsley, 2001), 14–26, 101–110. In this, his third sole authored book, he investigates the oral sources of Black experience, in order to use these traditions to affirm Black elders living in Britain, and to educate their young counterparts for the future journeys that await them. The reflection here is around a sketch, *Looking Ahead*, which the author wrote as part of this reflection, but is not included in this extract.]

The Birmingham Initiative (1995–1999) was a Methodist inspired, ecumenical research project that was concerned with the Christian Education and nurture of African Caribbean children in inner-city churches in

Birmingham. Whilst the work of the project was concerned primarily with the teaching and learning of the Christian faith amongst Black children, it was clear from the start that this work needed to be earthed within the experiences of the wider framework of Black family life. One could not attempt to work with Black children without reference being made to the older members of the family. These older members, often grandparents, were and continue to remain the bedrock upon which Black family life is lived in twentieth and twenty-first century Britain.

Given the initial focus of the research, it was not possible to investigate the claims and the importance of Black elders in their own right. At the back of my mind, however, there lay a dormant thought, namely, that this work must not be forgotten or allowed to disappear.

The 'Windrush' generation that are at the heart of this book are now in their dotage. As the ravages of time and chronology exercise their inevitable judgement, many of these pioneers are returning home. Some, to their cultural and spiritual home back in the Caribbean and in Africa; others, to the ancestral home in the next life. Whichever of the two eventualities has befallen them, it is vitally important that we acknowledge and affirm the achievements and the steadfastness of these epic heroes and heroines of an almost forgotten time. For without their courageous spirit, many of my peers and I would not be here today with the opportunity to express our experiences in writing. I am painfully aware of the irony that tinges the whole enterprise of this book. I am writing (and indeed have the opportunity to write) about the experiences of my elders and forebears, who themselves were often denied the opportunity to tell their own story: that of singing the Lord's song in a strange land.

This book, in one sense, has emerged at a strange time. In many respects, the most opportune time for the celebration of the Black presence in Britain seemed to be some years ago back in 1998. 1998 was a momentous year for this country, as we celebrated the fiftieth anniversary of the landing of the *S.S. Empire Windrush*. This ocean liner brought the first post-war migrants from the Caribbean to Britain. In the following two decades, close to a million people would join them. Our presence has enlivened a monochrome country.

But 1998 has gone and with it the plethora of television programmes, books and exhibitions that were commissioned, often for the first time, to mark our presence. If our moment in the sun has gone, why is this book being published now? I believe there are two reasons that make this publication a timely one. First, we need to be reminded, continually, that the presence, contributions and achievements of Black people, particularly Black elders, are ongoing ones. They cannot and should not be restricted to one-off events in the nation's consciousness. Are we to wait another fifty years for our next moment in the sun? The recognition of Black people in Britain and within the church during 1998 was an important moment for us all. Black people have not suddenly disappeared, however, and our presence needs to be noted and affirmed on a continual basis. Hence, the timely nature of this book.

Secondly, I feel this book makes an important contribution to the growing literature on the Black presence in Britain. Whilst a number of publications have been written, not least of all as a part of the 'Windrush' celebrations, very few of these pieces have dealt with the religious and spiritual dimension of Black people. Black people are incurably religious. A belief in powers higher than the temporal, mortal realm of humankind lies at the very heart of our understanding and relationship to the created world order. The struggles of our ancestors in Africa and in the Caribbean were forged in relationship with a belief in the benevolent power of the Creator. The stories of our travails and triumphs are contained in the narratives of these people throughout the ages.

Where It All Began

The occasion that prompted me to write the dramatic sketch *Looking Ahead* was the impending visit of the then Vice-President of the Methodist Conference, Ivan Weekes. Ivan was scheduled to attend my home church, Moseley Road Methodist, for a (Birmingham) District celebration event, as part of his semi-nomadic wanderings around the Methodist Church for that year. I, along with a group of young adults at the church, was charged with the responsibility of devising a programme of entertainment for that evening.

Very early in the planning stage, I was asked if I could write three short dramatic sketches, based upon the experiences of Black people in Britain. After much thought, I decided to base my pieces on the past, present and, hopefully, future experiences of Black people living in Britain. In the development of my writing, these pieces were of huge significance, for they were the first attempts to write explicitly about Black people. Prior to this, I had usually written my scripts and stories from what I have termed a 'spurious universalism'. By using this term, I mean to suggest that my writing was notionally geared to everyone and the characters within the pieces were largely nondescript, vague and very, very fictional. There was no context, no 'interior' to these stories and the people who populated them. There were no accents, no quirks of behaviour and no cultural reference points by which you might exclaim 'I know that person'. All that changed when I wrote *Looking Ahead*. For the first time, I began to write about people, situations and contexts that were familiar to me. These people were my people. Their stories were my stories.

When I wrote *Looking Ahead*, I drew upon the stories and anecdotes of my parents, aunties and uncles, and the wonderful people who inhabit my church, many of whom had become almost second parents to me since my own birth parents returned to the Caribbean in 1991. I looked into the eyes of these individuals, drew upon my memories and recollections, and began to write. What emerged is *Looking Ahead*. Were it not for *Looking Ahead* and this seismic breakthrough, there would have been no *Growing into Hope* and a cultural, Black perspective on Christian education, practical theology and spirituality, which emerged through the research and writing I undertook with the Birmingham Initiative.

Looking Ahead encapsulates what, for many, were the formative experiences of being Black, largely coming from the Caribbean, and living in Britain in the late 1950s and early '60s. The sketch touches upon a moment in time for that group of people who are now termed *The Windrush generation*.[3]

The importance of these individuals to the life of my own church and that of the many inner-city churches up and down the country is evidenced by the changing complexion of these institutions over the past twenty-five years. It has come increasingly the case that, were it not for the forbearance, faith and obstinacy of these individuals, such traditions as Methodist, Anglican, Baptist and United Reformed would no longer have any worshipping congregations in inner-city areas in Britain. The greater majority of these congregations are comprised of these older, fiercely proud, yet supremely loving and accommodating Black people, many of whom came to Britain from the Caribbean in the 1950s and '60s. These individuals, who were once overlooked and often despised, have now become the fulcrum and bedrock of these churches. 'The stone that the builders refused has now become the head cornerstone'.

Looking Ahead serves as an introduction to this book and a reminder to this country and the many churches and inner-city faith communities within these shores of the struggles of older Black people. In order to understand the stories of faith and experience, one needs to have a sense of the contexts from which these narratives have emerged. These contexts are ones of poverty, struggle, pain, hardship, and a grim determination to create a better life for one's offspring. When one of the characters in the sketch remarks that they came to Britain in order that their children might have greater opportunities than what was afforded them, herein lies one of the most basic truths of Black migration for the past 150 years. People have moved in order to create a new life for themselves and their children. People have left homes, loved ones, familiar spaces and worlds, moving to new pastures, in order that a new existence might become a reality. African and Caribbean people have never been 'little Islanders' or 'little villagers'. We are people who, from the smallness of our immediate surroundings, have always envisaged a huge world. We have been accompanied on our travels by a huge God, as we have moved from one context to another, in our struggles to create the 'new' in strange, often unpromising, environments.[4] The experiences of these older Black people are hugely important, for they provide the foundation for the post-Second World War mass Black presence in Britain.

To understand the present, we need to return to the past—to return to the era of the 1950s and '60s, and the time of early struggle. In many respects, we need to retreat even further back in time. We need to travel to the Caribbean. In the final analysis, we need to return to the continent of Africa. For the stories of faith and experience to which you will be exposed have their origins in Africa, in the era that predates slavery. So we need to travel back into the past—to engage in a process of reverse time-travel […]

Implications for the Work with Elders in Britain

A number of years ago, prior to my involvement with the Birmingham Initiative, I worked for a short time within a social services community care team for the elderly. As a social work assistant I visited a number of elders in their homes and in social-services-run residential homes. Given the catchment area covered by this team, I came into contact with a number of Black elders, the majority of whom had travelled from the Caribbean to Britain in the 1950s and 1960s. Whilst a number of the individuals I met seemed relatively contented with the situation and circumstances in which they found themselves, a larger proportion were somewhat dissatisfied and disaffected.

The latter were troubled at the sense of isolation and marginalization they were experiencing at this late stage of their life. Many of them had not come to Britain in order to grow old, or to die. A number of these individuals harboured intense hopes of returning to their homeland to spend their remaining years in the sunshine idyll of their youth. Given that many had come from relatively small rural communities in the Caribbean, the shock (for some) and disappointment of feeling isolated in their own home or in a residential home was a heavy psychological burden to bear.

The importance of this work, for the country as a whole, but particularly for those agencies charged with working alongside Black elders, is the necessity of taking seriously the wisdom and experience of these individuals. If Britain pays scant regard to older white people, what, then, will be the fate of the increasing number of Black elders? They belong to the Windrush generation that has grown old in this country, and for an increasing number the completion of their life will be in this country also. What of them? How can British society as a whole, including the church and her many partner agencies, meet the challenge of working creatively with Black elders? This research work has highlighted a number of important themes.

First was the importance of enabling Black people to tell their story. These are stories of faith and experience that have given meaning to, and defined the existence of, many Black elders. They are the stories of struggle. The stories of determination and overcoming. Stories that have shaped the Black post-Second World War experience in Britain. Stories that have enabled me to be here today undertaking this work. How can we affirm these stories, and what will be the effect of our doing so?

One of the most striking things to emerge from this section of my research was the sense of affirmation and confidence many of these individuals gained simply from the fact that an 'official' person wanted to converse with them about their experiences. I remember one woman saying, 'Why do you want to talk to me? Me is not anyone special.' I countered, 'You are special, because your story is special. You're special to God, so it is an honour for me to speak with you'.

The challenge for all agencies working alongside and with Black elders is to find ways in which they can encourage these individuals to share their stories of faith and experience. The oral traditions of people of African descent have their origins in Africa. Many of the traditions and the cultures that have shaped their lives are thousands of years old. Yet because of the effects of racism and marginalization, the manifestations of these oral traditions, contained in the form of stories of faith and experience, have rarely been given an opportunity to be expressed and affirmed in a public setting. Often the liturgies and theological reflections that are reflective of the mission and the ministry of the church are so grounded within a Eurocentric framework that they exclude the experiences and cultures of Black people.

In order to connect emotionally, spiritually and psychologically with Black people, it is essential to understand the world-view that influences and, in part, defines people of African descent. From my interaction with these elders I have seen that they are profoundly religious people. The blandishments of secularism and humanism have not penetrated their existence. The world of the spirit and the evidence of their spirituality and Christian convictions are very publicly on display.

A criticism that can be levelled at a number of organizations and agencies in their attempts to work with Black elders is that their practice rests upon social-scientific theories and models which are secular in character. Whilst there are many merits to this approach, its very perspective and the assumptions that follow from it are often at variance with the experiences and spirituality of the very people they are attempting to serve. One cannot work effectively with Black elders unless there is an appreciation of the theistic grounding of their existence. To put it bluntly, you cannot divorce Black people from God.

For those agencies that do acknowledge the theistic element, it is not sufficient to develop liturgies and theological reflection which assume that White European perspectives are the norm. Whilst these Eurocentric notions of God and the accompanying expression of the Christian faith and spirituality are more in keeping with African concepts of existence than, seemingly, social-scientific secularism, they nonetheless still fail to engage meaningfully with Black experience. Agencies such as the Church and her many sister organizations need to become conversant with the lived experience and the folk theologies of people of African descent.[5] To understand Black elders, one needs to understand the world from which they have emerged and the stories of faith and experience that have shaped them. By acknowledging oral traditions that have given rise to these stories, and the historical sources and experiences from which they have emerged, agencies will become more effective in their work. Of equal importance will be the affirmation and self-esteem Black elders will derive from having an opportunity to share their stories of faith and experience.

How to Facilitate the Stories and Experiences of Black Elders?

What I offer here are only examples and suggestions.

The most important way in which individuals, agencies and organizations can encourage and gain access to these stories and experiences is through the medium of pastoral care. There are a number of publications that can assist practitioners in gaining a greater understanding of the emotional, spiritual and psychological needs of Black people.

Without wishing to lose ourselves in great detail, for this is a somewhat complicated matter, practitioners and policy makers need to be aware of a crucial caveat when dealing with this issue. Due to the effects of racialized oppression and marginalization, many Black people may well be suspicious or even reluctant to talk in depth about personal stories or experiences. This reluctance will be exacerbated if the person seeking to initiate or facilitate the conversation is a White European. The sense of alienation and disaffection felt by Black people over the past five hundred years (from our forced removal and captivity in slavery, through to the period of British/European colonialism and imperialism of the more recent past) has manifested itself in a number of ways. One particular manifestation has been the tendency of Black people to submerge or disguise aspects of their existence and experience from the wider world which, often dominated by White people and their concerns, was viewed with suspicion. In order to gain access to those experiences and stories, one will need to exercise a great deal of patience. It may take some time for Black elders to become familiar with the notion of sharing their stories. Many of them may not have had a previous opportunity to share their experiences with people outside of their immediate circle.

Practitioners will need to display humility and exude a sense of genuineness and integrity when engaging with Black elders. In time, however, when a rapport has been established, individuals who once might have been quite diffident may become sufficiently confident to share their stories of faith and experience.

In addition to patience, one will need to develop the skill of persistence. It may well be the case that people who have been overlooked and marginalized for some length of time will view attempts to get them to share aspects of their lives with some suspicion. Some may hold the view that, 'By their fruits you shall know them'—if this person really wants to hear my story, then they will ask again. Black people are more than familiar with the tokenistic, cursory appeal to our better natures, which is underpinned by nothing more than paternalistic good intentions and a placating of one's conscience. Too many times I have heard the rather pathetic excuse, 'Well, I asked him or her.' Yes, you did. But if that person has been made to feel invisible and worthless for countless numbers of years, why should they suddenly wish to speak with you? Are they to be grateful? Are you really that important? The need for persistence can be irritating and time-consuming, but nevertheless, it is the only approach that will attest to one's genuineness and integrity.

In attempting to encourage Black elders to share aspects of their experiences, perhaps the most significant event in the course of my research within the Birmingham Initiative was the 'Storytelling Festival'. This event was held at my home church, Moseley Road Methodist Church in Birmingham, to mark the end of my work with the project. The stories from the many participants who took part in this final stage were acknowledged and affirmed in a more public setting, within a storytelling festival. The festival was organized by me and the many people who had played an active part in the research. The churches associated with the project were invited to this community evening. Many of the participants who had made a significant contribution to the research were present and shared a number of short extracts from the intergenerational conversations they had undertaken with me.

Nobodies to Somebodies: A Practical Theology for Liberation and Education

[These extracts are taken from chapters 1 and 3 of *Nobodies to Somebodies: A Practical Theology for Liberation and Education* (Peterborough: Epworth Press, 2003), 19–20, 73–84, 86–87, 90–92. A significant contribution of the 'early' Reddie literary output is his working on a new model of Christian Education that affirms the relationship between Black theology and education. Reddie's model is specifically informed by and reflects the needs of Black children and young people (of African-Caribbean ancestry) living in Britain and draws on the disciplines of Black, Womanist and liberation theologies and transforming education. What follows in this section are excerpts taken from Reddie's fourth sole authored book. This input is located in the broader thrust of Reddie's project of presenting a systematic approach to the teaching and learning of the Christian faith from a Black liberation perspective.]

Black Youth and Questions of Identity

An important issue that is often hidden, but remains a vital concern when discussing the Christian Education of Black youth, is the issue of Black identity. It is important that commentators are conscious of the individual struggles of Black people to define and embrace their Blackness. Without such awareness there is, I believe, limited scope for a clear and precise understanding of the necessity for a specific, Black, African-centred model of Christian Education. One must create strategies and teaching methods that assist Black people in their knowledge of self and the factors that have shaped their existence and experience.

As Clarice Nelson accurately surmises, the discovery of Black selfhood is primarily an exercise in justice, and, as such, is a theological task. She writes:

> This greater voice of protest is yet to come about and will, probably, not come until a theology, a Black theology relevant to the Black British situation, is developed.[6]

The importance and necessity for Black theology and its relevance to Christian Education, particularly as this discipline relates to Black youth, will be explored more fully in the second chapter of this book. At this point it is sufficient to say that Black theology has been of immense importance to this work. Black theology has served as the essential theological tool and the starting point for the struggle to create a new model for the Christian Education of Black people in Britain.

One of the inherent difficulties in attempting to understand the nature of the identity crisis amongst Black youth is the danger of seeing their condition as being abnormal. This tendency to view Black youth as if there is something wrong with them often leads to particular roles being imposed upon this section of British society. Such roles are based on the often unspoken assumption that deviancy and dysfunctional behaviour is inextricably bound up with Black youth. Odida Quamina has commented on this tendency in his analysis of the media and its treatment of Black people.[7] This tendency to demonize Black people is not a new phenomenon. Writing over twenty-five years ago, Hartman and Hubbard commented on the pernicious nature of the media's treatment of Black people. The authors referred to the ways in which newspapers tend to report only the negative aspects of Black life in Britain. This negative form of representation is based on particular forms of social construction in which Black people are presented as essentially the problem.[8] Similarly, with notions of identity crisis amongst Black youth, one must resist the alluring temptation to use such sociological and cultural theories to attack them. [...]

The Creation of *Growing into Hope*: An Example of a Black Christian Education of Liberation

Central to the aim of creating a new model for the Christian Education of Black youth is the creation of an African-centred scheme of teaching and learning. In this section, I examine the creative process that gave rise to *Growing into Hope*. I wish to demonstrate how many of the central ideas of Black and Womanist theology, coupled with Transformative education, informed this practical scheme for Christian Education. I intend to show the relationship and the creative tensions that exist between theory and practice.

In seeking to create this Black liberating Christian Education teaching and learning scheme, I was mindful of the associated difficulties of trying to convert theoretical concepts into models of good practice. Within the literature relating to Black Christian Education there have been relatively few instances of academic study giving rise to examples of practical schemes of teaching and learning.

In creating this curriculum I intended to combine the philosophical and ideological imperatives of Black and Womanist Theology[9] with the progressive notions of a liberating education. It was my hope to create a relevant, practical theology for inner-city churches in Britain. This enterprise was breaking new ground from the outset.

Black theological reflection as the content of the two books

In describing the creative process that gave rise to *Growing into Hope*, I have chosen to highlight the *Advent* (in volume one) and *Pentecost* (volume two) sections of the programme. These sections were the earliest attempts at turning Black theological thought and Christian Educational theory into practical teaching and learning material. While *Growing into Hope* was developed in five sections, the theological and educational process by which these two books were created relates most closely to the *Advent* and *Pentecost* sections. The later parts of the programme reflect the process that was initially devised, and which is described at this point in the book.

The task began with my reading the seminal work of James Cone. Black theology has sought to use the Black experience as an antenna for listening to Scripture and testing the truth claims of White theological discourse. In doing so, it has provided an invaluable framework by which Black people might seek to understand, in a more informed manner, their existence and their experience. A better understanding of the world in which Black people live provides opportunities for a greater engagement with the necessary tools that can be used to achieve freedom.[10]

Using a Black interpretative framework

Black theology provided the chief resource for the content of the curriculum. It was only after I had read and studied the writings of Black theologians that I began to appreciate more fully their method of re-reading Biblical texts and re-interpreting them for a different context or setting. That is, looking at Biblical texts again in order that they might speak to a different time and location from the one in which they originally emerged. This process is done by reflecting on the text in a self-conscious way, in the light of Black experience. This process of re-reading texts for a different setting (re-contextualization) was essential to the content and process of the curriculum and owed much to the pioneering work of the renowned African American scholar, Cain Hope Felder. Felder, in an important article on this crucial process of interpretation, writes

> The implication is that, whatever one may wish to say about the Bible, there
> is a need for a disciplined scepticism regarding western appropriations.[11]

This questioning approach to western methods of interpretation (a 'hermeneutic of suspicion') not only challenges and criticizes the norms and approaches of White Eurocentric scholars, but also asserts an alternative perspective that recognizes and affirms Black experience. Felder highlights particular texts that attest to the significance of Africa and people of African ancestry. The texts that he highlights illustrate the central place of Black people in the ongoing story of God's interaction with God's people. The psychological and emotional impact of this insight upon Black people, particularly Black youth, has been emphasized by Grant Shockley.[12]

The importance of Black Biblical interpretation is highlighted to even greater effect by Felder and others in a 1991 publication that has greatly influenced a number of theologians and Christian educators on both sides of the Atlantic.[13] These important contributions to Biblical studies, and the advancement of Black methods of interpretation (or hermeneutic), have opened up the Bible for people of African descent. It was through the influence of these writers, amongst many others, that I gained the confidence to engage in Black theological reflection. This confidence is displayed in the opening reflections in each new section of *Growing into Hope*. These small theological pieces were, in effect, Black Biblical interpretation linked to the themes of Black experience and existence.

The writing of this curriculum was also demonstrably influenced by my exposure to the *African Heritage Study Bible* (AHSB),[14] edited by Felder. The major portion of the Bible highlights themes and concepts that resonate with African cultures and experience as they arise within the Hebrew and Greek texts. When writing the early sections of Advent week three on the theme of *Heroes*, I decided to focus on the figure of John the Baptist.[15] The AHSB describes John the Baptist as 'An Afro-Asiatic or Edenic wilderness prophet.'[16] Identification of John the Baptist as an Afro-Asiatic man led me to use further material from the AHSB to develop this theme on *Heroes*. The section on *The Early Martyrdom of African Christians*[17] enabled me to create a link between this prototypical Biblical character and more modern heroes of African descent.

I used the figures of John the Baptist and more contemporary Black heroes to describe clearly the principles and means by which Black people have been able to surmount the oppressive situations that have confronted them. The resulting learning and affirmation for Black youth is hopefully self-explanatory.

A Black Christian Education of Liberation and the Bible Revisited

A number of these scholars have argued strongly for the need for Black people to engage with Biblical texts. They emphasize the need for Black youth to enter into dialogue with Scripture in order that their own experiences can be validated. This dialogue can help such individuals to see the relevance of Biblical material to the concrete realities of their lives. Among these, I note the efforts of Jeffrey Stinehelfer[18] and Peter McCarey.[19] Exposure to these attempts empowered me to adopt a similar approach in *Growing into Hope*. In volume two in the section on Pentecost, I scripted a short dramatic piece, re-writing the Pentecost narrative.[20] This sketch, entitled 'All Change', re-tells the Pentecost event in an alternative fashion using Jamaican Creole and elements of Black vernacular and speech patterns familiar to Black youth. The sketch sought to take seriously Earl Beckles' claim that Black speech patterns and dialects are not only vital components of Black identities, but also infer meaning, relatedness and affirmation.[21]

'Black English', according to Massey and Denton,[22] is not a corrupt derivation of standard received English, but an important idiom in its own right. Similarly, Carol Tomlin asserts that 'Black language' is an essential component in the identity formation and cultural practices of African peoples in the diaspora.[23] Consequently, the teaching and learning process needs to recognize ways of speaking if it is to engage successfully with children of African descent. Failure to incorporate these facets of African life leads to a loss of self-esteem and confidence amongst Black youth.[24]

Grant Shockley believes that self-esteem is vital to the development of Black youth. He argues that the practice of Christian Education should be linked to the ongoing experience of Black people.[25] Shockley highlights the inherent dynamism of Black Church worship and details the means by which this force interacts with an experience to create the raw materials for liberation.[26] The direct influence of Shockley's writings can be seen in *Growing into Hope* in the section written for the Sunday after Pentecost.[27] The theme for that Sunday is 'All Together'. In choosing this theme I wanted to highlight the importance of community, inter-dependence and the communitarian ethic amongst Black people. This corporate oneness, inspired by the Spirit of God, has enabled Black people of the African diaspora to surmount the oppressive situations that have confronted them. The writings of Shockley and others alerted me to the historical experiences of struggle, which found an antidote in corporate and collective response. These inter-communal responses have their origins in Africa.[28]

Joseph Crockett has undertaken some highly influential work that approaches the Bible from a Black perspective.[29] Crockett attempts to highlight themes within Scripture that reflect the African American experience since the era of slavery. When attempting to write the second week's material in the Advent section,[30] I was influenced greatly by Crockett's approach. He links the experience of 'Exile' of the African-American community with Psalm 137, which is seen as a primary example for the exile of the African diaspora.[31] His identification with Psalm 137 led me to use this passage in the thematic material for creating a Black Christian Education of Liberation. I was conscious of the historic resonance of this passage within diasporan African communities—one need only to reflect upon the traditional Black spiritual 'By the Rivers of Babylon', taken directly from Psalm 137, to see the importance of this theme.[32]

Henry Mitchell suggests that the development of Black Christianity which began in the era of slavery depended on oral transmission, with basic beliefs being formed and received through succeeding generations. This process of oral transmission is similar to the oral transmission of Bible stories and their development.[33] I adapted his persuasive argument to create material that looked directly at the storytelling element within the lives of Black communities in the diaspora.[34] Influenced by Mitchell, I used the notion of inter-generational storytelling in the Black community to link Psalm 137 to the Black experience of 'Exile' and migration.[35]

I was also influenced by Lawrence Jones, who argues that the notion of *hope* is an indispensable component of human existence and occupies even greater significance within the life experiences and expectations of dispossessed, minority communities.[36] I used his ideas to develop the theme for the first Sunday's material in the Advent section.[37] His work provided the main title for the completed work when it was published. The overall theme for this curriculum is 'hope'. A hope grounded in the strivings of oppressed Black people in every part of the world.

Developing the Teaching Strategy of the Two Books

I adopted a thematic approach because of my knowledge of, and commitment to, Black theology. In addition to the need to pay attention to this area, it was necessary to create a progressive teaching strategy that would bring this curriculum to life. Experience had shown me that worthy, self-righteous models of teaching which lend themselves to satisfying adults tend to have a nullifying effect upon the younger people for whom such schemes are created. This programme needed to possess a teaching strategy that would entice and attract Black youth to want to learn and develop. This approach would challenge, inspire and excite Black youth into a dialogical process, i.e. one where the teacher and learner share in the educational act.

The influence of Paulo Freire

Freire gave me a rationale and a method for creating appropriate strategies for teaching marginalized and disaffected Black youth. Freire argued that for oppressed people to be free, they must first recognize the condition in which they find themselves. One of the primary ways in which the oppressor controls the actions of the oppressed is by restricting the thinking of the oppressed.[38] Hence, the oppressed need to recognize the situation in which they find themselves before liberation can become a reality. This process of coming to an informed knowledge of one's condition, and the accompanying process of developing the necessary tools for liberation, has been termed by Freire as 'Conscientization'.[39] [...]

The force of Freire's writings had a profound influence upon the philosophy of education that underpins the teaching strategy of *Growing into Hope*. [...] Informed by this critical theory, I decided that the curriculum should adopt an approach which places historical analysis alongside contemporary situations.

Transformative education

In a more recent publication Freire, in partnership with Ira Shor, reflects upon the teaching and learning process as they proceed to highlight the major themes and issues in what they term 'transformative education'.[40] [...] They say that this form of teaching possesses the power to change the relationship between the self, external knowledge, and the wider society. This relationship in which there is a struggle for truth has the potential not only to transform the classroom and the resulting practice of the teacher, but also contains the seeds for a wider transformation.[41] [...]

James Banks provides a number of examples of how transformative teaching can enliven history and enable Black and minority ethnic students to reclaim their history. This type of teaching also enables them to see their historical roots and cultural experiences as being the norm and not some marginal distanced reality.[42] Banks argues that this kind of education enables Black students to become critically aware of how knowledge is constructed, and shows up the ways in which the voices of the marginalized and the oppressed are silenced.[43]

The example that Banks provides is instructive, for it relates directly to specific points in *Growing into Hope*. In this programme, Black youth are exposed to historical events and are presented with opportunities to engage in a dialogue which helps them to reshape their reality. In the section on Pentecost, the material relating to the second week (written for the oldest group) refers to the work of Harriet Tubman and Rosa Parks. Events from recent American history are placed alongside the contemporary struggles in the collective and corporate experiences of African Caribbean people living in Britain.[44]

Banks's assertions find accord with bell hooks,[45] who argues that this approach to teaching can liberate the thinking and the voices of women. This process gives rise to distinctive forms of knowledge and a re-shaping of reality that is neither conditioned nor silenced by the normative power of patriarchy.[46] Mindful of the charge of patriarchy and the male-dominated perspective that pervades a good deal of the content of most Christian Education material, I felt it important that positive images of women are included as core elements in the curriculum.[47]

Various sections of the programme are based on the assumption that dialogue is essential for effective teaching. In the first instance, dialogue operates as a specific teaching strategy. This approach invites adult leaders to use dialogue in their ongoing work. Secondly, dialogue is introduced at different points in the curriculum materials, through dramatic readings and sketches. These interactive forms of education provided Black youth with opportunities to become actors in both the figurative and the literal sense within the teaching and learning process.[48] [...]

My attempt to devise a curriculum that uses Freire's ideas in a practical, workable manner presented me with a challenge. Unlike Hope and Timmel's work,[49] mine had the additional challenge of working with children, some as young as five.

Moving beyond Freire—Black theology meets transformative education

A number of writers, particularly Grant Shockley, reminded me that Christian Education should be regarded as a theological discipline and not purely a social-scientific one. Shockley argues that if one wishes to develop a liberating model of Christian Education for Black people one needs to go beyond Paulo Freire.[50] Shockley outlines a five-stage programme for such a liberating model. This model uses not only educational theory, but clearly engages with Black theological ideas. It assumes that the God of love is involved in the struggles of oppressed and marginalized peoples. While Freire's work has provided an excellent ideological teaching strategy for the task of educating marginalized and oppressed peoples, it lacks a coherent theological rationale. He hints at the work of God, but does not explore this in an overt fashion. In many respects, his work is very human centred, with little or no conception of the transcendent nature of God manifested in the Holy Spirit, and God's continued involvement with humankind.[51]

In his theological argument for a programme of Black Christian Education, Shockley states that:

> The center of education for liberation occurs when persons are able to utilize their capacities of self-transcendence to evaluate reality, and as subjects, of naming the world instead of being named by it.[52]

This point is crucial. It inspired me to see why self-definition is an essential core component of the practical curriculum I sought to devise. There are a number of occasions in which this expressed intent is manifested within *Growing into Hope*. The most explicit example can be found in the section on Advent week one, in the material for the oldest group.[53] I wanted to find a practical way of dealing with issues of self-definition. I tried to achieve this through an exercise that portrays graphically how oppressed and marginalized people have their world defined for them. The exercise involves Black young people taking on the role of objects.

Shockley's vision for Christian Education finds its source in Black theology. He shares Black theology's view that God is predisposed towards poor and marginalized people.[54] This thinking led me to use Black theology to highlight the liberating impulse of the Gospel.[55] Shockley argues that appropriate Christian Education for people of African descent should be anchored to the realities of their experience. [...]

The Writing of *Growing into Hope*—a Balance between Idealism and Pragmatism

Christian Education programmes in many inner-city churches in Britain lack resources (both human and financial) and cater for decreasing numbers. A number of Junior Churches and Sunday Schools in Britain are still wedded emotionally to the halcyon days of the past. This was a seemingly prosperous time when the numbers of children attending church were considerably higher than is presently the case, and the effectiveness of Christian Education could be seen in the weekly 'conversions' to Christ.[56]

As one surveys the scene of Junior Church and Sunday School in many churches in Britain today, their halcyon days are clearly past. In attempting to create a curriculum that would have an impact upon the practice of Christian Education amongst Black youth, I was mindful of the historical resonance of the past that has clouded the perceptions of generations of Junior Church and Sunday School leaders.[57]

In addition to this difficulty, there was the inherently conservative nature of many of the older African Caribbean worshippers in the inner-city churches, where the material would be piloted. Many of these older people had migrated from the Caribbean, in the mass post-Second World War movement of the 1950s and '60s, having first been exposed to the full force of colonial miseducation. These older African Caribbean people had received the biased, self-serving teachings of British imperialism, which asserted the superiority of European aesthetics and culture. The pigmentation of Black people was disparaged in favour of White, which was depicted as being synonymous with purity and 'civilization'.[58]

My knowledge of the social and cultural environment, in which these older individuals had been nurtured, persuaded me that a very radical and overtly political Christian Education curriculum would alienate and frighten them. I could not afford to alienate this important group. These individuals are the primary influences upon Black youth in their church attendance and development of faith.[59] Many of the Black young people who are the focus of this study would not attend Church were it not for the continued diligence and faithfulness of these ageing believers from the Caribbean. In short, the challenge that faced me, in the writing of *Growing into Hope*, lay between the two extremes of principle and pragmatism.

The former represents the type of teaching and learning scheme that, as a principled position, refuses either to compromise or to acknowledge the inherent insecurities or weakness of the people (Black and White) who will use it. The result of such a stance is often a low take-up of the material. The latter is indicative of a position, which, in its attempt to engage with the potential audience, jettisons all the basic principles and ideas that lie at the heart of what one might term 'best practice'. This approach may lead to high demand and subsequent usage, but little if any integrity exists within the text itself. *Growing into Hope* needed to be principled and pragmatic. The pragmatism of which I have just spoken was juxtaposed with the need to remain faithful to the important sources that underpin this scheme of teaching and learning.

Another significant difficulty was the fact that the majority of the adult leaders who would be charged with the task of implementing *Growing into Hope* were White. My concerns regarding this group were somewhat similar to those stated previously. Namely, that a radical teaching strategy might alienate or disempower the very group I was dependent upon to implement the material in these inner-city churches.

Growing into Hope does not purport to be the ideal model or example for the Christian Education of Black young people or adults. The material was not written within a hermetically sealed, controlled environment. My knowledge of Black youth, and the insecurity and inhibitions of the adult leaders and the guardians who support these individuals in their Christian nurture, affected the writing of this experimental material.

Acting in Solidarity: *Black Voices*

[This extract is taken from *Acting in Solidarity* (London: Darton, Longman and Todd, 2005), 109–119. At the beginning of his book, Reddie outlines an approach to re-setting and interpreting the Bible from a Black, Jamaican/African Caribbean context. In that dramatic reading, the author commented on some of the negative aspects of Black cultural values and life. This extract takes up this issue even further, by looking at the different positions and values adopted by various people within diasporan Black British communities. Reddie does this by way of constructing a fictional social gathering—a party, or in Black speak, a 'dance', at which a variety of people and voices are present.]

One of the challenges facing Black theologians and cultural commentators is the necessity to develop a more honest and holistic view of Black cultures and the practices that exist within various Black communities. Too often, Black scholars (myself included) have concentrated our efforts (quite rightly, for the most part) on the external challenges that have confronted us, such as racism for example, with less emphasis being given to the internal issues and struggles that exist within our own communities.

For example, when seeking to describe and illustrate Black community living, great emphasis has been placed on the examples of solidarity and community. The many examples of homogeneity or sameness have been highlighted. This is particularly the case when scholars have spoken about Black and Black majority churches.[60] Our tendency to view Black communities as monolithic has meant that the diverse range of experiences and values that exist within the overall whole tends to be either downplayed or ignored altogether. I have addressed some aspects of this tendency to mythologize or romanticize aspects of Black culture in my previous book.[61]

On occasions, there is a type of hierarchy of 'Blackness' in Black communities, where some people are judged as belonging in a more complete fashion than others. There are many Black people who have been accused of not 'really being Black' or not being 'Black enough'.[62] Scholars such as Michael Eric Dyson[63] Kobena Mercer[64] and, most notably, Victor Anderson[65] have challenged us to see beyond the often strait-jacketed interpretations we place on Black cultural expression and lived experience. Anderson, in particular, has challenged the way in which Black religious, cultural critics have wanted to acknowledge only the 'positive aspects' of Black life, and have often sought to overlook or ignore those elements of which we are not so proud.[66] As Anderson reminds us, we cannot all be saints, heroes and 'trailblazers'.

Similarly, within the Biblical witness, there are as many flawed examples of humanity and 'fallenness', through which God's redemptive work is done, as there are so-called heroes and those of supposedly blameless character—King David is an obvious candidate that springs to mind in terms of the former. Michael Eric Dyson's honest account of the life of Martin Luther King is an important example of dealing with the wholeness of human experience, and not just the edited highlights.[67]

In a later book, the same author attempts a critical reassessment of the life of deceased rapper, Tupac Shakur. Dyson opens up new possibilities for us to see beyond the limitations of 'heroes' and 'villains', 'good people' and 'bad' ones.[68] Life, culture and cultural expression are complex and often contradictory. I have consciously sought to create a series of stereotypes in this sketch. I make no apologies for this, for I sense that beneath many stereotypes there usually resides an element (albeit relatively small) of truth. All these characters exist within the many Black communities of Britain. We all know some if not all of these people. Some will be familiar to us and we may possess affinity or fond feelings for them. In the case of others, the opposite will be the case. Without wishing to be overly pious or sanctimonious, that is exactly the point. The challenge of this sketch is to confront and acknowledge all these characters head on. Who are they and why do they act the way they do?

In writing *Black Voices* I wanted to find a way of illustrating the whole range of Black expression that may exist in any particular setting. Can we legitimately say that church is an expression of the Kingdom, when only certain kinds of people are permitted to attend, and be heard? How does our notion of 'being church' then compare with Jesus' inclusive instructions for those attending the wedding feast in Luke chapter 14? Are we guilty of being more prescriptive and concerned with correctness and acceptability than Jesus was—a man who kept company with prostitutes, tax collectors and other social undesirables? Who do we consider to be part of us, and who should not belong?

BLACK VOICES

[The scene... we see a bar. A tall man is standing nonchalantly behind the bar (a table with a few drinks on it) ... we are inside a house at a family party. We see two people, a man and a woman, at the bar. They are arguing.]

Mabel: Me noh know why me ever marry such a' wort'less piece a' man like yu... See yu... [Kisses her teeth]...

Barman: [Polite] Can I serve either one of you?

Lawrence and Mabel: [In unison] Shut up!

Lawrence: [Raising hand to fight] No bodder wrenk wi mi 'oman. If yu mek I raise fe my left han' an' clap yu t'ree kin' a' lik' cross yu neck back, yu go'n filt yu foot.

Mabel: [Boxes Lawrence first] Who yu go'n box hi? Mi? Yu tek mi fe fool… [Boxes him again]…Tek de lik, yu no shame, bruck down, mash up piece a' man.

[Barman attempts to intervene.]

Barman: Could I be of help here?

Lawrence and Mabel: [In unison] Shut up!

Mabel: Now me go'n ax yu again… [Looking around]… Wey she dey?

Lawrence: [Half hearted and pathetic] Me noh know wha' yu a' talk 'bout.

Mabel: [Slaps Lawrence again] Noh lie to me… Wey de man tiefing Jezebel? Me wan' drop three kin' a' lik innah she face. No one go'n tief my man, yu hear mi?

[Mabel slaps Lawrence once again.]

Lawrence: [Head bowed, totally defeated] Yes dear… [Mutters under his breath]… Diam miserable wretch.

Mabel: [To Lawrence] Wha' dat? Yu 'ave somet'ing fi sey? [Lawrence shakes his head slowly]… [Mabel looks into distance and sees someone coming. It is Janet]… A' she?

[Enters Janet.]

Janet: Hello Lawrence.

Mabel: [Leaps at Janet and grabs her around the throat] Tek yu han' off my man… Mi noh go'n warn yu again.

Janet: [Shaking Mabel's hands off her neck] I don't know what you're talking about.

Mabel: Noh lie to me. If dere's one t'ing mi cyan 'tan, and dat's a' laired…

Lawrence: 'top yu noise 'oman. Wha mek yu so miserable?

Mabel: [Boxes husband again... She leaps at Janet again] Now mi go'n warn yu fi de las' time... Tek yu han' off fe me man.

Janet: [Breaks Mabel's hold... Angry] Look! I don't know who you think you are. No one talks to me like that! Do you think I would be stupid enough to deal with an ugly, disgusting looking man like that?... [points to Lawrence's bedraggled and pathetic figure]... Look at him. Don't make me laugh. That man is nasty.

Mabel: [Thinking for a moment] Alright den. 'im nasty fi true...

> [Exit Mabel. There is a short interval as Janet and Lawrence pretend not to notice each other... then suddenly they leap into each other's arms. They begin to hug.]

Janet and Lawrence: Darling.

Barman: [Inquiring] Can I help either of you two?

Lawrence and Janet: [In unison] Shut up.

Lawrence: [Standing back and looking at Janet] Bwoy, yu look criss... Mi love yu, yu know.

Janet: But what about your wife? She knows about us?

Lawrence: Cho! Dat hugly 'oman? Mi noh care 'bout ar... She too diam fuhfool and chupid.

> [The two of them begin to hug again. Enter giles. Lawrence and Janet quickly break off their clinch. Giles approaches the bar. As he arrives, Mabel calls Lawrence off stage.]

Mabel: [Off stage] Lawrence! Tek yu frownsey cack off, broad batty over yahso... [slight pause]... NOW!

Lawrence: [Beginning to walk away...To Janet] Mi mus' go darling... De dragon 'oman a' call mi... Soon come.

> [Exit Lawrence... Giles stands next to Janet... Barman is peering at the two of them.]

Giles: [Posh Etonian accent] Hello! I was wondering if you could possibly help me?

Barman: [Intervening eagerly] I could help… I'm a barman. I'm trained to help people.

Giles: [To Barman] Now, now my good man, I was talking to the lady. I make it a point never to converse with the hired help. Now run along my good man and see if you can improve your education so that you can get a proper job… [To Janet]… I'm a little lost. Well, terribly lost actually. Is this the Henley-on-Thames Rotary club?

Janet: What?

Giles: The Henley-on-Thames Rotary club…

Janet: No.

Giles: Oh dash it… I knew I should have taken the fifth exit on the motorway… But when one is doing 150 miles per hour in a 1962 Aston Martin Lagonda, silver bullet, complete with eight litres, overhead cam, leather upholstered seats, aerodynamic foil, turbo boost, and sub sonic road tracking, one finds it rather perturbing to have to break the flow, change down through my six co-ordinated, hydraulic, air pressurized gears, and exit the motorway. I guess you find it quite perturbing as well?

Janet: What are you saying?

Barman: [Intervening eagerly] I know what he's saying. I'll translate for you. I speak fluent upper-class twit.

Janet and Giles: [In unison] Shut up.

Giles: [To Janet] Did you attend the Queen's garden party this year? I think I met you. Are you related to Lord Rothemere?

Janet: Are you for real, or are you pretending to be a stiff idiot?

Giles: My dear… I'm afraid I cannot divine the nature of your last remark. Are you calling into question the authenticity of my persona?

Janet: You're a stiff idiot for real. I've seen some big faced, no sense, small brain idiots in my life. Men who are practised jack asses. But you! You have a PhD in stupidity. I feel sorry for you.

Giles: [Pause] Oh! I have tickets to Wimbledon next year. Would you care to mash it up in a different style with I man?

Janet: [Kisses her teeth] Idiot.

[Enter a young ragga-ish youth, walking with a pronounced swagger. Walks up to Giles and Janet at the bar.]

Big Bwoy: [To Giles] Yo my main man. Shed some skin… [Holds out a hand in order to exchange the customary greetings with Giles, but Giles is non plussed] My man, Big Bwoy is the name, and cool runnings is my game. So what ya saying, Bro?

Giles: I wasn't aware one was required to engage in a dual discourse, in the form of a dialogue?

Big Bwoy: Come again, Bro?

Barman: [Still eager] I know what he's talking about. Please let me say something. Please, go on, please… Let me, let me…go on.

The other three: [In unison] Shut up.

Giles: Does one know the way to Hampton Court? Lord de Grenville is holding a coming-out party for his daughter… Lucinda Perringrow. I'm hoping to attend. One should come along… It will be absolutely spiffing.

Big Bwoy: [Nonplussed] Rewind and come again, selector. I don't understand the lyrics, Bro… You're chatting foolishness. Pure foolishness… You ain't no Black man. You're pure bounty. A real coconut. Black on the outside, White as chalk on the inside. Runwey man, runwey.

[Big Bwoy chases Giles out of the scene… he turns to talk with Janet.]

Big Bwoy: [To Janet] Wha'appen, Gorgeous… You're sweet and nice. Like ice cream… I could eat you up.

Janet: Get lost, creep.

Big Bwoy: Yo sweet thing, don't do me like that. I've been waiting all my life for a woman like you. So what do you say sweet thing? You and me? Mono on mono?

Janet: For such a bony pigeon-chested wretch, you sure have a big ego.

Big Bwoy: [Offended… exaggerated shock] What yu saying, Sis? You trying to dis me? Me…Big Bwoy?... [Begins to circle her]… Big Bwoy? Biggest and the baddest of all the bad men in town? What ya saying Sis, what you saying?

Janet: Look here, sparrow chest... If you didn't speak out of your bottom so much, your breath wouldn't smell so bad. At least your name is accurate. You are a boy... [Looking him up and down]... Only you're not very big, are you?

Big Bwoy: [Furious] What? What? Yu t'ink yu too nice or somet'ing? I should give you a taste of the back of my hand, sister...

    [Big Bwoy raises fist to hit Janet... suddenly there is a loud voice off stage.]

Luticia: [Shouting out] Cuthbert... Cuthbert... Is that you?

Big Bwoy: [Recoils in shame... Puts hands to head] Shame... Big shame.

    [Enter Luticia... Exit Janet at the opposite end. Luticia approaches Big Bwoy.]

Luticia: [to Big Bwoy] Cuthbert... Why don't you come when I call you?

Big Bwoy: [Looking around] Mum... Do you have to? You know all my friends call me Big Bwoy.

Luticia: Well I christen you Cuthbert, and dat is how you is going to stay... [Approaches Big Bwoy. Begins to look behind his ears and at the collar on his shirt]... You remember to wash behind your ears before you come out? And look 'pon your shirt collar? Pure nastiness. And did you change your brief this morning?

Big Bwoy: Clean underpants, Ma? Give it a rest.

Barman: [Leaning across eagerly] I changed my underpants this morning. Look, I'll show you.

    [Barman comes from behind the bar and begins to unzip his trousers.]

Luticia: [Slaps him quickly] Behave yourself, you blasted fool. What yu mek you t'ink I want to see your dutty brief?

Barman: [Going back behind the bar] But I thought...

Big Bwoy and Luticia: [In unison] Shut up!

Luticia: [To Big Bwoy] What would happen if you get knock down by a train tomorrow?... You want me to feel shame? And what about your socks? I can smell dem from here. And look 'pon you head. Not even Vaseline find itself in there... And look 'pon you face? Not even cream. Bwoy you have no shame. You need some good old fashion lick. Some bush lick... [begins to open her handbag]... Me have a piece a belt in here somewhere. Bwoy, you need some beating. You is not too old fe get lash you know.

[Big Bwoy runs off stage... Luticia calls after him.]

Luticia: Cuthbert, where you going? Me talking to you? Cuthbert! Come back here now!... Dat Bwoy? He need some bush lick me tell you. Some good old fashion lashing. When my mother used to beat me, lard, me couldn't walk, let alone sit fi three days... Dem English pickney get it easy you know.

[Luticia storms off stage... all silent, save the Barman. He walks out from behind the bar and walks centre stage, a big smile on his face.]

Barman: At last. My turn to talk. I've been dying to say something all night... So where shall I start? What can I say? Well, I could tell you about the time I met Bob Marley. I taught him how to play guitar you know. In actual fact, I don't want to boast, but I wrote 'Jamming' for him... [Begins to sing]... "Jamming, I'm jamming, and I hope you like jamming too. Yeah, I'm jamming..."

[Suddenly across the stage runs Janet, followed by Lawrence, who in turn is being chased by Mabel. All three stop momentarily to look at Barman.]

Janet, Lawrence and Mabel: [Stop and look at Barman. In unison] Shut up.

Lawrence: [To Janet] Run, darling. De mad 'oman go'n kill de both a' we.

Janet: [Begins to run again] I'm running, I'm running.

Mabel: [Also running now] Yu can run, but yu cyan hide. An' when mi ketch de two a' yu... Bwoy, yu betta run.

[Exit all three. Barman is about to speak again. He steps forward when, across the stage, runs Big Bwoy followed by Luticia.]

Big Bwoy and Luticia: [Both stop and look at Barman] Shut up!

Big Bwoy: [Continues to run] I can't stop, Ma... You're ruining my credibility. Big Bwoy is too cool to take any kind a shame.

Luticia: [Continues to run also] Cuthbert... Cuthbert... You remember to wash you cheesy feet? And you remember to put on your vest? You know how you easy fi catch cold?

> [Exit Big Bwoy and Luticia... Barman is about to speak again, when Giles enters the scene.]

Giles: [To Barman] Oh be quiet and run away my ignorant friend... [To audience]... Does anyone know the way to Buckingham Palace? Prince Charles and I are going to a Buju Banton concert... We are going to pick up some patties along the way... Charles does so like to niam. I'm partial to a bit of curry goat myself. Anyway, I must dash.

> [Exit Giles... Barman finally walks forward to talk.]

Barman: At last... As I was saying. I used to write songs for Bob Marley. We used to...

> [Enter all the other characters who walk in front of Barman and shout.]

Everyone except Barman: Shut up!

Barman: [Very sad] Alright then!

THE END

Post Sketch Reflections

One of the most obvious points that arise from a sketch such as this one is the fact that reactions to it are so clearly determined by the ethnicity or cultural location of the individual concerned. In the first instance, there is the sheer subject matter and identification with the characters concerned. Unlike many of the other pieces in this book (save for 'It Could Have Happened Like This') the characters in *Black Voices* are not generic people. The ethnicity of the people in this sketch is key to its composition, hence the rather unsubtle title of *Black Voices*. The reactions to this sketch, therefore, have varied greatly depending upon the composition of the group engaging with it.

   On the basis of my interaction with others in using this sketch, I would suggest that there have been two overarching categories of responses. First, when the groups have been monocultural, the reactions have differed, depending upon whether that group is a Black one or is comprised of White people. In terms of the latter, it has struck me that group participants have felt somewhat uneasy with the whole scenario. This is due in part to the cultural dislocation felt by many White people when exposed to self-consciously Black contexts.

Even within many western societies where many contexts (especially inner-city ones) are much more plural than they once were, it is still true that Black people know far more about White people and their cultural world than is the reverse. Many of the White people (particularly if they were older) knew relatively little about the cultural world which many Black people inhabit. A number of scholars have commented on the difficulty experienced by many White people in their attempts to engage meaningfully with Black people.[69] This lack of awareness has led many of the White participants to struggle when trying to respond in any meaningful way to the characters in the sketch.

Another important issue is that of language. Many of the characters speak in a variety of linguistic forms that are reflective of African Caribbean cultures and are an important signifier of their sense of identity. Scholars such as Willis,[70] Tomlin[71] and Callender[72] have all explored the importance of Black idioms to the identity construction of African Caribbean people in Britain. The linguistic traits of African Caribbean people are hugely important for the distancing effect they have exerted on White people. Basically, if people cannot follow what you are saying, then it becomes easier to sustain one's own self-determined identity, and to a lesser extent, one's destiny.[73]

The reaction amongst White-only groups is decidedly less marked when younger White people are involved. One of the clear effects of postmodernism is the realization that many cultural boundaries have been exploded, with young people being able to cross many different barriers.[74] I have noted the extent to which younger White people have expressed greater facility to engage with the Black characters in the sketch.

Amongst Black-only groups the reaction to the sketch has been as equally marked as that of White-only groups. For the Black participants, they have enjoyed being able to engage with this humorous and stereotypical sketch, which is very much reflective of the African Caribbean comic material of many contemporary Black comedians in the UK.[75]

The gusto and exuberant manner with which many Black people have engaged with this sketch is a reminder of the importance of Black religio-cultural settings, particularly the church, where Black identity and expression is given free rein. Robert Beckford's work, in particular, has been most notable for its critical assertion that the Black church in the UK is essential for providing a radical space in which Black selfhood can flourish.[76]

Black Voices has become for many a comedic template for what is the best and the worst of Black Christian expression. The strict moral climate of many Black churches is such that there appears to be a distinct chasm between those who are righteous (and saved) and those who are not.[77] It is a form of Christianity that rigidly adheres to a 'them and us' paradigm, which clearly makes judgements on the worthiness of particular people. *Black Voices* offers a useful framework for investigating the theology and practice of Black Christian contexts. For White people, this sketch challenges such individuals to reflect on how they relate to Black people, especially when they are in specific African and Caribbean contexts. How can we be brothers and sisters in Christ when there is limited or even no knowledge of the 'other'?

Accessing the Dramatic: Using Drama as a Medium for Doing Black Theology

[This extract is taken from *Dramatizing Theologies: A Participative Approach to Black God-Talk* (London: Equinox, 2006), 10–22. As is evident from the foregoing section, one of the ways in which Reddie seeks to develop an engaging and practical approach to Black theology is through the medium of drama. In this, one of his most recent publications, he theorizes around the nature of the disenfranchisement of ordinary Black people by White hegemony and the professional Black middle-class.]

Establishing the Identity of the Voiceless

This work outlines a new participatory approach for undertaking Black theological discourse with marginalized and oppressed peoples. My dialogue partners in this work are disenfranchised Black people of mainly Caribbean descent living in the UK.

The impetus for the work first arose a number of years ago when I first began to work alongside local church congregations in the West Midlands area of the UK. The majority of these church communities were Black majority, comprised mainly of African Caribbean migrants, many of whom had travelled from the Caribbean to the UK in the 1950s and 60s. They and their descendants now constitute the majority of the membership of these faith groupings, located primarily in inner-city, urban priority areas of large metropolitan cities.

On my travels with the various groups I noticed that an ongoing feature of these churches was the almost complete silence of the mainly older Black members.[78] In matters of theological reflection, worship, mission and pastoral care, particular groups of people (often a remnant of White middle-class persons living in suburbia and communing into the church) often dominated the discourse within the church. The articulation of spiritual and theological matters by Black people was largely absent.

What was also significant within these settings was the sense that what these Black people had to say was largely ignored or not considered to be of any import. It was not so much that they were ignored (which in many respects was the case), as their voice was not considered of sufficient importance to affect the discussion to any great extent. It is instructive to note that the individuals in these churches were the recipients of a pernicious phenomenon which sociologists and anthropologists have termed a 'hierarchy of credibility'.

In a previous piece of work I have identified this hierarchy of credibility as

> A social ranking that confers a greater degree of credibility and reliability upon some people often at the expense of others. The latter are perceived to have less status than the former.[79]

The social ranking within a hierarchy of credibility is linked explicitly to our notions of epistemology and what we assert as being truth. Black theologians have long argued that the alternate truths of Black experience (which often stand in stark contradistinction to White hegemony) are often disparaged or denigrated by those who possess the power to nullify the voice of the other.[80] As many Black people of Caribbean origin can testify, what is recognized as truth is linked directly to 'who you know and who knows you'.[81]

As I have stated elsewhere, the truths of the Black experience within a Diasporan context have always existed within a contested framework, which has demanded a range of socio-political and theological tools in order that it can be explicated and expressed with confidence and alacrity.[82]

What has become patently clear during the years when I was engaged in face-to-face work with predominantly Black Christian communities was the dual struggle under which many of these often marginalized and poor communities labour. That struggle was a dialectical tension between the more obvious forms of marginalization and estrangement from White authority on the one hand and the less obvious distance from and paternalism of Black professionalism.

In terms of the former, one can see this evident in the all-pervasive construction of White hegemony, which is documented in greater detail within this book. In terms of the more disguised features of the latter, Black professionalism has become no more adept at engaging with and conferring dignity upon poor, marginalized and detached Black people than their patrician thinking White counterparts.

In short, poor Black people have traditionally suffered from a form of 'double jeopardy'.[83] On the one hand, they are denied a voice by the claims of White hegemony, which has overlooked, disparaged and denigrated them; while on the other hand Black professionals have ignored the voice of poor Black people, on the grounds that it lacks the eloquence and the 'niceties' of their own particular type of discourse.

In terms of the latter, one can legitimately claim that there is at least a sense of solidarity and empathy for poor Black people, which is rarely found within the collective and corporate ranks of White power.

This sense of empathy and solidarity should not, however, disguise us from recognizing that this is still a perspective that is steeped in paternalism and pity. Black professionals often look down on and exhibit a form of embarrassment at their lowlier compatriots, recognizing in them aspects of their own journey from such relatively unpromising beginnings towards respectability and seeming acceptance.[84]

I have lost count of the number of occasions I have been on committees and consultative meetings when both White and Black middle-class professionals (one has to be middle class to be admitted to these particular arenas and engaged in the ensuing discourse) have taken delight in talking about poor and marginalized people (especially Black people) but rarely with them. The occasions when Black 'Community leaders' speak for their people (having rarely sought any mandate on which to make any pronouncements) is much too replete to detail at this point. Suffice it to say that on such occasions when such lofty, sententious rhetoric is uttered, poor, voiceless Black people are just that—voiceless people who are not present and not always consulted when their 'betters' are talking about them. I have addressed aspects of this phenomenon in a previous piece of work.[85]

The development of this attempt to create a more democratic and participatory approach to undertaking Black theological work with and alongside voiceless people arose from a particular incident a number of years ago. In the early 1990s I first became an active member of a Black caucus support group within the Methodist Church in Britain. The Black Methodist Group (BMG),[86] as it was then named, was founded in the mid-1980s by a group of Black Methodist ministers (initially called the Black Methodist Ministers' Group—BMMG) in order to challenge the endemic racism within the church. In the early 1990s at the time of my initial involvement, the group became embroiled in a relatively short, but intensely angry, debate with members of the White hierarchy of the church. A number of influential people within the BMG mounted a spirited and ultimately futile campaign to challenge the church hierarchy to change their minds over a particularly controversial decision that had been taken, which, it was felt, militated against the work of the BMG and Black people in general within the Methodist church in Britain.

Neither the details of the dispute nor particulars of the final decision need detain us at this point. What was quite instructive at the time was the seeming self-righteous rhetoric of both sides of the dispute. On the one side, members of the White hierarchy felt sufficiently emboldened to take a major decision without any seeming regard for the Black constituency that would be affected by their decision. On the other side, my peers and I were equally confident in our claims to speak for the many others who would be adversely affected, so we believed, by this erroneous decision.

I say 'so we believed' because, in truth, no attempt was made to consult with those who were not the leaders of this campaign. The campaign assumed that others were in agreement with our stance. We simply decided our course of action and implemented it without recourse to those for whom we claimed to speak.

Looking back, one might even cynically state that part of our reasoning, albeit in a sub-conscious vein, was the desire not to be encumbered by the innate conservatism and moderation of ordinary voiceless Black people. As I will demonstrate at a later point in this text, it is not uncommon for ordinary Black people to exhibit attitudes and theological beliefs that are markedly more moderate and conservative than their so-called intellectual betters.[87] Aspects of this tension are expressed by the Black practical/pastoral theologian Dale Andrews in his book *Practical Theology for Black Churches*.[88] I suspect that had we, the leaders of this campaign, sought out ordinary, poor, voiceless Black people, we might have found such individuals most inhibited, diffident and, perhaps, antagonistic to our desire to 'rock the boat'. Our refusal to consult with the group, for whatever motives, meant that we were no less complicit in the hierarchical and damaging process of ignoring the claims of the 'least of these'[89] than were our White adversaries.

The opening sketch *We Know Best*, which forms a part of the dramatic material that seeks to provide the substantive content for the process of 'dramatizing theologies', was written during the heightened months of that campaign. I have returned to it because within the few pages of highly charged polemic (the writing in this piece mirrored the blaze of anger that is detailed by James Cone in his first writings[90]) I sought to give voice to the leaders on both sides of the dispute. What is missing in this dramatic scenario is the voice of the voiceless.

In writing the sketch I quickly discounted the voice of those who are the most marginalized and oppressed. The setting of this piece and the fictional characters that populated it are both equally oblivious of the presence, and therefore the voice, of those who are the most vulnerable and least able to stake their claim in the world.

I remain clear that either sides of the debate are not equally culpable. I remain convinced that both the decision itself and the process by which it was taken by the White people with power were wrong. I am equally clear that it is the White people who hold the power in the sketch; just as I am clear that it is White people who hold all the 'aces' in the world. So I am not saying that the Black people in the sketch, any more than the actions of which I was a part over a decade ago, or those of Black Liberation theologians now, are wrong. Neither am I saying that we (both then and now) hold equal responsibilities for the voiceless, marginalized and oppressed condition of Black people in the world today.

The blame for such matters (if blame is the correct recourse—I feel that blame is not a particularly helpful construct with which to work, however) lies with White hegemony, not with Black Liberation theologians trying to engage in anti-hegemonic struggle.

And yet, despite these very necessary caveats, I remain struck by the alacrity of both groups, particularly the Black protagonists, to ignore the voices of those who are and remain the voiceless. It is often the case that many Black Liberation theologians are no more comfortable engaging in face-to-face with discourse with voiceless Black people than are the White experts, who are so easily criticized and critiqued by the former.

Often, Black Liberation theologians are no less armchair activists than the classical White theologians they denounce. I stand condemned on such grounds as do many others. This work is an attempt to create a participatory approach to Black God-talk, in which the voice of the voiceless is a crucial component in both the process and the substantive content of any theologizing.

So, as a way of introducing the central ideas in the process of dramatizing theologies, I offer you an extract of the script of *We Know Best*, my attempt to provide a fictional account of the dispute that raised my awareness of the voiceless nature of poor Black people in Britain and the world.

WE KNOW BEST

[Inside a committee room. We see five characters sitting together talking. Three are white and the other two are black.]

White man no. 1: The facts of the matter are as follows. Due to a number of personnel and budgetary difficulties, the central committee has to regretfully inform you that the Affirmative Action Development Scheme will have to close at the end of this month.

Black man: But you do have our best interests at heart?

White man no. 1: Am I right in assuming that I sense a little hostility here?

Black woman: I'd re-tune my radar if I were you. There's more than a little hostility in here.

Black man: Four hundred years of hostility to be precise.

White man no. 2: We understand your feelings, but you do have to see things from our perspective.

Black woman: And that is?

White man no. 2: [Looking at his two colleagues] Shall I explain our position?

White man no. 3: Go ahead, Roger.

White man no. 2: Obviously, it goes without saying that we are upset and saddened that such a decision regarding the Affirmative Action Development Unit has had to be taken.

White man no. 1: Your input would be greatly appreciated on this matter.

Black man: Why do you want our input?

White man no. 3: Well… Hmmmmmm.

White man no. 2: Well, because it does concern yourselves.

Black man: It's a bit late to be asking us for our concerns now. You've already made your decision.

Black woman: It's like inviting a guest to a meal, after you've already eaten all the food and cleared away the cutlery.

Black man: If you had really wanted our input, you would have invited us to a meeting before you made your decision.

White man no. 1: But it wasn't that simple.

Black woman: It never is. When you say 'it was felt', what you really mean is, you lot felt the unit was not achieving its specific aims. You didn't ask us what we felt about the work of the unit and, if you had, you would have found that we the practitioners on the ground, we the recipients of the Unit's activities, are more than happy with its work and the resulting achievements… But as I said, our opinion doesn't count.

White man no. 3: I think you're being slightly unfair.

White man no. 2: Not to mention unreasonable. I find your somewhat caustic attitude to be most unhelpful.

Black man: And now we get down to the crux of the matter. You find us to be unreasonable and unhelpful. Well, isn't that a shame? How dare we feel upset and suspicious at your decisions? After all, you the big chief knows best. We should be happy that you've made your executive decisions, without any recourse to our feelings, and closed down the unit. We should be grateful, because, after all, doesn't the big boss man know best? We should come into your room, all full of happy Caribbean smiles, do a quick limbo dance and then lie prostrate on the floor and tell you how grateful we are that you have decided to cut our unit. And people say that paternalism no longer exists?

White man no. 1: I think you are dealing in the realms of hyperbole. This has nothing at all to do with paternalism. This is simply a question of effective management of resources and seeking to find the best way forward.

Black woman: With you always holding the upper hand. You make the decisions and we have to take it and like it.

Re-reading *We Know Best* in Light of Robert Beckford's *God of the Rahtid*

On a recent re-reading of *We Know Best* I was struck by the polemical nature of the piece. What has become most notable in my analysis of this sketch is the passionate nature of the speeches made by the two Black characters.[91] On two occasions, they engage in lengthy rhetorical polemics, where the focus of their discourse is not on dialogue or elucidation, but rather is an exercise in didactic bombast! The White characters are unable to respond in a meaningful way as they are on the receiving end of a deluge of withering rhetoric.

Black British theologian and cultural critic, Robert Beckford, has explored the dynamics of Black rage and anger in the context of postcolonial Britain in his third book, *God of the Rahtid*.[92] Beckford argues that Britain is a country in which racialized oppression permeates the very fabric of the nation.[93] At the dawn of the twenty-first century, Black people are trying to come to terms with and exist within a context that both validates and legitimizes the institutional and casual incidences of racism against people of colour.[94]

It is within this climate that Black people are struggling with a phenomenon he terms 'low level rage'. Beckford defines the latter as 'related to internalized rage in that it is experienced in mind and body. It is manifested in anger, depression and anxiety'.[95] The high incidence of mental ill health (particularly schizophrenia) amongst African Caribbean communities in Britain adds substance to Beckford's contentions.

Having initially analysed the many contexts in which Black rage is to be located, the author outlines his own personal collision with the pernicious and debilitating nature of Black rage. In a moving section of the book, Beckford articulates the veneer of Black professional and personal mobility that encouraged him to suppress his rage at the altar of progress and advancement.[96] Personal circumstances, however, remind him of the fallacious nature of much that can be understood as Black acceptability.

Beckford draws upon Black theological insights concerned with the nature of the Kingdom of God, and argues that our understanding of the Kingdom provides the necessary tools and resources for a redeeming construct of Black rage.[97] Redemptive vengeance, argues Beckford, can be found within the notion of a realized eschatology, in which the agency of God, incarnated within the ministry of Jesus, provides the focus for harnessing the emotive power of Black anger.[98]

Re-reading this sketch in light of Beckford's *God of the Rahtid* has been quite instructive. When I had first composed this piece I did not possess the scholarly tools to provide a critically centred rationale for the actions and thought patterns of the Black protagonists in the drama. As I have outlined in my previous book, drama provides an opportunity to create a context and find words for that setting in order to unmask experiences and feelings that, hitherto, often remain unexplored.[99] Beckford's analysis of 'low level rage' is highly suggestive in the development of the process of creating a participative approach to undertaking Black theology, for lying beneath this transformative process is a desire to provide a schema that enables marginalized and oppressed Black people to discover their voice in order to articulate their pain and frustration.

Analysing *We Know Best* in light of Beckford's work reveals the cathartic, expiated desire of the Black characters in being liberated to 'speak words of truth'. This sense of release is manifested in a torrent of words in which the many years of pent-up, subterranean anger is set free, within the confines of a seemingly polite ecclesial meeting. When Beckford states:

> In my working adult life I have only ever once called an individual a 'racist' to their face. I have generally avoided accusatory politics, but on this occasion after four years of the subtlest racialized hostility, I erupted. My anger was full and volcanic[100]

he is re-enacting the very dynamics of this fictional sketch written a few years prior to his real life event. The cathartic sense of release in 'telling the truth and shaming the devil'[101] is reflective of Beckford's assertion that 'the truth shall set you free'.[102]

The Black characters in the sketch become critical subjective agents able to speak the truth in a challenging and dynamic way.[103] Yet their truth-telling remains individualistic and disconnected from the wider concerns of other Black people. This is not to suggest that they are not concerned with the hopes, aspirations and needs of poor, marginalized and oppressed Black people, but it is worth noting that throughout the drama we see no evidence that they have consulted with or taken counsel from others. To what extent are the two characters speaking for themselves or on behalf of others?

This question is more than a matter of simple semantics for it goes to the heart of the nature and intent of this enterprise. If the two Black characters are speaking with the cognizance of others then their discourse in this context is naturally imbued with a marked sense of mutuality and collegiality. If not (which I believe to be the case), then their discourse is a possibly presumptuous and somewhat detached form of rhetoric that reveals echoes of the kind of assumptions made by their White adversaries. By this, I mean, are the two Black characters acting in a manner that is informed by the best democratic traditions of consultation and consent, or are they acting as solitary agents content in the knowledge that they 'know what is best' for others? This dilemma and contextual struggle lies at the heart of this research.[104] Can Black Liberation theologians exhibit greater levels of engagement and mutuality with poor Black marginalized and oppressed people, which go beyond notions of tokenism, paternalism and condescension?[105]

I am not suggesting that *all* Black Liberation theologians are guilty of the sort of detachment and distance evidenced by the sketch and my previous comments. Black and Womanist scholars such as Lee Butler,[106] Jeremiah Wright[107] and Linda E. Thomas[108] are but three exponents (of many) who have engaged with Black subjects in their exploration of Black theological and religious themes. My central concern in this work is to move from the kind of close engagement with those who are the voiceless, in which one seeks to observe, interact and document, to a position where that very interaction becomes the means by which one's theological construction is undertaken. In short, the very dynamic with voiceless people creates the content of Black theology, not from an historic perspective,[109] but rather within the context of contemporaneous experience. Like Lynne Westfield,[110] it is my intention to use the contemporary experiences and discourse of, hitherto, Black voiceless people to assist me, by means of drama, to create a new approach to and a dynamic for the articulation and doing of Black theology.

8   Black Theology in Pulpit and Pew

There are two salient facts about Black Christianity in Britain—one, that matters of faith and practice matter intensely to Black people. Christian faith is not merely propositional nor consists only of existential musings. Faith is to be expressed and lived out with passionate commitment to God as revealed in the life, death and resurrection of Jesus the Christ. Second, this faith has to be proclaimed i.e. the kerygma of Black Christianity is central to its very own modus operandi. Implicit or surreptitious faith are not facets one usually finds within Black Christian discourse in Britain.

In light of these two bold assertions, the editors of this text would assert that Black theology in Britain, which emerges as the radical and prophetic wing of Black Christianity in this country, has always carried with it a distinct practical theological methodology. In using this term, we are making recourse to a body of knowledge and thought that falls within the purview of 'Practical theology'. Scholars such as Ballard and Pritchard,[1] Forrester[2] and Graham[3] have theorized around the development of Practical theology as a model of reflective activity in which the theologian interrogates the connections between the theory and practice of Christianity as it can be discerned within a diverse range of contexts and milieus. Practical theology is particularly adept as utilizing interdisciplinary approaches to theological reflection, especially those that are drawn from psychology, which has proved to be a durable dialogue partner for those engaged in pastoral theology (which is often taken as a synonym for Practical theology).

Within the broad field that is defined as 'Practical theology', 'Homelitics' or the theology of preaching is seen as one of the important areas of study. Preaching is both a theoretical arena for scholarly investigation in addition to being discerned as a phenomenon of consistent Christian practice in the plethora of Black and Black majority ecclesial settings up and down this country.

Preaching remains a key element of Christian practice within Black Churches in Britain. In fact, across the wider contours of the African Diaspora, preaching remains a key theological task for pastors, ministers, priests, deacons, lay readers or local preachers. Carlyle Fielding Stewart,[4] Dale Andrews[5] and Carol Tomlin[6] have all outlined the differing facets of Black preaching and the relationship between the preacher and the congregation. Within Black orality, there exists a mutuality and a connectedness between the principal speaker and the wider audience or congregation. The meaning and truth of any encounter does not reside solely with the preacher nor does it lie with the congregation. The preacher is not an active force nor is the congregation or audience a passive one. Conversely, there is an ongoing process of negotiation between the principal speaker and those who are in attendance. The congregation or audience are an active force. The congregation's engagement with the preacher is integral to the successful enactment of the sermon.

Within the Black milieu where aspects of Black cultural and religious practices are evident, it is not unusual to encounter explicit or implicit examples of a phenomenon many scholars have termed 'call and response'. Tomlin defines 'call and response' thus:

> In Call-response, the audience responds to the performer, who, in turn, shapes his or her performance according to the audience response. A favourable response will encourage the performer to continue in the same or similar vein; a muted response may suggest a change of course or new strategies.[7]

Whilst Black preaching comes in many forms and incorporates a wide variety of styles,[8] the expectations placed on Black preachers by their congregations are always high. Preachers are expected to be socially engaged, linking the story of the negated and troubled Black self with the ongoing narrative of redemption and transformation that comes from God's very own self.[9]

This chapter offers us a brief vignette of the dramatic impulse of Black preaching, which lies at the heart of the practical theological method of Black theology in Britain. The editors are aware of the irony of trying to capture the rhythmical cadences and verbal flourishes of Black preaching in static form on the page. Like Aldred before us, in his highly significant text *Preaching with Power*,[10] there is always something of the illusory promise of trying to capture what is essentially an oral practice within written text. It is not unlike the attempt to capture lightning in a bottle!

And yet, aware as we are of the philosophical and methodological contradictions in such an enterprise as this, we nonetheless want to affirm the importance of highlighting Black preaching and sermons in this Reader, for without it a major elemental feature of Black theology as liberative praxis is lost. In the words of African American pastoral theologian James H. Harris:

> Though black people can celebrate in good and bad times, the preacher has the responsibility of helping transform the bad times into good times where the oppressed will have jobs, adequate housing, and the ability to determine their own destiny. With the help of God this can be accomplished during our lifetime.[11]

Arise and Build (Isaiah 61:4, Nehemiah 2:20)

Kate Coleman

[This sermon is taken from Bishop Joe Aldred (ed.), *Preaching with Power: Sermons by Black Preachers* (London: Cassell, 2000), 111–21.]

The words of the prophet Isaiah resound with hope as we as people of God face the task that God, by His Spirit, has set before us in these days. The prophet pronounces 'They will rebuild the ancient ruins and restore the places long devastated, they will renew the ruined cities that have been devastated for generations' (Isa. 61:4 NIV). Because so much of what we see around us in our personal lives, our communities, our nation, is tinged with a sense of work that needs to be done, with a sense of changes that need to take place, these words from Isaiah are inspirational. What am I saying today?

I am saying that the people of God have one responsibility in these days. That is to be engaged with God and to be engaging with all that God is engaged in. As we follow Jesus we discover that we have been called to the task of restoration, to the task of rebuilding, to the task of putting right what has gone wrong, to the task of seeing individuals and communities restored. But how can we be God's answer to the world today? How can we be a part of God's solution and avoid simply being part of the world's problem?

Back in Jerusalem around 450 BC Nehemiah spoke these words to his Jewish brothers and sisters: 'Come let us arise and build' (Neh. 2:20). The hope pronounced by the prophet Isaiah became their hope, and the events in the book of Nehemiah demonstrate that this hope did not disappoint them. Many who have followed Nehemiah have subsequently found the courage to 'arise and build'. Nehemiah 1:2-3, 4:6-7, 13, 6:15: these few verses give us an overall sense of what some of these principles are. Allow me to set the scene for you.

Here in the book of Nehemiah we have moved from the events surrounding the first great Exodus of the Children of Israel from Egypt to the 'Promised Land' to the events surrounding the end of the last great Old Testament Exodus. This time the movement is from Babylon, but again it is to the same place of the promise. In other words, we meet the people of God back in the place of slavery. Not Egyptian slavery this time but Babylonian slavery; slavery by another name! We meet them back in the place of bondage, back in a place of trouble. As a result of their slavery the place of God's promise to them lies in ruins and in utter devastation. They had enjoyed it for a while; they had known that blessing for a short time but somehow and some way they had lost it.

God is not just the God of the first chance. He is also the God of the seventy-seventh! In many ways the book of Nehemiah is a book about second chances. After all you cannot rebuild what was not already built! And you cannot renew what was not once new! And the encouragement of this book is that God will stand with those who seek to flow in the hope expressed by the prophet Isaiah. How then do we rebuild?

Nehemiah's Story Begins with a Concern

Here is someone locked in slavery and servitude in a foreign land, in exile, and yet his thoughts are not for himself, nor for his personal condition. Instead, his thoughts are for his people, these people that God loves, not simply because they are 'the people of God' but because they are *his* people, people he identifies with culturally and historically, people who are a part of him. Sometimes I hear people speaking with fear as if identifying with a particular people-group is wrong or sinful, as if it is equal to prejudice or racism, as if to be for one group necessarily means to be against another. Jesus fully identified with a fallen humanity to the point of incarnation, but we do not accuse Him of such isms against nature or the animal kingdom! The focus here is not racism or destructive nationalism or ethnocentrism. Nehemiah was concerned for the *well-being of his people*. Are you? His concern is simply for whether or not they are going along OK.

Nehemiah 1:2: '...one of my brothers came from Judah with some other men and I questioned them about the Jewish remnant that survived the exile and also about Jerusalem'. When he hears the bad news about their condition he breaks down: 'When I heard these things I sat down and wept. For some days I mourned and fasted and prayed' (Neh. 1:4).

A man drenched in tears, not out of concern for himself but for his people. How often do you weep over the condition of God's Church? Weep, not of anger or frustration, not because someone has hurt you or irritated you, but weep because private enterprise, private empires and personal interest motivate us, it seems, more than a vision for building God's kingdom? I mean, have we ever wept simply because...we have failed to take our proper place within the purposes of God? Or wept simply because...of an all-too-common indifference to issues of righteousness and justice inside and outside the Church? Wept simply because 'hypocrisy' rather than 'integrity' is the word so linked with Christians by those outside the Church? When was the last time *you* wept, like Jesus did, over the condition of your own people? And even perhaps over the condition of your own heart?

Nehemiah WEPT, we are told. He wept and he mourned, but his tears were not the tears of despair and hopelessness. These were not the tears of spiritual and physical inactivity because we are told that he 'fasted and prayed to the God of heaven' (Neh. 1:4). But just look at how he prayed.

Not 'Lord, destroy *those* people who have destroyed Jerusalem', not 'Lord forgive my people because *they* have sinned' but '*I* confess the sins we Israelites *including myself* and my father's house have committed against you' (Neh. 1:6b).

But, perhaps you want to protest along with me 'hey, Nehemiah isn't to blame! After all, he's in the place of exile. He was carried off against his will. He isn't personally responsible, surely, for what is taking place in Jerusalem. He didn't torch the gates or break down the walls himself.' Yet he totally identifies with the sins that he acknowledges his own people have been guilty of committing, all the sins that have led up to the current state of affairs.

You know, we can't always conveniently absolve ourselves from blame over the state of the Church or of our people. We can't simply distance ourselves from the very real problems that our communities suffer from. Like Adam we cannot just point the finger accusingly at Eve, and like Eve we cannot simply blame the serpent for the state of affairs, because sin is not just about the things we do wrong, i.e. our sins of 'commission'. It is also about those things that we neglect to do, i.e. our sins of omission. Nehemiah recognizes that one manifestation of his own sin and that of his own people is the sin of neglect and inactivity. As far as we can tell, this is the first occasion that Nehemiah has even attempted to take steps to affect the situation.

Martin Luther King Jr wrote that 'Individuals have not started living until they can rise above the narrow confines of their individualistic concerns to the broader concerns of humanity'. Perhaps here is the turning point in Nehemiah's own heart. Have we come to the turning point in our own hearts where our concerns extend beyond our personal lives and circumstances? Have we come to the turning point in our own hearts where we are prepared to do more than just weep and mourn about surrounding circumstances? Have we come to the turning point in our own hearts where we are prepared to become agents of change?

We have good and legitimate reasons why we can't get to prayer. Or why we can't take time to encourage others. Or why we can't pursue justice. But if we don't, who will? If I don't, who will? If you don't, who will? We always *make* time for the things we think are important, like cinema, watching TV, listening to music, making phone calls and the rest of it. Perhaps the issue is not that we lack opportunity, perhaps the issue is that we lack willingness.

For Nehemiah, his Concern Became Availability

We all know that God cannot resist an available person because God is seeking out the people like David who, even as the giant Goliath blocks the path of advance, still doesn't understand what the word 'impossible' really means, in the light of God. He is seeking out people who haven't been put off yet by the words 'you are unsuitable for the task', people like

Mary Seacole who hear such words but go right ahead with the call of God anyway. You see, God isn't looking for skill, for wisdom or for strength.

1 Corinthians 1:27, 29 reminds us that if the world insists that you are the foolish, the lowly and the despised, if society doesn't think much of who and what you are, even if you feel useless: then you are just the sort of person God can use. You will do very nicely! Nehemiah prayed, he waited on God, he discerned what God required of him and he took up the challenge. As he did that, various things happened to him. Firstly—he overcame his own fear.

Nehemiah did not *lose* his fear, he *overcame* it. If we are human, we will feel the full force of fear from time to time, but to feel the *presence* of fear is not the same as feeling the *power* of fear. Fear can be felt and overcome, and God gives us the grace for it. 'I was very much afraid, but I said to the king...' (Neh. 2:2b-3). He did it anyway! It could have cost him his head to be downcast in the king's presence, yet he still stepped out. We see a similar incident in the book of Ezra, a few chapters earlier (Ezra 3:3): 'Despite their fear of the people around them they [the Jews] built the altar on its foundation and sacrificed burnt offerings on it to the Lord.' When the cause of God is strong in us, even fear can be overcome. So often we think that the opposite to fear is denial or some form of superhuman courage, but these people, like Nehemiah, acted on the strength of their conviction that God was directing and leading them and they did so with a *whole* heart!

Secondly, Nehemiah developed boldness. The king asks him what it is that he wants. Nehemiah begins by expressing his desire to go home but no sooner does he have the king's consent that he gains the confidence to add a number of further requests: For letters, for wood, for safe conduct.

As we seek to serve God's purposes we need to be bold in seeking out his provision to fulfil his purposes. It is often said that 'Where God guides, God provides'. But so many of us have never found out if it is true or not, because we have not dared to ask God for anything, not for strength, not for skill, not for wisdom, not for grace and not for finance. Yet we are still surprised when we discover that we have neither strength, skill, wisdom, grace or finance! It is God's to provide. Ours is to ask!

Finally, God granted him success, for when God's hand is on something he knows how to make a way for it. Nehemiah said 'God's hand was on me. The king granted my requests' (Neh. 1:8). But 'success' does *not* mean being trouble-free because wherever God opens a door. [...]

There is Always Opposition

There are a limited number of things that we can guarantee in this life. 'In this world', Jesus said, 'you will have trouble', and trouble arrives in all shapes and sizes. It is important that we understand that the experience of opposition is NOT the same as a closed door. Some of us are passively giving way to opposition when we need to resist it. On the other hand, many of us try to push open a closed door without success, a door that God has closed.

It takes discernment to tell the difference. A closed door cannot be opened even by prayer, but opposition can always be overcome. 'When Sanballat the Horonite and Tobiah the Ammonite official heard about this they were very much disturbed that someone had come to promote the welfare of the Israelites' (Neh. 2:10). It always amazes me when I read this verse. You'd think that other people would be pleased that someone somewhere has taken an interest in promoting the welfare of their own people, but instead we find that the reality is that they feel threatened, resentful and are sometimes even openly hostile! Sounds familiar to me!

External opposition in this instance comes from Sanballat and Tobiah (Neh. 6:1-4) and is, thankfully, fairly easy to identify and to counteract. By far the worst kind of opposition in the process of restoration is the opposition that comes from within the community; after all, some of the most significant and influential individuals in modern history such as Martin Luther King Jr and Malcolm X found that the fiercest and often most fatal opposition has come from within their own communities. Nehemiah experiences three forms of internal opposition.

Firstly, opposition comes from those who are simply not interested in doing any of the actual work. We read: 'The next section was repaired by the men of Tekoa, but their nobles would not put their shoulders to the work under their supervisors' (Neh. 3:5 Now these are the kind of people who are very happy to live in the house that you build! Inspiration and perspiration are not part of their vocabulary Too often I have met people who have enjoyed the labours of those who have fought for civil rights, for women's rights, or those who have struggled or liberty in so many places and yet have personally refused to take part in any struggle that will benefit the next generation who, after all, have to live in the houses that we build or, as the case may be, do not build effectively. The image of war behind it may be unhelpful, but surely Winston Churhill had a point when he said during the Second World War years, 'Never..has so much been owed by so many to so few'. It is unfortunate that churches and communities often operate in the same way. These people aid the opposition simply because they do nothing!

Secondly, opposition comes in the form of the scaremongers. We meet them in Neh. 4:10-11. Ten times they came! What for! It is not like Nehemiah and his co-workers were unaware of the external opposition. The scaremongers are like the people in the church and community who have the ministry of bad news. You may acquire a new car and they'll be the ones telling you why it will only last for two weeks; you'll share your vision and they will be the ones telling you why it can't work. These people are only able to criticize destructively! Who needs enemies when you've got friends like these?

The third kind of internal opposition comes from those who are supposed to be working with you but who are allowing the enemy to work through them. 'Also in those days the nobles of Judah were sending to Tobiah and replies from Tobiah kept coming to them' (Neh. 6:17). And if opposition in the work is inevitable, then vigilance is a necessity: 'Therefore I stationed some of the people behind the lowest points of the wall at the exposed places, posting them by families with their swords, spears and bows' (Neh. 4:13). Perhaps one of the most important things to note is [...]

In the Rebuilding Process Everyone has their Part to Play

Nehemiah may have been the catalyst just as Martin Luther King Jr, Olaudah Equiano and Harriet Tubman were catalysts in the process, but in the end, they weren't the sole players. They never operated entirely alone. Without the support of others nothing is possible. Someone once said that the definition of success is to 'find some like-minded people and stick with them'. Neither could Nehemiah have accomplished as much as he was able to do in such a short space of time without the help of others around him (Neh. 3:1; 3:12; 3:17). Men and women, priests and merchants, Levites and rulers: everyone has their part to play and as each one sets their hearts fully to the task at hand they are able to achieve a great deal in an incredibly short period of time. We are told that, surprisingly, the wall was rebuilt in 52 days (Neh. 6:15)! We can be encouraged and strengthened in the tasks that we face both because of the presence of others, whether they be friends, family, church or community members, i.e. those who stand around us right now and put their hands to the work, but we can also be encouraged by the examples and experiences of those who have gone before us.

In Any Community the 'House of Heroes' Becomes a Focal Point

As Christians we take our inspiration from Jesus and other biblical characters of faith such as Deborah, Moses, Zelophehad's daughters, Joseph, Priscilla and Paul. These heroes and heroines are those who have paved the way; they are those who have accomplished much. In turn, they become those who inspire us to move on.

In Ghana, where I was born, we have a symbol for the phrase Sankofa. The symbol means learning and wisdom from the past and it is an encouragement to return to 'pick up' or to learn from the past. Perhaps Nehemiah gained strength and encouragement from others who had shown the same concern as he had and who preceded him, others such as Zerubbabel who worked alongside the prophet Haggai, or Ezra alongside the prophet Zechariah.

My own house of heroes includes people like Mary Prince who published her autobiography in 1831 to aid the abolitionist cause, and Olaudah Equiano, a Nigerian Christian who sought the welfare of black people in eighteenth-century Britain. In addition, Sojourner Truth was spurred on by her faith in Jesus to fight both the abolitionist and women's cause in America, and of course there are countless others who have prayed, cared, persevered and resisted defeat, whose names we may never know.

Jesus is at work today, rebuilding and restoring the devastated lives of human beings. We are called to imitate this Jesus in his work by becoming involved in the repair of lives and communities, praying, taking action and paving a way that others can follow. Is it not, therefore, time for us as women and men of faith to 'arise and build'?

Reflecting on the Story of Ruth

Mukti Barton

[This sermon on Racial Justice was preached at the Queen's Foundation, Birmingham, Sunday September 2005.]

Today we have studied the book of Ruth. Outside the book of Ruth, Ruth is mentioned only once in the Bible and that is in Jesus' genealogy—in the first chapter of Matthew's Gospel. Matthew proudly declares that this poor, foreign woman was an ancestor, a foremother, of Jesus.

Matthew's account of Jesus' genealogy is comical. He starts in a very patriarchal fashion: Jesus, the son of David, the son of Abraham—a man in the line of all men. It seems that women are not needed in childbirth. However, this is not so striking, since in a male-dominated world that is how men write history. They try to write women out of history. What *is* striking is that from time to time Matthew remembers some mothers. He actually remembers altogether five mothers among whom Ruth is one. These four women are Tamar, Rahab, Ruth, the wife of Uriah, meaning Bathsheba, and Mary, the mother of Jesus.

If you look through the Old Testament, you will find all of them were rather dodgy characters—somewhat mischievous. Last Saturday, at the book launch of my book *Rejection, Resistance and Resurrection*,[12] Michael Jagessar became famous (or notorious!) for saying, God works in *mischievous* ways. Because of Michael saying these words, the Church scored high points with my young sons.

All through the Bible, and particularly in Jesus' genealogy, God does seem quite mischievous. When men begin to feel puffed up that Jesus was born in a patriarchal line, then God comes and writes in small print, 'Jacob, the father of Joseph, the husband of Mary, of whom Jesus was born' (Mt. 1:16). God has the last laugh. Joseph was simply the husband of Mary; Jesus was born of Mary, a woman. Luke writing Jesus' genealogy makes it clear, 'He [Jesus] was the son (as was thought) of Joseph' (Lk. 3:23). Both Matthew and Luke wrote patriarchal history in order to turn it on its head. No wonder we talk about God's upside down kingdom. When people say, 'each word in the Bible is the word of God', my question is, 'have you read the small print?'

The Bible is full of God's small print and the book of Ruth is one such small print. In an oppressive male-dominated world, poor women like Naomi and Ruth die of starvation and you search the history books and you won't find their names. Sharon Palmer, a Black poet in our diocese, wrote in *Rejection, Resistance and Resurrection*:

> Are there any statistics for YOUR crime? No
> I bet there isn't, my inquiries do not show, so who is to know.[13]

If you search the history books, you will see names of men who conquered the world and became famous; you won't read the history of the vanquished. The history of Ruth and Naomi is in the Bible because they refused to die quietly. They took their destiny in their hands and plotted together. When the powerless plot, amazing things can happen.

My book *Rejection, Resistance and Resurrection* is written because Black and Asian people in the Diocese plotted together. Aubrey Longe, a Black man who retold his experience, said, 'Now I believe that a people without a history is a people that's never existed. A people without a history is a people lost, so in an endeavour to share with you my experience of life within the Church of England I need to give you a background, a synopsis of myself.'[14]

Last year Black and Asian peoples said to me, 'Mukti, next year is the diocesan centenary. The powerful will write their history, but what about us? We want to write our history; you collect our stories and write a book'. *Rejection, Resistance and Resurrection* is a bit like the book of Ruth, which would not have been written, had the powerless not plotted.

Ruth and Naomi had to take the initiative and then twist the arms of Boaz pretty hard to make him give up some of his privileges and become the surrogate father of Ruth's son. This made Ruth come from the margins of society to the centre. Unless the over-privileged give up something, the underprivileged cannot get what is due to them. This giving up of something, the over-privileged really hate with their guts. In Ruth's story the next-of-kin is very keen to buy Naomi's land, but would not touch Ruth with a bargepole. He says, 'I cannot redeem it for myself without damaging my own inheritance' (Ruth 4:6). When the underprivileged gain their rights, the inheritance of the over-privileged is damaged.

As soon as *Rejection, Resistance and Resurrection* was written, *The Daily Telegraph* attacked Bishop Sentamu for writing the foreword in the book.

Their argument is, 'Institutional racism! What institutional racism! We don't have such a thing in our church and society.' This is next-of-kin reaction. If church and society admit that there is institutional racism, their over-privileged inheritance will be damaged.

It is very understandable that the over-privileged do not like their inheritance being damaged. Ruth had to become a tough cookie. A follower of mischievous God, Ruth was mischievous. She played all her tricks to make Boaz see that she was not going to let him go. Moreover, it is a relief that among the over-privileged there are a few God-fearing people like Boaz who give up their privileges to accommodate the demands of the poor and the hungry.

Including our Bishop Sentamu, we, Black and Asian people, are tough cookies. When *The Daily Telegraph* attacked the Bishop, instead of becoming silent, at the book launch he was more vocal. He said, 'When I talk about institutional racism, people say I have a chip on my shoulder. I say to them, "I don't have a chip on my shoulder, I have a whole forest!"'

Ruth, Naomi, Black people, women, poor people, gay people, disabled people—all people on the margins of our society—we have forests on our shoulders. We are not going to rest until there is justice in the unjust world. We are not powerful, but our inner strength cannot be compared with any pseudo power of the world. We have this soul power because our Jesus Christ is not born in the family of Herod. The Herods of the world might want to destroy human lives and kill Jesus. But they cannot really, because Jesus rises again and again—Jesus, who flouted patriarchy and was born in the line of Tamar, Rahab, Ruth, Bathsheba and Mary, will be born again and again in the rubbles of history. The word of God will make flesh

in every generation,
in the outcasts of the system,
on the margins of prestige and power,
on the downside of tradition.

When you read the book of Ruth and *Rejection, Resistance and Resurrection* ask yourself, 'Have I read God's small print in the Bible and the world?'

The Good Neighbour [Luke 10:25-37 (GNB)]

Bishop Wilfred Wood

[This sermon was preached in Westminster Abbey, Sunday 25 October 1983. It is taken from Wilfred Wood, *Keep the Faith Baby!* (Oxford: Bible Reading Fellowship, 1994), 28–33.]

If I were to name the subject of our meditation this morning the parable of the good *neighbour*, the chances are that you might be uncertain about which of Our Lord's parables I have in mind. On the other hand, should I make reference to the parable of the good *Samaritan*, you would recognize immediately the reference to the parable we have just heard read. The interesting thing is that Our Lord told this story in answer to the question, 'Who is my *neighbour?*'—and the answer surely is that the neighbour is anyone who acts with compassion towards a fellow human being. That would still have been the complete answer had Our Lord merely said that 'a third man' who came by helped the distressed traveller.

As it happens, Our Lord said that the third man was a Samaritan. But why is it that we today prefer to name this story, not the 'parable of the good *neighbour*', or even 'the parable of the *Samaritan* neighbour', but instead 'the parable of the *good* Samaritan'? Let us hazard a guess.

When the Hebrew people lived in slavery in Egypt, they did not divide themselves into Jews and Samaritans. They all knew a common oppression, and they all came to recognize the one true God who broke their chains, and set them free to love and serve him, first in their wanderings in the wilderness, and later in peace and prosperity in Palestine. Unfortunately, King Rehoboam surrounded himself with 'yes-men', lost touch with the common people, and soon had a civil war on his hands. The people of the north broke away and established Samaria as their capital city, and became a prosperous commercial people known as Samaritans. The people of the south retained Jerusalem as their capital and came to be known as Jews.

But the more the Samaritans outdid the Jews in prosperity, the more the Jews prided themselves on their *so-called* pure lineage and ancestry, and derided the northerners as a polyglot nation. So by the time of Our Lord, a Samaritan was, in the eyes of the Jews, the lowest form of life on earth. A Samaritan was a nothing, a nobody, not because of anything he did, but because of what he was—he was from a race that was at the bottom of the pile, and for the Jews that would always be the most important fact about him.

When Our Lord told this parable, and named the good neighbour as a Samaritan, there was only one way in which his Jewish hearers could accept the obvious point and yet keep their anti-Samaritan prejudices undisturbed. They could say, 'Ah, but he was not typical—he was different. He was a *good* Samaritan!'

My own sad conclusion is that today we too prefer the title 'the good Samaritan' rather than the good neighbour because our own thinking is so much like theirs. We, too, think and act on a basis of racial stereotypes, and not even superhuman feats of *individuals* in the fields of learning, craftsmanship, invention or sport will disturb our deep-seated prejudices. Such individuals are the exceptions which prove the rule, we say.

If proof were needed to support this claim, we need only to point to the position of black people in Britain today. Alongside the distinctive achievements of some black individuals, there is the daily experience of petty acts of racial discrimination which is the lot of most black people, the constant reminders that by your colour you are a member of a group of undesirables. You do not have to be a black member of a group of friends on a day trip to France, who with other black persons are denied admission and must remain at the quayside until your white friends return in the evening. You cannot avoid going into shops, even though you know you must make your selections with the store detective making no effort to conceal his interest in you, and his close attention to your every move. To be the teenage son of thrifty black parents who buy a house away from Brixton means being stopped by policemen and challenged to prove that you live where you say you live—to quote the telephone number, produce your house-key and so on.

Two weeks ago a fellow priest from Barbados learned the hard way not to be alone on an Underground station platform at 11 o'clock on a Saturday night—when he regained consciousness in St Bartholomew's Hospital the next day, following the attentions of a gang of hooligans.

Two weeks ago the national press reported that the government is going ahead with plans to divide people who claim unemployment benefit into racial groups. Staff at benefit offices will be asked to assess claimants visually and categorize them as West Indian, African, Asian, etc. Why is it so important that there should be recorded the colour of a man's skin when he claims the financial assistance to which unemployed people are entitled? Is it to provide some semblance of respectability to those that claim that black people are a drain on the economy of this country? Already I can hear certain members of parliament claiming that black unemployed people cost the country so many thousands of pounds and how much cheaper it would be to grand-aid them to leave the country.

So far as I know there has been no outcry or outrage against this blatant racism. *The truth is that this kind of behaviour on the part of both Government and individuals is possible only because there is a virus of racism in our national life that it is actively fostered by some people for their own ends, and is no longer a matter of concern or shame for the majority.*

By choosing a Samaritan, a member of a despised race, to be the benefactor in this story, Our Lord showed that neighbourliness is something which cuts across all barriers, racial and political differences, and even personal likes and dislikes. He shows that to do service to others in need is indeed neighbourly conduct, so the rich should help the poor, the strong should help the weak and so on. But he shows something else. He knew that such acts have in them the seeds of patronage and condescension, and this could lead to complacency and pride.

So this story has another lesson—the lesson of humility. There will be times when the neighbour will be someone from whom you will want to receive no favours, and to whom you will not want to be indebted. There are many people who enjoy being generous to others, but will accept no favours from them, forgetting that the other person's kindness and generosity are as important to his or her self-fulfilment as their own is to them.

This is a lesson which the Church accepts in theory but is reluctant to put into practice. True, we no longer hold crude theories about humanity being divided into 'superior races' and 'lesser breads', or that Europe is made up of 'nations' while Africa is made up of 'tribes'. But we still have a long way to go. We still have to recognize that it may please God to speak to us through the Samaritans of today's world—those whom we consider to be the despised or the inferior—and that we need to be humble enough to recognize and accept this.

I am continually being reminded of an episode in a book written almost twenty-five years ago entitled *The Lonely African*. The writer recalls how he was standing with a white farmer observing an African worker. The African wore only a pair of shorts, but around his neck was a tie! (probably a regimental tie!) The farmer commented that the silly fellow did not realize that one did not wear a tie without a shirt and collar! His more observant companion had already noted that for the African the tie was not a piece of clothing but had become a useful piece of equipment. He used it to tie bundles of wood, and it was only when it was not in use that he kept it around his neck!

Because the European so often looks at Africa through spectacles clouded by notions of racial superiority, he sees only the African's clumsy handling of European concepts and commodities, and has no perception of the African's ingenious adaptation of a new thread to be woven into the strong and authentic tapestry which has stood the test of time.

So it is with black people's experience of God. It is true that in Africa, the Caribbean and elsewhere there may be found church buildings modelled on ancient cathedrals in this country, and choirs robed in cassocks and Canterbury caps struggling with Anglican chants. It is true that there are records of priests going out from this country to minister to large black congregations overseas. But it is worth remembering that, even while theologians were debating whether or not black people had souls and were fit subjects for baptism, black people, by their existence of pain, of life and death in all its starkness, in the companionship which is bred in a common oppression, had laid hold upon the God unto whom all hearts are open, all desires known; the God who could, and would, exalt the valleys, and make plains of the mountains—the God who held them always in the hollow of his hand.

It was an easy mistake for the European to believe that they were receiving God at *his* hands—and for the first time—when they were allowed into the galleries of the churches, and therefore to assume that their religion was only a reflection of his. Now, Europe having pronounced God dead, or at any rate mummified in a religion which has no power to change the lives of men and women, it would not occur to them to look to the black presence in their midst for the authentic word of God today.

Yet the marks of true religion are to be found in Britain's black communities. *Suffering* there certainly is, but there is also *faith*. There is *hope* and, above all, there is *love*. There is *joy*, and although the rejection of sin and evil sometimes appears theatrical or sanctimonious, for *people*—including sinners—there is always *acceptance*. Moreover, there is a strong sense of the *indivisibility of truth*. Lies are always lies, and must necessarily lead away from God who is Truth. Even white lies are lies! There is a strong sense of *the place of weak persons*, as of right, in the life of the community, whether they be elderly people or small children. *Dependence upon God* is seen as strength and not as weakness, and *obedience to God's will* is a virtue, not something to be ashamed of. Where for others *to speak loudly to Jesus* as to a companion walking alongside might appear a form of mental illness, for a black Christian, conscious of the abiding presence of a living Christ, it is a perfectly reasonable thing to do.

For black Christians who are rooted in the life of the black community, the existence of God is not dependent upon the latest utterances of Cambridge theologians, and we can hear the word of God in holy Scripture with or without the aid of form criticism. So, in response to God's call, and with his help, we are determined, with a quiet confidence, that we shall always be good neighbours—Samaritans or not!

A Table in the Wilderness? (Psalm 78:9)

Inderjit Bhogal

[This sermon by Bhogal is taken from *A Table for All* (Sheffield: Penistone, 2000), 27–35. It was preached at the Methodist Conference, Huddersfield on Sunday 25 June 2000.]

What a marvellously crazy idea: a table in the wilderness. Community celebration—a party in the wilderness. It's about as crazy as having Conference in Huddersfield. It's about as mad as celebrating the holy eucharist in some of the contexts we represent. Like the Flower Estate in Sheffield where I share in ministry—a kind of waste land where houses have been knocked down, an area people are moving out of.

When the children of Israel were held captive in Egypt, Moses and Aaron went to Pharaoh and said 'thus says the Lord… Let my people go, so that they may celebrate a festival (feast) with me in the wilderness' (Exod. 5:1). What an image: to celebrate a festival, a party with God in the wilderness. God the party-goer wants a party—a rave-up in the open air. God chooses to celebrate in the wilderness, not in the place of captivity and oppression, even though the Psalmist could sing: 'You prepare a table for me in the presence of mine enemies, you treat me like an honoured guest'. While those in power might let me feed on scraps that fall off their table, you treat me like an honoured guest.

There were of course those who questioned this: 'Can God spread a Table in the wilderness? Even though he struck the rock so that the water gushed out and torrents overflowed, can he also give bread ...' (Ps. 78.19). Will there be food at the party? Can God spread a table in the wilderness?

Was this also the inward prayer of Elijah who fled 'a day's journey into the wilderness' and sat under a tree with an abject sense of failure, fearing for his life, feeling suicidal, wishing to die...when an angel came to him with bread and said 'Get up and eat'. Whatever else you do, when you are not well, don't stop eating.

And did all these images look back to Abraham sharing a meal with 'angels' in the wilderness, under the oaks of Mamre? Can we also anticipate in these meals Jesus eating food with multitudes in the countryside, in their homes, or on the beach?

There is a tradition in scripture of God providing manna, bread in the wilderness. The answer to the psalmist's rhetorical question would be clear to all the hearers: Yes. God can prepare a table in the wilderness, and a table in the midst of 'enemies' even, and treat people as honoured guests without laying any conditions except this: have enough for your need, don't be overcome with greed which leads to unfairness and waste. Have a party. But don't be greedy.

A table in the wilderness... That people may celebrate with me in the wilderness...

In the Wilderness!

In the place that people are inclined to steer clear of, to avoid, in the place where life is risky, in the place which can threaten to destroy life, in the place which can be beautiful but remote, arid and leave one exposed, vulnerable, in the place which can be vast, where one can get lost, and in which one may expect to be for a long time.

The Bible describes a desert as a wilderness and sees it in positive terms too: it is the place of encounter with God; it is the place where God's word is heard; it is where temptation is wrestled with; it is where God provides for people the miracle of water and food for each day; it is where prophets too find refuge and are ministered to by angels; it is where community with all its pitfalls is forged.

In the Wilderness

Can God provide 'a table in the wilderness'? Yes, God can prepare a table even in a place of oppression and in the presence of 'enemies' and treat you like an honoured guest. But will only prepare a table in order to *celebrate* where there is freedom from oppression, even if that means providing a table in the wilderness. There can be no party when there is oppression. Where is the wilderness for us, for you, for the church in which you worship and serve? What is the place you dread? The place you avoid? The place you would choose not to visit or live in? Is it that dull, monotonous, boring relationship which you find oppressive and which is exhausting? Is it the place of work in which you feel unfulfilled, or a new direction you are being pushed into? Is it the experience of unemployment? Is it the neighbourhood in which your church is set? Is it your congregation in which you feel isolated?

God wants to celebrate a feast with you there. This all sounds fun here in these surroundings. God at least gives honour and worth to you, and longs to celebrate a feast with you there. But can God prepare a table for those who have no home and no table? Can God prepare a table for the people in places of famine? Can God prepare a table for asylum seekers living in poverty and who have to beg in a hostile environment?

I decided to reflect on this by sitting where homeless people sit in Sheffield.

> *Graham is homeless. He says people call him a 'tramp' and sometimes give him money. He lives on the streets of Sheffield where I have got to know him well. As a walker, he gave me sound advice as I prepared to walk along roads from Sheffield to London. I saw him recently; he was sitting on a concrete bench in the city centre. He had a bandage round his head and one around a foot. 'Banged into a wall', he said.*
>
> *As we got into conversation I asked him to help me. I'm working on a sermon about tables and bread and parties in the wilderness, I said; it seems a bit odd, but can you help me?*
>
> *'I love bread' he said.*
>
> *He reached into a carrier bag beside him. His boots and walking stick were by the bag. Out of the bag he fetched bread.*
>
> *'I always have bread', he said. 'I know a shop. I turn up just before closing time. They give me a couple of loaves. With it I feed myself and my brothers and sisters who are poor.' He talked to me about all those homeless ones who walk at night as others sleep. He held out a large round cob.*
>
> *'This is made from rye. I love it—my favourite.' He said. 'Try some.' He broke off a large piece with his rugged hands and held it out to me. I received it and said 'Amen' and ate it in bits over several minutes. As I ate*

it, he unpacked his carrier bag and brought out different kinds of bread and placed it all on the concrete slab bench which had now become a table. Suddenly I was having a meal, and he was the host. Each loaf was held up and its contents were described. I was given a piece from each loaf.

'You need good red wine with this bread... it would be a good one for your communion at church'.

'You need to eat this bread with cheese...'

All around us a city centre environment with its own beauty, but a wilderness with a lifestyle of grabbing and greed and of profit before people. People racing about. Some sitting down to rest. Before me now a parable of the text: 'a table in the wilderness'.

I was being fed by one of the poorest people I know. I was a guest of honour at a table in the wilderness. 'You treat me like an honoured guest.'

After this feast I went and sat in a fast food bar for a while. What a contrast. The one described as a 'tramp' described himself as a 'connoisseur of bread'. We sat and talked for an hour. In the fast food restaurant people came and ate bland food made tasty by additives. They sat for 10–15 minutes to eat and went. They showed no respect for food, no respect for bread. They were not treated as honoured guests. They had no capacity to sit, to taste, to talk. No wonder that before Jesus fed a multitude with bread he said, 'Make the people sit down'.

The table is set/spread in the wilderness. In the midst of all that threatens: greed, decline, loneliness, homelessness, poverty, how asylum seekers are treated, church on broken-down housing estate, church in agricultural poverty, globalism, capitalism and socialism, selfishness, individualism, get-out-of-it-what-you-can culture, half a million tonnes of food are thrown away in UK each year.

We have to learn to celebrate and feast with God in our wilderness. The table is an important symbol in a culture dominated by chairs. Jesus sets a table in the midst of his community.

The eucharistic table: Is it the church's table which is so often an excluding one? Or Jesus' table which is an including one. Which is the table that Jesus turns over? The table that exploits, the table that excludes? The table that exists on 'trickle down' theory at which some eat the scraps that fall off? The unfair table which allows hunger? Can the Lord prepare a table in the wilderness?

Yes, and welcomes and treats all as 'honoured guests' as in Psalm 23, and as Jesus who eats even with those who betray him. It welcomes children. In the midst of all the shit celebrate eating with each other, drink wine, enjoy time with your lover, wear good clothes (Eccl. 9:7-9), build relationships, care for and provide for each other, end hunger so that no one has to eat the scraps that fall off tables.

The Lord's table is prepared in the midst of contexts and realities that threaten life, in contexts we may prefer to avoid. It challenges greed and seeks an end to hunger in a world of plenty. It challenges the scandal of church disunity. It calls for an end to economic structures that create hunger and famine.

God prepares a banquet in the wilderness. A celebration in the midst of all that threatens. It is in the wilderness God teaches much, woos people, calls, affirms, tests, feeds. Like the poor 'tramp', God feeds us out of God's bounty and treats us all with honour. A foretaste of the heavenly banquet prepared for all.

The (Un)forgiving King (Matthew 18:21-35)

Michael N. Jagessar

[This sermon was prepared for and is taken from the *Journal of the College of Preachers* 119 (July 2005), 64–66.]

I cannot recall ever hearing a sermon or reading a commentary on the *Parable of the Unforgiving Servant or Slave* where the 'wicked slave' has been given a chance to tell his or her story, even though almost all preachers tend to locate this parable in the context of forgiveness. Through Jesus, Matthew writes off the slave as wicked and unforgiving and deserving only to be handed over to be tortured until he could pay off his debt. Matthew then goes on to have Jesus saying to his disciples and to us: 'So my heavenly Father will also do to every one of you if you do not forgive your brother or sister from your heart.' There must be countless of these 'torture sites' with long queues of defaulted debtors! The King, on the other hand, is most forgiving.

Let us allow Black Martha—a house slave and a convert to the Christian faith, property of the Massa Christopher, owner of the Paradise Plantation—to share her 'insights' on this narrative.

> 'Black Martha is not my real name. I do not know my real name. This is the name my master and mistress and owner gave me as I was darker than most of the other house slaves who tended to be of a lighter hue. My friends told me that my real parents were killed when caught trying to escape to the mountains with me as a little baby. I was brought up by another slave mother—named Industry—who is now deceased. From age eight I have been working in the great house of Massa Christopher and family. "Work", not "lazy" is my other name. We work long, long hours—from sunup to sundown.
>
> 'The slave in the parable reminds me of my life and those of my friends and family—a hard, harsh and dehumanising life so far. I read the same

Bible as my master and his family and cannot understand how they treat us as lesser specimens of the human race to be forcibly managed. Whether house or field slaves, the fact is, we are property of Massa Christopher and bound to plantation Paradise. Our life is a real and present terror on Paradise. I can still recall that pregnant mother that Master Christopher whipped because she was unable to go to the fields. He had the other slaves dig out a hole to accommodate her belly when she was placed face down on the ground and whipped like hell. I have seen Tuba flogged and put to the stocks because she spent too much time breast-feeding her infant while she worked in the fields. I also recall that night when they caught Quashie, the runaway slave. We were all brought outside to witness how he was strung up-sided down and beaten with the cat-o-nine tails. I lost count after one hundred. I remember that after the beating salt was rubbed into his wound and he was left hanging until he died.

'The master or king in this parable may appear to be some kind and benevolent Father—willing to lend sums of money to his slaves to invest. I am yet to meet such a master. I may be wrong. If he is so kind why did the Master want to sell off this slave, his family and the little they had to pay off the slave's debt? Why did he hand the slave over to be tortured until he got back his money? If the slave could not pay up then the torture can only mean his eventual death and his family being sold to pay back the king. The fact is—whether we are house-slaves or managerial slaves—*we are slaves*. We are somebody's property. It is the master/king who has the *power*. His decision is calculated for his own benefit. It does not improve our condition. He would always get back his money. We pay either way: with money and/or life.

'This story reminds me of the naked force that is always dished out to literally whip us into submission. The reality is: we are at the mercy of the master/king. Our bodies are like punching bags—an object of abuse. So, I wonder if this is one reason why that slave brother, in desperation and fear, turned to force to get his money back from one of his own. He was terrified of the king and internalized the very thing that eclipsed his own life. I do not know what I would have done.

'I guess as a Christian, I am expected to forgive. And what can be more fitting than this image of debt to point out how costly is forgiveness. When someone is indebted to you—you have power over that person and to forgive is to give up that power. The problem here is whether the master or king had really given up power. Was his forgiveness genuine—from the heart? I am no expert—just a humble convert who has rescued my master's bible from collecting dust. But if true forgiveness is as Jesus said: "not seven times but seventy-seven times" then that king failed to forgive repeatedly and took back the forgiveness already offered when the slave failed to forgive just once.'

'In the end, by removing the slave the master/king re-established that he is "massa": powerful and ruthless. If you ask me this is not gospel and the Jesus way. This is not speaking rightly of God. Perhaps Jesus is doing a trick with the text to confound a wicked system and such wickedness with its own chains. By mimicry and mockery Jesus reveals the inconsistency in the world around him and subverts it. That is why he comes as a slave or servant. I still think that Jesus, whose body was brutalized and left hanging on the cross, knows our pains and loves us. Nothing can conquer such power of love. And Jesus loves plenty—that is the resurrection truth that is hope for me and my freedom'.

Freedom (Galatians 5:1-5)

Anthony G. Reddie

[This extract is taken from *Growing into Hope*, vol. II (Peterborough: Methodist Publishing House, 1998), 106–108. In this piece, the sermon takes a different and effective shape—that of drama in the context of 'Intergenerational Worship'. By 'performing the sermon', young and old learn about the links between Easter, the oppression of Black people, the people of South Africa and the significance of Jesus' mission to set all people free. Inspired by the life of Jesus, Black people did not believe all the lies that had been told to them. Recalling the life Jesus had led, the stories of Jesus in the Bible and how he was raised from the dead and, through the power of God, overcame all the difficulties and obstacles that had been placed in front of him, Black people knew in their hearts and souls that Jesus came to make them free.]

[The scene… we see a semi-circle of chairs, on which are sat four young adults/teenagers. At the apex of the semi-circle sits an adult/ teacher. In the middle of the semi-circle, there is a small table/chair on which is placed a small portable stereo/tape recorder. The sketch begins with a voice off-stage. The effect is to give the pretence that the voice is coming from the radio. Alternatively, the voice could be pre-recorded on tape and played on a cassette player.]

Voice: [Off stage] This is a historic day. One that many people here never expected to witness in their lifetime. The crowd is swarming all around this slight, dignified, elderly gentleman. The atmosphere is excited. The people are jubilant. This is a day many have dreamed, prayed and hoped for… Nelson Mandela is free.

[The adult rises from his/her seat and turns off the cassette player. He/she turns to the young adults.]

Adult: It will be Easter Sunday in a few days' time. You've heard the tape, about Nelson Mandela. What do you think the two events have in common?

Joanne: [After some silence] In common?... [Pause]... Nothing!

Adult: [Looking at the others] What does everybody else think?

Marlon: Of course they've got nothing in common. At least most people care about Nelson Mandela. Easter doesn't mean that much to anybody these days.

Adult: Is that what everybody else thinks?

[The young people look at each other, nod tentatively and then all nod in agreement.]

Adult: Why do you think Easter is not that important? You all heard what the Minister said last week. Jesus died for our sins. On Easter Sunday, we remember the time he rose from the dead. You don't think that is important?

Alicia: Well it is, but people have other things to think about when Easter comes.

Marlon: Like watching videos on TV.

Joanne: Going out raving with your friends... [Looking at the Adult]... You do know that Jungle is Massive?

David: Niaming a big chunk of bun and cheese, washed down with some sweet carrot juice. That's what Easter means to me.

Adult: I see... Like that, is it?

Alicia: You upset with us for saying that?

Adult: It's your prerogative to believe what you wish to.

Marlon: Are you for real?

David: Don't believe a word of it... He's/she's well vex, you can tell. Look at his/her nostrils, they're all flared up, like a horse... [To the Adult]... You're vex, aren't you?

Adult: I promise you... I am not vex as you put it... If that's what you think, then fair enough.

David: I don't buy any of this.

Alicia: Neither do I... It's your job to make us believe in Easter, and think it's important.

Adult: No… You're all intelligent people. You can think for yourself. If you say that Easter is not important, then fair enough. If you say that Easter and Nelson Mandela have nothing in common, then fair enough again.

[The Adult rises to his/her feet… There is silence. The young people look on suspiciously… The Adult turns and smiles.]

Adult: Can I ask you all to do this one thing for me?

Joanne: [Looking at the others] Hmmm… Yeah, sure.

Adult: Alright… This is what I want you to do… Just sit here.

David: Come again star?

Adult: Sit here…

Alicia: And do what?

Adult: Nothing… Simply sit and wait.

Marlon: For what?

Adult: You will see.

Joanne: Is that it?

Adult: Trust me.

David: I've heard that one before.

Adult: Trust me… Just sit here. You can talk, sleep, whatever, but you have to sit here.

[All the characters sit quietly, quite still. A young child walks across the front of the stage, with a white card held above their head. On the card are written the words, '20 minutes later'… The child then exits the stage. The scene comes to life again. All the young people are restless and fidgety.]

Marlon: How much longer do we have to sit here?

Adult: Not long.

Alicia: How long is that?

Adult: As long as a short piece of string.

Joanne: What does that mean?

David: This is pure wrenkness… When can we go?

Adult: Not long now. Just a little while longer.

[All characters sit quietly and still once again. Another young child walks across the stage, with a piece of card above their head. On this card are written the words 'another 20 minutes have gone by'. The child leaves the stage… The young people are still draped over their chairs, looking very dispirited and forlorn.]

David: This is slack.

Joanne: Out of order. You can't keep us here like this. I'm hungry. I want to go.

Marlon: I need some food… My belly a' pain mi.

Adult: I know… It won't be long now.

Alicia: You said that twenty minutes ago.

Adult: It won't be long. Trust me.

Joanne: You said that as well.

David: You can't hold us here like this. We have rights. You can't hold us. I want to be free.

Adult: Don't worry, it will soon come.

Marlon: My Dad always says that as he's leaving the house to go out. All eight hours later, he ain't set foot back in the house.

Adult: Trust me.

[All characters are still and quiet again… Another child walks across the stage with a white card above their head. On it are written the words, 'another 40 minutes have gone by'. The child walks off the stage. All the young people are lying, prostrate across their chairs. There are whines, sobs and snivels. All of them are dispirited and angry. They are desperate to leave. The Adult is standing in front of the group.]

All young people: [In unison] Let us go.

Adult: Soon... Not long now!

All young people: It's not fair.

Adult: I know... But just be patient.

All the young people: How long?

Adult: Not long.

> [David leaps to his feet and runs to an imaginary door and attempts to open it... We see him struggling, but he cannot escape... Reluctantly he returns to his seat.]

David: Please... Let us go.

All young people: [Shouting] Please!

Adult: [Pacing around] How do you all feel?

Joanne: Tired.

Marlon: Hungry.

David: Vex.

Alicia: Imprisoned.

Adult: Imprisoned... You're right... You were imprisoned. Denied your freedom... We all need our freedom. Freedom to think, freedom to speak. Freedom to move where you choose, freedom to be yourself. Why is Easter important? Why is Easter Sunday important?

All young people: Not sure.

Adult: Jesus came, gave up his position as the Son of God, died, and rose again on Easter Sunday, that we might be free. We all need to be free. Don't we?

All young people: Yes.

Adult: Very true. Now for the second question! What about Nelson Mandela? What has he got in common with Easter?

Alicia: Hmmmm... He's tried to set people free.

Marlon: Spent nearly thirty years in prison, trying to win Black people's freedom.

Joanne: I suppose they do have a lot in common.

Adult: God has called many people. From Harriet Tubman, through to Martin Luther King. God still calls people. People like Nelson Mandela, people who have made sacrifices and struggled to bring freedom for all people. On Easter Sunday, we remember the sacrifices and triumph of Jesus, to win our freedom. One day, you may be called upon to make such sacrifices and struggles for your freedom... [Pause] ... One last question. What about the wait?

Marlon: Terrible.

Joanne: Unfair.

Alicia: Frustrating.

David: Slack... Totally out of order.

Adult: Looking forward to leaving?

Young people: Yes.

Adult: Of course... You've waited for it. It was a long time coming. God is faithful and will always keep a promise. Sometimes, the wait makes the freedom all the more appreciated. Never forget that!

Young people: We won't.

Adult: Good... You can go.

Young people: [Shouting] Yes...

[All the young people rise from their seats and charge off stage, leaving the Adult standing alone... He/she looks forward at the congregation and begins to hum the tune to 'Freedom is coming'. The other characters return to join in and help sing. This will develop into the full song, which everyone is encouraged to sing, the congregation as well.]

THE END

9 Roots and Routes

Black theology in Britain has never been a purely internal, self-enclosed or self-referential enterprise. From the earliest writings, such as Grant and Patel's landmark texts *A Time to Speak*[1] and *A Time to Act*[2] (the first texts in Britain to use the nomenclature of Black theology in their title or subtitle), we have a very plural cast of players on show. Both texts utilize not only Black British voices but also those of Black and Asian people from the Caribbean and Asian Diasporas.

Black theology in Britain unlike its North American cousin has always been influenced by the Diasporan routes of postcolonial histories and the inter- and intra-culturality[3] that are a feature of hybrid subjectivities that arise from the discursive ebbs and flows of empire.[4]

The use of the term 'Black' in the UK context has invariably been used in a plural sense to connote identities and subjectivities that have transcended the seemingly ethnocentric boundaries that want to police such discourses around Afrocentric or Black nationalistic thought.

The term Black has to be understood within the context of Britain in a variety of ways. The use of the term Black does not simply denote one's epidermis but is rather a political statement relating to one's sense of marginalization within the contested space that is Britain. Using the term Black is to identify oneself as a socially constructed 'other' when juxtaposed against Eurocentric discourses that dominate the normative gaze and trajectory of what it means to be *authentically British*. This particular approach to the practicalities of coalition building and political mobilization can be traced back to the 1970s.[5] In effect, we are arguing, and acknowledging, that Black is not simply African or African Caribbean, nor is it solely about being born in the UK or having one's allegiances defined in any straightforward or single trajectory manner.

The development of Black theology in Britain has always been a plural affair. Indeed, the creation of the very first Black theology forum in Birmingham in the early 1990s was a product of the creative thinking and energy of two Black Methodist ministers from the 'World Church',[6] both of whom were resident in Birmingham at the time in educational establishments. Emmanuel Lartey, a Ghanian Methodist minister, was working at the University of Birmingham as a lecturer in Pastoral Theology, whilst George Mulrain, a Methodist minister from Trinidad, was the principal of Kingsmead College,[7] a Methodist mission college based in Selly Oak. These individuals were instrumental in giving birth to the development of Black theology in Britain, along with Inderjit Bhogal, another Methodist minister originally from Kenya.[8]

This chapter highlights the work of a number of 'Diasporan' scholars whose work has played an important role in the ongoing development of Black theology in Britain. The work of such scholars as Ron Nathan, George Mulrain, Michael Jagessar and Emmanuel Lartey (the 'Founding Father' of Black theology in Britain) illuminate this chapter and offer an inter-cultural and international scope to Black theology in Britain.

Caribbean Youth Identity in the United Kingdom: A Call for a Pan-African Theology

Ronald Nathan

[In this essay, taken from *Black Theology in Britain* 1 (October 1998), 19–34, Nathan introduces the idea of Pan-Africanism into Black British theological discourse with specific reference to the struggle of Caribbean youths in Britain for an authentic identity. His overarching plea is a call for a Pan-African theology as this would resonate with the experiences of people of African descent in Africa, the Americas, Caribbean and Asia and therefore be a model, among others, for the development of human identity, dignity and worth, especially where their social, political, economic and spiritual conditions are oppressive and degrading.]

The State of Black Youth in Britain

It is true to say that in the United Kingdom the most prominent attitude of Black Britons has been the belief in an integrationist ideal. The majority of Black British people have accepted conservative multi-culturalism as a good and progressive step towards equality with their White counterparts.

The quality of life of African/Caribbean youths in Britain tells a different and very bleak story. This is based on the combined social pressures of being Black in twentieth-century Europe and the perennial threat of racism with its long tentacles extending into areas of employment, education, health, social services, housing and the criminal justice system, the effects of global forces on the national economy and the British social class systems notwithstanding.

The participation of Black youths (aged 25 and under) in the society's social, economic, political and cultural institutions and structures is proportionate to the measure by which these facilities affirm and enhance their self-worth, self-identity and aspirations. Their reality in this context is of their aspirations thwarted, their dreams deferred and their desires squashed. Supporting documentary evidence shows the disproportionate ill-treatment of Black people in the criminal justice system and in immigration policies, exclusion from education facilities, employment opportunities and unemployment statistics, and lack of adequate provision as mental health service users.

No dialogue can take place with young black people without mention of their greatest aspiration, that of *respect*. This desire for *respect* is a cry for self-identity, self-worth, a sense of belonging and security which is heard loud and clear in their 'walk, talk, and dance'. One young man states, 'at home you're not yourself but you have to show respect. Out there with your peers, you can't be yourself either, but you have to get respect.' Often young people engage in activities solely in order to keep the *respect* of their friends. In other words, petty crime, for instance, can become a rite of passage to gain *respect*. This can be reflected in other ways that initiate conflict between themselves and their White teachers as, for example, in 'what the youths deemed to be cultural norms, particularly their tendency to question instructions, their mode of dress and their ways of walking'.[9]

Black Youths and the Black Church

British-born Caribbean youths of the first, second and third generations, by their absence from the Black churches and their removal of the Black church as their frame and point of reference, are indicating the existence of a social, political and cultural divide. Black young people are asking fundamental questions about the Black church's theology, priorities, institutions and its relevance for their spiritual, social, cultural and political livelihood today and for the future. The social and psychological impact of the perceived injustices they face does not square up with what is on offer as salvation. The living conditions of the growing Black underclass and working class and the psychological response of 'black rage' appear to be invisible to the Black church.

Respect has educational, social, cultural, economic, political and spiritual dimensions that have to be delivered in a language that engages the street culture. This, the church seems to regard as worldly and outside of its remit. To accept this call to a Pan-African theology is by definition to accept a radical agenda that is not offered to our youths through the normal process of socialization.

Cultural Agenda

The impact of the street culture of the United States of America upon youths on British streets cannot go unobserved. Drive-by shootings in our inner cities are now a reality. During a three-week period recently there were three drive-by shootings in Moss Side, Manchester. On 'Top of the Pops' one can find the use of music, dance and images in an attempt to gain *respect* by and for young Black people. This may not be on the terms established by middle-class society but it is certainly on the terms of the young people themselves. British hip-hop singer Ebony launched her record career with a new album entitled *RESPECT*. In the most thought-provoking and challenging book I have read in recent years, Caryle Fielding Stewart III quotes a young man as follows:

> Dignity, self respect, courage and honour. That's where God is and that's what God is about. We must do everything we can to worship and praise God. We can do this by protecting our lives the best way we can. The AK 47 is the highest form of protection of the sacred life God has given us. It puts everything into perspective and gives the innocent an edge in these streets of no return.[10]

Black youths are presenting a critique of the Black church's mission, priorities and practices. For many Black youths the Black churches' message of redemption without emancipation from mental slavery is unacceptable. Its equation of holiness with cultural abandonment in favour of Eurocentric systems, celebrations and norms is unacceptable. Its security in the comforts of middle-class aspirations culminating in social distance is unacceptable. Its conservative orientation towards social and political change, and preoccupation with a right-wing agenda without an 'in your face' challenge, is unacceptable. The colour-blind approach so cherished by Black churches is unacceptable. Therefore, Black youth's involvement in African spirituality, Rastafarianism and the Nation of Islam does not point to laziness or a lack of spiritual discipline but a choice based on relevance.

The spirituality young Black people perceive on offer from the churches separates off social justice and radical action and this they find unacceptable. Truly the biggest 'bogeyman' for the Black church is the understanding that to be Afrocentric and committed to the total liberation of people of colour is to be 'anti-white' or 'anti-anybody'. Commitment to total liberation is consistent with biblical teaching on people-hood, citizenship, righteousness and justice. There is among Black youths a feeling of disillusionment and isolation. They have developed an uncanny ability to see through governmental double speak and Christian religiosity. In this I hear a voice rustling in the mulberry tree calling for a Pan-African theology.

Cultural Identity: A Vehicle for Change and Liberation

C. Eric Lincoln in his essay 'Black Religion and Racial Identity' argues that identity within an Afrocentric tradition is communal, linking the Supreme Being, ancestors, divinities, clan, tribe, family and the individual and therefore it is an interlocking system of precise identification. He maintains that when this system is broken down or ruptured, the African sense of identity is lost and he or she is nowhere. Further on he makes the link between identity and church. He asserts that 'Religion is not race, but it is often made to function as if it were. In the African-American experience, where every critical index of racial and cultural identity had been forbidden, suppressed, or denied, religion became the closest approximation of African corporate identity.'[11]

William E. Cross Jr[12] identifies five stages in the psychology of Nigrescence. In other words, the stages Black people go through when they tear down their old identity and replace it with one that is more Black-orientated. These he names as (1) Pre-encounter, (2) Encounter, (3) Immersion-Emersion, (4) Internalization, and (5) Internalization-Commitment. What is vital for us to note with these stages is that their presence points to the fact that, due to diverse experiences and different stages Black people may be in, there is no one unified perspective of Blackness held by the Black community.

Paul Gilroy locates a vehicle for identity change in popular culture.

> Music dominates popular culture. It is central to this consideration of cultural identity because of its global reach, and because it is repeatedly identified as a special area of expressive culture that mysteriously embodies the inner essence of racial particularity... it is also in the music that the most intense legacy of the African past is concentrated... it is important, then, that the area of cultural production which is most evidently identified with racial authenticity and Black particularity is also the most mutable and adaptive of forms.[13]

Gilroy continues:

> Black popular culture does not determine the formation of social and cultural identities in any mechanistic way, but it supplies a variety of symbolic, linguistic, textual, gestural and, above all, musical resources that are used by people to shape their identities, truths, and models of community. This expressive culture is now a global phenomenon which, even when annexed by the corporate cultural industries, still hosts important conversations between constituencies that are closely linked, even if they are widely separated in space and time. It provides analysts with the means to explore the unequal exchanges that characterise the interactive, dialogical relationships between Black populations across the globe.[14]

Gilroy's statement has wide-ranging implications for those wishing to make an impact upon Black British youth culture. This popular youth culture incorporates a Pan-African hybrid of musical influences, reggae, hip-hop, soca, African high-life, world music and jungle drawn from the Caribbean, African-American street culture, British and Brazilian musical styles. The active participation of the Black church in the development of these popular cultural aesthetics is crucial to a street theology, a Pan-African theology.

It is important to stress that there are other aspects of Afrocentric cultural art forms that are attracting the attention of Black youngsters, including African names and naming ceremonies, Afrocentric influences in weddings and funerals, fashion, theatre, dance, drumming, Kwanzaa celebrations and alternative spirituality. This trend is highly visible in the popularity of groups such as Arrested Development, Sounds of Blackness, Desiree, Ebony, and The Fugees with their projection of an Afrocentric ideology and spirituality in their music, themes, stage settings, dress and movements.

An Afrocentric philosophy does not discard outright all postulates of European origin; it does, however, as Do Nascimento has argued, reserve to Africans the right to define which of these postulates might be valid for them, and the right to design and develop alternative principles based upon our own experience, methodologies and forms of knowledge. Our cultural goal should be to preserve, that is, to rescue and creatively reconstruct the positive aspects of our spiritual, philosophical, artistic, cultural and ethical values, rather than to fuse them with others in a context of inequality. We seek to respect and demand respect for ourselves as human beings with a specific history and identity, and to live in peace with other peoples respecting their identities as well.[15]

A Pan-African Theology

I now come to the theological formation that responds to the particularities of the situation as outlined above. Pan-African theology as a local theology has a unique perspective. It is not hung up on awaiting authentication in order to be. I do not claim that this is the only theology that would be formulated by Black people in the United Kingdom but I wish to stress that there is a voice crying in the wilderness of our urban centres. It is a call for a Pan-African theology from the underbelly of British life. In the Black tradition a call always demands a response. In the remaining part of this essay I will attempt to respond to the call by pulling together the various strands of thought previously mentioned in relation to a Pan-African theology.

I recognize *three* theological movements as having contributed to my thinking in this regard. These are: Black theology, Caribbean theology and African theology. The three hold in common a high regard for the interaction of the context (environment) with the interpretation of the text (hermeneutic) and the liberation of its subjects (praxis).[16]

Distinctive features of a Pan-African theology

All theologies are ideological in nature, for theology, the science and study of God, is a human construction. Western theology has historically been developed by White European males and as a result of Europe's political and economic ascendancy has been exported as classical theology. By contrast, a Pan-African theology is ideologically committed to the unity and well-being of people of African origin. I wish to share *four* distinctive features of a Pan-African theology. These are by no means exclusive or exhaustive as is evident in the proposed programme.

The first distinctive feature is *harmony*. Straddling an African worldview, African traditional religions and Afro-religions in the Caribbean, is the concept of harmony. This is harmony between all of the created order, that is, the Supreme Being (Creator), divinities, ancestors, the living dead, the living beings and those on their way to being and the environment. Thus 'harmony' as a value is identifiable in African religious systems and their hybrid cousins in the Caribbean and South America. Salvation and success is found in the creation of harmonious relationships be they communal, familial, individual, ecological or political.

The second distinctive feature is *Holism*. The dichotomy between, for example, Good and Evil, Secular and Spiritual, Heaven and Earth and Male and Female and so on does not exist within the world view of African societies and certainly not within an Afrocentric philosophy. These Hellenistic mythological imports were incorporated within the European Enlightenment and later Reformation Christian thought. This is the basis for tensions in our present society between religion and politics, for example. A Pan-African theology would be much more akin to the position of Process thinkers.

A third distinctive characteristic is that a Pan-African theology is fundamentally an *experiential theology*, as opposed to a dogmatic and systematic theology. In other words, it starts with the situation of the local context and the local people. It locates the gospel within their hearts and hands. It is democratic in the sense that it is not dependent on a learned class of specialists (e.g. clergy) to interpret, apply or develop it.

A fourth distinctive feature is that a Pan-African theology would be *action orientated*. It would seek boldly to address its concern in a proactive way, engaging Black British youths with a profoundly radical delivery mechanism. This is more fully illustrated below.

Methodologically, a Pan-African theology could not sidestep the matter of culture or race. It would see the Pan-African combination of cultures as a most accessible avenue for a liturgy of liberation. Here, I advocate the use of the arts as the primary medium for educational, evangelistic and communal salvation. I believe that in the pioneering work of Courtney Pine with the fusion of jazz and jungle music there is scope for cultural and religious fusion. As Charles Long[17] suggests, black music offers relatively unexplored expressions of black religion that intensify conceptions of certain creative possibilities within the religious existence of the Pan-African community. The importance of this for liturgical formation and worship is fundamental. 'Liturgy is the work of the people of God…and a space to struggle with political and social issues'.[18] Liturgy becomes the environment to contain corporate vision and to transmit social forms of believing. This creates an environment for belonging, history and memory and for telling our story.[19] Culture, liturgy and theology may either liberate people to rise to their fullest creative potential or else cohabit with the status quo to inhibit, dominate and exploit the masses.

A Pan-African theology church programme

According to Jawanza Kunjufu,[20] 'there are three types of black churches—the entertainment churches (sing, shout and holler), the containment churches (which only open their churches on Sundays) and the liberation churches (innovative churches)'. Liberation churches with a Pan-African theology will look distinctly different from their Black church or White-led Black church counterparts.[21] A transformation that begins with their theology would mean unhitching their denominational wagon from Eurocentric ideologies.

Liberation churches would have to develop liberation-centred theological institutions that produce Christian leaders who understand their mission to include community development and community leadership.

Liberation churches would be those that would celebrate their Blackness without apology for their African heritage. This would be reflected in their symbols, literature, architecture, theology, hymnology, music, worship and dance. They would resist cultural assimilation and integration and seek out ways of promoting cultural diversity. They would not seek to 'deny themselves' in order to be acceptable to White people or White churches. No greater avenue is open to articulate this cultural renaissance for social and political justice than in the church's liturgy and worship. They would consider liberating large numbers of people from social injustice as central to their mission. There would be a willingness to publicly elevate Black people from the quicksands of institutional racism and poverty.

In tackling the debilitating effects of unemployment, these churches will move beyond praying for jobs to being creators of jobs. Instead of wondering why there are no Black businesses in their communities and therefore no jobs, they would utilize their economic muscles to grow young businesses. Their investments would be targeted to bring business skills into the Black community. It would demand that businesses that enjoy the privilege of making profits in our communities make lasting contributions to those communities in a tangible way that empowers and resources us to do for ourselves.

A Pan-African theology will seek alliances beyond the shores of the United Kingdom to gain access to markets among their counterparts in the Diaspora and on the mother continent. Denominational affiliation will be sifted to facilitate new partnerships with the Black voluntary sectors and the Black business community instead of its divisive function of keeping one Christian community from the other.

Its involvement with the restoration of self-worth and dignity would be paramount in its rejection of the post-modern ideologies of Europe and the reclamation of that which is good from within our African and Caribbean heritage. Here I want to state that the art of the sermon will be truly an

Afrocentric collective experience, creative, dynamic and instructive in its application to the whole of Black life. The liberation church in its prophetic claims will tackle the reclamation of the Black male image linking it to the responsibility and accountability the Black male has as man, husband, father, brother, son and community developer.

With respect to Black women they will find in the Church (an institution to which they have given a disproportionate amount of time and resources) a community that will not burden them further with gender discrimination. The church will therefore be a seedbed for British womanist theologies that will challenge the triple jeopardy our women face of being Black, female and poor as well as the international feminization of poverty.[22]

These churches would reject a fortress theology that hides from the realities of the drug and gun cultures that terrorize our neighbourhoods with legal or illegal substances that dull the minds of our youth, corrupt their morals and captivate their bodies through addiction. Salvation will be reinterpreted to include the rescue, rehabilitation and resettlement of ex-offenders, prostitutes and homeless people, at the same time as tackling the social, moral and spiritual causes at the root of criminality, be that perpetuated by the state or individuals. Justice will reach out from the halls of prayer. The justice system will be challenged through the provision of lawyers, legal aid and policy advisors to put justice back into the system.

Liberation churches will tackle corruption in local and central government as well as within ecclesiastical circles. Liberation churches would call their members to community action by asking them to give themselves to prophetic action in soup kitchens, meals on wheels, room lettings, adoption and fostering, mentoring schemes, and supplementary education programmes. They would establish fresh-start programmes for those who have lost out on state education or have been incarcerated in prisons. They would require of the state education system not only an inclusion of the histories of people of colour but also the total overhaul of the policy of exclusion as a means of class control.

These churches will not lose their spirituality but would tap the gifts of all their membership which in turn would stimulate growth. Bible study would not be a bore but will take its place alongside empowerment conferences, Bible quizzes and political debates. Mission teams overseas will have as part of the good news ethical investment policies and a community development orientation. A keen interest will be taken on Black medical and mental health issues such as sickle cell anaemia.

Conclusion
I believe that Black youths in the United Kingdom reflect the sum total of black cultures which originate in Africa and the African Diaspora. Through their experiences of racism and alienation in British society they are calling

for a church that would deal with their identity crises as well as the socio-economic and political problems they face. A Church with a Pan-African theology would be Afrocentric in philosophy recognizing their heritages and histories and affirming their primary cultures. This theology will liberate the Black Church from its obsession with wishing to please and be admitted to the mainstream, which normally means white and Eurocentric.

Such theology will fully engage the cultural issues of the Caribbean youth in Britain. It will see art, drama, music and dance as a vehicle for reinforcing cultural orientation and utilize them for spiritual, social, educational, political and economic change. It would see as a natural part of its mission the creation of alliances and partnerships with Black communities at home and abroad. The participation in the small but vocal Pan-African Congress Movement (UK) would fill the spiritual vacuum so often highlighted in the movement's deliberations as well as energize this organization with hope.

It would foster links with African communities throughout the African continent and the African Diaspora and find practical expressions in solidarity with these communities. It would have a strong identification with Black street culture as this is the most vocal and yet vulnerable sector of the Black community. It will develop long-term strategies with the Black communities for the leadership and development of its communities and act as a buffer and mediator between governmental authorities and the local communities on behalf of its people.

The Music of African Caribbean Theology

George Mulrain

[This essay is taken from *Black Theology In Britain* 1 (October 1998), 35–45. George Mulrain is one of the Caribbean's foremost theologians, who lived and worked in the UK during the 1980s. In this article he argues a case for music that is relevant for the Caribbean theological task and by implications for Black British theology with its strong Caribbean presence.]

Introduction
Today there is an increasing appreciation for and commitment to the view that theology is not absolute but arises out of given contexts. Scholars from the so-called 'third world' have helped to promote the theories related to this new approach to theology. They have, for example, helped people from the west to realize that what used to be counted as universal theology was really the sum total of reflections about God by White, male, middle-class academics. God might be universal in the sense of being the one and only true God, but *God* talk certainly was not. In fact, there was

disagreement with the very premise that the *logos* of *Theos* meant verbal philosophical pronouncements. For some people, particularly those from the 'third world', doing theology entailed not just talk, but a continuous cycle of action, reflection, action, reflection—*the praxis* approach as it is commonly referred to. Theology is about how people experience and perceive God in the context of their daily lives.

I believe that I am right in assuming that there are no hurdles to overcome when I include *African Caribbean* theology in the description of my topic. What I hope to do in this presentation on *the music of African Caribbean theology* is to make two main points. The first is that music is the servant of theology in that it enhances our understanding of the God who is present and in control of the universe. The second is that in every given context where men and women do theology, there is a type of music that is best suited to affirming God's presence. I want to put forward some suggestions about music that is relevant to the Caribbean's theological task but which unfortunately has not been fully acclaimed as appropriate by people within the Caribbean region.

Theology and Music

I make the assertion that whenever men, women and children meet in chapels, churches, cathedrals, temples, synagogues, mosques and other buildings set aside for worship, they are engaged in doing theology. They are occupied in a quest designed to encounter God. Indeed worship is a theological activity. As far as Christianity is concerned, music plays a major role in worshipful endeavour. We dare not make the claim that music is essential, since members of the Society of Friends (or Quakers) will insist upon the authenticity of worship in silence. However, its invaluable contribution cannot be lightly dismissed. Take, for example, a church scenario that is not necessarily the norm, but which is fairly typical. There is a musical prelude that is played as the worshippers assemble. The choir sings an introit. In what follows, members of the congregation join in the singing of hymns and choruses, as well as in the chanting of psalms. Musical interludes and background music are included at different points in the worship. All of these musical offerings go towards creating an atmosphere conducive to an appreciation of the divine presence. It is not uncommon to hear persons, after such an experience, affirm that they have had a personal encounter with God.

A classic example of how theology can be communicated through music is found in the hymns of the Wesley brothers, John (1703–91) and Charles (1707–88). They both used their poetic skills, though Charles did so even more than John. Their hymns, which are sung in many churches today, do reflect their theological understandings. In fact, if one is to understand Methodist doctrine, attention must be paid to the hymns. The Methodist doctrinal emphasis on *Christian perfection*, also described as *perfect love*, suggests that all persons can be saved 'to the uttermost'. Methodists, as a singing people, recognize the value of music in theology. Bernard L. Manning had this to say:

> Why do Wesley's hymns confirm and restore our confidence, and build us up securely in our most holy faith? It is no doubt partly because they show us something of the life of one of the pure in heart who saw God. We may not see God. We cannot fail to see that Wesley saw Him. Purity of heart: we are near Wesley's secret there, scriptural holiness, purity of heart, inevitably reflected in his clear mind and limpid verse.[23]

Then there are the many pieces of sacred music produced by Johann Sebastian Bach (1685–1750), George Frederic Handel (1685–1759), Ludwig van Beethoven (1770–1827) and other great composers of the seventeenth, eighteenth and nineteenth centuries. These all emerged on the soil of Europe. As Christianity spread to the various parts of the world through European missionary ventures, the music of western theology came to be regarded as normative for worship. Any attempts to replace or supplement it with indigenous music met with stout resistance. The African drum, for example, was considered more of a threat than an ally in the offering of praises to God. It was considered by some to be the devil's instrument. Of course, the question rightly to be asked is: 'Why must the devil have all the good music?'

African Music in Caribbean Theology

During the period of slavery in the Caribbean, our African forebears were forbidden to worship God using the same pattern and symbols which obtained when they enjoyed their freedom in Africa. The message that came from the European slave owners was clear—no drumming, no dancing, no working yourselves up into frenzied states of excitement. The French, for example, had the Code Noir of 1685, which stipulated in Article 2 that all slaves 'shall be baptised and instructed in the Catholic religion, Apostolic and Roman'. They were expected to reject whatever they had been holding on to in Dahomey, Congo, Sudan, Senegal, Cameroon or wherever in Africa under the rubric of traditional religion. In attempting to stifle belief in the presence of African ancestral spirits, the slave owners did not succeed in extinguishing the fires of African spirituality. The slaves held their religious ceremonies under the cover of darkness, thereby succeeding in maintaining a grip on the spirituality that had been nurtured in the continent of their birth.

There are perhaps two strands of music that we today recognize as coming out of the slave period. First there are the Negro spirituals, many of which had liberation as a theme:

Oh, freedom, oh freedom, oh freedom over me
And before I'd be a slave, I'd be buried in my grave
And go home to my Lord and be free.

No more moaning, no more moaning, no more moaning over me
And before I'd be a slave, I'd be buried in my grave
And go home to my Lord and be free.
There'll be shouting, there'll he shouting, there'll be shouting over me

And before I'd be a slave, I'd be buried in my grave
And go home to my Lord and be free.

This song, like many of the spirituals, had a concept of freedom that was not available in the present life, but would be obtainable in the hereafter. There was something of a fatalistic twist to the theology of the slaves. They could do nothing to change the state of affairs, hence they sang about a God who, while not saying 'No' to their servile condition on earth, would certainly say 'Yes' to their achieving a state of glory in the hereafter. To emphasize this point, two other such songs will suffice:

I've got a shoes, you've got a shoes, all of God's children got a shoes
When I get to heaven goin' to put on me shoes
Going to walk all over God's heaven, heaven, heaven
Everybody talking 'bout heaven ain't going there
Heaven, heaven, going to walk all over God's heaven.

Steal away, steal away, steal away to Jesus
Steal away, steal away home, I ain't got long to stay here.
My Lord calls me, he calls me by the thunder
The trumpet sounds within a my soul
I ain't got long to stay here.

It is important to note, though, that in many of the songs there was an active message skilfully concealed under the seeming fatalism. 'Steal Away to Jesus' or 'The Gospel Train is Coming' could communicate a message other than that of passive acceptance of one's lot. Indeed the Haitians disproved the theory that all slaves were fatalistic when they won a resounding victory over the forces of Napoleon Bonaparte to earn them their independence on 1 January 1804. Certainly the success of the Haitian revolution has been attributed to the fact that the slaves were convinced that their ancestors were interested in their freedom. The ceremony of *Bo'is Caiman*, led by Boukman on the night of 14 August 1791, was a worshipful event in which the slaves all pledged to fight against their French captors.

The second type of music that flourished during the slave era is that which obtains in African traditional religions in the Caribbean—Vaudou in Haiti, Shango in Trinidad and Tobago, Santeria in Cuba, Pukkumina in Jamaica. Here, worship involves singing and dancing to the rhythm of the drums. Here is an example of a Haitian vaudou chorus:

Nan Guinee gin loa
Gin loa Congo a ki loa mouin
Nan Guinee gin loa
Gin loa Congo a ki loa mouin.

It says that in Guinea there are spirits, including the Congo spirit which is a personal spirit. The idea communicated in song is that each person has a protective spirit that functions like a guardian angel. The songs of African religions in the Caribbean are typical of the oral tradition, with repetitive phrases and choruses. They are simple in that they communicate one central theme rather than a complex set of theological ideas. One truth about Black culture everywhere—whether African, African American or African Caribbean—is that music is an expressive medium.

Throughout the ages, Black musicians, whether they are playing jazz, soul or the blues, have put heart and soul into their music. Black singers excel because they use singing to express their feelings. Singing has a deep-seated purpose, as the South Africans will tell us:

We have not sung because we are happy.
We have sung even when we cried.
We have sung so as not to allow ourselves to be broken.
We have sung to survive (WCC Statement, January 1994).

Indeed South Africans, during the heyday of apartheid, sang and danced with determination that one day they would be free.

The Wealth of African Caribbean Music

The Caribbean is rich in music that has developed from Africa. Chief among these are *reggae* and *calypso*. Reggae began as a Jamaican musical expression, relying very heavily upon the drums of Africa. People such as Bob Marley, the late singer who was a member of the Rastafarian movement, popularized it. Reggae is now well known throughout the Caribbean region and beyond. Calypso, also now a Caribbean phenomenon, began in the island of Trinidad. It made use of the rhythmic beat of Africa and included a chorus. It has had other influences, today bearing traces of the music of Jamaica, Venezuela, India and China. Within the past ten years or so, there has been the introduction of soca, a combination of soul music (so-) and calypso (ca). Both reggae and calypso have a prophetic function, in that the singers focus upon the happenings in society, commenting upon them while at the same time alerting the people to possible implications, good or bad. In the words of Keith Warner:

The calypsonian, then, in one of his roles, acts as a mirror for the society and provides the population with a voice and a platform. He also interprets that which is new, puzzling, controversial or foreign, as can be seen

from the many calypsoes commenting on newsworthy world affairs... It
is clear that the views expressed fall under the general banner of popular opinion, the type the average citizen holds and discusses with his
friends—views that also include those on religion, education, drug abuse,
unemployment etc. insofar as they affect the individual and his relationship with the rest of the society. As a result, there is no political harassment
of the calypsonian as individual, as private citizen and it is well known and
accepted that the calypsonian, too, is full of ambivalence. He can con-
demn in one stanza, condone in the next and still be listened to. His role
in shaping social and political consciousness is by no means unimportant
or insignificant. But, on the whole, the calypsonian does not dabble only
in social and political commentary, though some do only that; in fact he
often owes his international recognition largely to the *other* themes he
treats in his calypsos.[24]

Associated with the music of calypso is that of the steel band. The steel
pan was developed in Trinidad in the early part of the twentieth century.
In 1883 the colonial authorities had banned the African drum. Discarded
oil drums replaced African drums as percussion instruments. Eventually, it
was observed that constant striking of these metal drums altered the pitch.
It was not long before the idea was floated that if you applied heat to these
drums, the notes could be hammered out to produce a musical instrument.
The steel pan became popular at carnival time. Today steel bands include
a variety of pan instruments—tenor pan, double tenor, double second,
double guitar, four cello, quadraphonic, tenor bass, six bass, nine bass.
Steel bands play not only calypsoes but also the music of Bach, Beethoven
and other classical musicians.

The story of calypso and steel band is one of rejection in so far as the
Church is concerned. Influenced by the thinking of European missionaries,
these musical offerings were regarded as acceptable for secular events but
certainly not dignified enough for worship. This is the very issue I seek to
address. The story of reggae has been slightly different in that it found its
way into the Revivalist movement. The Great Revival in Jamaica was during
the 1860s when that country saw an upsurge of African Christian groups. In
their worship, they utilized the drums, they sang and clapped their hands.
The choruses that they sang were lively. The significant thing about Revivalists
was that they were more 'down to earth' in the sense that they appreciated
the African facets of Jamaican culture. When Jamaican *ska* music was in its
heyday in the 1960s and into the dawn of the reggae era of the 1970s, these
'little churches' were not afraid to proclaim the gospel in song using Jamaican
musical idioms. What was happening was a mutual sharing between so-
called *secular* and *sacred* music. Peter Manuel puts it this way:

> The Revivalist influence on popular music goes back to the early days
> of ska, when Revival-tinged recordings such as 'Six and Seven Books of
> Moses' and 'Hallelujah', by the Maytals, 'River Jordan' and 'Freedom',

by Clancy Eccles, and 'River to the Bank', by Baba Brooks, were among the mix of styles then to be heard on downtown sound systems. Even the Wailers, before fully embracing the Rastafarian faith, recorded a number of Revival-influenced spiritual songs during the ska period. With the ascendance of Rasta-oriented reggae, those elements of traditional Rastafarian music derived from Revivalist sources were transferred to urban popular music along with the rest, lending much of the reggae of the 1970s a hymn-like quality that would be familiar to the ears of churchgoers all over rural Jamaica. The melodies and chord progressions of many Rasta reggae songs, as well as the biblical language and prophetic messages that typify the genre, owe much to Revivalism.[25]

Despite the seeming success story of reggae, there is need for the music of African Caribbean people to be affirmed, to the extent that its idioms are regarded as acceptable within the context of Christian worship.

African Caribbean Music: A Vehicle for Doing Theology

African Caribbean music is a viable vehicle for doing theology within the Caribbean context. The interesting thing about the Caribbean is that it is a mixed cultural bag, yet it is only the music of Europe and North America which has so far penetrated and found acceptance within the churches across the region. Part of the reason is that the hymnbooks used by congregations originated in these two continents. Printing houses in the Caribbean have not been able, over the years, to compete with such enterprise in the developed nations. There have been some attempts, dating back to the 1970s, whereby theological students of the various denominations in training for the Christian ministry at the United Theological College of the West Indies (UTCWI) tried to affirm Caribbean music as God-given and therefore worthy of being used in worship. Some insisted on introducing Caribbean folk hymns to the accompaniment of guitars and drums. On Sunday mornings they would visit various Kingston churches and on Sunday evenings take part in folk mass at the University chapel. There was a mixed reception to this type of music. The more conservative element in congregations tended to question the calibre of young men and women being prepared for leadership of the Church in the Caribbean.

Following the lead given in the 1970s, the Caribbean Conference of Churches produced a series of booklets entitled *Sing a New Song*. This served as an encouragement to the hymnwriters of the region. A number of talented men and women emerged—Patrick Prescod, Noel Dexter, Doreen Potter, Ronald Gokool, Pearl Mulrain, Richard Ho Lung.[26] A few church choirs have included Caribbean hymns in their repertoire. However, the frustrating thing is that not many of the churches have made use of these as congregational hymns in worship. Why has the indigenous music not received full recognition as an authentic vehicle of theology? Some people felt embarrassed to sing songs that contained any of the local dialect. The song 'Blak Up' is a case in point. This Jamaican hymn recounts the happenings on the day of Pentecost:

> Blak up, blak up, sun a rise an' people say we blak up
> But a de spirit o' de Lord fly down like a fire
> Grab we in de spirit like a choir, singin' higher,
> Higher, higher, higher, Fire!

I recall one gentleman who found it offensive to sing the following lines in patois:

> For dem drop dem mout an' deni start fe shout
> Wat a hell a gwan roun' dis place.

I suppose a legitimate question to be asked is 'What makes any music usable as a tool of theology?' The answer would probably be 'the words with which it is associated'. Hymns that have entered into the Caribbean but have come out of a foreign context have only the association with God and things religious. The tune from the culture of origin might well have been associated with things secular rather than sacred. Some of the hymn tunes were originally dance hall music. However, in the new context it finds ready acceptance within worship. Since reggae, calypso and steel band music have been associated with the everyday, the ordinary and the mundane, this seems to have defeated the purpose of their being used in worship. To counteract this obstacle, it is important now to baptize indigenous music. If Caribbean people are intentional about it, they can make such local hymns so much a regular feature in worship that future generations will not be lumbered with some of the prejudices that are in existence at the moment.

Caribbean hymns are more likely to be sung today in Roman Catholic churches that have not had a longstanding tradition of hymn singing. A few years ago the Methodist Church in the Caribbean and the Americas put forward the suggestion of producing a hymnal in two parts. In one section there would be the traditional hymns of the Wesleys, Watts and so on. In the other there would be a repertoire of Caribbean hymns. To date, this hymnal has not been produced. It is, however, an idea well worth seeing through to completion. The fact is, such a hymnal would be a reminder that whereas the church ought to be indigenous, it ought also to be universal. The General Board of Global Ministries of the United Methodist Church, USA, has been making concerted attempts to educate its members that they belong to a global church. Global Music has so far produced two editions of a hymnbook including hymns from the Caribbean, parts of Africa, Asia, New Zealand and Latin America.[27]

I began this paper by acknowledging that the concept of *universal theology* is a misnomer. Theology does not emerge in a vacuum. The experience of God arises in context. What I have noted about music that has surfaced in the African Caribbean region is that although worthy of being used as a theological tool, there is still a long way to go before such a dream becomes a reality. We have not dismissed music from other contexts as useless. On the contrary, we have been enriched by the various theological offerings that others have couched in song. We cry out for greater recognition of what has come naturally from among us. When we are prepared to embrace the insights of others as well as of ourselves, we will better appreciate the idea of universal theology. It is something to which we must all strive as the people of God from around the world. When each one contributes to the sum total, there emerges a more complete picture of what the God of the universe is likely to be.

An Intercultural Approach to Pastoral Care and Counselling

Emmanuel Lartey

[Emmanuel Lartey was the first editor of *Black Theology in Britain* and former senior lecturer in Pastoral Theology at the University of Birmingham. He is a significant early voice in the development of Black theology in Britain. This essay is taken from his seminal work *In Living Colour: An Intercultural Approach to Pastoral Care and Counselling* (London: Jessica Kingsley, 2003 [1997]), 21–35.]

Essential Elements of Pastoral Care

It appears to me that there are five essential elements that any comprehensive definition of pastoral care needs to encompass. These would be, first, a declaration of *what kind* of activity it is. Second, a discussion of agency, exploring *who* are involved or engaged in it. Third, an indication of *how* it is done which includes pointing to resources and their employment in achieving the fourth' element of the definition, namely the *goals* aimed at. Last, but by no means least, is a setting forth of *motive*—why people do it.

In responding to these I will now set out the essential features of a definition of pastoral care which attempts to be intercultural in its nature and scope.

Pastoral care is an expression of human concern through activities

In pastoral care, it seems to me, deep concern about what it is to be human is expressed. Pastoral carers have a concern for what meets the eye about human persons as well as what may lie deeply buried within them. This implies that there is an aspect of pastoral care which may be hidden. The 'hiddenness' lies in the heartfelt desire for humanity to be truly and fully human. It is an all-encompassing passion that all people might live to the fullest of their potential. In the Christian Scriptures this is expressed in the saying of Jesus recorded in John 10:10, 'I have come that they may have life, and may have it in all its fullness' (REB). Pastoral care has to do with the total well-being of the whole person.

This concern is expressed in activity. Various helping activities such as counselling may offer such an expression but so are *celebrating, commemorating, rejoicing* and *reflecting*, as well as *mourning* or *being present with* people at different times of life.

Pastoral carers recognize transcendence

People who participate in pastoral care recognize a transcendent dimension to life. They realize that there is more to life than often meets the eye? They have an awareness that power, grace and goodness are often not found in the obvious places. They recognize that there is a mysteriousness about life which is not reducible to sociological, psychological or physiological analyses and explanations, important though these are.

This transcendence is real, although we have no objective and external means of gaining access to it and of verifying whether we are right or not. Different religious traditions have developed ways of speaking about it and have elaborated rites and rituals for signifying and participating in the recognized realities. The languages and rituals of spirituality, whether religious or non-religious, are attempts at coming to terms with it. The content of transcendence for many people is shaped by the formulations of the particular religious traditions in which they have been socialized. It is possible in terms of a given tradition to ascertain the degree of fit of any particular expressed viewpoint and as far, then, as that tradition is concerned there is truth and falsehood. Different religious traditions value different understandings of 'revelation' and hold their sacred scriptures to have been given by the Deity in specific ways. Each tradition is important and has valuable insights to offer. However, we have no direct access to an objective, external standard by which all viewpoints on transcendence may be judged as ultimately true or false.

In the pastoral care spoken of in this book, religious functionaries are significant participants although they are by no means the sole or even most important participants. There is a mutuality of participation in pastoral care. Leaders there may be, and their activity certainly merits careful study. However, being an official religious representative does not automatically confer pastoral ability upon one. As a matter of fact there are many who testify that those who have been of greatest pastoral relevance for them have not been the most obvious or recognized. It is crucial that we study the *pastoring function* and not simply the official pastoring functionaries. Pastoral care may be mediated through the least recognized source. Unless this reality is recognized and incorporated into the study of it, much that is of the essence of pastoral care will be lost.

There is a sense in which this recognition of a transcendent dimension to life characterizes and distinguishes *the pastoral* carer from other carers. This is not to suggest that the pastoral carer is superior nor that his or her efforts are couched in esoteric or otherwise overtly evangelistic terms. In point of fact pastoral carers are not overly anxious to be distinguished from other carers and most often work collaboratively with others in the attempt to mediate holistic care. The desire is not self-consciously to draw attention to themselves nor necessarily to make frenetic attempts to draw attention to the mystery they recognize. Rather, it is a deep consciousness which is as suspicious of superficial or facile interpretations as it is of pretentious ones.

Black psychologist Linda Myers has identified within Afrocentric thought a conceptual framework for the quest among transpersonal psychologists for a more holistic understanding of human experience. She describes this conceptual system as 'optimal psychology'.[28] In the antithesis to this system, which she describes as a sub-optimal world-view, reality is divided into spirit and matter, with matter being pre-eminent. Optimal theory, on the other hand, assumes the unity of spirit and matter, with spirit being pre-eminent. The primary means of gaining knowledge within a sub-optimal frame is by measuring and counting information provided by the five senses or their technological extensions. According to optimal theory, 'self knowledge is the source and basis of all knowledge'.[29]

These ideas provide an important link between forms of Eastern mysticism, Hebrew synthetic thinking, modern 'paradigm shift' physics and African traditional philosophy. In Chapter 6 I will take these ideas further and offer a more detailed discussion of transcendence and spirituality, which I am arguing is crucial to our understanding of pastoral care.

I recognize that the practitioners of pastoral care in educational circles, especially in Britain, would be of the view that their practice can be distinguished from 'religious activities'. They may even contest the view that they have any 'transcendental' ideas. However, many would be quite happy, in the current understanding, to describe their activities as catering for the 'spiritual' needs of pupils and students, even if they would want simply to point to their concern for the needs and well-being of the learners that lie beyond formal teaching activities and be about (among other things) 'the conscious effort to help young people in one way or another to develop as persons'.[30] Such an interest, which could be termed a concern for 'self-transcendence' among young people, is included in the sense in which the 'transcendent' is being used here. There is room here for minimalist, generalist or secularist understandings as well as maximalist, specialist or religious understandings of transcendence.

Intercultural pastoral carers, then, recognize transcendence and are prepared to examine the implications of transcendence for the particularities of daily human living.

Pastoral care entails multi-variate forms of communication

Verbal communication is a very important mode of communication. However, what has been somewhat pejoratively described as *non-verbal communication* is increasingly recognized as a most powerful mode of communication. Intercultural pastoral care explores the forms of communication present in any given society to ascertain their value within the society for caring interaction.

In many cultures, *indirect* forms of converse are very highly valued. In Gã and Akan (West African) societies, for example, the mark of maturity is the ability to use proverbs, sayings and allusions appropriately in public speech. An elder is not rebuked directly but instead is spoken to indirectly. A wise ruler can read and decipher the writing on the wall. Drama, poetry and other forms of imaginative literature may convey or mediate pastoral care of the highest order.

The use of *symbols*, such as works of creative art and sculpture, has largely been ignored in the study of pastoral care. It is most often literary works that have received attention. In intercultural study such neglect is deemed most impoverishing. Some of the most inspiring and liberative forms of discourse emanating from South and Central America are in symbolic art.

The motive is love

At the heart of the 'hiddenness' of pastoral care is love. The passion spoken of earlier is born of the compassion which lies at the centre of the universe deep in the heart of God, so to speak. In Christian terms, 'we love because he first loved us'.[31] Love is a thoroughly social phenomenon. Not only does it impel us into relationship with others, it also enables us to see injustice and to want to do something about it.

Christianity points to *agapê*, referring to the unconditional self-giving love of God, as the source and sustainer of the universe. The Christian teaching of incarnation seeks to convey an 'enfleshing' *of agape* in a historic person—Jesus Christ—who becomes the icon and enabler of such love for and in his followers. Such self-giving love is at the heart of the Christian gospel and is the impelling force behind Christian action.

The problem of course is the translation of this love into actual practice. It is evident that Christians have no monopoly on loving action. In fact evidence is plentiful of the exact opposite, especially in Christian relations with people of other faiths. Re-statement of ideals nevertheless may be a way of re-focusing and calling people to the true heart, soul and potential motivating force of their practice.

Pastoral care aims at prevention and fostering

Much of the literature and practice of pastoral care in the West has appeared to focus on *relief*. Pastoral care thus has a cliff-hanging or 'ambulance-service' image that is hard to escape. It would appear as if pastoral care is only needed after the devastating event has occurred.

Without losing sight of the importance of relieving anxiety or trauma once it has occurred, in this study pastoral care also aims at *preventing* distress, where possible, by creative anticipation and sensitive, non-intrusive awareness-building. This is an educative exercise of pastoral care which enables people to explore and examine situations imaginatively before they occur in order to be prepared if they were to happen. Pastoral carers, in this view, are also deeply involved in fostering or enabling human growth and the fulfilment of the potential of individuals as well as communities.

The definition which captures all these insights, one with which I have been working for a while, and which I see no reason to change at this stage, is as follows:

> Pastoral care consists of helping activities, participated in by people who recognize a transcendent dimension to human life, which by the use of verbal or non-verbal, direct or indirect, literal or symbolic modes of communication, aim at preventing, relieving or facilitating persons coping with anxieties. Pastoral care seeks to foster people's growth as full human beings together with the development of ecologically holistic communities in which all persons may live humane lives.[32]

Culture and Interculturality

It is necessary at this juncture for me to explain briefly my understanding of a concept which lies at the heart of our discussions—that *of culture*. The term is used in very many different ways, and is one of the most complex. In relation to our study this examination is offered so as to avoid the ambiguous and often misleading way in which the word is sometimes used and to indicate the way it is being used here.

By culture, I shall be referring to the way in which social groups develop distinct patterns of life and give 'expressive form' to their social and material life experience.[33] This way of speaking of culture has been described as an 'anthropological' one.[34] In this sense, the culture of a group of persons is the particular and distinctive 'way of life' of the group. This includes the ideas, values and meanings embodied in institutions and practices, in forms of social relationship, in systems of belief, in mores and customs, in the way objects are used and physical life organized. It has to do with the way in which patterns of life in a group are structured, with an emphasis on how these structures are experienced, understood and interpreted.

These structures and their meanings influence the ongoing collective experience of groups. They also, on the other hand, limit, modify and constrain how groups live and interpret their life experiences. Moreover, there is a constant historical interaction taking place between people and their changing social environment and circumstances. Culture is therefore never static. Instead there is a continual interplay resulting in dynamism, adaptability, re-interpretation, re-formulation and change. There is certainly continuity, but this is itself continually challenged by changing circumstances, so that new forms of expression, new perceptions and creative interpretations are emerging all the time.

It is also important to point out that membership of a particular social group does not imply endorsement of every aspect of the group's culture. There are significant individual differences within each social group.

An intercultural study attempts to capture the complexity involved in the interactions between people who have been and are being shaped and influenced by different cultures. It takes seriously the different expressions originating in different cultures, but then proceeds by attempting to make possible a multi-perspectival examination of whatever issue is at stake. It recognizes that it is impossible to capture the totality of any given social group's culture. It realizes also that dominant or powerful groups may deliberately or unwittingly seek to impose their culture and perspective upon all others or otherwise control and select what is to be allowed expression. Worse still, and yet most common, has been the attempt to universalize and 'normalize' a particular culture's experience and judge all others by that one culture's views. This has been the case most clearly in the Eurocentric enterprise, which has fuelled centuries of modernity. Such hegemonic attempts were pursued quite overtly in the period of Western expansionism but even now often continue in subtle ways.

The way an intercultural approach seeks to counter such developments and to enhance interaction therefore is by giving many voices from different backgrounds a chance to express their views on the subject under review on their own terms. It does not then rush to analyse or systematize them into overarching theories, which can explain and fit everything neatly into place. Instead, it ponders the glorious variety and chaotic mystery of human experience for clues to a more adequate response to the exigencies of human life.

An intercultural approach is opposed to *reductionism* and *stereotyping* in any form. It takes the view that stereotyping is a particularly neurotic form of reductionism, in which, as a result of an inability to cope with complexity or difference, an attempt is made to control by placing groups in hierarchical order, categorizing them and seeing any particular individual member of a particular group as bearing the presumed characteristics of that group. Some well-meaning attempts, adopted in many forms of 'multicultural training', to inform counsellors and other carers about 'ethnic minority clients', fall into this trap by perpetuating the myths, for example, about the angry underachieving Caribbean male, the Asian young woman's oppressive cultural role, the African student's problem with communication, the problems of the Asian extended family or the single-parent Caribbean family. As such, far from enabling attention to the particular client in question, these forms fuel stereotyping of the most heinous kind.

On the contrary, interculturality values *diversity* most highly. In an intercultural approach, culture's influence on belief and behaviour is taken very seriously, without it being seen as determining them, nor as the sole factor to be explored in examining them. Interculturality is a creative response to the pluralism which is a fact of life in present-day society. It calls for the affirmation of three basic principles, *contextuality, multiple perspectives* and *authentic participation.*

The principle of *contextuality* asserts that every piece of behaviour and every belief must be considered in the framework within which it takes place. It is within this framework of surrounding beliefs and world-views that its meaning and significance can be gauged.

The principle *of multiple perspectives* realizes that equally rational persons can examine the same issue and yet arrive at very different understandings. It goes on to insist that these different perspectives are equally deserving of attention. Through a process of listening and dialogue, one or other, or combinations of these perspectives, may prove more adequate in coping with a particular issue in a given context.

Finally, the principle of *authentic participation* is premised upon mutual concern for the integrity of the 'other', and affirms the right of all to participate in discussion and examination of an issue on their own terms, realizing that there are strengths and weaknesses in every approach.

Augsburger has argued quite rightly that one needs more than just information about another culture to become culturally aware. 'This change', he argues, 'comes from encounter, contact and interaction, not from programmic education or social engineering. It occurs on the boundary, not in the cultural enclave.'[35] For cross-cultural counselling it is necessary to be aware not simply of superficial, visibly different cultural traits, but also of significant and subtle issues of similarity and difference between people. Indeed it calls for an awareness of meaning within a different set of values and beliefs together with an ability to 'think and feel' the difference. As Augsburger puts it, 'The capacity not only to "believe" the second culture but to come to understand it both cognitively ("thinking with") and affectively ("feeling with") is necessary before one enters cross-cultural counselling.'[36]

Interculturality affirms a 'trinitarian' formulation of human personhood expressed by Kluckholn and Murray as far back as 1948.[37] Each assertion of the threefold statement is true and important in itself. Each needs to be held in relation to the others within a unity which holds together and transcends opposites.

Every human person is in certain respects:

- *like all others*
- *like some others*
- *like no other.*

In the first assertion testimony is borne to the universal characteristics which all human persons have in common. We are all born helpless, grow from dependence toward relative self-management, relate to other beings and to a physical environment and ten out of ten die!

The second assertion recognizes that precisely because we are human we are each shaped, influenced and patterned to some extent by the community within which we are socialized. This matrix of values, beliefs, customs and basic life assumptions which we call culture, as we have previously indicated, is shared to a large extent with those who share or have shared the community.

The third points to the uniqueness of each individual. Each person has a unique genetic code, voice pattern, fingerprint and dental configuration. Each person has a distinct life story, developmental history and particular lifestyle. No other person will ever see, think, feel, celebrate or suffer in an identical way.

It is dangerous to over-emphasize one of these to the exclusion of the others. On the other hand, in order to gain a fuller understanding of human persons, it is necessary to explore the 'unique and simultaneous influences of cultural specificity, individual uniqueness and human universality'.[38] Many attempts at multicultural or cross-cultural training have focused almost exclusively on the cultural aspect, often producing lists of culturally specific characteristics to be studied by Westerners to equip them to respond to 'specific minority cultures'. Such attempts often grossly over-emphasize and over-simplify cultural phenomena. Where the wrong-headedness of this approach has been recognized, the proposed solution for the problem has been to suggest an emphasis on existential or human universals.[39] However, in the long run such an emphasis is also inadequate precisely because it does not take culture or individual uniqueness seriously enough. Draguns wrestles with the dilemma of the universal versus the culturally distinctive and concludes: 'The best approach is somewhere in between, even though we do not yet know exactly where.'[40]

The most illuminating approach appears to me to be what I am calling interculturality. Here the complex interrelatedness and interconnectedness (pictured in the diagram on the cover) of the three spheres interacting in living, growing and changing human persons is what is expected, treated as the norm and attended to. Interculturality, therefore, while at various points in a discussion may focus on one or other of these aspects of our humanity, seeks always to have the others in view and therefore to hold all three in creative and dynamic tension.

Augsburger's cross-cultural counselling is an attempt to be 'at home on the boundary',[41] to have the capacity to enter creatively into each 'culture' and thus to function as one who mediates and reconciles. In spite of its clear strengths, even this approach is unable to escape the dangers of cultural stereotyping and the fostering of an 'us' and 'them' mentality. Interculturality, on the other hand, speaks *of living in the intersection* of the three spheres—being centred in the intersection of the universal, the cultural and the individual within living, colourful persons.

An intercultural approach to pastoral care and counselling, therefore, raises *three* kinds of questions of the persons and situations it encounters. Research based on this approach has to seek to respond to these three levels of experience and spheres of influence.

First, *what of the universal experience of humanity is to be found here?* To what extent is a particular experience common to all human beings? The forms of expression and configuration of the experience may differ, but what is universal about the core experience?

Second, *what is culturally determined about this way of thinking, feeling or behaving?* The task here is to attempt to figure out what in the experience being confronted is a function of social and cultural forces. Examples of these would include the influence of child-raising practices, socialization, gender and role expectations, and the processes and ideologies of racialization.[42]

Third, *what in this experience can be said to be uniquely attributable to this particular person?* Here, the practitioner needs to seek the differences which are due to individual particularities shining through the person's experience.

Navigating the World of 'White' Ecumenism: Insights from Philip Potter

Michael Jagessar

[In this essay, taken from *Wereld en Zending* 31.4 (2002), 32–41, Jagessar, who has done extensive research on the life, work and theology of Philip Potter, explores how Potter, a Caribbean person, navigated the turbulent waters of the then predominant white ecumenical world. Potter's significance to Caribbean and Black British theological discourse is yet to be fully acknowledged and studied. In terms of the British context, he was the first Black person to serve as a mission secretary for the Methodist Missionary Society. His influence on Methodism, mission and ecumenism in the UK has been far reaching. It is reasonable to suggest that Potter can be considered as one of the early voices in Black theological discourse in the UK.]

> Ah, Gregorias, you are genius, yes!
> Yes, God and me, we understand each other.
> (*Collected Poems 1948–1984*, London, 1986)

Introduction

In this essay I intend to briefly explore how Philip Potter, a black Caribbean person, navigated his way on the 'world scene', specifically in the ecumenical movement, and what are some of the lessons for our ongoing work *vis-à-vis* racial justice awareness. For the WCC was still a predominantly 'white' institution at the time of Potter's election as General Secretary (1973) even though it was in the process of moving towards including the younger churches from the two-thirds world. This process was further propelled by leaders such as Potter and the fact of the growing and vibrant churches in the former 'mission fields'.

Potter is an important church leader and ecumenical theologian of the twentieth century. He stands out as a significant *catalyst* in contemporary theological thinking, especially within the ecumenical movement. His contributions influenced the changing direction of mission, of ecumenical thinking, and of theology and doing theology in the latter part of the twentieth century.[43]

It is, however, necessary to note a couple of significant points. Firstly, Potter is from the Caribbean. He is quintessentially a Caribbean thinker, who comes from a region shaped by the 'archtectonic forces of conquest, colonization, slavery, sugar monoculture, colonialism, and racial and ethnic admixture'.[44] The region was 'the testing ground of colonialism, imperialism and capitalist racism'.[45] The stories of the Caribbean islands are essentially stories of the constant struggle for survival, cultural diversity/synthesis, subversion, nationalism, and black consciousness.[46] All these factors are significant in understanding Potter's leadership of the WCC as they have shaped his thinking and the ways in which he negotiated working in a predominantly 'white' western context.

Secondly, Potter has spent most of his working life outside of the Caribbean. It is reasonable to consider him as a missionary in Europe.[47] He served as the *first* Black SCM Overseas Secretary for Britain and Ireland (1948–1950), Executive Secretary of the Youth Department of the WCC (1954–1960), Field Secretary of the Methodist Missionary Society for West

Africa and the Caribbean (1961–1966), and Director of the Commission on World Mission and Evangelism (1967–1972). The significance of this observation is twofold. In the first instance, while there was the recognition of the need to include people from the 'mission field', Potter served in these key positions primarily because of his abilities, charisma and qualifications.[48] Likewise, Pauline Webb notes that Potter was elected as the General Secretary of the WCC (1973) not because he was from the 'third world' but because of his experience and qualifications for the job.[49] This was also the view of Willem Visser 't Hooft who noted that Potter who is from the 'third world' 'knows the other worlds intimately'.[50]

Further, it is reasonable to consider Potter as part of the Caribbean/Black Diaspora that lives and works in Europe. His work and theological articulation have been done in the context of 'homelessness' and displacement. In a real sense, wherever Potter lived (and is living) has been 'elsewhere'. The hybrid nature of Potter's life (including his genetic makeup) has affected all aspects of his life. Indeed, one can suggest that Potter led the WCC and wrote from the affective experience of social marginality and from the perspective of the edge offering alternative ways of seeing and thinking.[51] In Potter one finds a member of the Caribbean/Black Diaspora with the ability to slip into different contexts with a considerable amount of inside knowledge without being an insider—a person who can fish in several ponds, but they are never the right sort of ponds and he is the 'wrong' kind of fish for each. Hence, my claim that Potter should be considered a 'calypso' theologian.[52]

Sir, I Only Came with the Others

In his acceptance speech as General Secretary of the WCC, Potter told the story of the Caribbean person who arrived in heaven when various gifts were shared. While all the others in the group knew what they wanted, asked for it and got it, the Caribbean upon his turn merely gave a 'huge grin' and replied, '*Sir! I only came with the others*'. This comment was neither a self-depreciation of Potter's person nor the undervaluing of his gifts.[53] This was characteristically a Caribbean way of 'poking fun' at oneself when the joke was in fact on those who were laughing. It was a taste of genuine Caribbean 'Anancyism' at its best, that is, Caribbean sub-version. Anancyism is a signpost to surviving oppression. It is a pattern of behaviour that involves the ability to find the loophole in every situation so that the apparently disempowered individual manages to come out on top, in spite of the oppression. This is what Potter calls the 'in-spite of faith'.[54] It is also a philosophy of resistance and 'talking-back' or a sub-version of the dominant-version or dominant voices.

Potter may have had in mind his critics and those from the 'white' world of ecumenism who had reservations about his leadership of the

WCC. I think, however, that this was an indication of how Potter intended to navigate his way through the 'dominant white' ecumenical culture with all the usual baggage (subtle or overt) of superiority. His 'calypso' style leadership and thinking would refuse to fit into any pre-conceived moulds. The fact that he mostly wore a 'shirt-Jac' (some refer to it as 'Bush-Jacket') further underscored Potter's intention of non-conformity—a typical Caribbean way of subverting. As a *catalyst* or a *frontier theologian* he not only gave signals, but offered challenges and opened perspectives on: the inseparable relationship between faith and *praxis*, Jesus' offer of full life for the whole *oikoumene*, a sustaining spirituality, the necessity of a dialogue between cultures, the centrality of the Word of God for doing theology, the development of the concept of *koinonia* and the church as the house of living stones, and on social justice issues (economics, ecology, racism, sexism, etc.).

In his acceptance speech as General Secretary, Potter goes on to perceive his role as that of a 'servant', identifying the need to make the ecumenical community 'alive and real' and enabling each culture, nation and church in its context to be itself, 'not just the sum of parts but an organic relationship of interaction'.[55] The imagery of 'servant' was another hint at 'Anancy-ism'. While theologically/biblically one understands what he was saying, Potter's slave heritage must not be sidelined. The imagery of servant/slave (*doulous*) and Paul's words about Christ becoming a slave is not a theological dictum for a Caribbean person! Further, in the western context where the dominant version is characterized by power and the 'love of power', the call to a 'servanting' lifestyle is truly a sub-version. It is through the 'power of love' that Potter intended to negotiate his way—a way of living also espoused by the Christians in the west, but too often not practiced.

Beyond the Boundary

Potter suggests that the game of cricket has had a significant impact on his leadership of the WCC and the way he, as a Black Caribbean, was able to work and reflect theologically in Europe.[56] Implied here is more than the ideal of working as a team, enabling, and the insignificance of the end result. Cricket is at the nexus of colonial rule and the constructed precarious Caribbean/Black identity.[57]

C. L. R. James, a significant influence on Potter,[58] suggests that cricket's political resonance extends beyond the 'boundary' of the cricket pitch and interrogates the tenuous walls that separate culture from politics, race from class, high culture from low culture. The opposition of batsman and bowler serves as a metonym for the broader antagonism between not only colonizer and colonized, but between leader and led, between nation and individual, and between class and race factions. As James writes:

> The British tradition soaked deep into me that when you entered the sport-
> ing arena you left behind you the sordid compromises of everyday exist-
> ence. *Yet for us to do that we would have had to divest ourselves of our
> skins*... The cricket field was a stage on which selected individuals played
> representative roles which were charged with social significance.[59]

It is my view that Potter, who was nurtured in the British tradition, could
not (and rightly so) 'divest himself of his skin' and played a representative
role interrogating the barriers placed by the western world. Like many who
emerged from a colonial milieu, he reflected a contradictory consciousness—torn between the metropole and the Caribbean. Because of his
colour, his history and where he came from, he had no option but to 'take
on' the dominant western culture and traditions. He intuitively grasped
from his Caribbean heritage the incapacity of accompanying the 'master-
race' narcissism to encompass the many-sidedness of humanity. His critics,
mostly from the western world, did not (or did not want to) understand this.
Potter's leadership of the WCC confronted the tangible barriers that pre-
vented people from being fully human. He was criticized for his obsession
with third-world problems and with issues like racism, liberation struggles
(Southern Africa), development, human rights and poverty/debt. Western
critics were concerned about his unbalanced emphasis on activism and
social justice issues, the danger of his ideological/theological bias and his
weak emphasis on the unity of the church—especially with regard to the
older 'historic' churches.[60] In retrospect, the developments in South Africa
(among others) stand out as positive signs of Potter's insistence on the
Programme to Combat Racism. With the present focus on globalization,
poverty, world debt and ecological issues, Potter has demonstrated remarkable forward thinking. Today it is amusing and sad to read the western
white male critique of Potter in the light of dying and empty churches in
Europe and the growing 'black' and 'ethnic' Christian communities in their
midst.

Why could his critics not see the 'writing on the wall' and constructively
engage with the issues? Was the problem merely a matter of ideological/
theological differences or the 'evangelical camp' versus the 'liberal camp'?
Or was it because Potter is 'Black' and hails from the 'third' world? While
Potter was a respected leader, a very able theologian and had many 'white'
supporters, he often felt that the criticisms were unfair and specifically
directed to him because of his colour.[61] In a dominant 'white' environment, it is extremely difficult for Black and Asian minorities, from a context
of oppression (colonialism, racism, slavery, neo-colonialism) not to feel
despised because of their skin pigmentation and to display overt sensitivity
to criticisms or to be suspicious of the 'west'. This becomes even more
difficult in the context of subliminal and institutional racism. Moreover, the

insensitivity, arrogance and unconscious (or conscious) feeling of superiority of white sisters and brothers merely serve to exacerbate the situation. This would have certainly contributed to Potter's 'defensive attitude', hindered or stultified an honest and meaningful dialogue with western theologians and may have given the impression that he had a 'chip on his shoulder'.[62]

In discussing racism and slavery today, the threat of such polarization is still real. The difficulty of realizing a meaningful dialogue can also be attributed to the inability and unwillingness of the 'west' to *theologically* come to terms with its past *vis-à-vis* racism, slavery and her role in the impoverishment of Africa and the Caribbean. I am not aware of any serious effort by British and European theologians to deal *theologically* with their colonial past in order to break the cycle of their continuing superiority and domination. This becomes even more urgent given that Africa, Asia and the Caribbean are in Rotterdam, Paris, London and Birmingham. Potter's challenge was an attempt to move the discussion beyond a 'colonial' fixation and the monolithic moulds of oppressor/oppressed, hence his plea for and commitment to the search for authentic community and the 'dialogue of cultures' as the 'only hope for humankind to attain fullness of life in all its shared diversity in the Christ who contains and holds all things together'.[63] This is a tough and costly call. Potter, who has had to wrestle his own inner and outer struggles as a victim of racism and the consequences he displayed, knows this. As he told a gathering of decent English folks:

> I know in my inner being how hard it is to overcome the past and present, and the separation which this has caused between me and you, all the more hard because most of you in this country are so insensitive and complacent about it all… I know, too, how all this is woven into my own inability to forgive myself for the contempt I have for white people and the resulting contempt I feel for myself.[64]

While Potter is known to get passionate and angry when the issue of racism is being discussed, he seeks justice and reconciliation and not revenge. His genuine passion for seeking ways to give expression to full life for *all* is motivated by the power of love in Christ.

The Look in the Eyes

In one of his early sermons (1968), Potter cited a conversation that Laurens van der Post had with the last Governor of Indonesia. Van der Post records that the Governor was complaining bitterly that after 300 years, in which the Dutch had done so much for the Indonesians, they were being thrown out. In answer to his persistent 'why?', van der Post replied: '*It was the look in your eyes*'. That look had all the marks of self-sufficiency, self-regard, arrogance and superiority. The Governor did not have 'love or trust with seeing eyes'.[65]

In his ecumenical pilgrimage Potter encountered many 'white' folks who had 'love with seeing eyes'. Some of these folks have influenced his own life and thinking as he also influenced theirs. On the other hand, he has had to wrestle with the arrogance of those Christians with the western mindset of superiority. Potter was able to counter this by his genuine commitment in seeking ways to manifest the fullness of life in Christ. Even his sharpest critics and people who do not know him personally, but only see and hear him for the first time, see in Potter a man driven by the 'power of love'. Pauline Webb, who credits Potter for her ecumenical conversion and theological formation, shared an interesting anecdote with me (27 August 1990). At the Executive Committee Meeting of the WCC in 1979 (Oklahoma, USA), she was invited to the home of a conservative evangelical family who did not know much about the ecumenical movement. At that very time there was a programme ('60 Minutes') on TV in which Morley Safer interviewed Potter. Both the WCC and Potter were being criticized over the Programme to Combat Racism (PCR) with regard to the controversial support given to 'liberation' movements in Southern Africa. After the programme, Webb was struck by the comment of the family: 'We do not know much about the WCC and the programme under scrutiny, but we can recognize when something is said in Christian love and the second speaker (Potter) spoke in that manner.'

Motivated by the power of love in Christ, Potter, who had harsh things to say to the Western Christians and to his own people from the 'third world', was able to counter arrogance with humility and integrity—characteristics of his spirituality. The witness of Potter in the ecumenical movement is grounded on the belief that the labour of love begins with trusting that love is at the heart of the other. To counter cultural arrogance and the feeling of superiority we must re-discover this belief *and* live it out!

Two Letters: An Epilogue

In conclusion, I wish to cite the gist of two letters that, in my view, reveal a couple of insights related to the challenges underlying the assumption that 'white' folks unconsciously show an undercurrent feeling of superiority towards people of a different hue. In the early stages of the writing of my dissertation on Potter, I wrote to several people to arrange for interviews to discuss Potter's work and theological contributions.

One such person whom Potter succeeded as director of CWME/WCC wrote back refusing to give such an interview or to comment on Potter's work and theology. He claimed that he did not know a great deal about Potter's work and theological thinking and would not be able to help me in my research. One can read such a response in a variety of ways. I was struck by the thought that this respected British 'icon' (now deceased) did not know much about Potter's theological articulation even though Potter succeeded him in such a key position and the two would have met, spoken and written on the same ecumenical/missiological issues on the international scene. Is it possible that such a dismissive attitude is reflective of an unconscious sense of superiority and arrogance of some western theologians *vis-à-vis* the articulation of theologians from the 'third world', that is, that they would not even bother to listen to them, or read and respond to their presentations/writings?

The other piece of correspondence was from a very good German friend and former colleague (also deceased) of Potter. While he willingly shared his insights on Potter, he wanted to know how I could write a dissertation on the theology of a man who did not write theological books and queried which university would accept such. Indeed, Potter did not write *many* books, but his numerous articles, lectures and presentations are very impressive given that his working life was spent on the ecumenical frontier 'in posing and seeking to answer concretely the question: what is to be done?'[66] The comment of this theologian highlights another aspect related to the western feeling of superiority towards 'non-whites'. Scholarship and erudite theological articulation is associated with the written word. The spoken or oral word is viewed as 'un-scientific'.

Textualization and not oral articulation is the authority. Only a few western theologians (Raiser, Sölle, Webb) give credit to Potter for ideas that they later developed into articles or books. While it is Potter who very early (1960s) began to articulate the imagery of the church as the Household of God and the House of Living Stones in ecumenical circles, commentators would merely point to the books of Lange and Raiser for adopting the imagery.[67] There is still this tendency for scholars in the western 'book/text' culture to silently hijack the ideas of 'third' world theologians of the oral tradition and thus, through their written tomes, be acknowledged/recognized as experts on a subject or particular issue. Potter's response to these two letters has been quintessentially Caribbean: a silent smile that spoke volumes.

Potter's effectiveness as an ecumenical leader and theologian lies in a spirituality, which was effectively grounded in the Bible. This served as an indispensable source for his spiritual orientation in wrestling with western arrogance, racism and his own anger, in his ability to encourage, in breaking through an impasse, and in criticizing and being criticized. No wonder his life motto remains: 'We are unprofitable servants, we have only done that which is our duty to do' (Lk. 17:10b). Perhaps the insight of poet Laureate Derek Walcott is also true of Potter: *'Yes, God and me, we understand each other'.*

10 Future Trajectories

This last chapter is an attempt to try and offer some nascent thoughts for the future direction and development of Black theology in Britain. We offer these, our thoughts, in the hope that they will stimulate further reflection and action *vis-à-vis* the ongoing development of this academic discipline and form of contextual praxis into the future. Before we progress with this chapter, it is perhaps helpful to offer some preliminary reflections in order to put our perceptions into some form of context.

As we have been compiling this text we have been struck by the range of voices that have featured prominently in the ongoing development of Black theology in Britain. This discipline has never been reducible to only one individual, no matter what certain ill-informed authors may care to believe.[1] The collective and corporate nature of the British context has hopefully been illuminated from within the pages of this reader.

And yet, as we have compiled and reflected, it has struck us quite forcibly that any assessment of the future of Black theology needs to be informed by some of the significant formative developmental features that have defined the movement thus far. Essential to that development has been the 'absent guest' at this Black theology in Britain feast—namely, Emmanuel Y. Lartey.

As has been illustrated in a previous publication, Lartey was for many years the 'Grand Patriarch' of this movement. Whether in his capacity as the wise sage, one of only a few Black religious scholars in Britain with a PhD in religion and/or theology, working within the academy, to his supervision of students (both British and international), chairing the Black Theology Forum in Birmingham, creating the first MA programme in Black theology or as the founding editor of *Black Theology in Britain* (indeed, the only person suitably qualified to have taken on that post at the time), Lartey has been an intellectual giant in the development of Black theology in Britain. The editors of this work can attest to Lartey's nurturing and organizational skills in addition to his pioneering scholarly work in the area of Pastoral theology and care.

In this chapter, as we seek to outline an indicative future for the development of Black theology in Britain, we felt it prudent to return to Lartey's defining contribution from *Black Theology in Britain* where he outlines a manifesto for Black theology. We have chosen to return to Lartey's work for two reasons.

First, it possesses a clarity and a lucidity of thought that is still of benefit in the many years that have past since it was first written. Second, returning to Lartey's work is also an act of homage to one of our forbears in the struggle whose legacy is there for all to see, in the continuing work of the Black Theology Forum and *Black Theology: An International Journal*, both of which remain the most significant contexts in which Black theology work in Britain is undertaken.

Following Lartey's article, which is reproduced in full, we will then make some preliminary thoughts on this essay and then reflect on the implication of this work for an anticipated future for Black theology in Britain.

After Stephen Lawrence: Characteristics and Agenda for Black Theology in Britain

Emmanuel Y. Lartey

[This essay is taken from *Black Theology in Britain: A Journal of Contextual Praxis* 3 (November 1999), 79–91.]

Introduction

The murder of Stephen Lawrence on the night of 22 April 1993, and the subsequent police investigation, has ushered Britain into an era when it is no longer possible for the country to speak of itself as a haven of race relations and a beacon of tolerance. Since the publication of the report of the MacPherson Inquiry in February 1999, much has been written and said in response to this in sociological, political and psychological terms.

There have been gatherings of church and community leaders to consider their responses to and strategies against 'institutional racism' recognized as widespread in the county even if minimally in its 'unwitting' form. There was a valuable conference on the 'Bible and Racial Attacks' held in February in Birmingham under the aegis of the Bible Society and Black Christian leaders at which serious attempts were made to set racial attacks and racism in general in a biblical and religious context. Several illuminating papers were delivered on that occasion. However, little theological analysis and response have actually been offered.

For many black people, what happened to Stephen and the way in which the case was handled by the police actually was nothing new. Black folk live these realities on a daily basis and have done so for many years. What the Lawrence case did was to open up, largely to an incredulous white community, what black people in Britain had been experiencing and trying to express for years.

The Lawrences initially did not believe what was happening to them. When this whole drama began, they felt that they were good, law-abiding citizens and that these things only happened to those unlike themselves—criminals, gangsters and drug pushers. They were certain the killers would be caught. They believed in the justice and fair play touted as essentially 'British'. They had not savoured the experience of many black people in Britain.

Stephen Lawrence was young, black and Christian, living in England in the 1990s. It is necessary that black people particularly—and indeed all people of faith—living in Britain in the 1990s, reflect theologically on what may be learned from what has transpired. It is crucial that theological responses be made which will assist all institutions in the country, and beyond, to enter the 2000s with a new vision, and to work for a different future.

In this article I attempt to offer some theological consideration of the event. I go on to sketch characteristics of Black theology within the British context that I consider necessary for an adequate response to the realities surrounding us. In the final section of the paper I map out seven task areas that require attention if a comprehensive and effective theology is to arise from the experiences of 'being black' in Britain.

Racism is a Theological Matter

Any racial attack is a theological matter. This is true because a racial attack is essentially and in effect an attack on the Creator. God in his infinite and inscrutable wisdom created human persons with different skin hues. God appointed human persons to live and adorn the garden of God's creation. God created humanity in diversity and variety. None of us has a choice as to what our birth place, heritage, culture or skin colour will be. It lies within the providence of God. As such, when one created human person acting out of such hatred for God's creation of another human person, different to him/herself, decides to terminate the other's existence, it is not only an existential or criminal matter but also a deeply theological issue, requiring a theological response.

What Do We Mean by Black Theology?

A primary meaning of the term Black theology in Britain is one to which I have previously referred as what 'Black people in Britain are thinking, feeling, saying and expressing about God and their experience of God'.[2] In further elaboration on this it is necessary to assert that theology is a task of human persons as we reflect on our life in the light of faith. It is in life and about life that reflections on what God may be about are undertaken.

African American theologian, Gayraud S. Wilmore, makes the useful assertion that

> Black theology is not an unsophisticated, anti-intellectual reaction to whatever is happening at any moment in time—a mixture of emotion and pious propaganda. It is, rather, a hard-headed, practical, and pas-

sionate reading of the signs of the times in the white community as well
as the black. It is an elucidation of what we have understood God to be
about in our history, particularly in the history of our struggle against racist
oppression.[3]

This reading of 'the signs of the times' requires careful analysis and thoughtful engagement with other disciplines. Black theology is 'an elucidation' of
our understanding of the presence and activity of God and humanity's
response to this as it affects the black experience.

In this rendering, theologians are people who reflect upon their faith
and attempt to articulate it. As such, rather than theology being seen as
the preserve of a professional elite, it is recognized as something that many
thoughtful people do, even if they would neither recognize nor be recognized as such. Moreover, many theological productions are never given
such an ostensibly lofty title. Theology is expressed through many media
and in many forms. Art, music and drama are valid ways through which
the fruits of a theologian's efforts may be made known. These can in themselves be theological forms.

Who are Black?

The term 'Black' is one that continues to provoke passionate discussion
among people of different cultures and ethnicities. Often, paradoxically,
it is people who others would call 'Black' who most vociferously object
to the usage of the term. To such any assertion of black pride or dignity is
separatist and an affront to 'harmonious race relations'. In reality they are
more concerned with not upsetting white friends than they are with truth
or integrity. Such responses are wholly unhelpful in the quest for a theology
that in any sense reflects upon actual experience.

By 'Black' we refer in a general sense to people of African, Caribbean
and Asian descent as well as people who identify with 'the Black experience' in terms of heritage, oppression and domination. This is the widely
recognized political usage. In a more restricted and specific sense, as when
the term 'Black and Asian' is used, Black refers to people of African descent
whether on the continent or in the Diaspora.

It is important to point out that there are difficulties with any essentialist definitions that stress certain intrinsic attributes or characteristics
without which 'blackness' is denied to some. In as much as blackness has
been denigrated and used as a term of degradation, it must not now be
used as a label to exclude or beat people over the head with. The usage
here emphasizes biology, culture and politics taken together rather than
in isolation.

In the first part of this paper I shall sketch some characteristics of Black
theology in Britain. These reflect aspirations as well as what has actually
been realized in the activities and productions of black theologians.

Ten Characteristics of Black British Theology

1. Black theology in Britain begins with creation

'God created human beings in his own image, in the image of God he created them, male and female he created them' (Gen. 1:27).

Black theology in Britain affirms that to be black is to be created in the image of God. Consequently, as the Creator declares, it is good to be black. Black theologians affirm and celebrate our blackness. Since we bear the image of God, we reflect God's manifold and mysterious nature. Among other things I take this to mean that humanity, in its corporate and diverse nature, in some sense reflects the nature and image of God. A number of issues follow from this. The following are only three that will be considered at this stage:

First, to refuse to be what we are, as created by God, is a denial of God the Creator and a rejection of a loving relationship with God. Centuries of internalization of the negative stereotyping associated with 'being black' has resulted in the reality that some people go to great lengths to eradicate their skin colour, heritage, language or culture in order to be 'acceptable' to the dominant community. It is a reflection of the alienation from creation and Creator that is a source of much black self-hatred.

Second, such a response prevents an aspect of God's nature from being known. There are aspects of the nature of God that are reflected in blackness. To eradicate, efface, deny or destroy blackness therefore is to prevent an aspect of the glory of God from being revealed. It is thus to diminish the possibility to all of creation of a richer and fuller understanding of the multi-faceted nature of God. To the extent then that any theology ignores the realities of the black experience, to that extent does that articulation remain unduly partial and restrictive in its attempt to speak of God the Creator.

Third, to deny or to denigrate blackness is heresy. To try to be other than we were created (e.g. to mimic whiteness) is a grave insult to the Creator. Every attempt historically to force any human persons to be in essence or existence other than they are, as created by God, is a heinous sin against God who in his wisdom created all. All attempts to create after the image of some section of humanity (e.g. white western male) is in effect to make others 'be in the image of other humans, who declare themselves superior, the norm or the standard of civilisation' rather than after the image of God. This, I have suggested, was an aspect of the error of the Shemites recorded in the story of the tower of Babel (Gen. 2).[4] God created us 'different'. We must affirm our difference. It is necessary to recognize that such 'otherness' (difference) is crucial in the theological quest.

The challenge of creation is also the call to get real. To see things as they are rather than as we would wish them to be. It is a call to listen to and hear the realities of the experiences that 'only happen to other people'!

2. *Black theology in Britain is contextual theology. It arises out of and must attend to issues pertaining to the British context*

The term 'Black theology' arose within an American and South African context. Although much can be learnt from these countries, the realities of being black in Britain have their own peculiar character. The work of great founder and doyen of 'Black theology', African American theologian James Cone, can inspire us but we must look carefully at the British experience if we are to develop a useful theology. The black experience in Britain differs from that in the US or South Africa. Too often in Britain we have been tempted to claim that the black experience here is 'much better' than elsewhere (e.g. US, Germany and so on). Such attempts to calculate which is 'better', in my view, are futile and often serve to prevent us from looking closely at our context in this country. Things are not as glamorous and rosy as we are sometimes made to think. The Lawrence case, deaths in police custody and the recent bombings in Brixton, Brick Lane and Soho, among several other examples of racially motivated crimes, have made this fact even clearer.

Among the realities that need to be attended to is the fact of plurality within the 'Black community'. The trajectories of the journeys that have resulted in 'a Black community' in Britain are complex and diverse. Imperialism, slavery, colonialism, exploitation, trade, education, adventure, refuge, love, marriage, anger and romanticism have all played a part in these journeys. The countries and cultures that, through historic interaction with the British, yielded their nationals to the British nation are more numerous than is the case in other countries with a black population. Such diversity means that there is richness and complexity within the black British 'community' yet to be realized. Black British theology being contextual cannot be uniform.

3. *Black theologians in Britain employ all means at their disposal to understand, interpret, articulate and manifest their faith*

Black theologians are necessarily interdisciplinary in their approach. Studies in sociology, geography, history, politics, cultural studies, literary studies, psychology, the Bible and hermeneutics may all assist in the attempt to understand our personal and collective experience of living in Britain.

4. *Black theologians in Britain derive their values from their African, Caribbean and Asian roots*

Although it is dangerous to generalize, there are at least three value-streams that are discernible within these communities. These are, first, a communitarian ethos, which places more value upon 'the community' than 'the individual'. This value-preference is not without its problems. To recognize this tendency is not to extol its virtues above other values. It is simply to recognize a reality. Communitarians often find themselves at odds within the highly individualized society that western, post-industrial, postmodern cultures continue to be. Second, they tend to be affirmative of peoples' total experience including religious experience. Thus within these 'sub-cultures' religious experience flourishes even when it is being denied. There remains much religious and spiritual experience to be explored within black communities in Britain. Third, these cultures are expressive. In the midst of a nuanced argument that decries essentialism in black popular culture, Stuart Hall makes the following instructive assertion:

> However deformed, incorporated, and inauthentic are the forms in which black people and black communities and traditions appear and are represented in popular culture, we continue to see, in the figures and the repertoires on which popular culture draws, the experiences that stand behind them. In its expressivity, its musicality, its orality, in its rich, deep, and varied attention to speech, in its inflections towards the vernacular and the local, in its rich production of counter-narratives, and above all, in its metaphorical use of the musical vocabulary, black popular culture has enabled the surfacing, inside the mixed and contradictory modes even of some mainstream popular culture, of elements of a discourse that is different—other forms of life, other traditions of representation.[5]

5. *Black theologians in Britain embrace plurality, inter-faith interaction and dialogue*

A function of the multiplicity and diversity of the black community is the need for a broad-based approach to theological thinking and conceptualizing. An example of this is contained in Robert Beckford's *Jesus Is Dread*.[6] Beckford, a black male Pentecostal, engages seriously with Rastafarian thought, draws upon the works of Bob Marley and dialogues with Black Muslim art in the work of Faisal Abduallah. In point of fact, the central thesis of the book is premised upon the rasta concept of 'dread', namely upliftment, freedom and empowerment.

6. *Black theologians in Britain work carefully and conscientiously, examining and weighing material with close attention*

This is a requirement of all theological work. Any serious engagement with matters that are of enduring relevance must be done carefully and conscientiously. However, when such work is done in the context of centuries of 'unwitting' as well as deliberate misconception and misrepresentation, the importance of alertness and carefulness is thrown into sharp focus.

7. Women and men, young and old, work collaboratively on the Black theology project in Britain. Black theologians are prepared to work with any individuals and/or groups who share our vision and goals

One of the compelling features of James Cone's work since the late 1960s has been his openness to challenge and further thinking. In the preface to the 1986 edition of his now classic *A Black Theology of Liberation*, Cone wrote 'the most glaring limitation of *A Black Theology of Liberation* was my failure to be receptive to the problem of sexism in the black community and society as a whole'.[7] He had recognized the absence of the voice of black women in his early writings. In this area black theologians in Britain have from the beginning maintained the need for collaboration, even when black churches have perpetuated the male supremacy of traditional Western Christian teaching. Cone writes, 'When we truly recognise the limits of our experience without denying its revelatory power, we are then encouraged to reach out to others and connect with the transcendent in their experiences'.[8] Black theologians in Britain recognize the 'transcendent in the experiences' of women, men, young and old, and as such work collaboratively with all.

8. Black theology in Britain is an exercise in liberating praxis

Stephen Bevans's definition of praxis as 'reflected-upon action and acted-upon reflection'[9] is very appropriate in the work of the black theologian. Black theology seeks to bring theory and practice together in ways that promote liberation and well-being primarily for black people, but also for all. As such it employs the tools of critical social analysis, reflection on experience and practice as well as biblical and historical hermeneutics. Like all forms of liberation theology it seeks to be personally, socially and politically transformative. The prayer and activity of the liberationist is directed towards the transformation of all structures and forms of oppression and for the actualization of the reign of God wherein there is social justice, compassion and grace for all people.

9. Black theologians seek to engage seriously with all other theologians, as well as those of other disciplines whose work impinges on the black experience in Britain

Black theology seeks to be dialogical and to interact with all theologians in the quest for a just rendering of the varieties of encounter and expression of faith in God. Black theologians recognize varieties of methodologies in theology and seek to empower and facilitate the articulation and hearing of the less well-known voices in the wildernesses of theological discourse.

10. Black theologians seek to enhance authentic and creative approaches to theology, not merely to imitate white western liberal methods

Cone declares:

> [T]he great problem with dominant white theologians, especially white men, is their tendency to speak as if they and they alone can set the rules for thinking about God. That is why they seldom turn to the cultures of the poor, especially people of color, for resources to discourse about God.[10]

By contrast, black theologians explore different 'local' theologies and encourage a variety of methodologies for theologizing.

Having outlined crucial characteristics of Black theology as it emerges within the British context, I wish now to sketch some of the tasks that need to be done if a responsible and responsive Black theology in Britain is to emerge in the millennium. I am setting these out in the form of an agenda to enable the tasks and issues being faced to be seen clearly and cogently.

Seven Items on the Agenda of *Black Theology in Britain*

An agenda[11] sets out clearly items to be attended to. As such, what follows is a listing of crucial tasks to be achieved. In several cases they are receiving the attention of particular groups of persons.

1. There is a biblical task

It is a truism that black people love the Bible. Whether in Pentecostal, mainline or charismatic churches the love of the 'word' is clearly evident within the black community. Any perceived attempt to downgrade or challenge the 'authority' of Scripture is met either with incredulity or else with firm resistance. Rastafarians as well as members of the Nation of Islam, to cite just two other predominantly black religious traditions, read and quote the Bible extensively, raising serious hermeneutical questions for black and other Christian people.

Black youth is seriously questioning the way in which it has been approached. In spite of this plain fact, there are not that many biblical scholars within the black British community who have made the scholarly study of the Bible in its original languages their life's work. It is also the case that there are few African American biblical scholars, notable exceptions being Randall Bailey, Cain Hope Felder and Renita Weems.[12]

Contemporary biblical scholars highlight and position themselves in relation to text, authors or readers respectively. The importance and need for all three is, of course, recognized. Black theologians further recognize the need for the 'recovery of Black presence' in all three areas. Creative hermeneutic study and work is crucial.

2. *The historical task*

There is a need for careful work on the historical trajectories of black people in the UK. The fitting commemorations of the fiftieth anniversary of the arrival of the *Empire Windrush* in 1998 fuelled a number of oral as well as written histories.[13] However, they also perpetuated the misunderstanding that the black presence in Britain was merely 50 years old. Recent research and publications are attempting to set that record straight. Vincent Carretta has performed the service of re-editing and writing an introduction to the letters of Ignatius Sancho, who was born in 1729 on a slave ship bound for the West Indies. Sancho, orphaned by the age of two, was taken to England and rose from servitude to become the most celebrated African-Briton of his time.[14] In 1789 Olaudah Equiano had published his own *Interesting Narrative*[15] outlining his movements from African freedom through European enslavement on slave ships in the New World to eventual struggle for freedom in England. Mention needs also be made of the work of David Dabydeen, David Killingray, Hakim Adi, Marika Sherwood and Delia Jarrett-Macauley,[16] all of whom have made significant contributions to our understanding of the contributions that people of African descent have made to life in Britain. Several oral history projects are currently being undertaken. The Black and Asian Studies Association (BASA) can be mentioned as an important source of careful study in this area.[17] Historical studies of Africa before the advent of the European,[18] as well as Asian and Caribbean histories, have a bearing on this.

3. *Philosophical and cultural education*

Underlying much of Western philosophy and culture is a racist ideology. One demon in the belly of the Enlightenment was racism. As Hall has shown, Enlightenment thinkers believed that there was but one path to civilization and social development, and that all societies could be ranked early or late, lower or higher on this one scale.[19] The deconstructive task of exposing and analysing the ongoing effects of this way of thinking needs to be addressed. The work of Emmanuel Eze in gathering together relevant published essays by such well-known philosophers as David Hume, Immanuel Kant and Georg Wilhelm Friedrich Hegel, *inter alia*, has proved most instructive. The thoughts of these 'enlightened' European thinkers about Africa and Africans, as well as other 'inferior races', speaks for itself.[20] There is also the constructive task of recognizing, unearthing and articulating African and Asian philosophies. Black British theologians need to rise to this task.

4. *Socio-economic*

Black theology is a holistic enterprise. Every aspect of human experience and every means of promotion of black well-being needs to be addressed.

This includes black business promotion, housing provision, employment creation and health care, to mention areas of clear need. In Black theology 'Salvation' (soteriology) is a 'total person' concept.

5. Political

Black theology entails a commitment to the struggle for social justice, criminal justice and social well-being of all. At present the fact of black disadvantage and the complicity of the organs of state in black oppression are well documented. This struggle includes that against crime, drugs and the gun culture. A black political theology for the UK that takes the contemporary scene seriously is needed to mobilize us all in the struggle. The Black Christian Civic Forum, founded in London this year, is a welcome attempt to do just that. Such movements need the support of all who sincerely desire justice for all.

6. Psychological

The effects of black existence in Britain upon black people have yet to be fully worked out. Questions concerning the effects for different sections of the black communities of living in Britain need to be addressed. Psychological studies of the self-worth, self-esteem, identity and mental health of black persons within the country are beginning to appear from the work of black psychologists.[21] There is a need for further detailed and careful studies by black psychiatrists and educators of issues of psychological well-being affecting different sections of the community undertaken from a distinctively black perspective.

7. Aesthetic

The development and promotion of black music, drama, dance, film and the arts in Britain is a task which black theologians have largely ignored. Black creativity has often been condemned as 'worldly' by black theologians. There is a need for a reclamation of our heritage in all its varied dimensions, in the arts. There is also the task of engagement with the media concerning issues of representation, fairness, accuracy and consultation.

Conclusion

The task is as clear as it is daunting. However, if we are to respond to the realities that face us in nation, church and society, then we must engage all our powers to fulfil the mammoth and multi-dimensional task that lies ahead. We must resist a reductionistic approach to the theological task. It cannot merely be cerebral, conceptual and abstract. Engagement with the mind and theory is necessary, and we need many more black British people in that area of work. However, the praxeological is what is called for most in this regard. A final word then is that the interaction between theory and practice, faith and life, which lies at the heart of a wholesome and holistic theology, is what is needed.

Going back to move forwards: our reflections on Lartey's manifesto and beyond

Some critics of Black theology in Britain have dismissed Lartey's manifesto as nothing more than rhetoric. Our view is that such a position is based on misinformed analysis of the story of Black theology in Britain. Lartey's manifesto outlines a challenging future for the movement in this country. It is both descriptive and aspirational. In terms of the former, the manifesto delineates a number of the important salient characteristics of Black theology in Britain. His concentration is on the diverse roots of Black theology in Britain (as there is no single trajectory notion of the discipline as one might find in North America, where Black theology is synonymous with African Americans) or that Black British theologians (like the American counterparts) give priority to the Bible in their theological method.

Lartey's assertion that British Black theology begins with creation—with the very dust of the earth from which we and the whole of creation has been fashioned by God—is an assertion that finds echoes in the more recent work of Kate Coleman, one of the leading Black Women theologians in Britain in her comparatively recent doctoral thesis, an extract from which is published in Chapter 5.

Whilst Lartey's ten characteristics of Black British theology are descriptive (and normative) his follow-up seven-point assessment of the future agenda for this movement is more aspirational. It is on these seven principles and our reassessment of them, some eight years since they were published, that the rest of this chapter will focus.

A future trajectory for Black Theology in Britain

It is our opinion that the following represent some of the major challenges and opportunities with which Black theology in Britain must engage in the near future.

1. *Black theology in Britain must continue to grapple with the Bible.* Black Christianity, for the most part, approaches the Bible by means of quasi-literalist reading strategies, in which salvation is conceived solely in terms of adherence to Jesus Christ and his atoning death on the Cross. Whilst not wishing to discredit outright such reading practices, we, nevertheless, believe that it is imperative that Black faith regains its priceless ability of 'reading against the text', drawing especially on postcolonial biblical criticism in order to recover a dynamic and an explicit liberative agenda and praxis in our engagement with sacred text. Black theological engagement

with the Bible is one that holds in tension the sanctity of the sacred *text and that of the human (con)text*. We have placed the last few words in italics because it is essential that this assertion is greatly emphasized.

It is not our belief that the biblical text should take automatic precedence over the human text of experience and encounter. We know that many will want to assert that Holy Scripture is inspired by God's very self, but our counter assertion would state that 'being inspired tells one nothing of the provenance of that inspiration'. History and contemporary experience shows us clearly that all claims to be inspired by God are not necessarily the case. Claiming divine inspiration for one's actions simply informs one of that person's epistemological grounding for their actions not whether such assertions themselves are genuinely from or of God. Inspired narrators or writers are not disembodied spirits. They are flesh and blood humans located in particular cultural contexts. We are advocating that Black theology should assist Black Christians to distinguish between that which is the authentic 'Word of God' (i.e. that which promotes life and is redemptive) and that which might best be described as 'Word about God' (narratives that deny life and promote injustice). If Black Christianity can regain the 'commonsense wisdom' (what one might describe as an example of Prevenient grace) of being able to distinguish between the texts we can take literally, those we should re-interpret and hold in dialectical tension with human experience and those that are something less than the bounteous, gracious nature of God, then we will have retrieved the experiential wisdom of our slave forbears. Slaves in the eighteenth and nineteenth centuries did not believe in the literal word of God if the consequence of such readings was the diminution and negation of the Black self. They were not so much *biblical literalists* as *biblical realists*.

2. *Black theology must grapple with the nature of our Blackness*. In Lartey's manifesto, he argues that Black theology sees 'race' as a theological matter. We agree with him, but would press the matter even further and assert that just as 'race' is a theological matter, then as a corollary, Blackness and the theological anthropology of the nature of being Black are equally so. The editors would assert that any diminution of the complex reality and semantic struggle to decipher the theological meaning and the social constructed basis of Blackness is simply religious and emotional escapism. As Reddie has argued in a more recent piece of work, Black people are still being killed solely on the grounds of the politicized nature of their Blackness[22]—i.e. the darkness of the epidermis still arouses hostility, withering invective, much bile and even violence, and our faith in God *must* respond to these ongoing existential realities.

The editors have a noted a tendency in some quarters to argue for alternative nomenclatures when describing Black theological identity in Britain.

Some would want to push for 'Caribbean'. Whilst not wishing to discount or discredit these important advances, the editors would assert, however, the semantic problem of seeking to anchor one's theological identity to a region and its concomitant identities. Using such nomenclatures as 'Asian' or 'Caribbean', whilst important and not without merit, does not necessarily tell you anything about the nature, intent or positionality of the theological disposition of that particular understanding of the larger framework or family named 'Contextual Theology'.

Presumably, oppressive, authoritarian and paternalistic figures and groups of people who come from those regions and who might define themselves in terms that are consonant with that label could equally claim to belong to it. So, non-conscientized Brahmins or the upper class and usually lighter skinned and 'refined' postcolonial and un-deconstructed oligarchy in the Caribbean could claim that they are doing Asian and Caribbean theology respectively, just as repressive Afrikaans by dint of their birth could claim to be doing African theology.

Whilst we are not arguing that Black is the only valid nomenclature for defining and detailing the prophetic and subversive spirituality and religious ideals of people of African and Asian descent, we would assert that this term possesses an unambiguous ideological positionality that is not open to obfuscation, namely, that only those whose interests are ones of societal transformation and a prophetic, counter-cultural 'fullness of life theology' re-reading of history and contemporary reality can legitimately claim to be doing Black theology.

In short, as we have stated in the first chapter, simply being Black and engaging in theology does not make one a Black theologian or, indeed, engaged in the task of doing Black theology. There is a sharp difference between Black Christian religious experience (the general articulation of faith that is informed by and reflects the experiential and historical dimensions of Diasporan African experience) and Black theology, which although similar to the former, nevertheless carries with it an ideological dimension in terms of framing Blackness as the essential point of departure and norm in any talk about faith, spirituality and God.

3. *Black theology must remain committed to an expansive, generous and hospitable ecumenical vocation and vision.* This means that Black British theology must resist the temptation to fall into ecclesial camps and denominational myopic norms. We can learn from Black theology in the US. One of their strengths has been the extent to which the rivalries or camps, such as they exist, lie within methodological concerns[23] rather than collapsing theology into ecclesiology. In effect, their theologizing is concerned with the need to address how *all* Black people talk about and perceive God, rather than how *some* Black people (those with a similar ecclesial

tag) do so. The editors have noted a tendency amongst some writers and thinkers in the UK to assume a normative position for particular denominations and Christian traditions in their talk about Black faith in Britain. Such proclivities merely serve to destabilize the necessary ecumenical discourse of Black theology and stultify (and polarise) intra Black theological discourse.

Further, this tendency is unfortunate because it is symptomatic of an underlying theological disposition that is somewhat contrary and unhelpful to the very ideological intent of Black theology in Britain. For some, the concentration on particular manifestations of Black Christian religious experience in Britain is symptomatic of an underlying theology that is built upon notions of election and 'manifest destiny'. This form of theological construction holds to the view that only those who are 'saved' within a particular tradition are perceived as being the 'saints in the eyes of God', whilst all others, by crude process of elimination, are not. Previous writers have noted the pernicious elements of this religious phenomenon.[24]

The underlying problem with this particular form of theological construction is the way in which it separates people into two essential camps: those who receive God's grace and those who do not; those who are saved and those who are not; and those who are redeemed within that particular branch of the church and those who are not.

Whilst the editors do not doubt that there exists a strong theological tradition within Christianity, which traces its roots back to a certain strain of thinking with the Pauline canon, we would question the legitimacy of this understanding with reference to Black theology.

Any cursory reading of Diasporan African history will highlight the theological folly of attempting to divide Black people into those who are saved and those who are not. There is no compelling evidence to demonstrate that being saved offered certain Black people any particular form of amelioration from their contextual ills that was denied those who could not claim such an experience. Of perhaps even greater import is the assertion that Black theology does not believe in a God who makes those kinds of discrimination. God does not limit God's own love, care and concern for only those who say the right words, mimic the right liturgical actions and pontificate the correct declarations of faith. Black theology is concerned with working in partnership with God to declare the values and the reality of God's *oikonomia* (economy) here on earth as well as in heaven. In effect, the campaign is for life on earth, as heaven is ultimately God's business. We are campaigning for life before death—life for all, as opposed to the limited binary of life only for a select few and only after death. This is the theology of *hope-full living* that Black theology in Britain seeks to embody.

4. *One implication of the foregoing point is that Black theology must always be based on praxis.* The often-neglected section from the letter of James 2:14–26, especially in church lectionaries, clearly calls for the primacy of ortho-praxis as opposed to orthodoxy. Whether in terms of the 'Good Samaritan' (Luke 10:25–37) or 'The Rich Young Ruler' (Matthew 19:16–24, Mark 10:17–25 and Luke 18:18–25), the rubrics of the people of 'The Way' were predicated on praxis and not fossilized dogmas. This is not to deny the role of spirituality, faith and doctrine within the religious construction of Black people of faith in Britain. However, we do not hold to the view that believing certain things in isolation from the commitment to exhibit righteous actions in solidarity with those who are the 'least of these' (Matthew 25:31–46) is a true measure of the radical intent of the 'Jesus Way'. Walking the talk of the Jesus way, living the Jesus truth and modelling the Jesus lifestyle demands faith and faithfulness.

Whether in campaigning for an end to poverty or playing its part within the process that led to the MacPherson report,[25] Black Christian faith must be based upon a notion of reflective action and active reflection. Whilst an active participation in social events is of immense importance, there must also be the realization that simply responding to events without analysing the underlying structures and systemic fault lines that lead to particular forms of social inequalities is insufficient if Black faith is to proclaim the radical intent of the Economy of God. While Black theological discourse remains contextual and experiential, its vision is towards empowerment and transformation.

5. *Black theology in Britain must honour, respect and engage with the diversity of Black religiosity and spirituality within the ranks of all Black people.* Black theology must now take seriously the diversity within what we term 'Black' in the UK. Black theology needs to re-visit the complexity of contexts, ecclesial traditions, ethnicities, identities and experiences of Black people. For instance, the participants and focus of a recent gathering for 'A National Summit for Black and Minority Ethnic Church Leaders', called by Churches Together in England (October 2005), gives the erroneous impression of Black people as solely Pentecostals. The fact remains that that not all Black Christians are Pentecostals. Most Black Christians in the UK are in fact of the catholic ecclesial tradition (Anglo-catholic or Roman). There is an urgent need for a serious discourse on the intra-diversity in terms of religiosity, spiritualities, experiences and theological notions/terms.

Further, given the plural and religious diversity of present-day Britain it would not be surprising to note that not all Black people are Christians. Black people and their religious experiences cannot be reduced to mere Christian expressions.[26] The presence of Black Muslims from various parts of Africa, the Caribbean and via conversion in the British context poses sharp questions about Blackness, identity, faith and religiosity for Black theological discourse.

Moreover, Black British Christians of Caribbean ancestry ought to be aware of the significant presence and influence of Rastafarians in the UK. Indeed, the Caribbean Diaspora ought to be aware of the plurality and richness of Caribbean Black religious experience. Black Christians need to wake up to this and other African Caribbean religious streams that have nourished our faith journeys. Our religious identities are more plural than many of us would want to acknowledge.

Thus, Black theology's role is to give greater agency to and encourage more engagement with the diversity of Black religiosity and experience to enable Black Christian discourse to interrogate its own alliance with the inherited White Euro-centric Christianity.[27] In fact, Black British theological discourse needs to include any religious tradition in which Black people are immersed as the strictures of Eurocentric hegemony are not restricted to Christianity. Its own liberation and open-ended agenda demands no less, otherwise it falls into the trap of re-inscribing the very critique it offers to White hegemonic theology.

6. *Black theology must become a serious voice in interfaith conversations.* This is clearly one of the implications of the previous point, and a demand placed on Black theological discourse, mindful of the dialogical imperative that is necessary within diverse Black religiosity. As we have noted, the presence of the Rastafarians and the increasing numbers of Black Muslims through immigration and conversion do more than puncture any notion of the Black community as exclusively Christian. This development brings a new dimension to the spatial, contextual and historical paradigms of the Black British experience.

A challenge that Black Muslims and Rastafarianism pose to Black Christians and Black theology is related to the choice of identity and the un-deconstructed ways in which some aspects of Black Christianity have become reconciled or even subsumed within White Christianity. In the context of Black British people converting to Islam or Rastafarianism, we need to ask ourselves why these Black folks would opt to locate themselves as a double minority in Britain? Do these religious traditions offer more expansive frameworks to counter racism, economic exploitation and to re-define Blackness?

Closer scrutiny of interfaith or inter-religious dialogue in the UK would reveal a preponderance of largely White Christian voices (that are yet to interrogate its own Whiteness) speaking on behalf of Christians, and the lack of Black and Asian Christian participation in these conversations. Further, the interfaith conversations are yet to engage with Rastafarianism and the Black Muslim voices and presence. In effect, the interfaith discourse is taking place with little focus on issues of identities, cultures and race.

Black theology's engagement in interfaith conversations would do three things: (i) It would bring on the agenda of Black Christians the need to grapple with the rich diversity of Black (African and Asian) spirituality and religiosity and its relationship to the faith and faithfulness of Black people. (ii) It would demand of Black Christian discourse further interrogation of the inherited White Christianity and the concomitant cultural norms that may have been internalized. (iii) It would bring to the interfaith table the important place of ethnic identities, experiences and cultures, and challenge White Christians to interrogate their engagement with the religious 'other'. The fact remains that the preferential option of Black Christianity is to work in solidarity with all peoples who are marginalized and not fall into any tribal nature of things that separates 'us' from 'them' and assumes a privileged position for Christianity.

8. *Black theology must not neglect class analysis alongside its involvement in anti-racist struggle.* As the 'New World Order' continues to weave its toxic magic across the contours of the globe, material poverty and structural economic inequalities and injustice continue to be the lot of the bulk of predominantly Black peoples across the world. Black theology must not allow its practice to be fatally compartmentalized in such a fashion that the multi-dimensional analysis which has become commonplace, particularly in Womanist theology, is neglected.

One of the challenges for Black theology is to counter the worst excesses of 'Prosperity Teaching' within Christianity, which appears to have captured the imagination of the Black urban poor in many parts of the world. The likes of Beckford[28] and Reddie[29] have countered the predilection of particular Christian speakers and spokespersons to 'feed off' the very real struggles and desperation of the poor by offering them the enticing baubles of 'Cheap Grace' and disembodied religion. These forms of spirituality do not take seriously the root causes of poverty and exploitation. Rather, they emanate from the false doctrines of the market and rampant, unchecked capitalism. We are not arguing for a notion of faith that asserts the absurdity of there being 'dignity in poverty'. Poverty, like ignorance (the latter is never bliss), is simply a bad position to be in.

We note the tendency of polite White middle-class discourse to find ways of masking their own innate self-interest by taking refuge in theological obfuscation and escapism. The editors have lost count of the number of times they have witnessed comfortable—in some cases, very affluent—professional White middle-class clergy extolling the virtues of 'servant ministry' from within the confines of comfort and security. We find this form of theological construction nauseating and obnoxious. For many of us whose forbears were literally servants, we are not persuaded about the efficacy of invoking theological constructions that have no functional reality. In eschewing the dubious claims of servanthood, we nevertheless want to reassert the belief that nowhere in the Gospels does Jesus promise those who follow him riches or self-reward.

Black theology must continue to press for a balanced understanding of faith that rejects the extremes of non-indivituative material analysis expressed in some quarters of Liberation theology alongside the need to counter the hyper-spiritualized individualism of Charismatic Christianity.

9. *Black theology must remain prophetic, iconoclastic and protesting.* Black theology came into being, initially within the epoch of slavery, as a response to Black existential struggle and crisis. Black slaves knew first hand the tendentious and self-serving nature of the Christianity into which they were being inducted. Whether in the works of James Cone,[30] Jacquelyn Grant[31] or Robert Beckford,[32] Black theology has never been seduced by the blandishments of White patrician control. Reddie, for example, invoking the metaphor of the party, highlights the means by which the protesting, iconoclastic panache of Black theology was able to reject notions of trying to join the corrupt party of White power, choosing instead to construct an alternative party that becomes so compelling that the exclusionary White folks then want to come and join us![33] One only has to witness the ways in which White corporate capitalism has sought to market and endorse Black cultural production (as witnessed in hip-hop and RnB) that was once disparaged, in order to see the truth of this dynamic.

Black theology, at its best, has been a campaigning and subversive movement that has sought to re-interpret Christianity, the meaning of Christian faith and the nature and intent of the economy of God. Like the metaphor of the party invoked in the previous paragraph, Black theology seeks to re-imagine the very nature of reality, infusing what we see and experience as truth with an alternative vision where the first shall indeed be last and the last becoming first.

In terms of the latter, Black theology is rightly suspicious of all forms of human constructed hierarchies. If power corrupts, then Black theology needs to continue challenging and critiquing all forms of power, even if the people holding and dispensing that power are Black. We have noted that the old dictum of 'needing Black people in office' can become a false panacea given the ways in which ecclesial and secular examples often simply demonstrate that Black men and women who assume power and influence can be as authoritarian, non-collegial and myopic in their thinking and actions as the White people who preceded them.

Black theology must never seek to sit at the top table or luxuriate in the corridors of power. Black theology adopts the position of the prophet and not that of the priest. The editors note the means by which the Christian church was shorn of its radical, bottom-up iconoclastic nature once she became a part of the power structures courtesy of the imperial imprimatur following Constantine's conversion to Christianity. Whilst the Christian church 'sold out' her radical birthright at the altar of political power and societal influence, leading to an inability to challenge such abhorrent evils like slavery, Black theology continues to argue for a bottom-up model of structural change and societal and world transformation that eschews any sense of placating the status quo.

We note the tendency of particular branches of Black Christianity to describe themselves as conservatives. One of the editors in answer to such declarations would cite the private words of encouragement from Randall Bailey, the renowned African American Hebrew scholar, who states, 'When Black Christians describe themselves as conservatives, I always want to ask the question just what are they conserving? It was largely White males who invented this stuff and now we want to conserve it!'[34]

Black theology does not doubt the need for Black people to be involved in all forms of political processes, seeking to influence from the top, and engaging in the arenas of power, but we would remind all such persons that authentic change has always come from the bottom-up and not the top-down. Black theology must continue to align itself with the needs of ordinary rank and file Black people and not the blandishments of the powerful.

10. *Black theology in Britain must continue to pursue an interdisciplinary form of engagement in her methodological approach.* This is important as Black theology is not in the business of bringing closure on matters of faith nor does it major in exactitudes. It is our impression that the work of Beckford and Reddie, for example, and Black theology in Britain as a whole, exhibits a very eclectic nature. We are not 'pure' and 'suffocating' theologians: we are eclectic—in conversation with doctrines, bible, traditions, culture, the arts, literature, sociology, economics, etc. Unlike the African-American context, we are not developing a biblical or hermeneutic school as separate from a theological one. (This may be a shortcoming or perhaps not!) Many Black theologians in Britain are more biblical than many of the second and third generation African American scholars.

11. *And finally, in seeking to answer, perhaps the ultimate ethical question: How, then, shall we live?* We would respond by stating that as we strive towards that beloved community we dream of in the UK, Black theology in Britain needs to continue and build on this interdisciplinary dialogue with the world of films, music, art, myth, history, social sciences, cultural studies, etc. Our vision is beyond ourselves. It is a vision for all oppressed

peoples and for God's economy for the whole world. To that engagement Black theology brings narrative agency (our experiences), systemic thinking (engaging with structures, institution, dogmas, scholarship), inter-cultural engagement, the politics of location and positionality and the desire to work in partnership with God to transform the whole of creation.

Notes

Foreword

1.   See Anthony G. Reddie, *Dramatizing Theologies: A Participative Approach to Black God-Talk* (London: Equinox, 2006), 62–63.

2.   Further details on the monthly Black Theology Forum in Birmingham can be found in Anthony G. Reddie, *Black Theology in Transatlantic Dialogue* (New York: Palgrave Macmillan, 2006), 160–64.

Acknowledgements

1.   Living Out Faith is an Internet-based resource project that is seeking to document Black Christian life and Black theology in Britain and disseminate its unique transformative qualities for teaching and learning within schools in Britain, aiming particularly at Religious Education, Citizenship and Personal, Social and Health Education (PSHE). For further details on Living Out Faith see www.livingout-faith.org.uk. Further details can also be found in Carol Troupe, *The Contribution of Black Culture and Faith to Religious Education* (unpublished M.Phil thesis, University of Birmingham, 2005).

2.   See Reddie, *Dramatizing Theologies*.

Chapter 1

1.   Emmanuel Y. Lartey, *Black Theology in Britain: A Journal of Contextual Praxis* 1 (October 1998), 7.

2.   See Dwight N. Hopkins, *Down, Up and Over: Slave Religion and Black Theology* (Minneapolis: Fortress Press, 2000), 11–36.

3.   See Emmanuel C. Eze, *Race and the Enlightenment* (Oxford and Malden, MA: Blackwell, 1997).

4.   See Dwight N. Hopkins, *Being Human: Race, Culture and Religion* (Minneapolis: Fortress Press, 2005), 113–60.

5.   See Anthony B. Pinn, *Terror and Triumph: The Nature of Black Religion* (Minneapolis: Fortress Press, 2003), 1–25.

6.   Pinn, *Terror and Triumph*, 82–107.

7.   Pinn, *Terror and Triumph*, 82–107.

8.   John Wilkinson, James H. Evans Jr. and Renate Wilkinson, *Inheritors Together: Black People in the Church of England* (London: Race, Pluralism and Community Group Board for Social Responsibility, 1985), 10, emphasis added.

9.   Henry H. Mitchell, *Black Church Beginnings: The Long-Hidden Realities of the First Years* (Grand Rapids, MI/Cambridge, UK: Eerdmans, 2004), 24–45.

10.   See Anne H. Pinn and Anthony B. Pinn, *Fortress Introduction to Black Church History* (Minneapolis: Fortress Press, 2002), 6–8.

11.   Mitchell *Black Church Beginnings*, 8–45.

12.   Noel L. Erskine, *Decolonizing Theology: A Caribbean Perspective* (Maryknoll, NY: Orbis Books, 1983), 41–45.

13. Pinn and Pinn, *Fortress Introduction to Black Church History*, 32–43.

14. Pinn, *Terror and Triumph*, 90–93.

15. Pinn, *Terror and Triumph*, 93.

16. Harold Dean Trulear, 'African American Religious Education' in Barbara Wilkerson (ed.), *Multicultural Religious Education* (Birmingham, AL: Religious Education Press, 1997), 162.

17. See Anthony G. Reddie, *Black Theology in Transatlantic Dialogue* (New York: Palgrave Macmillan, 2006), 17–18.

18. See Reddie, *Black Theology in Transatlantic Dialogue*, 17, original emphasis.

19. See James H. Cone, *A Black Theology of Liberation* (Maryknoll, NY: Orbis Books. 1986).

20. See Delores Williams, *Sisters in the Wilderness: The Challenge of Womanist God-Talk* (Maryknoll, NY: Orbis Books, 1993).

21. See Robert Beckford, *Dread and Pentecostal* (London: SPCK, 2000).

22. James H. Cone, *God of the Oppressed* (Maryknoll, NY: Orbis, 1994), 183–94.

23. Williams, *Sisters in the Wilderness*, 161–77.

24. See Paul Gilroy, *Between Camps: Nations, Cultures and the Allure of Race* (London: Allen Lane, The Penguin Press, 2000).

25. See A. A. Sivanandan, *A Different Hunger: Writings on Black Resistance* (London: Pluto Press, 1982).

26. See Ron Ramdin, *The Making of the Black Working Class* (London: Gower, 1987).

27. See Kobener Mercer, *Welcome to the Jungle* (London and New York: Routledge, 1994).

28. Among R.S. Sugirtharajah's many publications see *Postcolonial Criticism and Biblical Interpretation* (Oxford: Oxford University Press, 2002).

29. Among Stuart Hall's many publications see *The Hard Road to Renewal: Thatcherism and the Crisis of the Left* (London: Verso, 1988).

30. See See Inderjit S. Bhogal, 'Citizenship', in Anthony G. Reddie (ed.), *Legacy: Anthology in Memory of Jillian Brown* (Peterborough: The Methodist Publishing House, 2000), 137–41 and Inderjit S. Bhogal, *On the Hoof: Theology in Transit* (Sheffield: Penistone Publications, 2001).

31. Mukti Barton, *Rejection, Resistance and Resurrection: Speaking Out on Racism in the Church* (London: Darton, Longman and Todd, 2005).

32. See James W. Perkinson, *White Theology* (New York: Palgrave, 2004). See also James W. Perkinson, *Shamanism, Racism and Hip-Hop Culture* (New York: Palgrave, 2005).

33. Paul Grant and Raj Patel (eds.), *A Time to Speak: Perspectives of Black Christians in Britain* (Birmingham: A Joint Publication of 'Racial Justice' and the 'Black Theology Working Group', 1990).

34. Paul Grant and Raj Patel (eds.), *A Time to Act: Kairos 1992* (Birmingham: A Joint Publication of 'Racial Justice' and the 'Black and Third World Theology Working Group', 1992).

35. See Inderjit S. Bhogal, *On the Hoof: Theology in Transit* (Sheffield: Penistone Publications, 2001).

36. See R. David Muir, 'Black Theology, Pentecostalism, and Racial Struggles in the Church of God' (unpublished PhD thesis, Kings College London, 2004).

37.   See chapter 2 of Reddie, *Black Theology in Transatlantic Dialogue*.

38.   The first issue was launched at the George Cadbury Hall, in Birmingham, on October 10, 1998.

39.   Reddie, *Black Theology in Transatlantic Dialogue*.

40.   Minutes of the Editorial Committee held at the Centre for Black and White Christian Partnership, Birmingham, England, October 27, 1997.

41.   Beckford, *Dread and Pentecostal*, 95–130.

42.   See Emmanuel C. Eze, *Race and the Enlightenment* (Oxford and Malden, MA: Blackwell, 1997).

43.   See James W. Perkinson, *White Theology* (New York: Palgrave, 2004), 154–84.

44.   Hopkins, *Being Human*, 144–60.

45.   This comment was made by Naboth Muchopa the Connexional (national) Secretary for Racial Justice in the Methodist Church.

46.   See Sylvester A. Johnson, *The Myth of Ham in Nineteenth-Century American Christianity* (New York: Palgrave, 2004).

47.   Johnson, *Myth of Ham in Nineteenth-Century American Christianity*, 27 50.

48.   Demetrius Williams, *An End to All This Strife* (Minneapolis: Fortress Press, 2004), 13–43.

49.   Mark Sturge, *Look What The Lord Has Done!* (London: SPCK, 2005).

50.   Renita J. Weems, *Battered Love* (Minneapolis: Fortress Press, 1997), 1–11.

51.   Beckford, *Dread and Pentecostal*, 99–101.

52.   See Emmanuel Lartey, 'Editorial', *Black Theology in Britain: A Journal of Contextual Praxis* 1 (1998), 7–9.

53.   See Robert Beckford, *Jesus Is Dread* (London: Darton, Longman and Todd, 1998).

54.   See Anthony G. Reddie, *Nobodies to Somebodies* (Peterborough: Epworth Press, 2003).

55.   See Reddie, *Black Theology in Transatlantic Dialogue*.

56.   See Robert Beckford, *God of the Rahtid* (London: Darton, Longman and Todd, 2001).

57.   Dwight N. Hopkins, *Introducing Black Theology of Liberation* (Maryknoll, NY: Orbis Books, 1999), 41–48.

58.   See Frederick Ware, *Methodologies of Black Theology* (Cleveland, OH: Pilgrim Press, 2002).

59.   See Itumeleng J. Mosala and Buti Tlhagale (eds.), *The Unquestionable Right to be Free* (Maryknoll, NY: Orbis Books, 1986).

60.   See Randall C. Bailey and Jacquelyn Grant (eds.), *The Recovery of Black Presence* (Nashville, TN: Abingdon Press, 1995).

61.   See Itumeleng J. Mosala, *Biblical Hermeneutics and Black Theology in South Africa* (Grand Rapids, MI: Eerdmans, 1989).

62.   It interesting to note that Alistair Kee in his assessment of Black theology in Britain makes no reference to any other scholar aside from Robert Beckford. The work of Anthony Reddie, editor of the journal and the most prolific writer in the British context, is completely overlooked. See Alistair Kee, *The Rise and Demise of Black Theology* (Aldershot, Kent: Ashgate, 2006).

63. Anthony G. Reddie, *Acting in Solidarity* (London: Darton, Longman and Todd, 2006), 38 and 39.

64. See chapter five of Reddie's *Black Theology in Transatlantic Dialogue*.

65. Joe Aldred (ed.), *Sisters with Power* (London: Continuum, 2000), v.

66. See Joe Aldred, *Respect: Understanding Caribbean British Christianity* (Peterborough: Epworth Press, 2005).

67. See Mitchell, *Black Church Beginnings*, 8–45. See also Noel L. Erskine, *Decolonizing Theology: A Caribbean Perspective* (Maryknoll, NY: Orbis Books, 1983), 41–45.

68. See Beckford *Dread and Pentecostal*, 95–130.

69. Elaine L. Graham, *Transforming Practice* (Eugene, OR: Wipf and Stock, 2002), 118–24.

70. See Robert Beckford, *Jesus Is Dread* (London: Darton, Longman and Todd, 1998).

71. See Robert Beckford, *Dread and Pentecostal* (London: SPCK, 2000).

72. See Robert Beckford, *God of the Rahtid* (London: Darton, Longman and Todd, 2001).

73. See Robert Beckford, *God and the Gangs* (London: Darton, Longman and Todd, 2004).

74. See Robert Beckford, *Jesus Dub: Theology, Music and Social Change* (London: Routledge, 2006).

75. Valentina Alexander, 'To Break Every Fetter? To What Extent has the Black-led Church in Britain Developed a Theology of Liberation?' (unpublished PhD thesis, University of Warwick, 1996).

76. See Kate Coleman, 'Black Theology and Black Liberation: A Womanist Perspective', *Black Theology in Britain: A Journal of Contextual Praxis* 1 (1998), 59–69; 'Black Women and Theology', *Black Theology in Britain: A Journal of Contextual Praxis* 3 (1999), 51–65. See also Lorraine Dixon, 'Teach it Sister! Mahalia Jackson as Theologian in Song', *Black Theology in Britain: A Journal of Contextual Praxis* 2 (1999), 72–89; 'A Reflection on Black Identity and Belonging in the Context of the Anglican Church in England: A Way Forward', *Black Theology in Britain: A Journal of Contextual Praxis* 4 (2000), 22–37.

77. See Hyacinth Sweeney, 'The Bible as a Tool for Growth for Black Women', *Black Theology in Britain: A Journal of Contextual Praxis* 5 (2000), 21–32.

78. See Valentina Alexander, 'Onesimus's Letter to Philemon', *Black Theology in Britain: A Journal of Contextual Praxis* 4 (2000), 61–65.

79. See Robert Beckford, 'Prophet of Dub: Dub as a Heuristic for Theological Reflection', *Black Theology: An International Journal* 1.1 (2002), 29–48.

80. Anthony Reddie, 'Editorial', *Black Theology: An International Journal* 4.1 (2006), 9.

81. See Anthony G. Reddie, *Dramatizing Theologies* (London: Equinox, 2006). See also *Black Theology in Transatlantic Dialogue*.

82. See Hopkins, *Introducing Black Theology of Liberation*, 42–43.

83. See Joe Aldred, 'Paradigms for a Black Theology in Britain', *Black Theology in Britain: A Journal of Contextual Praxis* 2 (April 1999), 9–32.

84. See Anthony G. Reddie, *Faith, Stories and the Experience of Black Elders* (London: Jessica Kingsley, 2001), 17–38.

85.   This term has been used on a number of occasions by one of the co-editors of this text in his description of the cross-cultural fertilization of peoples and the theological plurality and diversity of the Caribbean, in which he was socialized. For further analysis on this phenomenon see Michael Jagessar, 'Cultures in Dialogue: The Contribution of a Caribbean Theologian', *Black Theology: An International Journal* 1.2 (May 2003), 139–60.

86.   Paul Grant and Raj Patel (eds.), *A Time to Speak: Perspectives of Black Christians in Britain* (Birmingham: A Joint Publication of 'Racial Justice' and the 'Black Theology Working Group', 1990).

87.   Paul Grant and Raj Patel (eds.), *A Time to Act: Kairos 1992* (Birmingham: A Joint Publication of 'Racial Justice' and the 'Black and Third World Theology Working Group', 1992).

Chapter 2

1.   Bishop Christopher Lipscomb in Jamaica, and Bishop William Hart Coleridge in Barbados.

2.   Arthur C. Dayfoot, *The Shaping of the West Indian Church 1492–1962* (Kingston, Jamaica: University of the West Indies Press, 1999), 100, 107–108.

3.   Dayfoot, *The Shaping of the West Indian Church*, 150–51.

4.   Dale Bisnauth, *History of Religions in the Caribbean* (Kingston, Jamaica: Kingston Publishers, 3rd edn, 1996), 61.

5.   Keith Hunter, 'Protestantism and Slavery in the British Caribbean', in Armando Lampe (ed.), *Christianity in the Caribbean* (Barbados: University of the West Indies Press, 2001), 97.

6.   Francis J. Osborne and G. Johnston, *Coastlands and Islands* (Kingston, Jamaica: United Theological College of the West Indies, 1972), 46.

7.   Robert J. Stewart, *Religion and Society in Post-emancipation Jamaica* (Knoxville, TN: University of Tennessee Press, 1992), 6–11.

8.   Paul Curtin, *The Rise and Fall of the Plantation Complex* (Cambridge: Cambridge University Press, 1990), 150.

9.   Curtin, *The Rise and Fall*, 174.

10.   David Lowenthal, *West Indian Societies* (Oxford: Oxford University Press, 1972), 51.

11.   Johannes Meier, 'The Beginnings of the Catholic Church in the Caribbean', in Lampe (ed.), *Christianity in the Caribbean*, 49.

12.   Dayfoot, *The Shaping of the West Indian Church*, 113.

13.   Robert J. Stewart, 'Religion in the Anglophone Caribbean', in John W. Pulis, *Religion, Diaspora, and Cultural Identity* (Amsterdam: Gordon & Breach, 1999).

14.   See among others, Horace O. Russell, *Foundations and Anticipations: The Jamaica Baptist Story 1783–1892* (Columbus, GA: Brentwood Christian Press, 1993).

15.   Bisnauth, *History of Religions in the Caribbean*, 113–14.

16.   Dayfoot, *The Shaping of the West Indian Church*, 149.

17.   Horace O. Russell, 'Understandings and Interpretations of Scripture in Eighteenth-and Nineteenth-century Jamaica', in Hemchand Gossai and Nathaniel S. Muirrell (eds.), Religion, Culture and Tradition in the Caribbean (Basingstoke: Macmillan, 2000), 104.

18.   Shirley C. Gordon, *God Almighty, Make Me Free* (Bloomington: Indiana University Press, c. 1996), 119.

19.   For the following: Curtin, *The Rise and Fall*, 174–78.

20.   Stewart, *Religion and Society*, 96–105.

21.   Mary Turner, *Slaves and Missionaries: The Disintegration of Jamaican Slave Society, 1787–1834* (Urbana and London: University of Illinois Press, c. 1982), 58.

22.   Stewart, *Religion and Society*, 16–21, with reference to the English missionary James M. Phillippo.

23.   James Lawson, *Religion and Race*, 2.

24.   Mervyn Aleyne, *Roots of Jamaican Culture* (London: Pluto Press, 1988); cf. the American anthropologists Zora Neale Hurston and Melville J. Herkovits.

25.   Noel Erskine in Lawson, *Religion and Race*, x–xi.

26.   Paul Curtin, *Two Jamaicas: The Role of Ideas in a Tropical Colony, 1830–1865* (Cambridge, MA: Harvard University Press, 1955), 34.

27.   Such historians have included Peter Fryer, Gretchen Gerzina, Folarin Shyllon, Paul Edwards, James Walvin, Ron Randin and Norma Myers.

28.   Paul Edwards and James Walvin, *Black Personalities in the Era of the Slave Trade* (London: Macmillan, 1983), 13.

29.   Paul Gilroy, *The Black Atlantic: Modernity and Double Consciousness* (London and New York: Verso, 1993).

30.   Gilroy, *The Black Atlantic*, 4. It should also be noted that White cultures were themselves transformed by Black influence.

31.   Gilroy, *The Black Atlantic*, 16.

32.   Gilroy, *The Black Atlantic*, 16.

33.   Edwards and Walvin, *Black Personalities in the Era of the Slave Trade*, 76. One of the first fruits of this change in viewpoint is James Walvin's text *Making the Black Atlantic: Britain and the African Diaspora* (London and New York: Cassell, 2000).

34.   See Peter Fryer, *Staying Power: The History of Black People in Britain* (London: Pluto Press, 1984).

35.   Fryer, *Staying Power*, 5.

36.   Fryer, *Staying Power*, 8.

37.   Kenneth Little, *Negroes in Britain: A Study of Racial Relations in English Society* (London and Boston, MA: Routledge & Kegan Paul, 1972), 188.

38.   Folarin Shyllon, *Black People in Britain 1555–1833* (London, New York and Ibadan: Oxford University Press, 1977), 8. Shyllon draws on Eric Williams's seminal book *Capitalism and Slavery* (London: Andre Deutsch, 1964).

39.   Fryer, *Staying Power*, 9.

40.   There was not a real distinction in the experience of Black people according to Shyllon. As servants they were often unpaid unlike their White compatriots.

41.   Acts of the Privy Council of England, n.s. XXVI, 20–21. Quoted by Fryer, *Staying Power*, 11.

42.   Norma Myers, *Reconstructing the Black Past: Blacks in Britain 1780–1830* (London and Portland, OR: Frank Cass & Co., 1976), 18.

43.   Myers, *Reconstructing the Black Past*, 19.

44.   G. Francklyn, *Observations* (London, 1788), xi. Quoted by Myers, *Reconstructing the Black Past*, 20.

45. Little, *Negroes in Britain*, 189.

46. Little proposes that this fashion was probably connected to literary tastes of the period or even to create a distinction between the supposed intelligent master and the witless slave.

47. Little highlights an advertisement in the *London Advertiser* for 1756 which states that one Matthew Dyer fashioned silver padlocks or collars for Blacks and Dogs!

48. Edwards and Walvin, *Black Personalities in the Era of the Slave Trade*, 19.

49. Ignatius Sancho married a Black woman but this was probably an exception.

50. Those who had run away from slavery not only had to survive life on the streets but also had to be careful of recapture by those set on gaining monetary rewards.

51. See Shyllon, *Black People in Britain*, especially chs 4 and 5.

52. Institute of Race Relations, *Roots of Racism* (London, 1982), 21.

53. Institute of Race Relations, *Roots of Racism*, 21.

54. Fryer, *Staying Power*, 7.

55. Robert Miles, *Racism* (London and New York: Routledge, 1989), 14.

56. Miles, *Racism*, 16.

57. Miles, *Racism*, 17.

58. Miles, *Racism*, 21.

59. Both groups in their own way objectified and made Black people 'the other'; in other words to be Black was to be in some way not fully human because they were not White or part of the monied classes.

60. *The Daily Post*, August 4, 1720, quoted in Shyllon, *Black People in Britain*, 8.

61. Shyllon, *Black People in Britain*, 20.

62. Gretchen Gerzina, *Black England: Life Before Emancipation* (London: Allison & Busby, 1999), 183.

63. For an exploration of contrasting theories of religion as social cement see B. S. Turner, 'Religion as Social Cement', in Robert Bocock and Kenneth Thompson (eds.), *Religion and Ideology* (Manchester: Manchester University Press, 1985), 234–44.

64. For an insight into the psychological impact of the colour class dynamic on former slave societies see the classic text Franz Fanon, *Black Skins, White Masks* (London: Pluto Press, 1986 [1st edn, 1952]).

65. Professor Peter Wilson developed this thesis in his study of the Caribbean island of Providencia. His thesis is also relevant to other Caribbean societies. See Peter Wilson, *Crab Antics: The Social Anthropology of English Speaking Negro Societies in the Caribbean* (New Haven and London: Yale University Press, 1971); see also M. G. Smith, *Stratification in Grenada* (Berkeley and Los Angeles: University of California Press, 1965).

66. Wilson, *Crab Antics*, 102.

67. Dale Bisnauth, *History of Religions in the Caribbean* (Trenton, NJ: Africa World Press, 1996), 54.

68. See for example the Anglican rector Rev. T. Banbury, *Jamaica Superstitions; or the Obeah Book* (Kingston: Mortimer C. DeSouza, 1894).

69. E. W. Thompson, 'The Return of the West Indies', *International Review of Mission* vol. XXXIX no. 116 (October 1940), 445.

70. There are few detailed studies of Convince in the historical literature. I have therefore borrowed from William James Gardner, *A History of Jamaica* (Kingston: The Cass Library of West Indian Studies, 1971) and Donald Hogg, 'The Convince Cult in Jamaica', *Publications in Anthropology* 58 (1974), 3–24.

71. Gardner, *A History of Jamaica*, 357.

72. Donald Hogg, 'The Convince Cult in Jamaica'.

73. Robert Stewart documents missionary opposition to the importation of African and Indian labour in this period precisely because they brought with them these non-Christian influences which were counter to Christianity. R. Stewart, 'A Slandered People—"Views on Negro Character" in the Mainstream Churches in Post-Emancipation Jamaica', in Darlene Clarke Hine and Jacqueline McLeod *Crossing Boundaries* (Bloomington, IN: Indiana University Press, 1999), 5–6; see also William Green, *British Slave Emancipation* (Oxford: Clarendon, 1976), 267.

74. This discussion of Kumina draws upon the following: Edward Kamau Braithwaite, 'Kumina the Spirit of African Survival', *Jamaica Journal* 42 (1978), 44–63; Olive Lewin, 'Jamaican Folk Music', *Caribbean Quarterly* 14 (1968), 49–56; Monica Schuler, *Alas, alas, Kongo: A Social History of Indentured African Immigration into Jamaica 1841–1865* (Baltimore: The Johns Hopkins University Press, 1980).

75. For a detailed study of the origins of the term see Edward Braithwaite, *The Development of Creole Society in Jamaica, 1780–1820* (London: Oxford University Press, 1971), 61.

76. For a discussion of the varieties of Revival leaders see Mervyne Alleyne, *Roots of Jamaican Culture* (London: Pluto Press, 1989), 100–102.

77. G. E. Simpson, *Black Religions in the New World* (New York: Columbia University Press, 1978), 342.

78. According to Noel Erksine, Revivalism's toleration of cohabitation and premarital sex were important reasons for its appeal among the masses as opposed to the European denominations. Noel Erskine, *Decolonizing Theology* (New York: Orbis Books, 1983), 101–102.

79. Simpson, *Black Religions in the New World*, 56. One exception to this general rule: there were a small number of street preachers in Jamaica that combined revival preaching with political consciousness such as Warrior Higgins who was active in Jamaica between 1897–1902. For an account of these see W. Elkins, *Street Preachers, Faith Healers and Herb Doctors in Jamaica, 1890–1925* (New York: Revisionist Press, 1977). However, as reported by Chevannes, the influence of Revivalism has weakened considerably in this century. B. Chevannes, 'Revivalism: A Disappearing Religion', *Caribbean Quarterly* 24.3-4 (September–December 1978), 1–8.

80. This discussion of Pentecostal denominations draws upon the following: Roswith Gerloff, 'Religious Traditions in the African Diaspora', Kings College London Conference Paper presented at the Annual Conference of the Center for New Religions, 1994, 6; Virginia Becher, *Black Christians: Black Church Traditions in Britain*, a resource pack produced jointly by the Centre for Black and White Partnership and West Hill R.E. Centre, Birmingham, 1995.

81. Ian MacRoberts, *The Black Roots and White Racism of Early Pentecostalism in the USA* (Basingstoke: Macmillan, 1988), 51–52.

82. Speaking in tongues (diaglossia) sets Pentecostalists apart from other charismatic and evangelical groups. The main Sabbatarian church the Seventh Day Adventists, for example, do not place special emphasis on diaglossia but do recognize it as a spiritual gift.

83. See in particular ch. 7 'Black Birth, Interracial Infancy, Segregated Child-hood', in MacRobert, *Black Roots and White Racism*; see also Roswith Gerloff, 'The Holy Spirit and the African Diaspora: Spiritual, Cultural and Social Roots of Black Pentecostal Churches', *EPTA Bulletin: Journal of the European Pentecostal Theological Association* XIV (1995), 85–103, esp. 93.

84. Ira Brooks, *Where Do We Go From Here* (London: New Testament Church of God, 1983), 25. Detailed primary evidence is scant but there are references to white missionary activity in William W. Menzies, *Appointed to Serve: Story of the Assemblies of God* (Springfield, MI: Gospel Publishing House, 1971).

85. These census details are cited in Simpson, *Black Religions in the New World*, 48–49.

86. As in Jamaica the dissemination of Pentecostalism among other pre-rational peoples has been facilitated by its closeness to pre-existent religious traditions; see John Wolffe, 'Evangelicals and Pentecostals', in J. Wolffe (ed.), *Global Religious Movements in Regional Context* (Bath: Ashgate in Association with Oxford University, 2002), 14–108.

87. The power and effect of black preaching style has been substantially explored by Carol Tomlinson, 'Black Preaching Style' (unpublished doctoral thesis, University of Birmingham, 1989). My own attendance has shown that this is as true of Bristol's Afro-Caribbean communities as it is of churches elsewhere in Britain.

88. Rupert Lewis and Maureen Warner Lewis, *Garvey: Africa, Europe, The Americas* (Trenton, NJ: Africa World Press, 1997).

89. Horace Campbell, *Rasta and Resistance from Marcus Garvey to Walter Rodney* (London: Hansib Publications, 1985), 57–65; Richard Hart, *The Life and Resurrection of Marcus Garvey* (London: Karia Press, 2002), 73–75; Amy Jacques Garvey (ed.), *Philosophy of Marcus Garvey*, 2 vols. in 1 (London: Frank Cass, 1967).

90. Editorial in the *Blackman*, October 25, 1930; see Campbell, *Rasta and Resistance*, 64.

91. Leonard Barrett, *The Rastafarians* (Boston, MA: New Beacon Press, 1977 rev. edn, 1988), 81.

92. Precisely how this transmutation of ideas occurred is too complex for this brief description of the movement; however, E. Ernest Cashmore provides a summary of the literature describing the process in *Rastaman: The Rastafarian Movement in England* (London: Allen & Unwin, 1979), 20–26.

93. Barry Chevannes, *Rastafari* (Syracuse, NY: Syracuse University Press, 1994), 22–23 and ch. 9 'Repatriation and Divination'. Chevannes also documents Rasta-farian hostility to Revivalism for, among other things, its 'superstitions', 151–55.

94. Ibid., 109.

95. Campbell, *Rasta and Resistance*, 96.

96. For a more detailed discussion of the origin of dreadlocks see Chevannes, *Rastafari*, xi.

97. See Old Testament, Numbers 6:5.

98. Robert Owens, *Dread: The Rastafarians of Jamaica* with intro by Rex Nettleford (London: Heinemann, 1976), 80–81.

99. See Campbell, *Rasta and Resistance*, 99.

100. *The Guardian* (Weekend) February 19, 2000, 22–26.

101. From an oral history interview carried out in the course of the research in Jamaica, spring 2000.

102. P. Hennessy, *Never Again: Britain 1945–1951* (London: Vintage, 1993), 439.

103. From an oral history interview carried out in the course of the research in Brixton, autumn 1999.

Chapter 3

1. See Carol J. Tomlin, 'Black Preaching Style' (unpublished M.Phil. thesis, University of Birmingham, 1988) and Elaine F. Foster, 'Black Women in Black-Led Churches: A Study of Black Women's Contribution to the Growth and Development of Black-led Churches in Britain' (unpublished M.Phil. thesis, University of Birmingham, 1990).

2. See Anthony G. Reddie, *Black Theology in Transatlantic Dialogue* (New York: Palgrave Macmillan, 2006), 24.

3. See Mukti Barton, *Rejection, Resistance and Resurrection: Speaking Out on Racism in the Church* (London: Darton, Longman and Todd, 2005).

4. See David Isiorho, 'Black Theology in Urban Shadow: Combating Racism in the Church of England', *Black Theology: An International Journal* 1.1 (November 2002), 29–48.

5. See Glynne Gordon-Carter, *An Amazing Journey: The Church of England's Response to Institutional Racism* (London: Church House Publishing, 2003).

6. See John Wilkinson, *Church in Black and White: The Black Tradition in 'Mainstream' Churches in England—a White Response and Testimony* (Edinburgh: St. Andrews Press, 1993).

7. The Black-led Church is referred to throughout this essay as BLC.

8. Interview respondent, Shiloh Pentecostal Fellowship (SPF).

9. Interview respondent, New Testament Church of God.

10. C. Hill, *How Colour Prejudiced is Britain?* (London: Gollancz, 1963), 74.

11. M. Calley, *God's People: West Indian Pentecostal Sects in England* (Oxford: Oxford University Press, 1965), 121.

12. Calley, *God's People*, 145 (my emphasis).

13. Calley *God's People*, 145.

14. Roswith Gerloff has written several articles on the development of the BLC in Britain. However, her most significant contribution in this area is the substantial research thesis, 'A Plea for British Black Theologies: The Black Church Movement in Britain in its Transatlantic, Cultural and Theological Interaction with Special Reference to the Pentecostal Oneness (Apostolic) and Sabbatarian Movements' (unpublished PhD thesis, University of Birmingham, 1991).

15. Iain MacRobert has also published various articles and contributed to texts on religion in Britain. His major works are 'The Spirit and the Wall: The Black Roots and White Racism of Early Pentecostalism in the USA' (unpublished

MA dissertation, University of Birmingham, 1985) and 'Black Pentecostalism: Its Origins, Functions and Theology: With Special Reference to a Midland Borough' (unpublished PhD thesis, University of Birmingham, 1989).

16. Roswith Gerloff, 'The Black Church Experience in Britain', *Christian Action Journal* (Autumn 1982), 10.

17. For example, its rootedness in biblical faith and in African culture. See Roswith I. H. Gerloff, *A Plea for British Black Theologies: The Black Church Movement in Britain in its Transatlantic Cultural and Theological Interaction* (Frankfurt am Main and New York: P. Lang, 1992), 230–31.

18. MacRobert, 'Black Pentecostalism', 2.

19. This is a central theme in both of his major studies.

20. Wilkinson, *Church in Black and White*, identifies Black Christian faith as being 'a religion of the spirit'. In its liberative role 'its truth is not disclosed through speculative theology but through participation in the suffering and struggles of the oppressed', 14.

21. Roy Kerridge, *The Storm is Passing Over: A Look at Black Churches in Britain* (London: Thames and Hudson, 1995).

22. Cecil Cone, *The Identity Crisis in Black Theology* (Nashville, TN. Johnny Barbour, 2004). Cone's warning against understanding only a partial identity of the Black Church was used by Elaine Foster in the context of the Church in Britain. See Elaine Foster, 'Out of This World: A Consideration of the Development and Nature of the Black-led Churches in Britain', in Paul Grant and Raj Patel (eds.), *A Time to Speak* (Birmingham: A Joint Publication of 'Racial Justice' and the 'Black Theology Working Group', 1990), 60.

23. Iain MacRobert, in Paul Badham (ed.), *Religion, State and Society in Modern Britain* (London: Edwin Mellen Press, 1989), 129.

24. Foster, 'Black Women in Black-Led Churches', 58.

25. Selwyn Arnold, *From Scepticism to Hope: One Black Led Church's Response to Social Responsibility* (London: Grove Books, 1992). See also Foster, 'Black Women in Black-led Churches'; Ira Brooks, *Where Do We Go From Here?* (London: Charles Raper, 1982).

26. See Patricia Hill Collins, *Black Feminist Thought: Knowledge, Consciousness, and the Politics of Empowerment* (Boston, MA and London: Unwin Hyman, 1990).

27. See Hill Collins, *Black Feminist Thought*, 203.

28. Hill Collins, *Black Feminist Thought*, 208–17.

29. Hill Collins, *Black Feminist Thought*, 208, original emphasis.

30. Hill Collins, *Black Feminist Thought*, 215.

31. Hill Collins, *Black Feminist Thought*, 219.

32. Leonardo and Clodovis Boff, *Introducing Liberation Theology* (Tunbridge Wells: Burns and Oates, 1987), 27.

33. These characteristics have been identified as (1) community (2) identity (3) personal development (4) leadership (5) encouragement (6) incentive/hope.

34. Interview respondent, SPF.

35. Interview respondent, First United Church of Jesus Christ Apostolic (FUCJCA).

36. Ibid.

37. Interview respondent, New Testament Church of God.
38. Interview respondent, FUCJCA.
39. Interview respondent, New Testament Church of God.
40. Interview respondent, FUCJCA.
41. Interview respondent, FUCJCA.
42. Interview respondent, FUCJCA.
43. Interview respondent, SPF.
44. Interview respondent, FUCJCA.
45. Interview respondent, FUCJCA.
46. This phrase is used by Boff and Boff in their description of social analysis, *Introducing Liberation Theology*, 24.
47. James Cone, *God of the Oppressed* (San Francisco: Harper and Row, 1975), 2.
48. Boff and Boff, *Introducing Liberation Theology*, 34.
49. This kind of solidarity of the former oppressor with the oppressed is described by Freire as a prerequisite for liberation. He writes, 'The oppressor shows solidarity with the oppressed only when he stops regarding the oppressed as an abstract category...when he stops making pious, sentimental, and individualistic gestures and risks an act of love' (Paulo Freire, *Pedagogy of the Oppressed* [New York: Continuum, 1970], 26). In this way the conversion experience becomes a political act of repentance, carrying with it the assumption that the convertee will now 'walk right and live right'.
50. See MacRobert, 'Black Pentecostalism'. See also Bishop Kalilombe, *The Centre for Black and White Christian Partnership: 10 Years of Spiritual Challenge* (Birmingham: Centre for Black and White Christian Partnership, 1991), 27–31.
51. Taken from transcription of New Testament Church of God Youth service.
52. Taken from a popular chorus.
53. The edition mentioned carried a cover photograph of a Black family and inside the articles featured a fair number of Black evangelists.
54. J. D. Golden, 'Into the World with the Church of God Missions', *Church of God Evangel* (October 1, 1991), 14.
55. Ibid.
56. Martha Wong, in ibid., 11.
57. Charles Stewart and Rosalind Shaw, *Syncretism/Anti-syncretism: The Politics of Religious Synthesis* (London: Routledge, 1994), 21.
58. Boff and Boff, *Introducing Liberation Theology*, 24.
59. For example, the understanding of the early Church believers that they were brought to England 'for such a time as this', as was related by the former head of the African Caribbean Evangelical Alliance (ACEA), Joel Edwards.
60. John Wilkinson was Research Fellow at Queen's College, Birmingham, 1984–85 and Tutor in Mission and Pastoral Theology 1985–95. He co-ordinated the Black Christian Studies course 1987–92.
61. See Reddie, *Black Theology in Transatlantic Dialogue*, 19–32.
62. John Wilkinson, *Church in Black and White* (Edinburgh: St Andrew's Press, 1993).
63. Wilkinson, *Church in Black and White*, 185.
64. James H. Cone, *The Spirituals and the Blues* (San Francisco: Harper and Row, 1972), 52–54.

65. Gustavo Gutierrez, *We Drink from Our Own Wells* (London: SCM Press, 1984), 30.

66. *Faith in the City: The Report of the Archbishop of Canterbury's Commission on Urban Priority Areas* (London: Church House Publishing, 1985), 119.

67. Robinson Milwood, *Let's Journey Together* (London: Methodist Division of Social Responsibility and Zebra Project, 1980), 36.

68. Kenneth Cracknell, David Jennings and Christine Trethowan, *Blind Leaders for the Blind? Theological Education in Today's Plural Society* (Birmingham: All Faiths For One Race [AFFOR], 1981). There are no other publishing details to go with this text.

69. Peter Russell, George Mulrain, Maurice Hobbs and Heather Walton, *Race and Theological Education: A Discussion Paper* (London: Methodist Church Division of Social Responsibility, 1983). At that time Peter Russell was Principal of Kingsmead College Birmingham (Methodist Overseas Division), Maurice Hobbs was Chair of the Evangelical Race Relations Group (later ECRJ), and Heather Walton was Research Officer for the Working Party on Ethnic Minorities in Methodism.

70. See, for example, *Partners in Practice*, a discussion document produced by the British Council of Churches, arising from the visit of Overseas Theological Educators during 1987 (London: BCC, 1989).

71. Wesley Daniel, 'The Question of Race and Theological Education' (unpublished discussion paper, 1987).

72. See Bibliography for a detailed breakdown of the components of this course.

73. *Black Christian Studies at the Queen's College, Birmingham and the West Midlands Ministerial Training Course*, Queen's College Birmingham, November 1989, 5.

74. The course was also open to both spouses in any marriage where one partner, whether student or not, was Black.

75. This stands for the West Midlands Ministry Training Course—a semi-autonomous body along with full-time college that trained people for ministry on a part-time, non-residential basis.

76. Advisory Council for the Church's Ministry (ACCM)—a body which, under the authority of General Synod, had the responsibility for the selection and training of clergy.

77. *Simon of Cyrene Theological Institute*, introductory leaflet, SoCTI, 6.

78. James Walker, in a letter to Brian Russell, Secretary to the ACCM Committee for Theological Education, November 11, 1988.

Chapter 4

1. Queen's College has since been renamed the Queen's Foundation. The Foundation represents an integrated institution which houses the College (full-time residential ministerial formation), the West Midlands Course (part-time non-residential ministerial formation) and the Research Centre.

2. For further information visit Robert Beckford's website—see http://www.robertbeckford.co.uk/

3. See Paul Gilroy, *The Black Atlantic: Modernity and Double Consciousness* (London: Verso, 1993).

4.   Robert Beckford, *Jesus Is Dread* (London: Darton, Longman and Todd, 1998).

5.   Robert Beckford, *Dread and Pentecostal: A Political Theology for the Black Church in Britain* (London: SPCK, 2000).

6.   Robert Beckford, *God of the Rahtid: Redeeming Rage* (London: Darton, Longman and Todd, 2001).

7.   Robert Beckford, *God and the Gangs* (London: Darton, Longman and Todd, 2004).

8.   Robert Beckford, *Jesus Dub: Theology, Music and Social Change* (London: Routledge, 2006).

9.   See Paul Tillich, *Systematic Theology* (Chicago: Chicago University Press, 1967).

10.   See David Tracy, *The Analogical Imagination: Christian Theology and the Culture of Pluralism* (London: SCM Press, 1981).

11.   Tillich, *Systematic Theology*, 3.

12.   See Zoe Heller, 'A Family Affair', *The Independent on Sunday*, 8 December 1991. Heller identifies the complex legal problems of the Marley estate because of Marley's legacy of fathering many children to several different women.

13.   I have had numerous discussions with Black students who have told of their biblical studies lecturers' attitudes to Black and liberationist approaches to the text.

14.   S. Bevans, *Models of Contextual Theology: Faith and Culture* (Maryknoll, NY: Orbis Books, 1992), 69.

15.   See J. Cone and G. Wilmore, *Black Theology: A Documentary History, 1979–1992* (Maryknoll, NY: Orbis Books, 1992), 1–11.

16.   Elsewhere I have outlined the emergence of Womanist theology in Britain. See ibid., 153–65.

17.   L. Dixon, 'Mahalia Jackson: Neo-African Gospel Singer, Preacher and Theologian' (unpublished BD dissertation, University of Birmingham, 1998).

18.   See A. Gramsci, *Selections from the Prison Notebooks* (London: Lawrence and Wishart, 1971).

19.   Howard Kee, *The Living World of the New Testament* (London: Darton, Longman and Todd, 1974), 62.

20.   James Cone, *Black Theology and Black Power* (San Francisco: Harper & Row, 1989), 123.

21.   James Cone, *God of the Oppressed* (San Francisco: Harper Collins, 1975), 160.

22.   James Cone, *A Black Theology of Liberation* (Maryknoll, NY: Orbis Books, 2nd edn, 1986), 126.

23.   Karen Baker-Fletcher and Garth Kasimu Baker-Fletcher, *My Brother, My Sister: Womanist and Xodus God-Talk*, 284.

24.   Ibid., 290.

25.   Ibid., 293.

26.   b. hooks, *Killing Rage: Ending Racism* (New York: Henry Holt and Co, 1995), 16.

27.   Hooks, *Killing Rage*, 16.

28.   I have tried to explore this issue for black British people in *God of the Rahtid*.

29. See the discussion on the contemporary realities of multi-cultural Britain and the problems for African Caribbean and African people by Sunder Katwala in *The Observer*, 25 November 2001 at www.observer.guardian.co.uk/race/story/0,11255,605337,00.html.

30. See a report on racial discrimination in Britain in *The Observer*, 13 August 2000 at http://observer.guardian.co.uk/uk_news/story/0,6903,353751,00.html.

31. See Birgit Brander et al., *Making and Unmaking of Whiteness* (Durham and London: Duke University Press, 2001). See the introduction.

32. Arthur Asa Berger, *Cultural Criticism: Foundations of Popular Culture* (London: SAGE Publications, 1995), 74.

33. Henry Louis Gates Jr., *The Signifying Monkey: A Theory of African-American Literary Criticism* (Oxford: Oxford University Press, 1988), 74.

34. Tim E. D. Burton, *Afro-Creole* (London: Cornell University Press, 1997), 61.

35. Robert D. Pelton, *The Trickster in West Africa: A Study of Myth, Irony and Sacred Delight* (Los Angeles and London: University of California Press, 1980), 35.

36. See Louis Gates, *The Signifying Monkey*, 21.

37. Chris Potash, *Reggae, Rasta Revolution: Jamaican Music from Ska to Dub* (London: Books with Attitude, 1997), 146.

38. David Brain, 'Cultural Productions as "Society in the Making": Architecture as an Exemplar of the Social Construction of Cultural Artifacts', in Diana Crane (ed.), *The Sociology of Culture: Emerging Theoretical Perspective* (Cambridge, MA: Blackwell, 1994).

39. See S. Craig Watkins, *Representing: Hip Hop Culture and the Production of Black Cinema* (Chicago and London: University of Chicago Press, 1998), 215ff.

40. Linton Kwesi Johnson, *Tings an Times: Selected Poems* (London: Bloodaxe Books, 1991), 28.

41. Les Back and Michael Bull (eds.), *The Auditory Culture Reader* (Oxford and New York: Berg, 2003), 7.

42. See D. A. Cruse, *Lexica Semantics* (Cambridge: Cambridge University Press, 1986), 40ff., original emphasis.

43. See Cruse, *Lexica Semantics*.

44. Brian Blount, *Cultural Interpretation: Reorienting New Testament Criticism* (Minneapolis: Fortress Press, 1995), vii.

Chapter 5

1. See Mary Daly, *Beyond God the Father: Towards a Philosophy of Women's Liberation* (London: Women's Press, 1986).

2. See Daphne Hampson, *After Christianity* (London: SCM Press, 1996).

3. Elaine F. Foster, 'Black Women in Black-led Churches: A Study of Black Women's Contribution to the Growth and Development of Black-led Churches in Britain' (unpublished M.Phil thesis, University of Birmingham, 1990).

4. See Anthony G. Reddie, *Black Theology in Transatlantic Dialogue* (New York: Palgrave Macmillan, 2006), 29–102.

5. These are just a few of the questions I am presented with on a fairly regular basis. The interpretations may initially seem unfair and/or offensive; however, they are often borne out by the tone and content of ensuing conversations.

6.   See Olaudah Equiano's letter to *Time Public Advertiser*, 28 January 1788 in Paul Edwards and David Dabyden (eds.), *Black Writers in Britain, 1760–1890* (Edinburgh: Edinburgh University Press, 1991), 75.

7.   See Constance M. Carroll, 'Three's a Crowd: The Dilemma of the Black Woman in Higher Education', in Gloria T. Hull, Patricia Bell-Scott and Barbara Smith (eds.), *All the Women are White, All the Blacks are Men, But Some of us are Brave: Black Women's Studies* (New York: The Feminist Press, 1982), 115–28.

8.   Alice Walker, *In Search of Our Mother's Gardens: Womanist Prose* (London: The Women's Press, 1984), xi.

9.   Walker, *In Search of Our Mother's Gardens*, xii.

10.   'Introduction', in Cheryl J. Sanders (ed.), *Living the Intersection: Womanism and Afrocentrism in Theology* (Minneapolis: Fortress Press, 1995), 9–17.

11.   Debra Washington, 'Womanist Theology: Can White Women be Womanists?' (unpublished paper, Union Theological Seminary, 1996), 2.

12.   Walker, *In Search of Our Mother's Gardens*, xii.

13.   Washington, 'Womanist Theology', 8.

14.   Jacquelyn Grant, 'Black Theology and the Black Woman', in Beverly Guy Sheftall (ed.), *Words of Fire: An Anthology of African-American Feminist Thought* (New York: The New Press, 1995), 320–36.

15.   See Patricia Hill Collins (quoting Alice Walker), *Black Feminist Thought: Knowledge, Consciousness and the Politics of Empowerment* (London: Routledge, 1990), 37.

16.   Erlene Stetson, 'Studying Slavery: Some Literary and Pedagogical Considerations on the Female Slave', in Gloria T. Hull, Patricia Bell Scott and Barbara Smith (eds.), *All the Women are White, All the Blacks are Men but Some of us are Brave: Black Women's Studies* (New York: The Feminist Press, 1982), 61–84 (65).

17.   Alice Walker, *In Search of Our Mother's Gardens* (New York: Harcourt Brace Jovanovich, 1983), xi. Also see Kelly Brown Douglas and Cheryl J. Sanders, 'Introduction', in Cheryl J. Sanders (ed.), *Living the Intersection: Womanism and Afrocentrism in Theology* (Minneapolis: Fortress Press, 1995), 9–17 (9). In outlining some of the contemporary developments in Womanist theory, Kelly Brown Douglas and Cheryl J. Sanders write that 'While the term Womanist was coined by Pulitzer Prize-winning novelist Alice Walker in her 1983 volume, *In Search Of Our Mother's Gardens*, its usage now goes beyond her definition. African American women have adopted the term as a symbol of their experience. Womanist signals an appreciation for the richness, complexity, uniqueness, and struggle involved in being black and female in a society that is hostile to both blackness and womanhood' (xi).

18.   Gustavo Gutierrez is a Peruvian priest and theologian. He is sometimes referred to as the 'Father of Liberation Theology' and has authored a number of texts on Liberation Theology. See Leonardo Boff and Clodovis Boff, *Introducing Liberation Theology* (Tunbridge Wells: Burns and Oates, 1992).

19.   James Cone, *God of the Oppressed* (New York: Seabury Press, 1975), 39.

20.   Hazel Carby, 'White Woman Listen!' Black Feminism and the Boundaries of Sisterhood', in Heidi Safia Mirza (ed.), *Black British Feminism: A Reader* (London: Routledge, 1997), 45–53.

21.   Katie G. Cannon, *Black Womanist Ethics* (Atlanta, GA: Scholars Press, 1988), 2.

22. Delores S. Williams, *Sisters in the Wilderness: The Challenge of Womanist God-Talk* (Maryknoll, NY: Orbis Books, 1994).

23. Williams, *Sisters in the Wilderness*, 4.

24. Cheryl J. Sanders, *Living the Intersection: Womanism and Afrocentrism in Theology* (Minneapolis: Fortress Press, 1995), 130.

25. Jacqueline Grant, *White Women's Christ and Black Women's Jesus* (Atlanta, GA: Scholars Press, 1989), 12–18.

26. Grant, *White Women's Christ and Black Women's Jesus*, 203.

27. This includes African feminist theology, Mujerista theology, emerging out of the specific experiences of American Latino women, Jewish and Asian women's theologies.

28. Mercy Amba Oduyoye, 'Reflections from a Third World Woman's Perspectives: Women's Experience and Liberation Theologies', in Ursula King (ed.), *Feminist Theology from the Third World: A Reader* (London: SPCK; Maryknoll, NY: Orbis Books, 1994), 23–34 (34).

29. See Robert Beckford, *Jesus Is Dread: Black Theology and Black Culture in Britain* (London: Darton, Longman and Todd, 1998), 153–59. Also Kate Coleman, 'Black Theology and Black Liberation: A Womanist Perspective', *Black Theology in Britain* 1 (1998), 56–69.

30. Valentina Alexander, 'A Mouse in the Jungle: The Black Christian Woman's Experience in the Church and Society in Britain', in Delia Jarratt-Macauley (ed.), *Reconstructing Womanhood, Reconstructing Feminism: Writings on Black Women* (London: Routledge, 1996), 85–108 (85).

31. The Church Army is a lay society of evangelists that has existed within the Church of England since the 1880s. It was founded by Prebendary Wilson Carlile, who was soon joined by his sister Marie Carlile to start a women's section.

32. bell hooks, *Ain't I a Woman: Black Women and Feminism* (Boston: South End Press, 1981). The title comes from a speech advocating social justice for all women including slave women delivered by Sojourner Truth at the second annual convention of the women's rights movement at Akron, Ohio in 1852.

33. Kelly Brown Douglas, 'Womanist Theology: What is its Relationship to Black Theology?' in James Cone and Gayraud Wilmore (eds.), *Black Theology: A Documentary History. II: 1980–1992* (Maryknoll, NY: Orbis Books, 1993), 292.

34. bell hooks, *Killing Rage: Ending Racism* (London: Penguin Books, 1996), 10–11.

35. hooks, *Killing Rage*, 10–11.

36. hooks, *Killing Rage*, 272.

37. A 'sista' is a Black sister, i.e. a woman. The term emanates from the Gangsta rap fraternity of the Hip-Hop community. Words are often changed to reflect the importance of the sounds of words. Thus words like 'sista', 'gangsta', 'xodus', etc. will reflect the rhythm of African-American orality as expressed in rap.

38. Iyanla Vanzant, *The Value in the Valley* (New York: Simon & Schuster, 1997).

39. Stella Dadzie, 'Searching for the Invisible Woman: Slavery and Resistance in Jamaica', *Race and Class* 32.2 (1990), 21–38; Barbara Bush, *Slave Women in Caribbean Society 1650–1838* (London and Kingston: James Currey, 1990).

40. Itumeleng Mosala, 'The Implications of the Text of Esther for African Women's Struggle for Liberation in South Africa', in R. S. Sugirtharajah (ed.), *Voices from the Margin* (London: SPCK; New York: Orbis Books, 2006), 168–78.

41.   Beverley Bryan, Stella Dadzie and Suzanne Scafe, *The Heart of the Race: Black Women's Lives in Britain* (London: Virago, 1985), 6.

42.   See Andre LaCoque, *Esther in the Feminine Unconventional: Four Subversive Figures in Israel's Tradition* (Minneapolis: Fortress Press, 1990).

43.   David Clines, 'Reading Esther from Left to Right: Contemporary Strategies for Reading a Biblical Text', in David Clines, Stephen Fowl and Stanley Porter (eds.), *The Bible in Three Dimensions: Essays in Celebration of the Fortieth Anniversary of the Department of Biblical Studies in the University of Sheffield* (Journal for the Study of the Old Testament Supplement Series, 87; Sheffield: JSOT Press, 1990), 41.

44.   Bryan, Dadzie and Scafe, *The Heart of the Race*, 184.

45.   Dadzie, 'Searching for the Invisible Woman', 29.

46.   Bush, *Slave Women in Caribbean Society 1650–1838*, 142.

47.   Ibid., 141.

48.   Dadzie, 'Searching for the Invisible Woman', 30.

49.   Dadzie, 'Searching for the Invisible Woman', 30.

50.   Itumeleng J. Mosala, 'The Implications of the Text of Esther for African Women's Struggle for Liberation in South Africa', in R. S. Sugirtharajah (ed.), *Voices from the Margin: Interpreting the Bible in the Third World* (London: SPCK; New York: Orbis Books, 2006), 169.

51.   'Quasheba' and the male equivalent 'Quashee' were names 'derived from Kwasi, a popular name among Akan-speaking slaves of Ghanaian origin'. Bush, *Slave Women in Caribbean Society*, 52. Used as a perjorative by massa but took on a subversive nature among Blacks.

52.   Bush, *Slave Women in Caribbean Society*, 61.

53.   Cheryl Townsend Gilkes, 'We Have a Beautiful Mother: Womanist Musings on the Afrocentric Idea', in Cheryl Sanders (ed.), *Living the Intersection: Womanism and Afrocentrism in Theology* (Philadelphia: Fortress Press, 1995), 21–42.

54.   Gilkes, 'We Have a Beautiful Mother', 26.

55.   See Valentina Alexander, 'A Mouse in the Jungle: The Black Christian Woman's Experience in the Church and Society in Britain', in Delia Jarrett-Macauley (ed.), *Reconstructing Womanhood, Reconstructing Feminism: Writings on Black Women* (London: Routledge, 1996), 85–107.

56.   Herbert Ekwe-Ekwe and Femi Nzegwu, *Operationalising Afrocentrism* (Reading: International Institute for Black Research, 1994), 9.

57.   Molefi Kete Asante, *Afrocentricity* (Trenton, NJ: Africa World Press, 1988), 48.

58.   See bell hooks, *Black Looks: Race and Representation* (London: Turnaround, 1992).

59.   These are: (1) The concept of the spirit-filled universe, (2) death as a transition period, (3) communication with the spirit world through dreams and visions, (4) the extended family structure alongside the spirit of polygamy, (5) evil as a real and potent force in the universe, (6) time awareness that centres around kairos…opportune time or event, and (7) worship as an occasion for celebration made more enjoyable by the presence of a representative from the spirit world. George Mulrain, 'African Cosmology and Caribbean Religion', *Caribbean Journal of Religious Studies* 10.2 (1989), 8–9.

60. Ekwe-Ekwe and Nzegwu, *Operationalising Afrocentrism*, 10–12.

61. This was demonstrated, for example, in my research findings. See Valentina Alexander, 'Breaking Every Fetter? To What Extent Has the Black-led Church in Britain Developed a Theology of Liberation?' (unpublished PhD thesis, Warwick University, 1997), under the headings of community, identity, personal development and leadership, encouragement and incentive/hope.

62. See in particular Delores Williams's critique entitled, 'Afrocentricism and Male-Female Relations', in Sanders (ed.), *Living the Intersection*, 43–56.

63. bell hooks, *Yearning: Race, Gender, and Cultural Politics* (London: Turnaround, 1991), 78, makes a similar point when speaking about narrative in popular culture as an effective means of engaging students in critical and meaningful reflection.

64. Jacquelyn Grant, 'Black Theology and the Black Woman', in Gayraud S. Wilmore and James H. Cone (eds.), *Black Theology: A Documentary History, 1966–1979* (Maryknoll, NY: Orbis Books, 1979), 423; Pauli Murray, 'Black Theology and Feminist Theology: A Comparative View', in Gayraud S. Wilmore and James H. Cone (eds.), *Black Theology: A Documentary History, 1966—1979* (Maryknoll, NY: Orbis Books, 1979), 399.

65. See Heidi Safia Mirza, *Young, Female and Black* (London and New York: Routledge, 1992), especially her chapter 'The Myth of Underachievement'.

66. James H. Cone, *A Black Theology of Liberation* (Maryknoll, NY: Orbis Books, 1986).

67. The only subjects I was taught at GCE level. I could not get any higher than a C in the other four subjects. So in all six subjects I obtained the highest grade possible!

68. The prevalence of the matriarchal family structure and the significant number of pupil pregnancies amongst the African-Caribbean communities is well pathologized in the research field of education and 'race', and certainly within the schooling community to which I belonged. See Mirza, *Young, Female and Black*, 16–18, 36, 72.

69. The lives of fictional characters like Janet and John and their dog at the heart of the reading scheme I was put on never engaged me.

70. I prefer to use the word refuse rather than resist to convey the point made by Heidi Safia Mirza, *Black British Feminism: A Reader* (London: Routledge, 1997), 275 that 'black women do not accept the dominant discourse, nor do they construct their own identities in opposition to the dominant discourse. They redefine the world, have their own values, codes and understandings, *refuse* (not resist) the gaze of the other' (original emphasis).

71. See John Holt, *How Children Fail* (Middlesex: Pelican Books, 1969), 165.

72. The enquiry focused on the local park's regeneration. It was relevant to all my pupils because even if they neither lived locally nor visited the park out of school hours, for half the year they had swimming lessons at the leisure centre situated on the park grounds.

73. The Conservative government introduced the National Curriculum in 1990 and in 1998 and 1999 the New Left-leaning Labour government introduced its recent companions the National Literacy Strategy (NLS) and the National Numeracy Strategy (NNS).

74. As an interpretative tool, standpoint theorists have found this approach invaluable in representing reality from a subjugated perspective.

75. Such a standpoint allows an educational approach to emerge in a similar fashion to what Raj Patel and Paul Grant claim must develop for theology, 'from the context of Black life rather than the dictates of White…academe'. Quoted in Robert Beckford, *Dread and Pentecostal: A Political Theology for the Black Church in Britain* (London: SPCK, 2000), 24.

76. My mother's reading of the Bible is an African-Caribbean cultural practice that reflects the hermeneutics of Black churches. Beckford, *Dread and Pentecostal*, 192.

77. Cited in Patricia Hill Collins, *Black Feminist Thought: Knowledge, Consciousness and the Politics of Empowerment* (London: Routledge, 1991), 97.

78. Brain-based learning (using what we know about the brain to enhance learning) advocates, such as the 'University of the First Age Birmingham', point out how the brain needs to rest often since on average it can only concentrate for twenty minutes at a time. Furthermore, advocates are also aware that the brain processes information subconsciously so turning off from your focus of study can actually help you digest information and comprehend the subject of study better.

79. Beverley Bryan, Stella Dadzie and Suzanne Scafe, *The Heart of the Race: Black Women's Lives in Britain* (London: Virago, 1985), 59.

80. Her view of scholarly learning reflects a tradition within Black Atlantic communities who interpret Adam and Eve's pursuit of knowledge that leads them to succumb to the devil's temptation as madness, because as a result they lose all they had, notably each other. Furthermore, as Iain MacRobert, *The Black Roots and White Racism of Early Pentecostalism in the USA* (London: Macmillan, 1988) recognizes, this anti-scholarly tradition flourished within the infancy of the Black Pentecostal movement, because 'Among the Pentecostals, black people were no longer disadvantaged because of their colour or lack of education, for the Spirit could minister through whoever was yielded to Her [His] influence' (84).

81. See Karen Baker-Fletcher, *Sisters of Dust, Sisters of Spirit: Womanist Wordings on God and Creation* (Minneapolis: Augsburg Fortress Press, 1998), 116.

82. Holt, *How Children Fail*, 163.

83. Justification for my suspicious stance has been presented by academics, Paul Gilroy and Kenan Malik, as cited in Beckford, *Dread and Pentecostal*, 84–85.

84. Quoted in Maureen Stone, *The Education of the Black Child: The Myth of Multiracial Education* (London: Fontana, 1981), 25.

85. See Mirza, *Young, Female and Black*.

86. Mirza, *Young, Female and Black*, 15–16.

87. Notably, the Afrocentric masculinist notion that female-headed households are doomed to fail its members and the community because they go against the social order of things for the African community at home or abroad. Whilst in stark contrast, an African-centred nuclear household, headed by a strong male, will naturally promote its members because it is in harmony with the social order. A view shared by many Black Majority Churches (BMCs) whose patriarchal reading of the Bible means they believe males should lead in church and society as God ordained it. See Womanist and Feminist scholars' criticism of this patriarchal hermeneutics, such as Jacquelyn Grant, 'Womanist Jesus and the Mutual Struggle

for Liberation', in Randall C. Bailey and Jacquelyn Grant (eds.), *The Recovery of Black Presence: An Interdisciplinary Exploration* (Nashville: Abingdon Press, 1995) and Valentina Alexander, 'A Mouse in the Jungle: The Black Christian Woman's Experience in the Church and Society in Britain', in Delia Jarrett-Macauley (ed.), *Reconstructing Womanhood, Reconstructing Feminism: Writings on Black Women* (London: Routledge, 1996).

88. See Tony Sewell, *Black Masculinities and Schooling: How Black Boys Survive Modern Schooling* (Stoke on Trent: Trentham Books, 1997), 214–17.

89. See Mirza, *Black British Feminism: A Reader* and Alexander, 'A Mouse in the Jungle'.

90. Data collected in 1994 by the Assessment Unit for Birmingham Local Education Authority (LEA) shows 38.9 per cent of African-Caribbean LEA nursery children score 5+ in the baseline tests for English compared to 26.3 per cent Bangladeshi, 29 per cent Indian, 17.2 per cent Pakistani, and 35.3 per cent White.

91. Both my brothers at the age of 27 and 34 respectively have returned to education, one to do an access course and the other an initial teaching training course. The eldest brother and my sister and I actively encouraged him to enrol on the course and the other brother was inspired and encouraged by his girlfriend who is a law graduate. It may have taken longer for them to desire to fulfil the academic potential but they have reached it in the same single female-headed family in which they have been raised.

92. Though there is no real consensus within the Pentecostal movement on what exactly constitutes authentic evidence of spirit baptism, generally it is understood to include speaking in tongues—glossolalia (unintelligable blabbering) and xenoglossia (lucid speech) and the nine gifts listed in I Corinthians 12:8-10) which the apostle Paul qualifies with love (presented in I Corinthians 13) and other qualities that make up the fruit of the spirit (presented in Galatians 5:22-23). See Iain MacRobert, 'Black Pentecostalism in Britain' (unpublished thesis, University of Birmingham, 1988), 107–109.

93. Baker-Fletcher, *Sisters of Dust, Sisters of Spirit*, 112.

94. MacRobert, 'Black Pentecostalism in Britain', 110.

95. Veli-Matti Karkkainen, *Pneumatology: The Holy Spirit in Ecumenical, International and Contextual Perspective* (Grand Rapids: Baker Academic, 2002), 122.

96. This is evident in Ephesians 6:10-20 and the call to put on the armour of God.

97. See Karkkainen, *Pneumatology*, 33–34 for a description of Paul's pneumatology.

98. This political pneumatology is embedded in the Womanist image of God 'as empowering, sustaining, life-giving and strengthening, delivering bodies and souls from the pit of death, whether such death is imposed from outside by oppressive forces or from within by self-destructive, suicidal tendencies' (Baker-Fletcher, *Sisters of Dust, Sisters of Spirit*, 116). Beckford, *Dread and Pentecostal*, refers to the political pneumatology I am alluding to, as 'dynamic pneumatology [which] introduces the concept of dread pneumatology, that is, conceiving the Spirit of God and possession by using it as a mandate for radical activity consistent with a "strong dread" [Rastafarian/Christological cultural and political praxis] analysis. Such a conception is prophetic in so much as it challenges the status quo and offers an alternative vision of social relationships'.

99. See MacRobert, *Black Roots and White Racism*, 87.

100. There is a lot of debate around the use of the label Womanist to describe the work of Christian Black feminists. The opinions of Kelly Brown Douglas, *Sexuality and the Black Church: A Womanist Perspective* (Maryknoll, NY: Orbis Books, 1999) and Cheryl Sanders, 'Christian Ethics and Theology in Womanist Perspective', in Gayraud S. Wilmore and James H. Cone (eds.), *Black Theology: A Documentary History. II: 1980—1992* (Maryknoll, NY: Orbis Books, 1992) illustrate both sides of the debate well. However, the description of Womanist theology by Delores S. Williams, 'Womanist Theology: Black Women's Voices', in Gayraud S. Wilmore and James H. Cone (eds.), *Black Theology: A Documentary History. II: 1980–1992* (Maryknoll, NY: Orbis Books, 1992) best reflects the understanding of Womanist taken in this study. Namely that it is an efficient tool to be used by Womanist theologians rather than a label to describe the essence of the theologian. In this way the term Womanist operates as a verb rather than a noun with regards to the theologian labelled as a Womanist.

101. A key duty of a priest was to ensure through prayer and supplication that the people prospered and came to no harm. Calling on God to help the people deal with social issues and enjoy their lives was therefore an essential role of the priest. As Baker-Fletcher, *Sisters of Dust, Sisters of Spirit*, shows, this priestly understanding of the Spirit has been integral to the lives of Black women.

102. See the work of Black liberation theologians, especially James H. Cone, *A Black Theology of Liberation* (Maryknoll, NY: Orbis Books, 1986); Jacquelyn Grant, 'Black Theology and the Black Woman', in Gayraud S. Wilmore and James H. Cone (eds.), *Black Theology: A Documentary History, 1966—1979* (Maryknoll, NY: Orbis Books, 1979) and Jacquelyn Grant, 'Womanist Jesus and the Mutual Struggle for Liberation', in Randall C. Bailey and Jacquelyn Grant (eds.), *The Recovery of Black Presence: An Interdisciplinary Exploration* (Nashville: Abingdon Press, 1995) for a more detailed account of this liberation message within the gospel as it applies to Black men and women.

103. Black Atlantic refers to the shared geopolitical and historical location of my foremothers and sisters in the UK, USA and Caribbean. Namely, Black women from these Atlantic communities share a common African heritage, history of slavery and dynamic traditions that reflect their experiences of oppression and hope for a better tomorrow.

Chapter 6

1. See Noel Erskine, *Decolonizing Theology* (Maryknoll, NY: Orbis Books, 1981), 27–51. See also Dianne M. Stewart, *Three Eyes for the Journey: The African Dimension of the Jamaican Religious Experience* (New York and London: Oxford University Press, 2005).

2. See Anne H. Pinn and Anthony B. Pinn, *Fortress Introduction to Black Church History* (Minneapolis: Fortress Press, 2002), 102–122. See also Clarence E. Hardy III, *James Baldwin's God: Sex, Hope, and Crisis in Black Holiness Culture* (Knoxville: University Tennessee Press, 2003).

3. See James H. Cone, *God of the Oppressed* (San Francisco: Harper Collins, 1975), for his use of the Bible in his theological method.

4. See Frederick L. Ware, *Methodologies of Black Theology* (Cleveland, OH: Pilgrim Press, 2002), 66–114.

5.   Anthony G. Reddie, 'Editorial', *Black Theology: An International Journal* 4.1 (2006), 9.

6.   This tradition of engaging theologically in creative and discursive fashion with the Bible can be seen in more recent work by the likes of Robert Beckford and Anthony Reddie. See Robert Beckford, *Jesus Dub: Theology, Music and Social Change* (London: Routledge, 2006), 93–100. See also Anthony G. Reddie, *Acting in Solidarity: Reflections in Critical Christianity* (London: Darton, Longman and Todd, 2005), 45–53.

7.   J. S. Croatto, *Biblical Hermeneutics: Towards a Theory of Reading as the Production of Meaning* (Maryknoll, NY: Orbis Books, 1987), 1.

8.   The main source for womanist theological studies is found in the African American context. My research therefore is made up of most of that literature.

9.   A. Walker, *In Search of our Mother's Gardens* (London: The Women's Press, 1995), xi–xii.

10.   For further studies consult Randall C. Bailey and Jacquelyn Grant, *The Recovery of Black Presence: An Interdisciplinary Exploration* (Nashville: Abingdon Press, 1995).

11.   See works of feminists Mary Daly and Daphne Hampson.

12.   Howard Thurman, *Jesus and the Disinherited* (Nashville: Abingdon Press, 1949), 30–31.

13.   Professor Renita Weems, 'Reading as an Act of Rebellion'. Lecture at Queen's College, Birmingham, 1997. See also C. Michelle Venable-Ridley, 'Paul and the African American Community', in Emilie E. Townes (ed.), *Embracing the Spirit* (Maryknoll, NY: Orbis Press, 1997).

14.   A point to bear in mind, however, is that if one is going to raise the standard of biblical interpretation for women, then the same must be carried out on an equal basis for men, especially black men.

15.   Venable-Ridley, 'Paul and the African American Community'.

16.   Brad R. Braxton, *No Longer Slaves: Galatians and African American Experience* (Collegeville, MI: The Liturgical Press, 2002), 30.

17.   R. S. Sugirtharajah, 'Biblical Studies after the Empire: From a Colonial to a Postcolonial Mode of Interpretation', in R. S. Sugirtharajah (ed.), *The Postcolonial Bible* (Sheffield: Sheffield Academic Press, 1998), 15.

18.   James H. Cone, *God of the Oppressed* (San Francisco: Harper SanFrancisco, 1975), 38.

19.   See chapter 2 of R. S. Sugirtharajah, *Postcolonial Criticism and Biblical Interpretation* (Oxford: Oxford University Press, 2002). He argues that until postcolonial biblical criticism, biblical scholarship has never escaped the Christiandom model governed by the mission motif of the colonial era. See also Part 1 entitled 'Readings for Liberation', in Norman K. Gottwald and Richard A. Horsley (eds.), *The Bible and Liberation: Political and Social Hermeneutics* (London: SPCK; Maryknoll, NY: Orbis Books, 1993).

20.   Robert Morgan and John Barton, *Biblical Interpretation* (Oxford: Oxford University Press, 1988), 286–87.

21.   Ann M. Clifford, *Introducing Feminist Theology* (Maryknoll, NY: Orbis Books, 2001), 67.

22.   Richard A. Horsley, 'Submerged Biblical Histories and Imperial Biblical

Studies', in R. S. Sugirtharajah, *The Postcolonial Bible* (Sheffield: Sheffield Academic Press, 1998), 153.

23. Karen Baker-Fletcher and Garth Kasimu Baker-Fletcher, *My Sister, My Brother: Womanist and Xodus God-Talk* (Maryknoll, NY: Orbis Books, 1997), 86.

24. Loren Wilkinson in Maxine Hancock (ed.), *Christian Perspectives on Gender, Sexuality, and Community* (Vancouver: Regent College Pub., 2003), 105.

25. I am italicizing this phrase in recognition that it is one of a number of plausible translations of *ha'adam* including 'earthling', 'earth creature' and 'human'. It is the latter that is preferred here. See Ronald A. Simkins's discussion in 'Gender Construction in the Yahwist Creation Myth', 32–52 in Athalya Brenner (ed.), *A Feminist Companion to the Bible* (Sheffield: Sheffield Academic Press, 1998), 40.

26. Quoted in Peter J. Paris, *The Spirituality of African Peoples: The Search for a Common Moral Discourse* (Minneapolis: Fortress Press, 1995), 103.

27. Clifford, *Introducing Feminist Theology*, 68.

28. Lisa Isherwood and Dorothy McEwan, *Introducing Feminist Theology* (Sheffield: Sheffield Academic Press, 2001), 110.

29. Mercy Amba Oduyoye, *Hearing and Knowing: Theological Reflections on Christianity in Africa* (Maryknoll, NY: Orbis Books, 1986), 90.

30. Dolores S. Williams, *Sisters in the Wilderness: The Challenge of Womanist God-Talk* (Maryknoll, NY: Orbis Books, 1993), ix.

31. See Walker, *In Search of Our Mother's Gardens.*

32. Oduyoye, *Hearing and Knowing*, 136.

33. Emmanuel Lartey, *In Living Colour: An Intercultural Approach to Pastoral Care and Counselling* (London: Cassell, 1997), 37.

34. Derek Kidner, *Genesis: Tyndale Old Testament Commentaries* (Leicester, England and Illinois: Intervarsity Press, 1967), 60.

35. Musimbi Kanyoro, *Introducing Feminist Cultural Hermeneutics: An African Perspective* (Cleveland, OH: Pilgrim Press, 2002), 75.

36. John Parrat, *A Reader in African Christian Theology* (London: SPCK, 1997), 41.

37. Baker-Fletcher and Baker-Fletcher, *My Sister, My Brother*, 137.

38. Gustavo Gutierrez, 'Where Hunger is God is Not', *Witness* (April 1976), 6, cited in Elisabeth Schussler Fiorenza, *In Memory of Her: A Feminist Theological Reconstruction of Christian Origins* (New York: Crossroad, 1984), xix.

39. Mukti Barton, *Scripture as Empowerment for Liberation and Justice: The Experience of Christian and Muslim Women in Bangladesh* (Bristol: Centre for Comparative Studies in Religion and Gender, Dept of Theology & Religious Studies, University of Bristol, 1999), 154.

40. Renita J. Weems, 'Womanist Reflections on Biblical Hermeneutics', in J. H. Cone and G. S. Wilmore (eds.), *Black Theology: A Documentary History*, II (Maryknoll, NY: Orbis Books, 1993), 216.

41. Weems, 'Womanist Reflections on Biblical Hermeneutics', 219–20.

42. Jurgette Honculada, 'Martha and Mary: The Burden and Blessing of Gender', in Lee Oo Chung et al. (eds.), *Women of Courage: Asian Women Reading the Bible* (Seoul: Asian Women's Resource Centre for Culture and Theology [AWRC], 1992), 218.

43. Honculada, 'Martha and Mary', 218.

44. All biblical references are from the New Revised Standard Version with Apocrypha. However, the quotes from Wisdom of Jesus son of Sirach are from the Good News Bible with Apocrypha/Deuterocanonical Books.

45. Compare Mt. 26:1-13, Mk 14:1-11, Lk. 7:36-48, Jn 12: 1-8; for Mary Magdalene see Lk. 8:1-3.

46. Ben Witherington, *Women in the Earliest Churches* (Cambridge: Cambridge University Press, 1998), 115.

47. Weems, 'Womanist Reflections on Biblical Hermeneutics', 222.

48. James Strong, *The New Strong's Exhaustive Concordance of the Bible* (Nashville, TN: Thomas Nelson, 1984), 18.

49. Sinclair B. Ferguson and David F. Wright (eds.), *The New Dictionary of Theology* (Leicester: InterVarsity Press, 1988), 367.

50. Raymond M. Pruitt, *Fundamentals of the Faith* (Cleveland: White Wing Publishing House, 1988), 240–41.

51. *The Bethany Parallel Commentary* (Minneapolis: Bethany House Publishers, 1983), 97.

52. Laurie Green, *Power to the Powerless* (Basingstoke: Marshall Pickering, 1987), 57.

53. Eric Lowenthal, *The Joseph Narrative in Genesis* (New York: Ktav Publishing House, 1973), 191.

54. Mervyn Alleyne, *Roots of Jamaican Culture* (London: Pluto Press, 1988), 69.

55. Bruce C. Birch, *Let Justice Roll Down* (Louisville, KY: Westminster/John Knox Press, 1991), 282.

56. Peter R. Ackroyd, *Exile and Restoration* (Philadelphia: Westminster Press, 1968), 239.

57. Louise Spencer-Strachan, *Confronting the Color Crisis of the African Diaspora* (New York: African World Infosystems, 1992), 30.

58. Selwyn Arnold, *From Scepticism to Hope* (Nottingham: Grove Books, 1992), 13.

59. Arnold, *From Scepticism to Hope*, 13.

60. Arnold, *From Scepticism to Hope*, 112.

61. John Marshall Holt, *The Patriarchs of Israel* (Nashville, TN: Vanderbilt University Press, 1964), 175.

62. Ira V. Brooks, *Another Gentleman to the Ministry* (Birmingham: Compeer Press, 1989), 77.

63. This is a tradition in the United Reformed Church, where a prospective minister is invited by a potential congregation to 'preach with a view'.

64. David, Buttrick, *Homiletic: Moves and Structures* (Philadelphia: Fortress Press, 1987), 41.

65. David Tracy, *Plurality and Ambiguity* (San Francisco: Harper & Row, 1987), 79.

66. Cleophus LaRue, *The Heart of Black Preaching* (Louisville, KY: WJK Press, 2000), 2.

67. James Cone, *God of the Oppressed* (San Francisco: Harper San Francisco, 1975), 29.

68. Susan Niditch, *A Prelude to Biblical Folklore: Underdogs and Tricksters* (Chicago: University of Illinois Press, 2000), xvi.

69. See Anthony Reddie, *Faith Stories of the Experience of Black Elders* (London: Jessica Kingsley, 2001).

70. Philip Potter, *Life in All its Fullness* (Geneva: WCC Press, 1981), 141.

71. For e.g. religiosity, thought patterns, cultural practices, oral tradition, literature, arts and symbols etc.

72. Walter Brueggemann, *Finally Comes the Poet* (Minneapolis: Fortress Press, 1989).

73. Edouard Glissant, *Le Discours Antillais* (Paris: Editions du Seuil, 1980).

74. See the works of Caryl Phillips, Hanif Kureishi and Sunetra Gupta, *inter alia*.

75. See Joy Cowley, 'The Hitchhikers', in Penny Scown (ed.), *Beyond the River* (Auckland: Ashton Scholastic, 1994) for Joy Cowley's use of story-teller as a thief, magician, seamstress and liberator.

Chapter 7

1. All the books by Reddie are cited in the bibliography included in this volume.

2. *Growing into Hope*, vols 1 and 2 (Peterborough: Methodist Publishing House, 1998).

3. See Peter Freyer, *Staying Power* (London: Pluto Press, 1984). These two pieces offer insights into the historical development of Black post-war immigration to Britain, and the experiences of these Caribbean migrants in Britain since the landing of the *S.S. Empire Windrush* on these shores in 1948.

4. See Anthony G. Reddie, 'An Unbroken Thread of Experience', in Joan King (ed.), *Family and All That Stuff* (Birmingham: National Christian Education Council [NCEC], 1998), 153–60. In this article, I discuss my understanding of family, using my own familial experiences as my first point of departure. In this article, I refer to the migratory impulse of Black people, who, since the dawn of the twentieth century, have travelled from their places of birth, in order to create new lives and develop fresh experiences in contexts radically different from the ones in which they were first nurtured.

5. See Henry H. Mitchell, *Black Belief* (San Francisco: Harper and Row, 1975).

6. Clarice T. Nelson, 'The Churches, Racism and the Inner-cities', in Paul Grant and Raj Patel (eds.), *A Time to Speak: Perspectives of Black Christians in Britain* (Birmingham: A Joint Publication of 'Racial Justice' and the 'Black Theology Working Group', 1990), 9.

7. Odida T. Quamina, *All Things Considered: Can We Live Together?* (Toronto: Exile Editions, 1996), 201–212.

8. Paul Hartman and Charles Hubbard, *Racism and the Mass Media* (London: Davis Poynter, 1974), 146.

9. Womanist theology can be seen as a related branch of Black theology. It is an approach to theology that begins with the experience of Black women and women of colour. Womanist theology utilizes the experience of Black women to challenge the tripartite ills of racism, sexism and classism. This discipline is influenced by (Black) feminist thought. On occasions, Womanist theology has been

inaccurately caricatured as *Black feminism*. Some important works by Womanist theologians include Katie G. Cannon, *Black Womanist Ethics* (Atlanta, GA: Scholars Press, 1988); Emile M. Townes, *Womanist Justice, Womanist Hope* (Atlanta, GA: Scholars Press, 1993); Jacquelyn Grant, *White Women's Christ, Black Women's Jesus: Feminist Christology and Womanist Response* (Atlanta, GA: Scholars Press, 1989); Delores Williams, *Sisters in the Wilderness: The Challenge of Womanist God-Talk* (Maryknoll, NY: Orbis Press, 1993).

10. Kortright Davis, *Emancipation Still Coming* (Maryknoll, NY: Orbis Books, 1990), 103–104.

11. Cain Hope Felder, 'The Bible—Re-Contextualisation and the Black Religious Experience', in Gayraud S. Wilmore (ed.), *African American Religious Studies: An Interdisciplinary Anthology* (Durham and London: Duke University Press, 1989), 158.

12. Grant S. Shockley, 'Black Theology and Religious Education', in Randolph Crump Miller (ed.), *Theologies of Religious Education* (Birmingham, AL: Religious Education Press, 1995), 333.

13. Cain Hope Felder (ed.), *Stony the Road We Trod: African American Biblical Interpretation* (Minneapolis: Augsburg Fortress, 1991).

14. Cain Hope Felder (ed.), *The African Heritage Study Bible* (Nashville, TN: James C. Winston Publishing Co, 1993).

15. See volume 1 of *Growing into Hope: Believing and Expecting*, for opening section on *Heroes*, week three of Advent, 59.

16. Felder, *The African Heritage Study Bible*, 'The Gospel of Matthew' 3:1, p. 1379.

17. Felder, *The African Heritage Study Bible*, 1827–32.

18. Jeffrey N. Stinehelfer, 'Dig This: The Revealing of Jesus Christ', *Religious Education* 64.6 (Nov.–Dec. 1969), 468.

19. P. K. McCarey, *The Black Bible Chronicles: From Genesis to the Promised Land [Book One]* (New York: African American Family Press, 1993). P.K. McCarey, *The Black Bible Chronicles: Rappin' With Jesus [Book Two]* (New York: African American Family Press, 1994).

20. See volume 2 of *Growing into Hope: Liberation and Change*, for section on *Pentecost*, week one, 128.

21. Earl Beckles, 'The Language Needs of Children of West Indian Origin', *Multicultural Teaching* 8.2 (Spring 1990), 38–41.

22. D. S. Massey and N. A. Denton, *American Apartheid* (Cambridge, MA: Harvard University Press, 1993), 164.

23. Carol Tomlin, *Black Language Style in Sacred and Secular Texts* (New York: Caribbean Diaspora Press, 1999).

24. Massey and Denton, *American Apartheid*, 164.

25. Grant S. Shockley, 'Christian Education and the Black Religious Experience', in Charles R. Foster (ed.), *Ethnicity in the Education of the Church* (Nashville, TN: Scarritt Press, 1987).

26. Grant S. Shockley, 'From Emancipation to Transformation to Consummation', in Marlene M. Mayr (ed.), *Does the Church Really Want Religious Education?* (Birmingham, AL: Religious Education Press, 1988), 234–36.

27. See volume 2 of *Growing into Hope: Liberation and Change*, for section on *Pentecost*, week two, 137–56.

28. Ella P. Mitchell, 'Oral Tradition: Legacy of Faith for the Black Church', *Religious Education* 81.1 (Winter 1986), 100–101.

29. Joseph V. Crockett, *Teaching Scripture from an African-American Perspective* (Nashville, TN: Discipleship Resources, 1990).

30. See volume 1 of *Growing into Hope: Believing and Expecting*, for section on Advent, week two—'Words and Stories', 34–57.

31. Crockett, *Teaching Scripture*, 15–26.

32. It should be noted that not all Black and Womanist theologians (in different locations of the world) feel that the theme of 'exile' is the dominant motif in Black theological reflection. Writers such as Lorraine Dixon prefer the theme of 'migration', viewing that as more representative of the African Caribbean experience. See Lorraine Dixon, 'Are Vashti and Esther Our Sistas?' in Anthony G. Reddie (ed.), *Legacy: Anthology in Memory of Jillian Brown* (Peterborough: Methodist Publishing House, 1998), 97.

33. Henry H. Mitchell, *Black Belief* (New York: Harper and Row, 1975), 49. Anthony G. Reddie, *Faith, Stories and the Experience of Black Elders: Singing the Lord's Song in a Strange Land* (London: Jessica Kingsley Publishers, 2001), 43.

34. See volume 2 of *Growing into Hope: Liberation and Change*, for the section on *Pentecost*, week two, 137–56.

35. The issue of inter-generational storytelling is addressed in greater detail in my previous book *Faith, Stories and the Experience of Black Elders*.

36. Lawrence N. Jones, 'Hope for Mankind: Insights from Black Religious History in the United States', *Journal of Religious Thought* 34.2 (Fall–Winter, 1978), 59.

37. See volume 1 of *Growing into Hope: Believing and Expecting*, for section on Advent, week one, 14–32.

38. Paulo Freire, *Pedagogy of the Oppressed* (New York: Herder and Herder, 1993 [1970]), 31.

39. Paulo Freire, *Education for Critical Consciousness* (New York: Continuum, 1990 [1973]), 18–20.

40. Paulo Freire and Ira Shor, *A Pedagogy for Liberation: Dialogues for Transformative Education* (New York: Macmillan, 1987), 8–9.

41. Freire and Shor, *A Pedagogy for Liberation*, 35–44.

42. James A. Banks (ed.), *Multicultural Education: Transformative Knowledge and Action* (New York: Teachers College Press, 1996), 340–41.

43. Banks, *Multicultural Education*, 342–44.

44. See volume 2 of *Growing into Hope: Liberation and Change*, for section on Pentecost, week two, 154–55.

45. This is the author's preferred presentation of her name. An explanation for this is given in Robert Beckford, *God of the Rahtid* (London: Darton, Longman and Todd, 2001), 94–97.

46. bell hooks, *Teaching to Transgress: Education as the Practice of Freedom* (New York: Routledge, 1994), 93–128.

47. See volume 1 of *Growing into Hope: Believing and Expecting*, particularly pp. 78, 83 and 88. See volume 2 of *Growing into Hope: Liberation and Change*, particularly pp. 18, 20, 29, 56, 128, 142 and 154.

48. See volume 1 of *Growing into Hope: Believing and Expecting*, particularly pp. 26–27, 52–55 and 100. See volume 2 of *Growing into Hope: Liberation and Change*, particularly pp. 54, 59, 82–83, 104, 106–108, 128–29 and 139.

49.   Anne Hope and Sally Timmel, *Training for Transformation: A Handbook for Community Workers* (4 vols.; Gweru, Zimbabwe: Mambo Press, 1999).

50.   Grant S. Shockley, 'Christian Education and the Black Religious Experience', in Charles R. Foster (ed.), *Ethnicity in the Education of the Church* (Nashville, TN: Scarritt Press, 1987), 36.

51.   Cheryl Bridges Johns, *Pentecostal Formation: A Pedagogy among the Oppressed* (Sheffield: Sheffield Academic Press, 1993), 49–52.

52.   Shockley, 'Christian Education and the Black Religious Experience', 37.

53.   See volume 1 of *Growing into Hope: Believing and Expecting*, 29–32.

54.   James H. Cone, 'Black Theology and the Black Church: Where Do We Go From Here?' in Gayraud S. Wilmore and James H. Cone (eds.), *Black Theology: A Documentary History, 1966–1979* (Maryknoll, NY: Orbis Books, 1979), 350–59.

55.   See volume 1 of *Growing into Hope: Believing and Expecting*, 29–32. Note the Bible passages that are highlighted from Matthew's Gospel and how these are linked to the exercise and the overall theme for that Sunday's lesson.

56.   Recent documentation has shown this to be a classic case of historic romanticism. In a report of the 'Joint Commission of the Three Methodist Churches on Sunday School Work to Conference 1931', it was noted that between them, the three traditions were writing off over '100,000 young people from their Sunday-School registers each year'. John Sutcliffe, *Tuesday's Child: A Reader for Christian Education* (Birmingham: Christian Education Publishing, 2001), 25–26.

57.   For a useful description and analysis of the development of children's work within churches in Britain, see *The Child in the Church* (London: British Council of Churches, 1976); *Understanding Christian Nurture* (London: British Council of Churches, 1981); *Children in the Way* (London: The National Society and Church House Publishing, 1988); *All God's Children?* (London: The National Society and Church House Publishing, 1991); *Unfinished Business* (London: CCBI Publications, 1995).

58.   Winston James, 'Migration, Racism and Identity Formation: The Caribbean Experience in Britain', in Winston James and Clive Harris (eds.), *Inside Babylon: The Caribbean Diaspora in Britain* (London: Verso, 1993), 234–35.

59.   See Anthony G. Reddie, *Faith, Stories and the Experience of Black Elders* (London: Jessica Kingsley Publishers, 2001).

60.   See Peter J. Parris, *The Social Teaching of the Black Churches* (Philadelphia: Fortress Press, 1985) and Dale P. Andrews, *Practical Theology for Black Churches* (Louisville, KY: John Knox Press, 2002).

61.   Anthony G. Reddie, *Nobodies to Somebodies* (Peterborough: Epworth Press, 2003), 29–36.

62.   See Isaac Julien, 'Black Is, Black Ain't: Notes on De-essentializing Black Identities', in Gina Dent (ed.), *Black Popular Culture* (Seattle: Bay Press, 1992), 255–63.

63.   Michael Eric Dyson, *Reflecting Black: African American Cultural Criticism* (Minneapolis: University of Minnesota Press, 1993).

64.   Kobena Mercer, *Welcome to the Jungle: New Positions in Black Cultural Studies* (London: Routledge, 1994).

65.   Victor Anderson, *Beyond Ontological Blackness: An Essay on African American Cultural Criticism* (New York: Continuum, 1995).

66.   Anderson, *Beyond Ontological Blackness*, 118–31.

67. Michael Eric Dyson, *I May Not Get There With You: The True Martin Luther King, Jr* (New York: Simon and Schuster, 1999).

68. Michael Eric Dyson, *Holler If You Hear Me: Searching for Tupac Shakur* (Pittsburg: University of Pennsylvania Press, 2002).

69. See Dennis L. Ockholm (ed.), *The Gospel in Black and White: Theological Resources for Racial Reconciliation* (Downer's Grove, IL: Intervarsity Press, 1997).

70. Lerleen Willis, 'All Things to All Men? Or What has Language to Do with Gender and Resistance in the Black Majority Church in Britain', *Black Theology in Britain* 4.2 (May 2002), 195–213.

71. Carol Tomlin, *Black Language Style in Sacred and Secular Contexts* (New York: Caribbean Diaspora Press, 1999).

72. Christine Callender, *Education for Empowerment: The Practice and Philosophies of Black Teachers* (Stoke-on-Trent: Trentham Books, 1997), 65–95.

73. See Anthony G. Reddie, *Nobodies to Somebodies* (Peterborough: Epworth Press, 2003), 97–99, 105–106.

74. See Jonathan S. Epstein, *Youth Culture: Identity in a Postmodern World* (Oxford: Blackwell, 1998).

75. The BBC programme *The Real McCoy* was a very popular Black comedy sketch show, which emerged in the early 1990s. Since the demise of this show, individual comedians such as Curtis Walker, Angie Le Mar and Felix Dexter have emerged as major comedians on the separate and distinct Black comedy circuit in the UK.

76. See Robert Beckford, *Jesus is Dread* (London: Darton, Longman and Todd, 1998). See also *Dread and Pentecostal* (London: SPCK, 2000).

77. Robert S. Beckford, 'Theology in the Age of Crack: Crack Age, Prosperity Doctrine and "Being There"', *Black Theology in Britain: A Journal of Contextual Praxis* 4.1 (Nov. 2001), 9–24.

78. See Anthony G. Reddie, *Nobodies to Somebodies: A Practical Theology for Education and Liberation* (Peterborough: Epworth Press, 2003), 120–31.

79. Reddie, *Nobodies to Somebodies*, 138.

80. Robert Beckford, *God of the Rahtid: Redeeming Rage* (London: Darton, Longman and Todd, 2001), 31–40.

81. See Anthony G. Reddie, 'Introduction: In Memory of One Who Was Truly Unique', in Anthony G. Reddie (ed.), *Legacy: Anthology in Memory of Jillian Brown* (Peterborough: Methodist Publishing House, 2000), ix.

82. Anthony G. Reddie, 'Editorial', *Black Theology: An International Journal* 2.2 (July 2004), 135–38.

83. This phrase has been borrowed from the writings of many Womanist theologians who state that Black women suffer from double jeopardy (i.e. being Black and a woman) and often triple jeopardy (being Black, a woman and poor). For further information see Frances Beale, 'Double Jeopardy: To be Black and Female', in Gayraud S. Wilmore and James H. Cone (eds.), *Black Theology: A Documentary History—1966–1979* (Maryknoll, NY: Orbis Books, 1979), 368–76. See also Theressa Hoover, 'Black Women and Churches: Triple Jeopardy', in Gayraud S. Wilmore and James H. Cone (eds.), *Black Theology: A Documentary History—1966–1979* (Maryknoll, NY: Orbis Books, 1979), 377–88.

84. For a critique of the illusory nature of Black professional acceptability see

Robert Beckford, *God of the Rahtid: Redeeming Rage* (London: Darton, Longman and Todd, 2001), 31–37.

85.   See section entitled 'A Problem Shared' in Anthony G. Reddie, *Acting in Solidarity: Reflections in Critical Christianity* (London: Darton, Longman and Todd, 2005).

86.   This group has since been renamed the BMLU—'Black Methodists for Liberation and Unity'.

87.   See section entitled 'Complaints—Post Sketch Reflections' in Reddie, *Acting in Solidarity*.

88.   Dale P. Andrews, *Practical Theology for Black Churches: Bridging Black Theology and African American Folk Religion* (Louisville, KY: Westminster/John Knox Press, 2002), 1–30.

89.   Matthew 25:31–46.

90.   See James H. Cone, *Black Theology and Black Power* (Maryknoll, NY: Orbis Books, 1989 [1969]) and *A Black Theology of Liberation* (Maryknoll, NY: Orbis Books, 1990 [1970]).

91.   The full text of the script can be found in Anthony G. Reddie, *Dramatizing Theologies: A Participative Approach to Black God-Talk* (London: Equinox, 2006).

92.   Robert Beckford, *God of the Rahtid* (London: Darton, Longman and Todd, 2001).

93.   Beckford, *God of the Rahtid*, 1–10.

94.   Beckford, *God of the Rahtid*, 11–30.

95.   Beckford, *God of the Rahtid*, 8.

96.   Beckford, *God of the Rahtid*, 31–38.

97.   Beckford, *God of the Rahtid*, 40–47.

98.   Beckford, *God of the Rahtid*, 40–65.

99.   See section entitled 'So Why Christian Drama', in Reddie, *Acting in Solidarity*.

100.   Beckford, *God of the Rahtid*, 31.

101.   Anthony G. Reddie, 'Editorial', *Black Theology: An International Journal* 2.2 (July 2004), 135.

102.   Beckford, *God of the Rahtid*, 32.

103.   This type of speech is reflective of the account provided by James H. Cone in 'Theology's Great Sin: Silence in the Face of White Supremacy', *Black Theology: An International Journal* 2.2 (July 2004), 139–52.

104.   The search for a more egalitarian, non-patrician approach to undertaking theological discourse with poor Black people has been the subject of a number of research projects and publications. See Reddie, *Nobodies to Somebodies* (2003), *Acting in Solidarity* (2005) and *Dramatizing Theologies* (2006) as recent examples of this intent.

105.   It is worth noting the pioneering work of Womanist Practical theologian Lynne Westfield in this regard, whose work includes the use of poetry as a means of engaging with marginalized and oppressed African American women. See N. Lynne Westfield, *Dear Sisters: A Womanist Practice of Hospitality* (Cleveland, OH: Pilgrim Press, 2001). See also N. Lynne Westfield, 'Towards a Womanist Approach to Pedagogy', *Religious Education* 98.4 (Fall 2003), 519–32 (520).

106.   Lee H. Butler, 'Testimony as Hope and Care: African American Pastoral Care as Black Theology at Work', in Linda E. Thomas (ed.), *Living Stones in the*

Household of God: The Legacy and Future of Black Theology (Minneapolis: Fortress Press, 2003), 24–32.

107.   Jeremiah Wright Jr., 'Doing Black Theology in the Black Church', in Thomas, *Living Stones in the Household of God*, 13–23.

108.   Linda E. Thomas, 'Womanist Theology, Epistemology, and a New Anthropological Paradigm', in Thomas, *Living Stones in the Household of God*, 35–50.

109.   See Dwight N. Hopkins and George L. Cummings (eds.), *Cut Loose Your Stammering Tongue: Black Theology in the Slave Narrative* (Louisville, KY: Westminster John Knox Press, 2nd edn, 2003), Will Coleman, *Tribal Talk: Black Theology, Hermeneutics, and African/American Ways of 'Telling the Story'* (University Park, PN: Pennsylvania State University Press, 2000) and Dwight N. Hopkins, *Down, Up and Over: Slave Religion and Black Theology* (Minneapolis: Fortress Press, 2000).

110.   Westfield, 'Towards a Womanist Approach to Pedagogy', 519-532 (520).

Chapter 8

1.   See Paul Ballard and John Pritchard, *Practical Theology in Action: Christian Thinking in the Service of the Church and Society* (London: SPCK, 1996).

2.   See Duncan B. Forrester, *Truthful Action: Explorations in Practical Theology* (Edinburgh: T & T Clark, 2000).

3.   Elaine L. Graham, *Transforming Practice: Pastoral Theology in Age of Uncertainty* (Eugene, OR: Wipf and Stock, 2002).

4.   Carlyle Fielding Stewart, III, *Black Spirituality and Black Consciousness* (Trenton, NY: Africa World Press, 1999), 105–120.

5.   Dale P. Andrews, *Practical Theology for Black Churches: Bridging Black Theology and African American Folk Religion* (Louisville, KY: John Knox Press, 2002), 6–23.

6.   Carol Tomlin, *Black Language Style in Sacred and Secular Contexts* (New York: Caribbean Diaspora Press, 1999), 125–66.

7.   Tomlin, *Black Language and Style*, 126.

8.   See Joe Aldred (ed.), *Preaching with Power* (London: Cassell, 1998).

9.   Ermal Kirby, 'Black Preaching', *The Journal of the College of Preachers* (July 2001), 47–49.

10.   See Aldred (ed.), *Preaching with Power*.

11.   James H. Harris, *Pastoral Theology: A Black Church Perspective* (Minneapolis: Augsburg Fortress, 1991), 99.

12.   Mukti Barton, *Rejection, Resistance and Resurrection* (London: Darton, Longman and Todd, 2005).

13.   Barton, *Rejection, Resistance and Resurrection*, 107.

14.   Barton, *Rejection, Resistance and Resurrection*, 42.

Chapter 9

1.   Paul Grant and Raj Patel (eds.), *A Time to Speak: Perspectives of Black Christians in Britain* (Birmingham: A Joint Publication of 'Racial Justice' and the 'Black Theology Working Group', 1990).

2.   Paul Grant and Raj Patel (eds.), *A Time to Act: Kairos 1992* (Birmingham: A Joint Publication of 'Racial Justice' and the 'Black and Third World Theology Working Group', 1992).

3.   See Emmanuel Y. Lartey, *Pastoral Theology in an Intercultural World* (Peter-borough: Epworth Press, 2006).

4.   See Anthony G. Reddie, *Black Theology in Transatlantic Dialogue* (New York: Palgrave Macmillan, 2006).

5.   See Harry Goulbourne, 'Collective Action and Black Politics', in Doreen McCalla (ed.), *Black Success in the UK: Essays in Racial and Ethnic Studies* (Birmingham: DMee: Vision Learning and Cambridge University Press, 2003), 9–38.

6.   This term refers to what one might describe as 'Global Christianity'. The use of this term is mainly used in Methodist (and Anglican to a lesser extent) circles, in order to denote the spread of Christianity and the church particularly in those areas of the world that are linked inextricably with missionary activity during the era of empire and colonialism. The British Methodist church has a desk within the Connexional/National team called 'The World Church Office'. This deals with the relationship between British Methodism and her partner Methodist churches across the world, particularly in Africa, the Caribbean, Asia and Europe.

7.   Kingsmead has since closed.

8.   Details of the development of Black theology in Britain, particularly the birth of the first Black Theology in Britain forum can be found in Reddie, *Black Theology in Transatlantic Dialogue*.

9.   *This is Where I Live: Stories and Pressures in Brixton* (London: The Runnymeade Trust, 1996), 10–11.

10.   Caryle Fielding Stewart III, *Street Corner Theology* (Nashville, TN: James C. Winston Publishing Co, 1996), 23.

11.   C. Eric Lincoln, 'Black Religion and Racial Identity', in Herbert W. Harris, Howard C. Blue and Ezra E. H. Griffith (eds.), *The Psychology of Black Identity Change in Racial and Ethnic Identity* (London: Routledge, 1995), 209–21 (219).

12.   W. E. Cross, Jr., 'Encountering Nigrescence', in J. G. Ponterotto *et al.* (eds.), *Handbook of Multicultural Counseling* (Thousand Oaks, CA: Sage, 2001), 30–44.

13.   Paul Gilroy, 'Roots and Routes: Black Identity as an Outernational Project', in Harris, Blue and Griffith, *The Psychology of Black Identity*, 15–30 (25).

14.   Gilroy, 'Roots and Routes', 26.

15.   Kofi Baku, 'Pan-Africanism towards Afrocentrism', The W.E.B. Du Bois Memorial Lecture, *West Africa* (14–20 November 1988), 21–42.

16.   Kwame Bediako, *Christianity in Africa: The Renewal of a Non-Western Religion* (Edinburgh: Edinburgh University Press, 1995), 256 and Josiah Ulysses Young III, *A Pan-African Theology: Providence and the Legacies of the Ancestors* (New Jersey: Africa World Press, 1992).

17.   Joseph M. Kitagawa and Charles H. Long, *Myths and Symbols: Studies in Honor of Mircea Eliade* (Chicago and London: University of Chicago Press, 1969).

18.   Robin Green, *Only Connect* (London: Darton, Longman & Todd, 1987), 8, 13.

19.   Green, *Only Connect*, 15–17.

20.   See Jawanza Kunjufu Adam, *Where Are You? Why Most Black Men Don't Go to Church* (Chicago, IL: African-American Images, 1994).

21.   Andres Tapia, 'Soul Searching', *Christianity Today* 40.3 (1996), 26–30 (27).

22.   Theressa Hoover, 'Black Women and the Churches: Triple Jeopardy',

in James Cone and Gayraud S. Wilmore (eds.), *Black Theology: A Documentary History* (Maryknoll, NY: Orbis Books, 1993), 293–303 (293).

23. Bernard L. Manning, *The Hymns of Wesley and Watts* (repr. London: Epworth Press, 1942), 47.

24. Keith Warner, *The Trinidad Calypso* (London: Heinemann, 1982), 87–88.

25. Peter Manuel, *Caribbean Currents: Caribbean Music from Rumba to Reggae* (London: Latin America Bureau, 1995), 170.

26. Patrick Prescod (ed.), *Sing a New Song* (Bridgetown: CEDAR Press, 1980), Joyce Bailey (ed.), *Sing a New Song* (Jamaica: Christian Action for Development in the Caribbean (CADEC), 1973), Pearl Yvonne Mulrain, *Out of My Faith* (Trinidad: The College Press, 1989), Garfield Rochard, *Caribbean Hymnal* (Great Wakering: House of McCrimmon, 1980).

27. David Peacock and Geoff Weaver, *World Praise* (London: Marshall-Pickering, 1993), S. T. Kimbrough, and Carlton R. Young (eds.), *Global Praise* (New York: GBGMusik, 1996).

28. For a fuller discussion of this see Linda Myers, *Understanding an Afrocentric World View: Introduction to an Optimal Psychology* (Dubuque, IA: Kendall/Hunt, 1988).

29. Linda Myers, '"Transpersonal" Psychology: The Role of the Afrocentric Paradigm', in A. Kathleen Hoard Burlew *et al.* (eds.), *African American Psychology: Theory, Research and Practice* (Newbury Park, CA: Sage, 1992), 10.

30. See, for example, Richard Pring's comprehensive discussion of 'personal development' in M. Marland and P. Lang (eds.), *New Directions in Pastoral Care* (Oxford: Basil Blackwell, 1985), 130–41 (134).

31. 1 John 4:19.

32. A slight modification of E. Y. Lartey, 'African Perspectives on Pastoral Theology: A Contribution to the Quest for More Encompassing Models of Pastoral Care', *Contact* 112 (1993), 5.

33. See Stuart Hall, 'Cultural Studies: Two Paradigms', in T. Bennett *et al.* (eds.), *Culture, Ideology and Social Process* (London: Batsford and Open University Press, 1981). Also Rosamund Billington *et al.*, *Culture and Society: A Sociology of Culture* (Basingstoke and New York: Macmillan, 1991).

34. For a concise and useful introduction to various usages of the term see S. Hall and B. Gieben (eds.), *Formations of Modernity* (Cambridge: Polity Press and Open University, 1992), 229–37.

35. David Augsburger, *Pastoral Counselling Across Cultures* (Philadelphia: Westminster Press, 1986), 25.

36. Augsburger, *Pastoral Counselling Across Cultures*, 26.

37. This is presented and discussed helpfully in Augsburger, *Pastoral Counselling Across Cultures*, 48–78.

38. S. L. Speight *et al.*, 'A Redefinition of Multicultural Counselling', *Journal of Counselling and Development* 70 (September/October 1991), 11.

39. See M. A. Fukuyama, 'Taking a Universal Approach to Multicultural Counselling', *Counsellor Education and Supervision* 30 (1990), 6–17; C. E. Vontress, 'Existentialism as a Cross-cultural Counselling Modality', in P. B. Pedersen (ed.), *Handbook of Cross-Cultural Counselling and Therapy* (Westport, CT: Greenwood, 1985), 207–12.

40. J. G. Draguns, 'Dilemmas and Choices in Cross-cultural Counselling: The Universal versus the Culturally Distinctive', in P. B. Pedersen *et al*, *(*eds.), *Counselling Across Cultures* (Honolulu: University of Hawaii Press, 1989), 14.

41. Augsburger, *Pastoral Counselling Across Cultures*, 47.

42. For a recent useful discussion of 'racialization' see Stephen Small, *Racialised Barriers: The Black Experience in the United States and England in the 1980s* (London and New York: Routledge, 1994), esp. 29–39.

43. Michael Jagessar, *Full Life for All: The Work and Theology of Philip A. Potter* (Zoetermeer: Boekencentrum, 1997), 15.

44. Gordon K. Lewis, *Main Currents in Caribbean Thought* (Kingston: Heinemann Educational Books [Caribbean], 1983), 3.

45. Philip Potter, *Life in All its Fullness* (Geneva: WCC, 1983), 141.

46. Dennis Benn, *The Growth and Development of Political Ideas in the Caribbean 1774–1983* (Jamaica: Institute for Social and Economic Research (ISER), 1987).

47. Jagessar, *Full Life for All*, 72.

48. Cyril Davey, *Changing Places: Methodist Mission Then and Now* (Basingstoke: Marshall Pickering, 1988), 20.

49. Jagessar, *Full Life for All*, 80.

50. William Gentz, *The World of Philip Potter* (New York: Friendship Press, 1974), 83.

51. See Roger Bromley, *Narratives for a New Belonging: Diasporic Cultural Fictions* (Edinburgh: Edinburgh University Press, 2000).

52. Jagessar, *Full Life for All*, 302.

53. Pauline Webb (ed.), *Faith and Faithfulness: Essays on Contemporary Ecumenical Themes* (Geneva: WCC, 1984), viii.

54. Potter, *Life in All its Fullness*, 141.

55. Philip Potter, 'Dear Friends', *Ecumenical Review* 24.4 (October 1972), 472.

56. Potter, *Full Life for All*, 90.

57. See C. L. R. James, *Beyond a Boundary* (London: Hutchinson, 1963).

58. Jagessar, *Full Life for All*, 130.

59. James, *Beyond a Boundary*, 72, original emphasis.

60. For more on the critics and the criticisms, see Potter, *Full Life for All*, 89–94.

61. M. M. Thomas, *My Ecumenical Journey* (Trivandrum: The Ecumenical Press, 1990), 410.

62. Jagessar, *Full Life for All*, 297.

63. Potter, *Life in All its Fullness*, ix.

64. Philip Potter, *The Alex Wood Memorial Lecture* (Surrey: Fellowship of Reconciliation, 1974), 18.

65. Philip Potter, 'Work out your own Salvation', Sermon preached at the Assembly of the United Board of World Ministries of the United Church of Christ, Greensboro, North Carolina, Sunday, 10 November 1968 (General Secretary Files, WCC Archives, Geneva), 12.

66. Potter, *Life in All its Fullness*, vii.

67. Jagessar, *Full Life for All*, 158.

Chapter 10

1.   See Alistair Kee, *The Rise and Demise of Black Theology* (Aldershot, Kent: Ashgate, 2006), 137–67, where the author's assessment of Black theology in Britain does not extend beyond the work of Robert Beckford.

2.   See E. Y. Lartey, 'Editorial', *Black Theology in Britain* 1 (1998), 7.

3.   Quoted in Thomas Langford, *Practical Divinity: Readings in Wesleyan Theology* (Nashville: Abingdon Press, 1999), 226.

4.   See E. Lartey, 'Pastoral Care in Multi-cultural Britain: White, Black or Beige?', *Epworth Review* 25.3 (1998), 42–52.

5.   Stuart Hall, 'What is this "Black" in Black Popular Culture?', in David Morley and Kuan-Hsing Chen (eds.), *Critical Dialogues in Cultural Studies* (London: Routledge, 1996), 465–75 (470).

6.   Robert Beckford, *Jesus Is Dread: Black Theology and Black Culture in Britain* (London: Darton, Longman and Todd, 1998).

7.   James Cone, *A Black Theology of Liberation* (Maryknoll, NY: Orbis Books, 1990), xv.

8.   James Cone, 'Preface to the 1997 Edition', in *God of the Oppressed* (Maryknoll, NY: Orbis Books, 1997), xiv.

9.   Stephen Bevans, *Models of Contextual Theology* (Maryknoll, NY: Orbis Books, 1992), 65.

10.   Cone, *God of the Oppressed*, xiv.

11.   'Agenda' literally means 'things to be done' and comes from the Latin 'agere', 'to do'. It is as such a schedule or list of items to be attended to; matters to be attended to (as at a meeting).

12.   See, for example, Cain Hope Felder (ed.), *Stony the Road We Trod: African American Biblical Interpretation* (Minneapolis: Fortress Press, 1991).

13.   For example, Onyekachi Wambu (ed.), *Empire Windrush: Fifty Years of Writing about Black Britain* (London: Victor Gollancz, 1998).

14.   See Vincent Carretta (ed.), *Letters of the Late Ignatius Sancho, an African* (Harmondsworth: Penguin Books, 1998). The Letters were first published in Britain in 1782.

15.   See 'The Interesting Narrative of the Life of Olaudah Equiano or Gustavus Vassa, the African', written by himself in Henry Louis Gates (ed.), *The Classic Slave Narratives* (Harmondsworth: Penguin Books, 1987).

16.   E.g. David Dabydeen and Paul Edwards (eds.), *Black Writers in Britain: 1760–1890* (Edinburgh: Edinburgh University Press, 1991), David Killingray, *Africans in Britain* (Ilford: Frank Cass, 1994), Hakim Adi, *West Africans in Britain: 1900–1960* (London: Lawrence and Wishart, 1998), Marika Sherwood, *Pastor Daniels Ekarte and the African Churches Mission, Liverpool 1931–1964* (London: Savannah Press, 1994), and Delia Jarrett-Macauley, *The Life of Una Marson, 1905–1965* (Manchester: Manchester University Press, 1998), which marks the life of 'the leading Black feminist in London in the 1930s'.

17.   See Black and Asian Association Newsletter (published three times a year) (BASA, c/o ICS, 28 Russell Square, London WC1B 5DS).

18.   See Basil Davidson, *West Africa before the Colonial Era: A History to 1850* (London: Longrnan, 1998).

19.   See Stuart Hall, 'The West and the Rest: Discourse and Power', in Stuart

Hall and Bram Gieben (eds.), *Formations of Modernity* (Cambridge: Polity Press, 1992), 275–320 (312).

20. Emmanuel C. Eze, *Race and the Enlightenment: A Reader* (Oxford: Basil Blackwell, 1997).

21. See Lena Robinson, *Psychology for Social Workers: Black Perspectives* (London: Routledge, 1995) and *Race, Communication and the Caring Professions* (Milton Keynes: Open University Press, 1998).

22. See Anthony G. Reddie, *Black Theology in Transatlantic Dialogue* (New York: Palgrave Macmillan, 2006), 136–37.

23. See Frederick L. Ware, *Methodologies of Black Theology* (Cleveland, OH: Pilgrim Press, 2002).

24. See Robert Beckford, *Dread and Pentecostal* (London: SPCK, 2000), 204. See also Anthony G. Reddie, *Acting in Solidarity: Reflections in Critical Christianity* (London: Darton, Longman and Todd, 2005), 109–119.

25. See Reddie, *Black Theology in Transatlantic Dialogue*, 136–37.

26. See Anthony Pinn, *Varieties of African American Religious Experience* (Minneapolis: Fortress Press, 1998).

27. See Dianne M. Stewart, *Three Eyes For the Journey: African Dimensions of the Jamaican Religious Experience* (New York: Oxford University Press, 2005).

28. See Robert Beckford, 'Theology in the Age of Crack: Crack Age, Prosperity Doctrine and "Being There"', *Black Theology in Britain: A Journal of Contextual Praxis* 4.1 (Nov. 2001), 20.

29. See Reddie, *Acting in Solidarity*, 144–53.

30. James H. Cone, *God of the Oppressed* (San Francisco: Harper Collins, 1975).

31. Jacklyn Grant, *White Women's Christ and Black Women's Jesus* (Atlanta: Scholars Press, 1989).

32. Robert Beckford, *Jesus Is Dread* (London: Darton, Longman and Todd, 1998).

33. See Anthony G. Reddie, *Nobodies to Somebodies: A Practical Theology for Education and Liberation* (Peterborough: Epworth, 2003), 162–65.

34. Private conversation in Birmingham, October 2005.

Supporting Material

The undertaking of this Reader highlighted for us the level of inadequacy that underpins all one's best attempts to create a coherent and fulfilling piece of work. Despite the size of this work, for example, we have had to make extremely difficult decisions regarding what to include and omit from this Reader. We are also aware of the invidious nature of all definitions that seek to clarify (in the most laudable of ways) and yet also conclude by being restrictive and discriminatory (the underside of such attempts at categorization).

We acknowledge that whilst this text is concerned with Black theology in Britain, the largely Christian enterprise of a radical re-interpretation and articulation of Christianity, achieved through the lens of Black existential experience, is one that draws its roots and strength from the larger commitment of ordinary Black people of faith. Black theology cannot and should not become divorced from the faith truth-claims and religious practices of ordinary Black people, most of whom would not adhere or subscribe to the basic tenets of this discipline.

By way of attempting to 'solve this problem' of recounting what should and should not be included in this Reader, we have sought to construct a comprehensive, yet not exhaustive, section that includes supporting material and a broader bibliography. This section offers a range of resources for potential researchers and scholars. Whilst it is always a thankless undertaking to attempt any completist task of including 'everything', we have, nonetheless, sought to identify as many works as our meagre resources have permitted, in order to offer a detailed list that will provide the overarching backdrop from which the extracts that populate this text have been drawn.

We hope that the following resources will excite many of you to consider your own archival search for sources that will enhance future studies in Black religious studies and Black theology in Britain.

This section begins with archive material from the Black Christian Studies course which ran at Queen's in the late 1980s through to the late 90s. It was overseen by The Revd John L. Wilkinson and Dr Robert Beckford.[1] As we have stated in the introduction to Chapter 3, and reiterated here, we have included this material not as a form of negation of the important developments in Black theological curricula since that time, but rather as

---

1. Details of this narrative detailing the development of Black Theology at the Queen's College (Foundation) have been recounted in Chapter 3 by John Wilkinson.

a means of recognizing the pioneering work that was undertaken in this course, almost twenty years ago.

Black Christian Studies

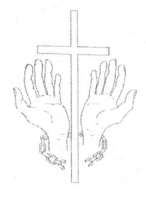

at

THE QUEEN'S COLLEGE, BIRMINGHAM

and the

WEST MIDLANDS MINISTERIAL TRAINING COURSE

QUEEN'S COLLEGE
Principal:
The Rev Dr James Walker

WEST MIDLANDS MINISTERIAL TRAINING COURSE
Principal:
The Rev Andrew Wingate
The Queen's College, Somerset Road, Edgbaston, Birmingham B15 2QH
Tel: College 021 454 1527 Course 021 454 8597

BLACK CHRISTIAN STUDIES COURSE
Associate Tutors:
The Rt Rev. Dr Patrick Kalilombe
Director, Centre for Black & White Christian Partnership, Selly Oak, Birmingham

The Rev. Rajinder Daniel
Bishop's Adviser for Black Ministries,
Diocese of Birmingham

The Rev. Nduna Mpunzi
Vicar, St Mary's Parish Church,
Bilston, Wolverhampton

Co-ordinator:
The Rev. John Wilkinson
Tutor, Pastoral Studies, Queen's College

Visiting Lecturers:
The Rev. Roderick Hewitt
Council for World Mission, London

The Rev. David Moore
HM Inspector of Schools

February 1989
(revised November 1989)

Cover design by Eve Pitts

Principal's Introductions

For me, who was born in Malawi, there is something incredibly moving about a Black Christian Studies course at Queen's, where one of the consultants is a Catholic bishop from Malawi. The course has become one of the most fruitful areas of life at Queen's. A whole new perspective and depth has been growing, as Jesus Christ is more clearly illuminated and light is cast into the shadows of much of our white understanding and life.

St Paul, in his letter to the Church at Colossae, having rejoiced in the fullness of the life of God in Jesus Christ, wrote that Christians must not live a lie. The lie exists whenever any person, through race, gender or class is excluded from Christ's body. Sadly this has all too often happened as many Black people can testify, and thus the body of Christ has been wounded. Our prayer is that, through this Black Christian Studies course, and its impact both in Churches and in the ongoing life of our study and worship at Queen's, there will be a recovery of a Church in which visibly and truly 'Christ is all, and in all' (Col. 3:11).

How this course will make its impact in Britain lies in the hand of Almighty God, but it is exciting to feel a part of one small step in the growing together of all Christians into Christ, that the world may believe.

James B. Walker, Queen's College

When I came to the West Midlands Ministerial Training Course seven years ago, it had never had a Black student. When research by Renate and John Wilkinson indicated the large numbers of Black Anglicans in Birmingham, and parallel Methodist research reached similar conclusions, students from the course's sponsoring Churches expressing their sense of deprivation by the course's monochrome whiteness. We now have three Afro-Caribbean students (out of 57), which is inadequate, but is at least a beginning. It is encouraging that all Churches are now examining their structures and looking at how these may hinder Black candidates, Afro-Caribbean and Asian.

It would, however, be irresponsible to have Black candidates if we did not also recognize their particular gifts, history and theology, and help them to grow further in these areas as they prepare for ministry. This happens in various ways on the West Midlands course, but particularly through the Black Christian Studies course. This has been invaluable as it has helped its members grow in confidence. They are then able to bring their particular challenge to their fellow students on the main course. The balance of history and theology, affirming and listening to experience, extending and deepening that experience, reflecting on questions related to society and the church, gives an essential grounding that would not be available in any other way I therefore commend this course greatly and look forward to its development in the coming years.

                                          Andrew Wingate, West Midlands course

Foreword
by the Rt Rev. Patrick Kalilombe
Director of the Centre for Black and White Christian Partnership

This two-year programme of Black Christian Studies is a pioneering venture developed under the auspices and within the context of Queen's College. In its present form it is largely tentative and exploratory. Nevertheless it represents a development that is overdue in a theological college like Queen's, which seeks to prepare ministers for the highly multi-cultural and multi-racial Christian community of the West Midlands.

The importance of the Black presence in the mainline churches has become more and more accepted over the past few years. This presence is a call to the churches to identify, respect, accept and include, in their way of understanding the Gospel and living the faith, those variations which are the result of diverse human cultures and histories. No one culture or set of cultures can claim to be the sole and comprehensive embodiment of God's Word in Christ and the response in faith and obedience which it calls forth in human society. By its very nature Christ's church is 'Catholic' in the true sense of the word. And so the Black presence in the churches deserves a commensurate share in the ministry and leadership as well as in giving shape to the faith, worship and witness of Christian communities.

As more and more candidates for the ministry began to come forth from the Black communities and joined the theological college, it was necessary to seek ways and means of making it possible for them to discover what special contributions they could make to the common programme of ministerial training and formation at Queen's College. 'Black Christian Studies' is part of this adventure of discovery.

The programme is being developed in two main stages. In the first stage, the present one, the Black candidates are studying and searching in a group of their own, for they cannot be expected to offer a valid contribution if they have not first 'put their act together' and discovered who they are and what their communities have to offer. But a second stage will have to follow, when the Black contribution will be open to the whole College. 'Black Christian Studies' should become part of the common programme, available to all and not restricted to the Black students. Hopefully this will help in the process whereby the Black Christian tradition becomes an enriching ingredient in the whole of ministry training and church life generally.

Patrick Kalilombe
February 1989

Black Christian Studies

1. *Aims*
The Black Christian Studies course aims to provide Black students with the opportunity to:

    a. study the inheritance of Black Christianity and explore their own experience,
    b. study theology and prepare for ministry on the basis of a Black identity,
    c. work collaboratively towards a British Black theology,
    d. find mutual support.

2. *Origins*
The course originated with a desire to respond to the needs of Black students, and to encourage potential Black ordinands, by providing facilities for studying theology on the basis of a Black identity. Reflections from Wesley Daniel, a Black Methodist ordinand at Queen's College from 1985 to 1988, were especially valuable. The establishment of the course was agreed by the College staff in July 1987, and began the following October.

Early meetings were taken up with determining basic principles, aims and methods. Four issues were especially important: eligibility for the course, its relationship to other studies, assessment, and teaching staff. These have been provisionally resolved as follows:

(a) *Eligibility.* For the first two-year cycle of the course, only Black students were admitted. This was necessary: particularly for the fulfilment of the fourth aim (mutual support for Black students). From September 1989 a small number of white students with appropriate experience have been admitted. However, the course will continue to be made up of a majority of Black students. The course is normally restricted to students of Queen's College and the West Midlands Ministerial Training Course (WMMTC), though applications from others are considered.

(b) *Relationship to other studies.* Students are able to take the course without adding to their total workload. Normal commitments may therefore be modified, by arrangement with the student's personal tutor. Enrolment for the course is not obligatory.

(c) *Assessment.* Each student is to submit one seminar presentation or one essay per term, to be marked in the usual way. Tutors in other subjects may be asked to agree essay titles to which a student could respond from a Black perspective, whilst covering College essay requirements for that subject. Second-year students, additionally, choose a study topic in the first term in consultation with the course tutors and students. A paper of up to 5,000 words is submitted on this topic at the beginning of the third term.

(d) *Teaching staff.* The participation of Black clergy with appropriate theological skills is sought, whilst the role of the tutor from College (who is not Black) is primarily to coordinate and administer. The collaborative style of the course should make it the 'property' of all participants.

3. *Tutors*

The coordinator of the course is the Rev. John Wilkinson, Tutor in Pastoral Studies at Queen's College. In the first year the principal external staff were the Rt Rev. Patrick Kalilombe of the Centre for Black and White Christian Partnership, and the Rev. Barney Pityana, then Vicar of Immanuel Parish, Highter's Heath, Birmingham. Other contributors have been the Rev. Rajinder Daniel, Birmingham Diocesan Adviser on Black Ministries and the Rev. Roderick Hewitt of the Council for World Mission.

In October 1988, the Rev. Nduna Mpunzi, Vicar of Bilston, Wolverhampton replaced Barney Pityana who now works in Geneva as Director of the World Council of Churches' Programme to Combat Racism.

4. *Course methods of study and reflection*

(a) It is intended that the following elements are present in the study process:

(i) *encounter with recognized Black theological thought*: although little written Black theology from Britain is yet available, guidance and inspiration is sought from reflection which has already been recorded elsewhere, notably the United States, the Caribbean and South Africa.

(ii) *systematic study*: the course investigates the subject matter of the principal theological disciplines (systematics, liturgy, pastoral studies, biblical studies, church history) from a Black perspective.

(iii) *experience*: the categories of theological thought and the received wisdom of Black theologians is constantly in dialogue with the experience of students, both individually and collectively.

(b) The course meets *every* Tuesday in term-time from 3.30pm to 4.45pm. Each meeting begins with prayer led by course members and appropriate short contributions of music, poetry etc. are welcomed. A student normally 'moderates' each meeting.

(c) For each curriculum topic an amount of required reading for all students is given weekly. In addition, other books and articles are recommended. Normally a student presents a seminar paper which is then responded to by a staff member and by students. Alternatively, a topic is covered by a lecturer.

(d) An important part of each meeting is the exchange of news and experience, through which course members support each other. Black students preparing elsewhere for ministry, and other guests, are welcomed on appropriate occasions.

(e) Visits may be arranged to congregations, cultural events, significant sites, etc.

(f) The course aims to be in dialogue with people from the wider Black community, particularly from Black-led churches and from community groups. These exchanges can be opportunities for testing the course's findings, for developing ecumenical relations, and for mission.

(g) The course may, from time to time, share something of its life with the College and the WMMTC. This was done successfully in the first year of the course through a Tuesday Preaching Service to commemorate the twentieth anniversary of the death of Martin Luther King.

(h) A booklist of relevant literature from Britain, the United States, the Caribbean, South Africa and elsewhere has been compiled and will be updated annually. The College Librarian is attempting to obtain as many as possible of these books for the College Library. Additionally, relevant journals may be purchased, or indication given where these are already available in Birmingham. It is hoped that this will become a resource for the wider Church.

The course acknowledges with gratitude a grant of £500 from the Christendom Trust for the purchase of books.

5. *Curriculum*

Year 1

A. *Introduction*

1. The Black theological enterprise for Britain today, including methodology, the meaning of 'Blackness'[1], liberation, celebration, history and culture, community groups, context.

2. The resources we bring, including student hopes, aspirations, understandings, experience, personal and practical resources.

B. *History*

1. Historical method, Black people and the writing of history.

2. Subjects:
(a) Our African Heritage
(b) Slavery and the Birth of Black Christianity
(c) From Slavery to Colonialism in the Caribbean and the Emergence of the Colonial Church
(d) From the Caribbean to Britain, and the Formation of the Black Church in Britain ('Black-led' and 'mainstream')
(e) The Black Christian Presence in Britain Today
(f) North America: the Black Church, Black Radicalism and Black Theology
(g) The Experience of British Christians of Asian Origin
(h) Black Christian Voices from South Africa plus (i) Marcus Garvey, (ii) Martin Luther King, (iii) Malcolm X

C. *Black theology*

1. Methodology, the aims of Black theology, its relationship to the tradition of the Black Church, to other liberation theologies, and to White theology.

2. The content of Black theology:

(a) God the Creator
(b) The Fall, Sin and Bondage
(c) God the Liberator
(d) The Human Being
(e) Jesus Christ
(f)   The Holy Spirit
(g) The Church
(h) Eschatology
(i)   Liberation and the Christian Ethic
(j)   The Black Use of the Bible

Year 2

D. *Mission, ministry and life in the church*

1. Whither the Black Church in Britain?—developments and hopes in 'Black-led' churches and in mainstream, esp. Anglican and Methodist.
2. The responsibilities of the Black Minister—pastor, educator, community leader, role with white Christians, his/her spiritual sustenance and support, networking.
3. Particular topics:

(a) Black Preaching
(b) Prayer, Praise and Worship
(c) Baptism and Eucharist
(d) Healing, Illness and Death
(e) Black Music and the Gospel
(f)   Handing on the Tradition: Young People and the Context of Faith

E. *Black people in a white society*

1. Sociological method, social analysis, sociological tools in Black perspective.
2. Racism—how it is operative in British society.
3. Specific issues:

(a) education
(b) health provision
(c) the law, the police and justice
(d) citizenship
(e) housing
(f)   business and enterprise, employment
(g) Black art: music, drama, fine art

6. *Wider links*

The course seeks to cooperate with and to complement others working in the field of Black theology and training for ministry.

Through Bishop Patrick Kalilombe it has links with the Working Party on Black Theology set up by the Community and Race Relations Unit of the British Council of Churches, and with the Centre for Black and White Christian Partnership in Selly Oak.

Through the Rev. Rajinder Daniel it has links with the work of Mrs Glynne Gordon-Carter, Secretary to the Race and Community Relations Committee of the Board of Social Responsibility and Secretary to the Black Anglican Concerns Committee, with the ecumenical group responsible for the establishment of the Simon of Cyrene Centre and with the Association of Black Clergy.

The course is also in contact with the Methodist Black Ministers' Group.

Some Student Testimonies

In September of 1987 I was invited with three other students to join a course at Queen's College, Birmingham. The subject was Black theology. I went with a lot of anxieties because I was not sure what this would involve. After the first session I became less nervous and wanted to go back. We explored many areas in our history, looking on our African heritage, the move to the West Indies, the Americas and later to the United Kingdom. By this time my adrenalin was really active because I could connect a lot of history to today's living. We studied the life and work of many of our freedom fighters such as Malcolm X, Marcus Garvey and Martin Luther King.

Not only did we study in these areas, we also looked at the biblical implications and its relevance to us and our 'blackness'. What is Jesus Christ saying to me as a black person and how black would he have to be to liberate me?

We were able to use all these materials in our context and match them beside our life. This course has transformed me not only in my thinking but in my general lifestyle and attitudes. It has been a year of pain and joy, a time of tremendous growth and healing.

I now look forward to another year, this time with eagerness. From the syllabus for this year I know more will be revealed about the God of the oppressed—the God who promises to set his people free.

Carl Ramsay CA

As preparation for a ministry which neither devalues nor diminishes my experiences as a black person, I find Black Christian Studies relevant and stimulating.

Sonia Hicks

The black group of Bishop Patrick Kalilombe, clergy and students of various denominations now meeting at Queen's College in Birmingham is part of a black theological process now taking place in Birmingham and throughout the country. Those attending are experiencing a degree of emancipation and liberation that has brought about a measure of confidence and boldness not hitherto experienced. The Church and the country can only benefit from this.

The Rev. Rolston Deson

When I arrived at Queen's eighteen months ago it was clear that any serious attempts to study theology had to include my perspective of God and what he means to me as a black woman training for ministry. My experience of life had to be taken seriously by the College and consequently the quality of training I received. It must be said then that without the Black Christian Studies group on Tuesdays I would not have survived with my integrity intact.

This group gave me the opportunity not only to find the right books, but it also gave me the chance to explore my faith in the light of my black experience. The group helped me to organize my thoughts—it gave me a chance to deal systematically with the issues, for example, 'What does God mean to me when society would have me believe that others are more in the image of God?'

But above all the group is a place of refuge. Refuge because in an all-white environment it would be easy to go under or play the 'We are all one in Christ' game. Of course we are, but the fact remains that as black people we need to plug into our own spiritual and cultural tradition if we are to remain sober, or if our theology is to remain authentic. We must learn to be, and to love the company of our own people. This group gives me that chance—without it I would not have survived College. It is not supposed to be all things to all of us, but it means a lot to all of us.

Anon

Appendix 1

Black Christian Studies Students 1987–92
(names of White students are italicized)

Steve Tash 1989–91
Novette Thompson 1989–92
Gill Warren 1990–92
Rob Hilton 1990–92
Vicky Merriman-Johnson 1991–93
Denise Neale 1991–93

Chris Shannahan 1991–93
Mary Shannahan 1991–93
Zahida Mallard 1991–93
Adrian Perry 1991–93
Karen Best 1992–94
Eve Pitts 1987–89
Rolston Deson 1987–88
Elsie Watson 1988–89
Carl Ramsay 1987–90
Walter Burleigh 1988–89
Pat Ward 1987–90
Sonia Hicks 1988–91
Rose Wilkin 1989–91
Lorraine Dixon 1989–91
Yvette Poole 1989–91
Conrad Hicks 1989–91

Black Religion/Black Theology: A Bibliographical Survey

1. Books

Aldred, Joe, *Respect: Understanding Caribbean British Christianity* (Peterborough: Epworth Press, 2005).

Aldred, Joe (ed.), *Praying with Power* (London and New York: Continuum, 2000).

——*Sisters with Power* (London and New York: Continuum).

——*Preaching with Power* (London and New York: Cassell, 1998).

Arnold, S. E., *From Scepticism to Hope: One Black-led Church's Response to Social Responsibility* (Nottingham: Grove Books, 1992).

Barton, Mukti, *Scripture as Empowerment for Liberation and Justice: The Experience of Christian and Muslim in Bangladesh* (Bristol: University of Bristol, 1999).

——*Rejection, Resistance and Resurrection: Speaking Out on Racism in the Church* (London: Darton, Longman & Todd, 2005).

Becher, Virginia, *Black Christians: Black Church Traditions in Britain* (Birmingham: Centre for Black and White Christian Partnership, Westhill College and RE Centre, 1995).

Beckford, Robert, *Jesus Is Dread: Black Theology and Black Culture in Britain* (London: Darton, Longman & Todd, 1998).

——*Dread and Pentecostal: A Political Theology for the Black Church in Britain* (London: SPCK, 2000).

——*God of the Rahtid: Redeeming Rage* (London: Darton, Longman and Todd, 2001).

——*God and the Gangs* (London: Darton, Longman and Todd, 2004).

——*Jesus Dub* (London: Routledge, 2006).

Bhogal, Inderjit, *A Table for All: A Challenge to Church and Nation* (Sheffield: Penistone Publications, 2000).

——*On the Hoof: Theology in Transit* (Sheffield: Penistone Publications, 2001).

Blakebrough, Eric, *Church for the City* (London: Darton, Longman and Todd, 1995).

Brooks, Ira V., *In Chains They Shall Come Over* (Birmingham: New Testament Church of God, 1970).

——*Where Do We Go from Here? A History of 25 Years of the New Testament Church of God in the United Kingdom 1955–1980* (London: Charles Raper, 1982).

Campbell, Horace, *Rasta and Resistance: From Marcus Garvey to Walter Rodney* (London: Hansib Press, 1985).

Carretta, Vincent (ed.), *Olaudah Equiano: The Interesting Narrative and Other Writings* (New York and London: Penguin Books, 1995).

——*Letters of the Late Ignatius Sancho, an African* (New York and London: Penguin Books, 1998).

——*Quobna Ottabah Cugoano: Thoughts and Sentiments on the Evil of Slavery* (New York and London: Penguin Books, 1999).

Centre for Black and White Christian Partnership (CBWCP), *Black Majority Churches UK Directory* (London: CBWCP, 2000).

Centre for Caribbean Studies, *A Handbook of the Afro-West Indian United Council of Churches* (London: Macmillan, 1972).

Centre for Contemporary Cultural Studies, *The Empire Strikes Back: Race and Racism in 70s Britain* (London: Routledge, 1992).

Charman, Paul, *Reflections: Black and White Christians in the City* (London: Zebra Project, 1979).

Church of England, *Serving God in Church and Community: Vocations for Minority Ethnic Anglicans in the Church of England* (London: Church House Publishing, 2000).

Clarke, Austin, *Twice Round the Black Church: Early Memories of Ireland and England* (London: Routledge & Kegan Paul, 1962).

Clarke, Clifton, *The Reason Why We Sing: Introducing Black Pentecostal Spirituality* (Cambridge: Grove Books, 1997).

Coleman, Kate, *Being Human: A Black British Christian Woman's Perspective* (Oxford: Whitley Publications, 2006).

Coombs, Orde, *Is Massa Day Dead? Black Moods in the Caribbean* [1st edn] (Garden City, NY: Anchor Books, 1974).

Dabydeen, David (ed.), *The Black Presence in English Literature* (Manchester: Manchester University Press, 1985).

Edmead, Peter L., *The Divisive Decade: A History of Caribbean Immigration to Birmingham in the 1950s* (Birmingham: Birmingham Library Services, 1999).

Edwards, Joel, *Let's Praise Him Again: An African Caribbean Perspective on Worship* (Eastbourne: Kingsway, 1992).

——*The Jamaican Diaspora: A People of Pain and Purpose* (Kingston: Morgan Ministries International, 1998).

——*Lord Make Us One—But Not All the Same* (London: Hodder and Stoughton, 1999).

——*The Cradle, the Cross, the Empty Tomb: A Faith We Can be Proud to Proclaim* (London: Hodder and Stoughton, 2000).

Edwards, Paul, and James Walvin, *Black Personalities in the Era of the Slave Trade* (London and Basingstoke: Macmillan, 1983).

Evans, James H., *Inheritors Together: Black People in the Church of England* (London: Race Pluralism and Community Group of the Board for Social Responsibility of the Church of England, 1985).

Field, F., and P. Haikin (eds.), *Black Britons* (London: Oxford University Press, 1971).

Fryer, Peter, *Staying Power: The History of Black People in Britain* (London and Sydney: Pluto Press, 1984).

Gerloff, Roswith, *A Plea for British Black Theologies: The Black Church Movement in Britain in its Transatlantic, Cultural and Theological Interaction, with Special Reference to the Pentecostal Oneness (Apostolic) and Sabbatarian Movements*. Studies in the Intercultural History of Christianity, 77 (2 vols.; Frankfurt am Main: P. Lang, 1992).

——*Partnership in Black and White*. Home Mission Occasional Papers, No. 29 (Westminster: Methodist Home Mission, 1997).

Grant, Paul, and Raj Patel, *A Time to Speak: Perspectives of Black Christians in Britain* (Birmingham: A Joint Publication of 'Racial Justice' and the 'Black Theology Working Group', 1990).

——*A Time to Act: Kairos 1992.* Birmingham: A Joint Publication of 'Racial Justice' and the 'Black and Third World Theological Working Group', 1992.

Green, Jeffrey, *Black Edwardians: Black People in Britain 1901–1914* (London and Portland, OR: Frank Cass Publishers, 1998).

Gordon-Carter, Glynne, *An Amazing Journey: The Church of England's Response to Institutional Racism*. A report on the development of the Committee for Minority Ethnic Anglican Concerns (CMEAC), the former Committee on Black Anglican Concerns (CBAC) (London: Church House, 2003).

Harris, C., and W. James (eds.), *Inside Babylon: The Caribbean Diaspora in Britain* (London: Verso, 1993).

Haslam, David, *Race for the Millennium: A Challenge to Church and Society* (London: Church House Publishing, 1996).

Hill, Clifford, *West Indian Migrants and the London Churches* (London and New York: Oxford University Press, 1963).

——*Black Churches: West Indian and African Sects in Britain.* A CRRU booklet, no. 1 (London: Community and Race Relations Unit of the British Council of Churches, 1971).

Howell-Baker, M., and T. Bolton, *Am I My Brother's and Sister's Keeper: Black Majority Churches and Development* (London: Christian Aid & Centre for Black Theology, 2003).

Jackson, Anita, *Catching Both Sides of the Wind: Conversation with Five Black Pastors* (London: British Council of Churches, 1985).

Jagessar, Michael N., *Full Life for All: The Work and Theology of Philip A. Potter: A Historical Survey and Systematic Analysis of Major Themes* (Zoetermeer, Netherlands: Boekencentrum, 1997).

Jagessar, Michael N., and Anthony G. Reddie (eds.), *Black Theology in Britain: A Reader* (London: Equinox, 2007).

Jagessar, Michael N., and Anthony G. Reddie (eds.), *Postcolonial Black British Theology: Textures and Themes* (Peterborough: Epworth Press, 2007).

James, W., and C. Harris (eds.), *Inside Babylon* (London: Verso, 1993).

Kerridge, Roy, *The Story of Black History* (London: Claridge Press, 1998).

Lartey, Emmanuel, *In Living Colour: An Intercultural Approach to Pastoral Care and Counselling* (London: Jessica Kingsley, 1997).

——*Pastoral Theology in an Intercultural World* (Peterborough: Epworth Press, 2006).

Leech, Kenneth, *The Fields of Charity and Sin: Reflections on Combating Racism in the Church of England*. Theology and Racism 3 (London: Church House & Board of Social Responsibility, 1986).

——*Struggle in Babylon: Racism in the Cities and Churches in Britain* (London: Sheldon, 1988).

Lobo, A. (ed.), *Black Catholics Speak: Reflections on Experience, Faith and Theology* (London: Catholic Association for Racial Justice, 1991).

McCalla, Doreen (ed.), *Black Success in the UK: Essays in Racial and Ethnic Studies* (Cambridge: DMee: Vision Learning and Cambridge University Press, 2003).

Milwood, Robinson A., *Let's Journey Together* (London: Division of Social Responsibility of the Methodist Church, 1980).

——*Liberation and Mission* (London: African Caribbean Educational Resource, 1997).

Mirza, Heidi Safia, *Black British Feminism* (London: Routledge, 1997).

Murray, Leon, *Being Black in Britain: Challenge and Hope* (London: Chester House Publication, 1995).

Parekh, Bhikhu, *The Future of Multi-Ethnic Britain* (London: Profile Books, 2000).

——*Rethinking Multiculturalism: Cultural Diversity and Political Theory* (Basingstoke: Macmillan, 2000).

Ramdin, Ron, *The Making of the Black Working Class in Britain* (Aldershot, Hants: Gower, 1987).

——*Reimaging Britain: 500 Years of Black and Asian History* (London and Sterling, VA: Pluto Press, 1999).

Reddie, Anthony G., *Growing into Hope: Believing and Expecting*, vol. 1 (Peterborough: Methodist Publishing House, 1998).

——*Growing into Hope: Liberation and Change*, vol. 2 (Peterborough: Methodist Publishing House, 1998).

——*Faith, Stories and the Experience of Black Elders: Singing the Lord's Song in a Strange Land* (London: Jessica Kingsley Publishers, 2001).

——*Nobodies to Somebodies: A Practical Theology for Education and Liberation* (Peterborough: Epworth Press, 2003).

——*Acting in Solidarity: Reflections in Critical Christianity* (London: Darton, Longman and Todd, 2005).

——*Black Theology in Transatlantic Dialogue* (New York: Palgrave, 2006).

——*Dramatizing Theologies: A Participative Approach to Black God-Talk* (London: Equinox, 2006).

Reddie, Anthony (ed.), *Legacy: Anthology in Memory of Jillian Brown* (Peterborough: Methodist Publishing House, 2000).

Root, John, *Building Multi-Racial Churches* (Oxford: Latimer House, 1994).

Selwyn, Arnold, *From Scepticism to Hope: One Black-led Church's Response to Social Responsibility*. With a commendation by the Archbishop of Canterbury and a foreword by Prebendary Pat Dearnley and Bishop Wilfred Wood (Bramcote, Nottingham: Grove Books, 1992).

Sherriffe, Hugh, *Faith in the Black Country: Development Work with Black-led Churches and Communities 1989–1991*. Faith in the Black Country Community Project (Halesowen: Barnardos, 1992).

Smith, I., with W. Green, *An Ebony Cross: Being a Black Woman in Britain Today* (London: Mashall, Morgan and Scott, 1989).

Smith-Cameron, Ivor, *The Church of Many Colours* (London: Ivor Smith-Cameron, 1998).

Sturge, Mark, *Look What the Lord Has Done: An Exploration of Black Christian Faith in Britain* (Bletchley: Scripture Union, 2005).

Sykes, Homer, *The Storm is Passing Over: A Look at Black Churches in Britain* (London: Thames and Hudson, 1995).

Vincent, John, *The Race Race* (London: SCM Press, 1970).

Walvin, James, *An African Life: The Life and Times of Olaudah Equiano 1745–1797* (London and New York: Continuum, 1998).

Westhill RE Centre, *Black Christians: Black Church Traditions in Britain* (Birmingham: Centre for Black and White Christian Partnership and Westhill RE Centre, Selly Oak Colleges, 1995).

Wilkinson, John L., *Church in Black and White: The Black Christian Tradition in 'Mainstream' Churches in England, a White Response and Testimony*, Windows on theology, Fenster zur Theologie Series (Edinburgh: Saint Andrew Press; Bonn: Pahl-Rugenstein, 1993).

2. Journal Articles

Aldred, Joe, 'Paradigms for a Black Theology in Britain', *Black Theology in Britain: A Journal of Contextual Praxis* 2 (April 1999), 9–32.

Alexander, Valentina, 'Afrocentric and Black Christian Consciousness: Towards an Honest Intersection', *Black Theology in Britain: A Journal of Contextual Praxis* 1 (October 1998), 11–19.

——'Onesimus's Letter to Philemon', *Black Theology in Britain: A Journal of Contextual Praxis* 4 (2000), 61–65.

Barton, Mukti, 'I am Black and Beautiful', *Black Theology: An International Journal* 2.2 (July 2004), 167–87.

Beckford, Robert, 'Black Sexual Representation and Pastoral Care', *Contact* 118 (1995), 15–24.

——'Theology in the Age of Crack: Crack Age, Prosperity Doctrine and "Being There"', *Black Theology in Britain: A Journal of Contextual Praxis* 4.1 (November 2001), 9–24.

——'Prophet of Dub: Dub as a Heuristic for Theological Reflection', *Black Theology: An International Journal* 1.1 (November 2002), 79–82.

Channer, Yvonne, 'The Youth and the Church: Impact of External Forces on Personal Beliefs', *Black Theology in Britain: A Journal of Contextual Praxis* 6 (2001), 9–24.

Chike, Chigor, 'Black Theology in Britain: One Decade On', *Black Theology: An International Journal* 4.2 (July 2006), 192–209.

Coleman, Kate, 'Black Theology and Black Liberation: A Womanist Perspective', *Black Theology in Britain: A Journal of Contextual Praxis* 1 (1998), 59–69.

——'Black Women and Theology', *Black Theology in Britain: A Journal of Contextual Praxis* 3 (1999), 51–65.

——'Black to the Future: Re-Evangelizing Black Youth', *Black Theology in Britain: A Journal of Contextual Praxis* 6 (2001), 41–51.

Dixon, Lorraine, 'Teach it, Sister!': Mahalia Jackson as Theologian in Song', *Black Theology in Britain* 2 (1989), 72–89.

——'A Reflection on Black Identity and Belonging in the Context of the Anglican Church in England: A Way Forward', *Black Theology in Britain: A Journal of Contextual Praxis* 4 (2000), 22–37.

——'Reflections on Pastoral Care from a Womanist Perspective', *Contact* 132 (2000), 3–10.

Gerloff, Roswith, 'The Early Vision of the Centre for Black and White Christian Partnership', *Journal of the Centre for Black and White Christian Partnership* 2 (Birmingham, 1995/96), 5–6.

——'An African Continuum in Variation: The African Christian Diaspora in Britain', *Black Theology in Britain: A Journal of Contextual Praxis* (4 (May 2000), 84–112.

——'Open Space: The African Christian Diaspora in Europe and the Quest for Human Community', (guest-editor), *International Review of Mission* LXXXIX.354 (July 2000), 275–81.

Howell-Baker, M., 'Towards a Womanist Pneumatological Pedagogy: An Investigation into the Development and Implementation of a Theological Pedagogy by and for the Marginalized', *Black Theology: An International Journal* 3.1 (January 2004), 32–54.

Isiorho, David, 'Black Theology in Urban Shadow: Combating Racism in the Church of England', *Black Theology: An International Journal* 1.1 (November 2002), 29–48.

Jagessar, Michael N., 'Navigating the World of "White" Ecumenism: Insights from Philip Potter', *Wereld and Zending* 4 (2002), 32–40.

——'Cultures in Dialogue: The Contribution of a Caribbean Theologian', *Black Theology: An International Journal* 1.2 (May 2003), 139–60.

——'Spinning Texts—Annacy Hermeneutics', *The Journal of the College of Preachers* (July 2004), 41–48.

——'Bound Coolie: Resistance, Liberation and the Religious Imagination of Bechu (1894–1901)', *Humanitas: The Journal of the George Bell Institute* 7.2 (April 2006), 158–79.

Johnson, Janet, 'Unity and the Regeneration of Black Youth', *Black Theology in Britain: A Journal of Contextual Praxis* 4 (2000), 66–83.

Kaur-Mann, Cham, 'Who Do You Say I Am? Images of Jesus', *Black Theology: An International Journal* 2.1 (January 2004), 19–44.

Lartey, Emmanuel Y., 'African Perspectives on Pastoral Liturgy', *Contact* 112 (1993), 3–12.

—— 'After Stephen Lawrence: Characteristics and Agenda for Black Theology in Britain', *Black Theology in Britain: A Journal of Contextual Praxis* 2 (1999), 79–91.

Leech, Kenneth, 'From Chaplaincy Towards Prophecy: Racism and Christian Theology over Four Decades', *Race and Class* 41/1-2 (1999), 131–42.

Lewis-Cooper, M., 'Diaspora Dialogue: Womanist Theology in Engagement with Aspects of the Black British and Jamaican Experience', *Black Theology: An International Journal* 2.1 (January 2004), 85–109.

McCalla, Doreen, 'Black Churches and Voluntary Action: Their Social Engagement with the Wider Society', *Black Theology: An International Journal* 3.2 (July 2005), 137–75.

Morrison, Doreen, 'Resisting Racism—By Celebrating "Our" Blackness', *Black Theology: An International Journal* 1.2 (May 2003), 209–223.

Mulrain, George, 'Bereavement Counselling among African Caribbean People', *Contact* 118 (1995), 9–16.

——'The Music of African Caribbean Theology', *Black Theology in Britain: A Journal of Contextual Praxis* 1 (October 1998), 35–45.

Nathan, Ron A., 'Caribbean Youth Identity in the United Kingdom: A Call for a Pan-African Theology', *Black Theology in Britain: A Journal of Contextual Praxis* 1 (October 1998), 19–34.

Potkay, Adam, 'Olaudah Equiano and the Art of Spiritual Autobiography', *African-American Culture in the Eighteenth Century* (Summer, 1994), 677–92.

Reddie, Anthony G., 'The Oral Tradition of African Caribbean Elders as a Resource for Christian Education', *Caravan: A Resource for Adult Religious Educators* 12.47 (Summer 1998), 12–13.

——'The Oral Tradition of African Caribbean People as a Resource for Black Christian Formation', *British Journal of Theological Education* 10.1 (Summer 1998), 16–25.

——'Towards a Black Christian Education of Liberation: The Christian Education of Black Children in Britain', *Black Theology in Britain: A Journal of Contextual Praxis* 1 (October 1998), 46–58.

——'The Case for a Contextualised Christian Education Curriculum for Black Children in Britain: A Survey of the Literature', *Black Theology in Britain: A Journal of Contextual Praxis* 3 (October 1999), 66–78.

——'Peace and Justice Through Black Christian Education', *Black Theology in Britain: A Journal of Contextual Praxis* 6 (June 2001), 73–85.

——'Creating a New Paradigm for the Christian Education of Black People in Britain', *The British Journal of Theological Education* 12.2 (February 2002), 119–31.

——'Singing the Lord's Song in a Strange Land', *Black Theology in Britain: A Journal of Contextual Praxis* 4.2 (May 2002), 186–93.

——'Developing a Black Christian Education of Liberation for the British Context', *Religious Education* 98.2 (May 2003), 221–38.

——'God-Talk and Black Empowerment', *The Epworth Review* 30.4 (October 2003), 53–62.

——'Jazz Musicians of the Word', *The College of Preachers—The Journal* (January 2004), 21–28.

——'Profile: Robert S. Beckford', *Epworth Review* 31.4 (October 2004), 25–34.

——'A Contextualised Approach to Black British Theology by Means of Dramatic Engagement', *Journal of Adult Theological Education* 2.1 (April 2005), 11–30.

——'A Dramatic Approach to Black Theological Reflection', *Contact* 146 (June 2005), 16–28.

——'Another Way of Doing Black God-talk', *Theology* CIX.850 (July/Aug 2006), 252–61.

Robinson, Lena, 'Black and Mixed Parentage Adolescents in Britain: An Overview of Racial Identity Issues', *Black Theology in Britain: A Journal of Contextual Praxis* 4 (May 2000), 113–25.

Sweeney, Hyacinth, 'The Bible as a Tool for Growth for Black Women', *Black Theology in Britain: A Journal of Contextual Praxis* 5 (2000), 21–32.

Toppin, Shirlyn, 'Soul Food' Theology: Pastoral Care through the Sharing of Meals: A Womanist Reflection', *Black Theology: An International Journal* 4.1 (2006), 44–69.

Troupe, Carol, 'An Exploration of Black Theology and its Contribution to the Education of Young People', *Black Theology: An International Journal* 4.2 (July 2006), 173–91.

Watt, Diane, 'Traditional Religious Practices Amongst African Caribbean Mothers and Community Other Mothers', *Black Theology: An International Journal* 2.2 (July 2004), 195–212.

Willis, Lerleen, 'All Things to All Men? Or What has Language to Do with Gender and Resistance in the Black Majority Church in Britain?', *Black Theology in Britain* 4.2 (May 2002), 195–213.

——'The Pilgrim's Process: Coping with Racism through Faith', *Black Theology: An International Journal* 4.2 (July 2006), 210–32.

3. Reports and Pamphlets

Ackroyd, Sandra, Marjorie Lewis-Cooper and Naboth Muchopa, *Strangers No More: Transformation through Racial Justice* (London: The Methodist Church, 2001).

Anglican Diocese of Birmingham, *Faith in the City of Birmingham: The Report of a Commission set up by the Bishop's Council of the Diocese of Birmingham* (Exeter: Paternoster Press, 1988).

Archbishop's Council, *Called to Act Justly: A Challenge to Include Minority Ethnic People in the Life of the Church of England* (London: The Archbishop's Council, 2003).

Archbishop's Council and Committee for Minority Ethnic Anglican Concerns (CMEAC), *Serving God in Church and Community: Vocations for Minority Ethnic Anglicans in the Church of England* (London: The Archbishop's Council, 2003).

British Council of Churches (BCC), *The New Black Presence in Britain: A Christian Scrutiny*. A statement by the British Council of Churches' Working Party on Britain as a Multi-Racial Society (London: BCC, 1976).

——*Building Together in Christ: A Report on the Sharing and Transfer of Church Buildings, the Joint Working Party between White-led and Black-led Churches* (London: BCC, 1978).

——*Coming Together in Christ: A Report of the Joint Working Party between White-led and Black-led Churches* (London: BCC, 1978).

——*Rainbow Gospel* (London: BCC, 1988).

——*Partners in Practice* (London: BCC, 1989).

——*Account of Hope: Report of a Conference on the Economic Empowerment of the Black Community* (London: Community and Race Relations Unit of the British Council of Churches, 1990).

——*Equal Partner: Theological Education and Racial Justice* (London: BCC, 1992).

Catholic Association for Racial Justice (CARJ), *Building Bridges: Dialogue with Black-led Churches* (London: CARJ, n.d.).

Catholic Truth Society, *The Church and Racism: Towards a More Fraternal Society* (London: Catholic Truth Society, 1989).

Church of England, *Inheritors Together: Black People in the Church of England* (London: Race, Pluralism and Community Group Board for Social Responsibility, 1985).

——*Seeds of Hope: Report of a Survey on Combating Racism in the Diocese of the Church of England* (London: Church House Publications, 1991).

——*The Passing Winter: A Sequel to Seeds of Hope* (London: Church House Publications, 1996).

Claiming the Inheritance: Ten Years On (West Bromwich: Claiming the Inheritance, 1997).

Committee on Black Anglicans Concerns, *Roots and Wings: Report of the Black Anglican Celebration for the Decade of Evangelism*. University of York, 22-24 July 1994 (London: General Synod of the Church of England, 1994).

Deson, Rolston, *Claiming the Inheritance: Ten Years On*. Pamphlet. West Bromwich, n.d.

Gerloff, Roswith, *Learning in Partnership*: third report from the Joint Working Party between black-led and white-led churches (London: British Council of Churches, 1980).

——*Report of the Proceedings of the Consultation between the World Council of Churches and African and African Caribbean Church Leaders in Britain*, 30 November–2 December 1995, eds. R. Gerloff and H. van Beek (Geneva: WCC, 1996).

Greater Bristol Ecumenical Council, *Grasping the Nettle: Racial Justice and the Church in Bristol* (Bristol: Greater Bristol Ecumenical Council, 1988).

Howard, Vanessa, *A Report on Afro-Caribbean Christianity in Britain*. Community Religions Project research papers No. 4 (Leeds: Dept. of Theology and Religious Studies, Leeds University, 1987).

Leicester Consultation, *The Church of England and Racism* (London: Board of Social Responsibility, 1981).

Methodist Church, *Faithful and Equal: The Report Adopted at the Portsmouth Methodist Conference* (London: The Methodist Church, 1987).

Muchopa, Naboth, *Making a Positive Difference* (London: The Methodist Church, 2001).

Parry, Tony, *Black-led Churches in West Yorkshire* (Leeds: Church and Neighbourhood Action Project, 1993).

Pontifical Commission, *The Church and Racism: Towards a More Fraternal Society* (London: Catholic Truth Society, 1989).

Sentamu, John, 'The Stephen Lawrence Inquiry Report: Towards an Agenda for Action for the Church of England' (General Synod: Church of England, July 1999).

Walton, Heather, *A Tree God Planted: Black People in British Methodism* (London: Ethnic Minorities in Methodism Working Group, The Methodist Church, 1984).

World Council of Churches (WCC), Report of the proceedings of the consultation between the World Council of Churches (Office of Church and Ecumenical Relations at the General Secretariat) and African and African-Caribbean church leaders in Britain, at the New Testament Church of God, Harehills, Leeds, England, 30 November–2 December 1995 (Geneva: Office of Church and Ecumenical Relations, World Council of Churches, [1996?]).

4. Theses and Dissertations

Alexander, Valentina, 'To Break Every Fetter? To What Extent has the Black-led Church in Britain Developed a Theology of Liberation? (unpublished PhD thesis, University of Warwick, 1996).

Andrews, G. A., 'The Condition of Black Pentecostal Churches in Britain. The Time has Come: A Study of the Development and Advance of the Black

Pentecostal Church in Britain' (unpublished MA thesis, King's College, London, 1999).

Barnes, Clarice V., 'The Montserrat Volcanic Disaster: A Study of Meaning, Psycho-social Effects, Coping and Intervention' (unpublished PhD thesis, University of Birmingham, 2000).

Burton, Edson, 'From Assimilationism to Anti-Racism: The Church of England's Response to Afro-Caribbean Migration 1948–1981' (unpublished PhD thesis, University of West England, 2004).

Evans, Maitland M., 'Counselling for Community Change: A Study which Engages African-Caribbean Beliefs and Core Values to Construct a Missio-cultural Counselling Model and to Further Examine its Effectiveness in Engendering Mature Personhood and Community Change' (unpublished PhD thesis, University of Birmingham, 1999).

Foster, Elaine, 'Black Women in Black Led Churches: A Study of Black Women's Contribution to the Growth and Development of Black Led Churches in Britain' (unpublished MPhil thesis, University of Birmingham, 1990).

Grant, Lilieth, 'Pastoral Work Undertaken by the Clergy of Black Majority Christian Churches in Birmingham' (unpublished MA thesis, University of Birmingham, 1999).

Griffiths, Herbert, 'The Impact of African Caribbean Settlers on the 7th Day Adventist Church in Britain 1952–2001' (unpublished PhD thesis, University of Leeds, 2003).

Howard, John David, 'Black Leadership in an Inner City Methodist Church' (unpublished MA thesis, University of Sheffield, 1995).

Isiorho, David, 'Deep Anglicanism: A Sociological and Political Analysis of the Mode of Involvement of Black Christians in the Church of England with Special Reference to English Ethnicity' (unpublished PhD thesis, University of Bradford, 1998).

MacRobert, Iain, 'Black Pentecostalism: Its Origins, Functions and Theology' (unpublished PhD thesis, University of Birmingham, 1989).

Muir, David, 'Black Theology, Pentecostalism, and Racial Struggles in the Church of God' (unpublished PhD thesis, King's College, London, 2004).

Pemberton, Eric, 'A Study of Caribbean Religions' (unpublished MPhil thesis, University of Birmingham, 1988).

Timothy, James John, 'Pastoral Care and Counselling in Black Churches in Britain. With Special Reference to those in Leeds' (unpublished PhD thesis, University of Leeds, 1990).

Taylor, Claire T., 'British Churches and Jamaican Migration: A Study of Religion and Identities, 1948 to 1965' (unpublished PhD thesis, Anglia Polytechnic University, 2002).

Tomlin, Carol J., 'Black Preaching Style' (unpublished MPhil thesis, University of Birmingham, 1988).

Troupe, Carol, 'The Contribution of Black Culture and Faith to Religious Education' (unpublished MPhil thesis, University of Birmingham, 2005).

Ward, Tim, 'Where the Saints have Trod: Black-led Churches as Agencies of Community Development' (unpublished dissertation, Westhill College, Birmingham, 1987).

5. Television/Films

BBC Production, *Colour in Britain* (London: BBC, 1965).

——*Black Britain* (London: BBC, 1997). Videocassette, 30 min.

——*All Black: White Church, Black Magic* (Pebble Mill: BBC2, 1994) Videocassette, 30 min.

——*What's It Like to Be a Christian in a Black-led Pentecostal Church?* (London: BBC, 1993). Videocassette.

Beckford, Robert, *Britain's Slave Trade* (Channel 4, 1999).

——*Black Messiah* (BBC 4, 2001).

——The BAFTA award winning *Test of Time* (BBC Education, 2001).

——*Blood and Fire* (BBC 2, 2002).

——*Ebony Towers* (BBC 4, 2003).

——*God Is Black* (Channel 4, 2004).

——*Who Wrote The Bible?* (Channel 4, 2004).

——*The Empire Pays Back* (Channel 4, 2005).

——*The Gospel Truth* (Channel 4, 2005).

——*The Real Patron Saints* (Channel 4, 2005).

——*The Passion: Films, Faith and Fury* (Channel 4, 2006).

Index

You are invited to:

COFFEE MORNING

Saturday 4th February

10.30 – 12noon

United Reformed Church

Armour Road

Printed in the United Kingdom
by Lightning Source UK Ltd.
129793UK00001B/73/A